MAN-MADE AMERICA

MAN-MADE AMERICA
CHAOS OR CONTROL?

An Inquiry into Selected Problems of Design
in the Urbanized Landscape

by Christopher Tunnard and Boris Pushkarev

In association with Geoffrey Baker, Dorothy Lefferts Moore,
Anthony H. Penfold, Ann Satterthwaite, and Ralph Warburton

Foreword to the Harmony Books edition by Wolf Von Eckardt

With drawings by Philip Lin and Vladimir Pozharsky,
and photographs by John Reed and Charles R. Schulze

H

HARMONY BOOKS/NEW YORK

In February 1979 Christopher Tunnard lost his long, brave struggle against cancer. Only sixty-eight, he was full of ideas and planned to spend his retirement traveling and writing. His death was followed by that of his wife, Lydia Evans Tunnard, in June 1980.

Although my father was the quiet observer and writer, my mother's constant support, ebullient spirit, and shrewd eye made it possible for him to create books such as this one. I was privileged to be with them on many of their worldwide journeys, and I shall always remember the great rapport and frequent exchanges of thoughts and views that made these travels rewarding and enjoyable for them and a remarkable education for me.

To commemorate their lifelong partnership, and with the blessing of our great friend Coleman Woodbury, this new edition of Man-Made America *is dedicated, with love, to the memory of my parents.*

CHRISTOPHER R. TUNNARD

Originally published with assistance from the foundation established in memory of Philip Hamilton McMillan of the Class of 1894, Yale College.

First paperback edition published in 1981 by Harmony Books by arrangement with Yale University Press.
Copyright © 1963 by Yale University.
Foreword copyright © 1981 by Wolf Von Eckardt.

Inquiries should be addressed to Harmony Books, a division of Crown Publishers, Inc., One Park Avenue, New York, New York 10016

Printed in the United States of America
Published simultaneously in Canada by General Publishing Company Limited

Library of Congress Cataloging in Publication Data

Tunnard, Christopher.
    Man-made America, chaos or control?

    Reprint of the ed. published by Yale University Press, New Haven.
    Bibliography: p. 452
    Includes index.
    1. Architecture—Environmental aspects—United States.   2. Urban beautification—United States.   3. Architecture—United States—Conservation and restoration.   4. Regional planning—United States.
I. Pushkarev, Boris, joint author.   II. Title.
NA2542.35.T86   1981   711'.3'0973   80-26145
ISBN: 0-517-543796

10 9 8 7 6 5 4 3 2 1

Contents

Foreword by Wolf Von Eckardt   vii
Preface   xiii

Part One

The Urbanized Landscape: An Esthetic for Man-Made America   1
  1. The Contemporary Scene   3
  2. Landscape as Art   5
  3. The American Landscape   10
  4. Emerging Landscapes of America   13
  5. Beauty Spots   31
  6. The New Settlement Pattern   36
  7. The Non-Beautiful   45

Part Two

The Dwelling Group: The Esthetic of Low-Density Housing   53
  1. The Growth of Low-Density Housing   57
  2. The Morphology of the Urban Fringe   72
  3. Visual Principles of Small House Groupings   98

Part Three

The Paved Ribbon: The Esthetic of Freeway Design   157
  1. The Development of Freeway Form   159
  2. The Internal Harmony of the Freeway   177
  3. The External Harmony of the Freeway   206

Part Four

The Monuments of Technology: The Esthetics of Industry and
                     Commerce in the Landscape   277
  1. Industrial Location   279
  2. Industry as an Element of Urban Design   284
  3. Commercial Facilities in the Urban Fringe   311
  4. Possibilities of Planned Design   316
  5. The Need for Visual Order   326

Part Five

The Outlines of Open Space: Esthetics and Recreation   337
  1. Present Trends in Recreation   339
  2. General Factors Affecting Design   355
  3. The Framework of Open Space Design   361
  4. Opportunities for Design   387

Part Six

Something for the Future: The Preservation of Visible History   401
    1. Changing Attitudes   403
    2. Losses and Gains   406
    3. Inventory and Design Survey   412
    4. Method   416
    5. Preservation and Renewal   427
    6. Private Enterprise Preservation and Urban Design   431

Conclusion

The Emergence of Form: Esthetics and Planning   441
    Shaping the Urban Region   444

Photographic Credits   449

Bibliography   452

Index   461

Foreword

Many things have changed since this book was written in 1961, but the need for it is not one of them.

Chaos or control is still one of the foremost questions America must answer before greed and public indifference run it to the ground. Christopher Tunnard and Boris Pushkarev were among the first to say this, specifically as it applies to the problems of urban sprawl, housing, freeways, industrial parks, open space, and historic preservation in America. They say it clearly, forcefully, and convincingly —quite without the subsequent Chicken Little alarms that cried of falling skies and dyings oceans and that, unfortunately, discredited very real environmental concerns.

Man-Made America owes its considerable influence on public opinion, environmental design, and legislation to its restrained forcefulness and forceful restraint. It is a model for effective instruction and arousal of both professionals and what librarians call general readers. This new edition of the book will therefore surely further strengthen the environmental movement here and abroad. It needs strengthening.

Technically, of course, we can control waste, ugliness, and pollution almost as easily as we spread them. There is nothing insurmountably difficult about regional planning, landscape design, or urban design.

Our problem is political. It challenges democratic thought and involves the survival of our free-enterprise system. In the end, we must control chaos. The question is only whether we do it voluntarily, with our civic and economic liberties intact, or whether we must call a militia to save our lives.

Before the end, the voters must therefore muster the will, the sustained will, to put public need before private greed. We must learn that the public's unquestionable right to health, beauty, and serenity must take precedence over the questionable private right to ravage the land for quick profit. We must adjust our values and employ wealth and technology to raise not only the standard of living but also the standard of life.

Compared with that of other democratic countries, our standard of life leaves much to be desired. We are "a Croesus on a garbage heap," as John Gardner once said, referring to the way we allowed America the Beautiful to become a mess. Great Britain, France, and particularly Holland have national urban policies, designs, and plans to guide urban development. We still think a national urban policy un-American and effective regional planning an impossible dream. We don't even try to control the ever-accelerating, literally sickening noise in our cityscape. We still quarrel about billboard control, surely a matter civilized people should not even have to discuss. We are still rich. But we don't live like rich people. Like boorish *nouveaux riches,* we show off our gadgetry.

Our national will to clean house is not ill but shaky. God knows, we have our share of criminals. But the vast majority of Americans, who kill the majestic stillness of a winter landscape with the racket of snowmobiles, would not poison drinking water. The manufacturer who dumps his new factory heedlessly into a green valley is likely to be a good neighbor at home. He meticulously manicures his front lawn and spends time in zoning meetings to protect his neighborhood against a commercial highrise invasion.

The county council member, who votes for yet another needlessly sprawling shopping center or subdivision, does so to increase the county's tax income and teacher salaries. The highway engineers, who slice up city neighborhoods with hideous concrete ribbons, do so to get trucks off residential streets, accelerate business, and ensure highway safety.

It doesn't help to ask these people to control themselves or to vote for government control. As the young environmentalists of the 1970s have learned, confrontation politics often hardens resistance. You cannot ask Americans *not* to ride around in the snow, build factories, raise the local tax base, or build dangerous roads. They are likely to lash back.

The best hopes for environmental sanity are the patient hopes for education and design.

Good education is essential to getting along in this Promethean age of technological sophistication. But a good education must aim for more than teaching skills and holding up a mirror to what we are, as is currently fashionable. It must also impart a measure of knowledge about the millennia of human experience, as distilled in history and literature, so that we can know what we may be, as Shakespeare put it. Humanistic knowledge alone can give us both humility to keep our technical prowess in perspective and confidence in the potentials of our humanity. Solid knowledge alone, not the promiscuous relativism of social psychology, can hone our often blunted ethnics and instill us with greater respect for human dignity.

A more widely accepted sense of ethics and human dignity has, in the past few decades, advanced civil rights and women's equality in America. The same sense of ethics and dignity must be applied to livability and order in our cityscape and landscape.

Design is creative problem solving. It is often confused with decorating, or "form-giving," or "styling," in other words with making things *look* attractive. It is not mere engineering, which is the straightforward application of scientific principles to practical problems, an often ingenious but also simple-minded way to make an engine, or a freeway, or a subway function. It tends to omit the human factor and ecological relationships.

Design is more. It is the art of making technology livable. (The modern movement in architecture and industrial design assumed that "honest" and purely "functional" products of technology are ipso facto beautiful and practical and therefore marvelous to live with. That is simply not so.) Design, in the sense in which the word is used here, is a comprehensive, if you will, a holistic, and if you must, a *gestalt* approach to the things people use and surround themselves with.

Design, for example, is not merely selecting the color of the tile for a subway station. It is not even merely creating the configuration of the station to make it convenient and pleasing. It is fitting the subway system efficiently and esthetically into what should be a clockwork of regional transportation and into the urban and natural ecology.

Design, in the broad sense in which Tunnard and Pushkarev use the word, "includes land-use relationships, financing, legal provisions, operation, and even fire and accident prevention." The authors do not directly say it, but, as I understand them, design is synonymous with planning, or, at least, it is the prerequisite of any plan for constructive human intervention to shape the human environment, be it a house, village, city, urbanized region, or landscape.

Environmental design, or planning, requires not only architects and landscape architects but also teamwork. The team includes engineers, urban planners, biologists, ecologists, economists, and other specialists.

Environmental design, or the environmental approach to design, is capable of solving esthetic and ecological problems in the environment that cannot be solved by ignoring, denying, shouting, or wishing them away. Its ultimate aim, as Tunnard and Pushkarev put it, is "to establish an equilibrium in a constantly changing world." It seeks to maintain a balance between the demands of technical and economic progress and the demands of nature, including human nature.

Design, then, can presumably silence or at least quiet snowmobiles—their consumers willing. It can certainly fit a factory into a green valley so that sensitive souls can live with it and progressive esthetes might even find it beautiful. (A generation of European architects fawned over American silos.)

Competent regional design, or regional planning, is quite capable of satisfying our county council member if only he or she knew it and gave it a chance. Contrary to conventional wisdom, we are *not* caught in a hopeless predicament between ugly growth and dreary no-growth. Design can reconcile demands for profit and tax revenue with demands for open space to regenerate the air, water, and human spirit. Design can turn a freeway from an unattractive nuisance to an attractive convenience. The cost-benefit equation only comes out better in the end.

The American public was scarcely aware of what was happening to our habitat when Christopher Tunnard began to work on it in the 1950s. Nobody talked about an urban crisis, let alone an environmental crisis, in the cocky Eisenhower years. Tunnard, who taught landscape architecture and directed the graduate program in city planning at Yale University, was among the first to conduct various investigations into the new phenomenon of the urban region, or Megalopolis.

But he went further and determined what can be done about it. He set out to prove, as he put it in his preface, "that Americans are not powerless before the 'mindless juggernaut of subtopia'—that much can be done by a combination of private and public interest to redeem the landscapes which are rapidly being absorbed by urban growth, and to give the new fabric a practical and agreeable form."

Boris Pushkarev, an architect who studied with Tunnard and assisted him in these searches and researches, collaborated in converting these studies into a book. This volume was first published in 1963.

Man-Made America joined a small but potent shelf of books, all published at about the same time, that brought new insights and some relief. John Kenneth Galbraith showed us that *The Affluent Society* was wanting. Michael Harrington pointed to abject poverty in *The Other America* for shocking evidence. Rachel Carson told movingly in *The Silent Spring* how chemical insecticides and other deadly progress poisons nature's ecology. Lewis Mumford's lifework, but particularly *The City in History,* made us aware of the urban ecology. Jean Gottmann discovered and described the dynamics of *Megalopolis: The Urbanized Northeastern Seaboard of the United States.* Peter Blake charged that these dynamics were turning the country into *God's Own Junkyard.*

William H. Whyte and his collaborators at *Fortune* magazine showed that *The Exploding Metropolis* left downtown in shambles. Jane Jacobs, in her *The Death and Life of Great American Cities,* opened our eyes to the fact that urban revitalization, as prescribed by modern architecture, was killing the cities, and that their true life springs from their old, organic neighborhoods. The revelation shocked the city planners but came just in time to stop cataclysmic "urban renewal" and launch urban conservation and recovery.

Most of these authors, including Tunnard and Pushkarev, came to Washington in the spring of 1965 at the invitation of Mrs. Lyndon B. Johnson to participate in the White House Conference on Natural Beauty for America. They did not talk to themselves. Nor did they talk about cosmetic beauty. Joined by prominent architects and environmentalists, they held a sort of seminar for government bureaucrats, who found it difficult to refuse the President's wife's invitation to attend.

The device worked. "Beautification" caused much excitement in government and out. Seldom before had new thought so quickly risen to the heads of power.

In President Johnson's Great Society, The Environment became a cause that nobody could openly oppose. The Cities became a political concern, elevated to a crisis. Urban Sprawl became dirty words. A rebellion against urban freeways arose, flaring into bitter battles in San Francisco, New Orleans, and Washington, D.C. The proverbial little old ladies of historic preservation societies were joined by a growing number of young intellectuals. Their interests began to encompass entire historic districts and towns, such as Savannah, rather than only houses George Washington was alleged to have slept in. Led by Johnson's Secretary of the Interior, Stewart L. Udall, the nation began to extend Theodore Roosevelt's concepts of nature conservation to urban conservation.

The slowly changed public opinion of the sixties roused the ground swell of the seventies. An emotional, popular movement set out to rescue "Spaceship Earth" from certain doom caused by pollution and the exhaustion of natural resources.

The movement received added momentum from what might be called the American Youth movement. Suddenly and intensely, middle-class students, who had traditionally been apolitical in America (at least compared with other countries) became active in civic issues. They marched in Selma. They rallied against the war in Vietnam. On April 22, 1970, they celebrated Earth Day, a national, environmental teach-in, as they called it.

The teach-in became global when the United Nations, in 1972, held a conference on the environment in Stockholm, followed four years later by Habitat, a UN conference on human settlements, in Vancouver.

The commotion did not, as René Dubos, the wisest of the environmentalist leaders, has said of Earth Day, provide new insights or factual knowledge. But it did help to mobilize concern for environmental quality, and it did lead to a beginning of reform.

The Arabs also helped. The oil embargo imposed by OPEC, the Organization of Petroleum Exporting Countries, late in 1973, and the subsequent skyrocketing increase in the cost of oil caused the American people to take a critical look at their gas-guzzling pet and the wasteful ways of modern architecture. That added energy to the ecology crisis.

Two further things happened to help the cause Tunnard and Pushkarev espouse: the birth rate dropped and middle America fell in love with old buildings. The former means that there were fewer households to settle in suburbia (which is paradise only for innocent children). The latter sends young householders to the inner city to make old Victorian houses their homes.

The federal government, as always in America, was quick to respond to the changed views and mood of the governed. It established an Environmental Protection Agency and a Department of Energy. It demanded environmental impact statements on everything being built with the help of federal money. The words "quality of life" became part of the bureaucratic jargon.

As to Tunnard and Pushkarev's specific concerns, I suppress only slight qualms when I say that the American government has recognized the dangers of urban sprawl. It is making sticks-and-carrots efforts to arrest the continued centrifugal forces. As yet, they have not been effective. But at least the virtue of environmental design is now widely recognized.

In the early seventies, in fact, Congress called for, the Department of Housing and Urban Development administered, and the Nixon administration killed a federal program to assist planned communities, or new towns. The idea was that reasonably compact settlements, where people can work, play, and shop as well as sleep, are more efficient and livable than the dispersal of human activities all over the landscape and the consequent disintegration of human community. New towns have proven successful in Great Britain and elsewhere. Two privately built planned communities in America, Reston in Virginia, and Columbia in Maryland, both launched in the sixties, are meeting most of the social goals new towns are supposed to meet. They also made evident that, as in England, new towns can be built only in public-private partnership. A prominent commission on "Development Choices for the Eighties" recently recommended just that, calling for "urban villages."

Oddly, Tunnard and Pushkarev never mentioned new towns in their book.

On freeway design, the authors won their point. It became an important issue in Mrs. Johnson's beautification campaign. And the "beautniks," as one highway engineer called them with more anger than insight, won the day. Pushkarev's design criticisms are now the federal highway administration's guidelines. Beautniks, Arabs, and inflation finally established a more reasonable balance between paved ribbons and public transportation.

Equally gratifying is that the surge of interest in historic preservation, discussed in the final chapter of this book, has become a storm that has blown the federal freeway and urban renewal bulldozers out of the city. The rehabilitation of old neighborhoods and districts, the conversion of worthy old buildings to valued new purposes (the jargon calls this adaptive reuse), and most of all a new interest in "ambience," amenities, and old-fashioned urbanity are restoring life to the hearts of many old cities, notably Boston, Baltimore, Pittsburgh, and Philadelphia.

An alliance between nature conservationists and urban conservationists is in the making, as I write. In the face of a backlash against environmental controls, as evidenced by the conservative (but not conservationist) victory in the 1980 national elections, this coalition is likely to hold the ground gained with the help of this book.

May this new edition contribute to the further advance of livability.

WOLF VON ECKARDT

Washington, D.C., January 1981

Preface

If we are to justify modern American civilization before our own growing population and in the eyes of the world, the creation of a more appropriate physical shape for that society is one of the most urgent tasks ahead. In the following pages we hope to prove that Americans are not powerless before "the mindless juggernaut of subtopia" —that much can be done by a combination of private and public interest to redeem the landscapes which are rapidly being absorbed by urban growth, and to give the new fabric a practical and agreeable form.

Our interest in the appearance of rapidly-developing urban regions—the subject of this book—dates formally from 1950. In that year a joint Yale University-Connecticut Development Commission conference was held to discuss the expanding "urban core" of the state, which we described as being made up of several cities and many towns, stretching along the coast and up the central valley into Massachusetts. In the same year, an illustrated visual survey of this man-made scene was prepared with the help of students in the Graduate Program in City Planning, and was published in the English journal, *Architectural Review*.[1] In more than its title alone, this special issue of *Architectural Review* was a precursor of our book.

These two threads—regional growth and urban esthetics—were thenceforth interwoven, and occupied our available time for research until the Fall of 1961, when this book was completed. During this period, our interest in Megalopolis, as the urban region has been termed, extended to other parts of the United States, and in particular to the Atlantic Urban Region, stretching along the eastern coastline from Maine to Virginia. Preliminary studies of this region were discussed at a second Yale conference held in 1955;[2] since then more detailed aspects of its form and spatial character have been examined. On the esthetic side, while *Architectural Review* turned its attention in 1955–56 to the British urbanized landscape,[3] a joint committee of the American Institute of Planners and the American Institute of Architects, of which one of the authors was a committee member, was preparing its report on community appearance in the United States.[4] At Yale, studies were carried out on the possibilities of creating visual design surveys with plans for their adaptation in the community planning process; a third conference, "Civilizing the American Roadscape," was held later to discuss this special problem.

With these individual and collaborative efforts as antecedents, the case studies for the present volume were begun in 1957. They would not have been possible, nor

1. Tunnard, Christopher, Part 2, "Scene," in "Man-Made America," special number of *Architectural Review*, December, 1950.

2. Tunnard, Christopher ed. *The Atlantic Urban Region:* Papers Presented at a Conference of the Graduate Program in City Planning, Yale University, 1955. City Planning at Yale, No. 2, New Haven, 1956.

3. "Outrage," special number of *Architectural Review*, June 1955. See also "Counter-Attack," special number of *Architectural Review*, December, 1956.

4. Fagin and Weinberg, eds., *Planning and Community Appearance*, Regional Plan Association, Inc., New York, 1958.

would the scope of the work have been as wide, without the aid of a grant from the Humanities division of the Rockefeller Foundation, which we wish to acknowledge first and foremost among the many debts we owe to helpful individuals and institutions.

Our philosophy of design will become apparent in the following pages, but a brief preamble may be in order to prepare the reader for what is to come. Today's esthetic failures are not in the "pure" design problems, but rather in those areas which are generally considered "non-design" and hence are left to decision makers who fail to take esthetic values into account. Meanwhile, land-use relationships, financing, legal provisions, operation, even fire and accident prevention, *are* to some extent visual design problems, and should be considered as such. A great deal of educational work must be done to acquaint designers with "utilitarian" problems on the one hand, and to make non-design experts visually sensitive on the other. This book is an attempt to do so, in that we deal with the visual as well as the non-visual side of urban design. The esthetic ideas presented are offered within a planning framework; they are not necessarily the ideas of an architect, a landscape architect, or an engineer, but deal with spatial and structural characteristics in general terms. We are not concerned here with particular styles of architecture, or with the merits and deficiencies of aluminum siding or clapboards; we *are* concerned with the position of man-made objects in space and in the values of scale in the landscape: with streets, open spaces, and large-scale industrial and commercial facilities—in other words, with the esthetic values of man-made elements which have received very little attention in the recent past. We believe that the design of urban regions can be improved by consideration of these broad esthetic principles on the part of all decision makers, and we advance them here in the hope that they may contribute to the practical tasks of laying out highways, parks, subdivisions, and other space-consuming facilities in the contemporary world.

One other clarification of our approach should also be made at the outset. This concerns the density of urban development. While we believe with others that centers of more intensive interaction should henceforward be planned for suburban and semi-rural parts of the region, and that many of these areas could well be "urbanized" in the sense of containing higher densities than are now common, our attention has necessarily been focused on low-density development in those parts of the region where the greatest population increase is taking place and where the greatest urgency for design improvement occurs. While we do not ignore the crying need for good design in the older central cities, this study is largely concerned with their rural-urban fringes—the present-day "wasteland" of the design world, where professional talent has so far been conspicuous by its absence.

In choosing the components of the urban scene to be studied, our criteria included their visual prominence, their neglect as artifacts, their space-consuming importance, and the amount of investment demanded. Low-density residential development, for instance, occupies some forty per cent of the urbanized land in the United States; freeways occupy only a small fraction but are visually extremely prominent.

Historic sites have been neglected in a materialistic generation and, despite the considerable investment that goes into new industrial plants, the visual aspects of their siting are frequently left to chance. Some components are only a generation old—regional shopping centers, limited access freeways; others are older, but are achieving new significance as our population moves—open space reservations, industrial parks, and large-lot subdivisions. Much that once seemed to be outside the province of design, we now see should fall within it; and if we continue to neglect these facets of the expanding American "community" we do so to the detriment of society as a whole.

Although the two authors acted in large part as catalysts for the indispensable work of others, they alone are responsible for the findings and conclusions reached. The project was initiated by Christopher Tunnard, who, as Director of the Graduate Program in City Planning, established its policy and scope. He is the author of that part of the book which presents the theory of the investigation, and he supervised the preparation of the sections dealing with open space and historic preservation. Boris Pushkarev is the author of the parts dealing with low-density housing and freeway esthetics; abstracts of the latter have appeared in the magazine *Landscape* (Winter 1960–61) and the *Proceedings of the Highway Research Board* (1962). He is also responsible for the studies of regional structure in Part One, and for the section dealing with technological elements in the landscape. The conclusion was written jointly by the two authors.

Important preliminary studies on the internal harmony of the highway were carried out by Anthony H. Penfold. Preliminary material on industry was assembled by Ralph Warburton, while the section on commercial development was prepared by Geoffrey Baker. Dorothy Moore and Ann Satterthwaite did the research and basic text on open space and historic preservation respectively. Exploratory studies in related fields were carried out by James Frost, David Gosling, Morton L. Isler, Anthony Penfold, Earl Rush, Malcolm Strachan, and Rachel Weiler, and other research assistance is gratefully acknowledged to Richard Bader, Hyung Chung, Paul Finney, Stanley Greimann, Norman Jackson, C. N. Rao, Eugene Ujlaky, and Alexei K. Vergun. The graphic material was prepared by Philip C. Lin and Vladimir J. Pozharsky. In addition to illustrative matter received from government agencies and numerous commercial firms, photographs were specially taken for the book by John Reed and Charles R. Schulze, and by graphic design students at Yale under the direction of Alvin Eisenman and Herbert Matter. Secretarial work and editorial assistance was provided by Jeannette Nichols.

Aside from the individuals directly involved in the study, credit is due many people and organizations who willingly supplied suggestions and information. For the section on low-density housing, valuable suggestions were made by Walter D. Harris; the manuscript of this section was critically reviewed by Brent Friedlander of New York University and by Stanley B. Tankel and Dick Netzer of the Regional Plan Association, Inc. The latter organization and its Executive Vice President, C. McKim Norton, supplied valuable information and assistance as did numerous county and municipal planning agencies and private consulting firms. The original draft of the section on freeways was reviewed by Frederick W. Hurd, Director of the Bureau of Highway Traffic at Yale; Nelson Miller Wells, former Director of the Landscape Bureau, New York State Department of Public Works; Robert G. Mitchell, Assistant Chief Engineer, Connecticut State Highway Department, and Regierungsbaudirektor Dr.-Ing. Hans Lorenz, Autobahnbauamt Nürnberg. Extensive sets of working drawings were given to the study by the Bureau of Public Roads, Washington, D.C.; the Connecticut State Highway Department; the New Jersey State Highway Department; the New York State Department of Public Works; and Autobahnbauamt Nürnberg, Germany.

Richardson Wood, of Program Research, Inc., reviewed a preliminary draft of the industrial section; especially generous help was given to Dorothy Moore in acquiring material and references for the section on open space by Karl J. Belser, Director of Planning, County of Santa Clara Planning Department, by Milton Breivogel, Director of Planning, Los Angeles County Regional Planning Commission, by Charles W. Eliot, Planning Consultant and Professor at Harvard University, by Stephen A. Kaufman, Deputy Director, and Melvin Roebuck, Chief Planner, Cleveland Regional Planning Commission, and by Philip Lewis, Landscape Architect with the Department of Resource Development, Recreation Division, State of Wisconsin (formerly of the University of Illnois); the manuscript on historic preservation was read by Mrs. William Slater Allen, Vice President of the Providence Preservation Society and Board Member of the National Trust for Historic Preservation, Washington, D.C.; and Mrs. Robert Penn Warren discussed with us many problems of rural-urban fringe living.

The authors' thanks go to all these people and to many more who in conversation or correspondence have helped us in our work. Special gratitude is due to Coleman Woodbury, of the University of Wisconsin, who, as Visiting Professor in City Planning at Yale, guided our early thoughts into constructive channels. Last but not least, we wish to record our appreciation of the facilities afforded by the Yale University Press under the aegis of its Director Chester Kerr; to its Arts Editor and expert counselor Edward Trafford McClellan; and to the designer of these pages, John O. C. McCrillis.

C. T.
B. P.

New Haven, March 1962

PART ONE

The Urbanized Landscape: The Esthetics of Man-Made America

1. The Contemporary Scene

2. Landscape as Art

3. The American Landscape

4. Emerging Landscapes of America
   The Center
   The Middle Ground
   Suburbia
   Elements of the Fringe
   The Rural Landscape
   Unsettled Country

5. Beauty Spots

6. The New Settlement Pattern

7. The Non-Beautiful

1. The Contemporary Scene

Visitors to the United States are impressed by our skyscrapers and our superhighways, the vast scale of our harbors and cities, and our dramatic conquest of half a continent by technological invention and adaptation. The availability of so many goods in the stores, the vast numbers of automobiles in the streets, and the relative speed and quantity of building construction are also noticeable in comparison with many other countries.

But if the informed visitor gives us high marks for the production of goods and for the spectacular conquest of difficult technical problems, he is not so likely to give wholehearted approval to the environment which is the result of this production. As the Parisians are apt to say of their most famous nineteenth-century planner, Baron Haussmann, "It is not that he wasn't a creator, but his creations were without soul." The traveler from Europe may with justice reprove us for being too hasty in our reliance on technology to solve every problem, or if he is from a developing nation in Asia or Africa he may prayerfully hope that advancing technology in his own country will not produce an environment like this one.

For the expertly engineered automobiles are seen against a background of ramshackle slums, the winding rivers are dark with pollution, the waterfronts are crowded with ancient factories, and the spreading suburbs seem to have no centers of life or evidence of individual distinction. The tall buildings stand next to vacant lots and the highways are strung out between billboards and shoddy commercial salesrooms.

Instead of placing man at the center of the American environment, we apparently have left it either empty or cluttered with waste. Not only are our creations without soul, but they seem to be aimless and without forethought.

If the visitor looks further, he will find that this was not always so—that along with rough exploitation of the land has often gone a careful husbandry and a fitting taste in man-made houses and towns. He has only to look at the landscape of Vermont, where farming and nature have combined to make views in all directions a delight, or at the early settlements of Alexandria, Virginia, or the later development of the Back Bay in Boston, where, as in a hundred other places, an appropriate townscape has been evolved, to know that Americans have contributed agreeable things to Western cultural history.

These distinctive earlier differentiations of the settlement pattern, which achieved an urban atmosphere in the town and a rural beauty of the countryside, have given way to an entropic form of growth, the characteristics of which are chaos and sameness. In recent times a very loose rein has been held on the forces which shape our environment, and the economic determinism which has unleashed these forces has produced a confusion in men's minds between personal liberties and wider freedoms. Even the recent applications of welfare capitalism have not been effective in creating anything but very small enclaves in which the tendency to organization has increased rather than deteriorated, and these exhibit few esthetic results, being mostly in the nature of social legislation and improved economic status on limited scales.

It is to be expected, therefore, that in spite of the efforts of planners and others who wish to improve the environment, the modern city will show few aspects of definite, coordinated form, but rather an indeterminate, atomized pattern of change, working toward the destruction of any earlier coherent forms which may exist within it, and the concomitants of this process are waste, ugliness, and decay.

Economic forces account for much, but not everything. Perhaps the informed visitor will think that the American population has increased so rapidly in recent years that we have not been able to catch up with ourselves. Certainly an urban revolution has been under way, spilling over into the small towns and countryside. But this is no real excuse for lack of taste and wild disorder.

Other societies have successfully handled sudden increases in population as far back as Hellenistic times, when, with more limited resources, hundreds of new towns of a planned nature were founded to urbanize the Middle Eastern and North African world. Nor was Hellenistic society at all niggardly in providing places of public gathering, libraries, theatres, or items of public adornment in even the most remote parts of the ancient landscape. Therefore, if our traveler goes on to blame public apathy, he will be partly right—it is all too obvious that recent generations of dedicated teachers have not been able to inculcate a desire on the part of the American people to care for anything to do with appearance except in the matter of their own homes and home appliances, their automobiles, their cosmetics, and their clothes. A public indifference to public beauty is a most obvious lack in the nation at the present time and is certainly prime cause for concern on the part of those who wish to see the countryside properly cared for and the cities appropriately rebuilt.

Apart from the already-mentioned reliance on technology and innovation as a panacea, it seems clear that another lacuna exists in the public mind to block the achievement of a wholly satisfying environment. Our undoubted talents in economic production and in organization, the strength of our churches and ethical institutions, our eagerness and generosity in helping the less fortunate, all leave out a wide area of human endeavor concerned with the application of taste in the visual world. This is a lack often to be found in new democracies; Jefferson warned us of it and Santayana made a wry joke of the matter when he said that in a democracy "people can do as they wish and (therefore) do not get what they want." It has thus too often happened that all personal demonstrations of beauty by a Stanford White or a Frank Lloyd Wright have either quickly gone out of fashion because no standards of beauty exist or have been laughed at because they do not conform to the low level of popular taste.

It is with some aspects of art in the environment, therefore, that the present book is concerned, in the belief that design must be applied to a wider field than that of architect-designed houses, office buildings, or schools if we are to create a man-made landscape of which we can be proud. It is written with the conviction that there are principles of order, which, if understood and consciously used, can bring art into the landscape in such a way that there will be plenty of room for individual expression without resulting in the disturbing anarchy (or monotony) which now exists. To this end, we have examined selected man-made phenomena: the low-density subdivision, the highway, industrial and commercial facilities, recreational systems, and historic districts—all of regional significance, appropriate to the type of settlement pattern now evolving. It is our belief that if the underlying esthetic principles are examined against the background of our changing economic and physical needs, the first step toward a public sympathy and understanding for a better-looking America can be won.

2. Landscape as Art

How shall we look at the landscape, natural or man-made?

Can we indeed be objective about it? We know that a Chinese Buddhist monk, an eighteenth-century traveler on the Grand Tour, the occupants of a covered wagon

Olympic National Park, Washington: Delabarre Glacier on the east side of Mount Christie.

going west, and a modern businessman looking out an airplane window would all see something different in the same stretch of countryside. To one, a mountain range would provide a symbol for the expression of thought, to another a picture of delight, to the third a fearsome barrier, and to the last perhaps only a landmark on an aerial map. We discover that attitudes toward nature are constantly changing, making it hard for any of us to be objective about even the simplest of natural phenomena.

Religious symbolism, animism, cosmolatry, romantic morality, psychological transference, and a host of other factors may be involved in our attitude to the landscape.

It is man's world, after all.

Our mountain range may receive the attention of the hydraulic engineer or of Gutzon Borglum, of the skiing enthusiast or of Robert Frost—each will see it differently: as a utilitarian, a hedonist, a conceptualist, or a moralist, whatever he may be, connecting the phenomenon with his own intuitions and ideas.

Some few men have looked at the landscape objectively, it is true—that is, objectively, but with humanitarian concern. From Patrick Henry to Harold Ickes there have been individuals and groups who have promoted soil conservation, reforestation, national parks, and even preservation in the cities. Through their efforts public policies have been formed and public improvements made. We have reached a stage of civilization in which great numbers of people have been educated to look at the landscape in a new way, and to realize that man and his environment today are so inextricably interwoven that the mountain range has become more than a symbol and is a vital element of man's existence on earth. The conquest of nature, of space, of time, and of distance, and the achievement of population and production balance—all these will serve only to wed man still closer to nature, and, even as he appears to emancipate himself from earthly ties, to make him more dependent than ever on the materials of earth and air. This necessary coordination of effort is becoming especially apparent in our atomic age, as we see that the activities of man, instead of achieving balance, could produce an unendurable imbalance of the physical world, creating a nightmarish universe in which certain elements, certain processes, could become so important that society might engage in the destruction both of nature and of itself. Some will say that this reckless tinkering with nature is already in an advanced stage, but it is not too late to adopt another attitude and to command the forces of nature by more humanized concepts.

Certainly, man's imprints on the landscape are often detrimental to the future in lesser ways. After the collapse of Roman civilization in Tripolitania, overgrazing and the neglect of soil control measures led to erosion of the wadis and the deterioration of a large part of the northern Sahara. The nineteenth-century American pioneer made a practice of burning down the forest, cropping the soil until it was exhausted, then moving on to virgin land; and when "suitcase" farmers expanded their holdings to grow wheat and overgraze thin-cover grasslands in Oklahoma and Texas during an eight-year drought in the 1930s, the ensuing race against their creditors produced the disaster of millions of acres of dust, ready to blow in every breeze.

Against these examples one can place the careful methods of Dutch and Japanese farmers, whose elaborate methods of irrigation, intercropping, and fertilization of the soil have kept it in production through many centuries; in this country, one can point to the enrichment of their farm land by the Pennsylvania Dutch and the proper maintenance of farming in parts of Iowa, where agricultural land is so valuable that it is only rented to farmers who guarantee to maintain soil fertility. And it is largely due

Kaiser Steel Plant at Fontana, California, in farm landscape before suburbanization.

to the example of the national government and the efforts of private farmers using good cultivation practices that the American "dust-bowl" has been reclaimed. But eroded land, marginal land, scrub-forests, and the scars of surface mining all over the world are testimony to the fact that we have not yet come to consider the total land-scape as a productive unit in the scheme of human progress.

When man does try to establish an equilibrium in a constantly changing world, we call this activity planning. And, somehow, in our new way of looking at the landscape, we must include the possibility of planning everywhere, even though it be planning in the sense of conserving the wildest nature, untouched by the hand of man.

Conservation of wild nature, unknown when man's numbers were still small and he was fighting against the wilderness, becomes increasingly important as we enter a period of intensified urbanization in all the earth's countries. The need for increased food production, born of the population explosion, demands that the land not wild be made productive; thus we have a two-pronged approach to the landscape of the future—through conservation and through increased productivity.

It should be mentioned that there is in theory no incompatibility between the enlargement of towns and land fertility. It has been pointed out by agriculturists that land fertility actually increases with the size of towns, and not with the number of persons engaged in farming. Money from urban consumers flows back to the farmers, and, as long as this process is continuous, allows them to put more back into the land than they take out of it. In view of the development of urban regions to be described later it is interesting to realize that the world of 100 years hence with its population of perhaps some 20 billion people will be able to feed itself, provided that most people live in cities and offer enough money for the production of their food.

In our approach to the landscape nowadays, therefore, it is important to develop attitudes more fitting to the realities of man's relationship to nature than those which merely evoke a mood or a psychological reaction. The latter will be present in any case. Certain melancholy feelings will presumably always arise at the prospect of miles of dismal swamp, and feelings of reassurance will be induced by landmarks, natural or man-made, in the surroundings of towns. But beyond this, we should be seeking more productive attitudes and taking a new look at nature to see how it can nourish our emerging settlement patterns and satisfy the demands of modern life.

This new attitude surely must include the concepts of productivity and usability. It may not be inappropriate to invoke Jefferson's dictum, "Utility to man is the standard and test of virtue." The virtue of man-used landscapes should be precisely that they are fitting in this respect—that they contribute to his vision of the order of the world. The concept of utility to man does not merely envisage nature as a provider of food and shelter but also as a part of man's progress and destiny; nature, when well-used, is a reflection of his noblest aspirations. Violations of nature are the reverse—symbols of his inhumanity, selfishness, or greed.

It follows from this that a sense of the usefulness of nature must be a prerequisite to man's actions in building and shaping his surroundings. This principle must underly the design esthetic which we have seen to be a missing quality in public attitudes and actions in dealing with the physical world.

What, then, is the nature of design within this concept of the environment?

In the broadest sense, we can say that design enters the picture when man's imprints on the landscape are congenial, rather than careless. Accepting the fact that we live in a world of perpetual change, we must achieve an equilibrium where we can. This will express our intentions clearly, and within this action lies the esthetic element we are seeking. Square diked rice paddies, rows of grain, the broad sweep of reforested hillsides, highway ribbons, planned cities—these express our sense of order, our intentions. Any action that humanizes the landscape or puts it to its highest productive use may contain esthetic values—a very ancient concept of beauty which derives from Greek civilization.

We should not always expect to find the highest forms of art in specific man-made landscapes. This would be utopian and impossible of realization. In most cases we should expect to achieve nothing more than a congenial form, and only occasionally, where the form is endowed with imagination, a true work of art—like the acqueducts of Roman times, the forest landscapes of certain French chateaux, or the completeness of a well-designed residential square. Where esthetic values are dominant we can talk of art or fine art, but in the case of the macro-landscape it is difficult to separate the esthetic from the useful, and we have had to be content with those values, low in the scale of art though they may be, which increase man's comfort, knowledge, and pleasure. They may be nothing more than the value of order—it is order which makes the irrigated surroundings of Isfahan or the reforested areas of the T.V.A. so attractive to the eye and to man's sense of fitness.

But man is a learning animal, and nowadays there is no reason to be content with landscapes which are not of a higher level than before. Many skills are involved in the shaping of the environment today—engineering, architecture, urban planning, forestry and scientific agriculture, landscaping, and conservation, as well as just plain

Black dirt area, Orange County,
New York.

building. The physical products of all these activities, it is true, are in varying degree determined by the realities of natural science and by the social realities of politics and economics. But while in certain exact disciplines like aerodynamics close adherence to physical determinism almost automatically produces pleasing forms, the physical and economic realities of our large-scale man-made environment, in spite of their inherent order, are incapable of producing beauty by themselves. Here, beauty can only emerge from a deliberate effort to express the encounter between society and environment in significant form.

Hence, these pages will touch upon elements of engineering, human geography, and the other disciplines involved, but their emphasis will remain visual, and the basic method to be employed will be that of formal esthetic analysis. The environmental types considered will be analyzed from the viewpoint of harmonious visual relationships within themselves, and from the viewpoint of their coordination with the micro-landscape as well as the macro-landscape. They will be measured against abstract esthetic criteria, such as those of continuity, contrast, rhythm, balance, articulation, proportion, and focus, and the resulting conclusions will be checked back against the functional requirements of the activity or technological form in question, and against their potential for human use and enjoyment.

3. The American Landscape

How shall we look at the American landscape? What conditions make it a specialized type of landscape and what indications are there that it may require a special treatment?

First, it is too large a land mass to be considered as a whole. What do we think of when we hear the words "American landscape"? Fields of corn, hunting bear, canoeing on lakes, Route 66, the Rocky Mountains, San Francisco, the Jersey flats, Texas oil fields, the Everglades? All these images and many more, probably. There are more climatic, geological, and vegetative differences within the United States than in almost any other country, from Alaska's ore fields to the steamy Florida peninsula, from New England's rocky pastures to the Mojave Desert. Almost any kind of crop can be cultivated somewhere within its borders, almost any mineral dug, and almost any type of manufacture operated.

At the same time it is the country which has gone farthest along the road toward elimination of differences in standards of living and culture, so that repetitive elements are bound to occur in the man-made scene. Roads, farm machinery, vehicles of all kinds, factories, and even houses will look alike in every section, and, although regional differences do exist, there is more and more a sameness about man's changes in the earth's surface. All our recent revolutions in the economic and social order have tended to produce this sameness—new forms like oil cracking plants or shortwave relay stations are continually being introduced, but they tend to be cast in exactly the same mold; even their disposition on the ground will vary little from a standard pattern.

The suburbs of Anchorage are similar to those of New York, the only difference being that the houses in Alaska are more expensive, having been shipped in from "outside." All the newer manifestations of mass culture—trailer parks, shopping centers, marinas, or motels—tend to be laid out on a similar plan, and even regional differences in their architecture have disappeared as they tend more and more to become chain operations.

The major regional differences in this large country today tend to be found in the elements which were present before the white man came, ironically enough—in land formation, natural vegetation and crop production, although the two last have changed considerably in their components. Differences in habitation and economic patterns are to be found less and less. Certain variations in land division tend to linger and leave their mark: the sections and quarter sections of the Midwest as opposed to strip layouts in French Canada or the metes and bounds system of New England. Strip mining and a few other extractive operations are not carried on everywhere and may mar a regional landscape distinctively, but nowadays it will be mainly

Baby Doe Tabor's cabin at the Matchless Mine, Leadville, Colorado, where she died in 1930; the site is now a tourist attraction.

the difference in pattern of a cranberry bog and sand dune area of Cape Cod from a San Bernardino County orange grove which will stand out sharply in the memory, or the distinctive texture of a northern pine forest and the deciduous hardwoods of the Southern Appalachians which will mark one region from another.

True, a white New England village center around an irregular green and a Texas courthouse town with its central building on the square are still very different habitation patterns, but now that both have been invaded by standardized subdivisions, identical gas stations, garages, restaurant chains, stainless steel "diners," auto courts, and parking lots, their distinctive character has largely been dissipated. And if the ghost towns of Arizona and Colorado lend color to the desert and mountain regions of the West it is our sentimental attachment to a riotous period in American history rather than their small, scattered, and crumbling forms which mark the landscape as a special place. Much more significant in the West today are the trailer camps for uranium workers, which move from site to site as new mines are opened up and old ones are exhausted.

However, there are still enough differences from European and other countries to make the American scene distinctive *in itself.* The New England landscape, for instance, is shaggier, more woodsy, and somewhat wilder than anything to be found in old England, while its settlement pattern (houses of all periods scattered on country roads throughout a whole township) is completely different. Our open-lot tradition of separated houses is distinctly non-European, although it is fairly close to the traditional practice of some Asian countries. The scale of our harbors, docking, railroad facilities, and warehousing is much larger, on the whole, and even the scale of our buildings, after the Colonial period, is much bigger than Europe's—compare the frame house for middle- and low-income families since 1900 in the United States with its modest European counterpart. The skylines of our cities and towns are taller, our streets often wider. Beyond the inner ring of old brick row houses and apartment buildings in most American cities, everything seems looser and more spread out; the vacant lot is practically unknown in Europe. You might say that parts of California have a superficial resemblance to the French, Italian, and Lebanese rivieras, but this is mainly because all are littorals, dry and with the ocean at hand. However, this resemblance ends with closer inspection of the micro-landscape—a few hours' driving from, say, Hollywood toward Palm Springs, reveals a landscape with very special characteristics. After leaving the downtown area you pass walled and fenced subdivisions, abandoned orange groves, vineyards (much more extensive than the European vineyard), a giant Convair plant, houses appearing on the tops of hills—only the San Bernardino Mountains (protected) give any reassurance that wild nature still has any part to play in the design. Even a glimpse of the nostalgic and beautiful civic center at Pasadena or the calculated layout of the town of Riverside will seem different to a visitor from a planned city in Europe—the architecture will be unfamiliar, at least, and at Palm Springs, if he hasn't heard about it, he will find himself in such a never-never land as he scarcely expected to see on this earth. The advanced development of mass production and mass distribution in the United States is producing a completely new landscape, bearing little relation to older California traditions, prodigal, amazing, but at least in part predictable. "In part" because we are only now beginning to understand what is happening, somewhat after the event. This process will be described later.

If, as Victor Jones suggests, the European city and its physical area of influence is beginning to develop growth characteristics similar to those now special to the United States, we can expect many of the present differences to disappear in time. Already the apartment houses springing up on the edge of Damascus have the look and scattered siting of their Arroyo Seco counterparts, and the villas up the hills beyond Beirut are very similar to the individual houses being built in the foothills beyond San Bernardino. Land controls and real estate development do not function any better in Lebanon than in California, not that this should be any consolation to Americans. The man-made landscape of the United States, although still distinctively different, leaves much to be desired as human geography, and it is in the direction of a more humanized landscape (the term, of course, includes the concept of wild nature) that our efforts should be directed before it is completely twisted out of shape.

4. Emerging Landscapes of America

Proceeding from these general remarks on the American settlement pattern, we will now turn to an examination of its component parts and their changing forms.

Growth of the nature which we see going on all around us inevitably brings certain changes in the landscape, not all of which are immediately visible but which have their symbols nonetheless. Most of them are necessary changes, too, and have to do with our increasingly specialized economy and new forms being developed in the exchange of goods. That these changes are seldom foreseen accounts for much of the visual chaos and confusion of modern America—we do not hold anyone responsible for this thoughtlessness, but by allowing the "process" of the free market to take place without consideration of its byproducts in social and physical terms we encourage untidiness and waste. An undertaking such as the British Town & County Planning Act, which requires a proposed physical use for every acre of land in Great Britain, would be unwelcome here because of our illusions of freedom to expand in any way we like, and because of our reliance on local communities to do the job in their own way. But there is no local community in the older sense—we are still living mentally in the old rural America of the town meeting, which has gone into the past as surely as a horse and buggy creaking down the lane. Today's community is a broader affair altogether —its interrelationships with the outside world suggest the "higher provincialism" of Josiah Royce—and it is an unwilling host to new economic and social forces not always understood.

If, as Robert McIver suggests, the mark of a community is that one's life *may* be lived wholly within it, most American families today have a stake in a much larger piece of the land than ever before—their mobility, working hours, leisure-time pursuits, and economic scale have all contributed to ripping the old communities apart. Their new sphere of activity is a community which has taken on the dimensions of a region.

THE CENTER

At the heart of this region is the central business district of the older cities. Will this central "market place" continue to exist in its present form? In many cities it is quite thoroughly being rebuilt, or plans for rebuilding are under way and millions of dollars are being poured into clearance and redevelopment. Why? Because it has found itself recently in competition with new retail sales centers in suburban areas or outside the city altogether. In some cities this trend has been accepted as inevitable and the rebuilt areas at the center are concentrating on commercial activities other than retail—on specialized services, like banking and "communications" industry, or on supporting office uses, services, such as wholesale distribution, regional markets,

Central business district of Philadelphia, with new construction in progress; in the foreground, the Penn Center office building complex.

medical centers, and so on. (These are as a rule just outside the central business district, but are a part of what planners call its "frame.") "Perhaps the central business district of the future will be a central office district," the economic geographers speculate, "an area in which the business enterprises of the city will maintain their offices, accompanied by only enough retailing to serve the immediate needs of the people who work in the office buildings," although they qualify this by stating that, if retailing is on the decline in very large cities, this function can possibly be maintained in the centers of moderate-sized cities.

All this indicates change, and a very important change, since the heart of the city has always been considered the center of our civilization. That it should alter from the conglomerate mixture of shops, wholesale commerce, theatres, hotels, libraries, and city offices which have somehow maintained themselves as a market and civic center for all the people of the city for so many years is tragic in one sense and a mirror of the times in another. Many people are deliberately shunning the central business district today, even those who live well within the city limits. Its convenience has disappeared—the old easy-going days of city living in which a housewife could call up a store and have a package delivered by the streetcar conductor at the end of the street are gone forever, and such new "convenience" devices as drive-in tellers and pigeon-hole parking garages have not proved an adequate substitute. New attractions which might have brought more people to the central business district have seldom been forthcoming—the movie houses have been turned into television studios, the best restaurants are likely to be out on the highway with plenty of free parking; when these new attractions have been desperately conjured up by city fathers in the form of amusement centers and the like, they usually require too much space to be feasible in the city center.

The central business district is also being pruned of its earlier manufacturing plants, built at or near the center in the days when they relied on an urban work-force for their labor supply. Usually a loft-type building which neither suits today's manufacturing processes nor allows enough parking for the more mobile factory worker, the manufacturing plant has abdicated its position as a prime city use and gone to the suburbs or even further out. Most of the residence has gone too. Many planners think this is a good thing—that the valuable land at the center should only be used for activities that promote greater prosperity at the center—all else should go. But the fact remains that the center will lose much of its glamour and interest if it has no residential life and is occupied merely by a daytime population of people who work in offices and distribution centers.

In the process of change and being created anew the central business district is being given a new shape by an opening out and by new entrances, brought about by the construction of new highways. Elsewhere will be found an account of their prog-ress through the interurban landscape, but nowhere have they done as much to cre-ate the new city as at the center. Both radial feeder highways and interurban freeways converge at the center, but since present-day traffic volumes do not permit concentra-tion at one point, the older idea of bringing traffic into a central plaza, as in Philadel-phia, Detroit, and elsewhere, has been abandoned by the traffic engineers in favor of a device called the Inner Connector Loop, a highway circumferential to the central business district. This facilitates traffic movement in or very near the heart of the city and enables motorists to drive directly into strategically placed garages or parking lots serving the central business district. This is the best answer we have had so far to the pull of suburban facilities, although it is only a partial answer. The Inner Connector Loop has tended to increase values within the portion of the central business district which it encloses, and to encourage the erection of supporting facilities—warehousing, service industries, and so on—on the exterior. This highway usually runs through old slums or industrially-blighted areas just outside the commercial-cultural center and has often been constructed as part of a redevelopment program for these problem areas. Since the alignment of a six- or eight-lane facility of this kind can seldom follow the gridiron pattern of the average city and since very large interchanges are necessary at the entrance to the central business district itself, the whole appearance of this part of town has been changed, new views opened up to the motorist (often of the backs of huge warehouses or office buildings, set at non-conforming angles to the high-way), and a great deal of the former closed-in feeling of the center has been dissipated.

The center of the average American city can thus easily become a series of not-very-skillfully related projects of a commercial-servicing nature, separated by surface park-ing lots and garages and containing a huge population in daytime and almost none at night. It is not easy to make such a center beautiful, except with much greater vision that our cities have so far shown. It has been recommended by a group of architects and planners that the cities embark immediately on the preparation of visual design plans which would involve the necessary research of proposals to improve relation-ships at the center, the proposals to be incorporated in the master plan of the community. Much stronger control over private redevelopment will also be necessary; strict landscaping provisions will have to be written into redevelopment contracts; and developers made to conform in height, bulk, and general appearance to the over-all design plan. No city, with the possible exception of Philadelphia, Detroit, and a few others, has made any strong move in this direction at present.

Meanwhile, it will be helpful in our consideration of the center of the city if we look at it as a somewhat more specialized, denser part of the urban continuum. In

Grey areas of today and tomorrow: *above,* Astoria, Queens, seen from the tracks of the New York Connecting Railroad; *below,* suburbs of Philadelphia seen from the Pennsylvania Turnpike.

some cases it may become nothing more than a regional shopping center, so great have been the efforts of the Downtown Merchants' Associations to compete with the threat of the suburbs. In others the new center may conform more to the logic of the service function sketched above, which will enable it to play a changed but still active part in the city's economy. In still others, especially the centers of older cities in which cluster many important buildings and institutions of historic or regional importance, a balance may be reached between new demands and the continuing use of the center as a cultural nucleus. In all cases, a coordinated effort by planners, highway engineers, architects, and redevelopment authorities will be necessary to improve the center's appearance. The economic pressures have so far been given priority over esthetic considerations, but it is the latter which will insure the place of the center in the community's esteem and its ultimate success in attracting people.

Very few design devices for high-density areas have yet been tried, particularly those which would take advantage of the multi-dimensional nature of city centers—the introduction of depressed pedestrian plazas, for instance, which would open the entrances of subway tunnels to light and air, with utility channels below and automobile circulation above, opening onto small pedestrian parks with water and intimate views.

The parks and malls and fountains; the temples of God, of government, and of commerce which have marked the central city at its greatest periods; the squares and avenues and vistas—if these are forgotten or merely given lip-service, we can only turn our backs on the center of the city and accept the village culture we deserve.

THE MIDDLE GROUND

The urbanized areas of the American landscape extend from the center of the cities to the edge of a well-defined street pattern, or, in the words of the 1950 Census, in which they were described for the first time, "Each urbanized area contains at least one city with 50,000 or more inhabitants. . . . Each urbanized area also includes the surrounding closely settled incorporated places and unincorporated areas. . . . Its boundaries were established to conform as nearly as possible to the actual boundaries of thickly-settled territory, *usually characterized by a closely-spaced street pattern* [italics added]."

This is a convenient definition for the extent of the city proper, including the "pure" suburbs, and excluding the haphazard development usually termed the "rural-urban fringe," with its discontinuous street and building pattern, where different problems are to be found.

Outside the "frame" of the central business district, where warehousing, mixed commercial, and terminal facilities are usually located, lie the city's middle-aged residential neighborhoods, which today are subject to blighting influences and are in danger of deteriorating into "rock-bottom slums." They are tending to overcrowding, as the centers are rebuilt and former central area residents move out, their housing is in need of repair, there is traffic congestion and insufficient off-street parking and "a declining faith in the future of the neighborhood, leading to a high rate of move-outs and a low rate of maintenance." The older, in-city neighborhoods are plagued by a mixing of commercial and industrial uses with residences and apartments, while the farther-out quality residence districts are subject to pressures for new institutional uses—private, educational, religious, and semi-commercial insurance, hospitals, and medical and charitable office buildings, which often destroy, rather than enhance, historic areas of civic beauty.

These parts of the city, lying as they do between the center and the newer suburbs, are in the throes of change and are becoming a focus of municipal attention in desperate efforts to stabilize them, on the one hand by rehabilitation and "conservation" measures and stricter enforcement of housing codes, and on the other by new zoning provisions which allow modified conversion of existing buildings and require off-street parking provisions. It is likely that government funds will be increasingly used to assist home owners in "conservation" areas where private lending institutions fear the risk involved, and that rehabilitation advisory services will be set up to provide technical assistance for the process of stabilization.

Whether these efforts, which are being made late in many cases, will succeed in preventing "the middle ground" from becoming a vast slum is problematical. Granted that there are people now moving out to the suburbs who would prefer to live closer to the center of the city, the people who can conveniently live in the city are by force of circumstances narrowed down at present to young married couples without children and retired people, who do not have to consider the problem of obsolete school buildings and major traffic hazards. This relatively small group is vastly outnumbered by people of low incomes who are forced to live in second-hand housing and converted dwellings in the grey areas because they have no automobile or cannot afford to own their own homes. As William H. Whyte has put it, "the city is becoming a place of extremes—a place for the very poor, or the very rich, or the very odd," although recent figures indicate an increasing middle income group.

By contrast with nineteenth-century developments in European cities like Vienna or Paris, where mobility is far less common and structural permanence greater, the deterioration of the American central city moves much faster than clearance and redevelopment can correct. Although European cities also face immense reconstruction problems, their middle ground areas are often at once more livable and more esthetically pleasing, since their reconstruction efforts have been in the direction of blending the new with the old. The high cost and "drop in the bucket" aspects of redevelopment in American cities have caused some authorities to suggest completely new uses for the middle ground, such as accessible in-city airfields and rural parks in town, or, alternatively, retaining much of the fabric and providing free public transportation, which in some cases would be cheaper than drastic rebuilding and would provide a stimulus to home improvement. To such extremes have responsible theorists been driven by the multiplying problems of the older cities.

If "conservation" and rehabilitation are combined with major traffic reorganization, school modernization, new park acquisition, better and cheaper rapid transit facilities, and other progressive ideals, living conditions in the grey areas may be improved sufficiently to bring back a modicum of order and beauty into the lives of the people who need it most in our society. Even so, we should not consider these areas as "central city oriented" any longer. The factory worker living in the middle ground will need the new highway facility in order to drive out daily to his job in the rural-urban fringe, and the housewife can be counted on to use it also for a weekly shopping trip to the suburbs. An urban region of increased "flow" and mobility will mean that these older areas of the city, now teetering on the brink, must be bolstered by vast public improvements as well as self-help in order to survive. But outlining neighborhoods and city districts with new or improved traffic arteries will not be the extent of public improvement needed. Imaginative rebuilding as well as conservation is a critical necessity in the older parts of the city—balancing off new squares and pockets of old-age housing, for instance (there is a high proportion of elderly people in these areas), with careful preservation of suitably-built residential districts like Society Hill in Philadelphia or Wooster Square in New Haven. Extremely successful new residential squares have been built in the East End of London by the London County Council, much less institutional-looking than the earlier public housing in England or the United States. Only a view of the city as a whole, and as an artifact, will produce such interesting results on a nationwide scale. Otherwise, we may expect the critical middle ground to deteriorate into a nightmare problem area, as parts of it have indeed already become.

SUBURBIA

With the inner suburbs on the urban fringe of the city we come to the beginning of the landscape which is the main concern of this book and also to significant anti-city attitudes on the part of the region's inhabitants. Suburbanites as a group want no part of the central city, although there are many exceptions among individuals to this generalization. They are protected and encouraged in this attitude by local political boundaries, taxation policies, and other devices of municipal particularism, stemming from the days when America's economy and political outlook was agrarian, when the city and the country town were separate and distinct entities. The myth persists that grass-roots democracy has its home in the suburban town, and newcomers from the city are quickly indoctrinated with the supposed virtues of small-town living, the higher-paid teachers, the lack of urban corruption, the generally superior facilities for modern family life.

In spite of inevitable growing pains and rising taxes, the dwellers in suburbia *are* better off in many ways than the in-city resident. They do not live in such crowded conditions as the inhabitants of the grey areas. They have some access to open space, if not always in an intensive park system, at least in the grounds of their own homes. They can enjoy certain leisure-time activities denied to central city dwellers or apartment-house renters—gardening, boat-building, alfresco dining. There is more encouragement to entertain friends, join civic groups, participate. For many people, suburbia offers the best possible milieu for bringing up children, for social advancement, and for the enjoyment of living. It represents "the apotheosis of the family," as

Henry James remarked of the country club (a suburban institution) many years ago.

Yet, in any attempt to foresee the future of the suburban landscape, certain important "hidden costs" of the true suburb must be taken into account. The suburban dweller is, of all social groups, the most dependent on other parts of the urban region for earning a living. The largest single expenditure arising as a result of suburban growth is for highways and other transportation to tie together the scattered elements of the living and working pattern. Suburbia is thus the home of the commuter, the white-collar worker who can afford to live outside the central city and drive or ride to work in town. In recent years he has been able to share to some extent in new employment opportunities in the rural-urban fringe and in some of the former "bedroom" suburbs, where jobs are now increasing faster than population. He is thus both an escapist and a prisoner at the same time. His children will see little of him, and they will miss other opportunities, too—seldom meeting children of other social groups, for instance, and having to travel long distances to visit museums and other necessary cultural facilities or go without doing so. The suburb is deficient in many things—it will rarely contain a public housing project or a superior public art collection. At the same time, it runs the risk of attracting blight, especially near its old village center which over the years has remained the only part of the suburb resembling a high-density area. If boarding houses, gas stations, and shoddy commercial ventures exist in a suburb, they will be found here, as well as along the highway which serves as a main artery into town.

Although it is the image all suburbs hold of themselves, it should not be imagined that they consist exclusively of substantial citizens living on leafy lanes with a fire hydrant on each corner and an eighty-foot frontage of green lawn. Beside every select Bronxville there exists a Tuckahoe, and beside every Lake Forest a part of the county in which the garbage collectors and cleaning women live, in contrast to the older cities where they may live around the corner. Less dramatically, a large tract of suburbs will show many gradations of income, but few mixed areas. This is a reflection of the way suburbs are built, subdivision by subdivision, some with higher restrictions than others, and all of them geared to special income levels. This is a very different living pattern from the ones Americans knew before 1920, but it is also the one which is producing the nation's managerial class and which has conditioned social standards and attitudes among middle-income groups in this country for a full generation.

Physically, therefore, the suburban areas may be described as a mosaic of rather large pieces of land, segregated by income and class, and held together with the cement of housing prices and zoning. The mosaic is broken by parks, shopping centers, occasional industries, golf courses, and public and private institutions which follow the major road patterns. Within the mosaic are raw new suburbs and settled older suburbs, ranging in size from a few hundred people to several thousand, representing entire political entities or quasi-political subgroups within a suburban community. There is variety here, but also a sameness; together with its low density and preponderance of single-family houses on similar-sized lots, this makes for a pattern

The suburban mosaic in New Jersey. Predominantly residential, many suburbs nevertheless contain industry and commerce. At right center is the planned community of Radburn with its interior park strips (1928); at the upper left is Fair Lawn Industrial Park (McBride Associates), built in the 1950s, with its manufacturing plants surrounded by green lawns; below this can be seen an apartment-house group. Several schools are also visible among the subdivisions.

of uniformity on the scale of the macro-landscape, however varied the individual pieces of the mosaic may be.

Two problems of the suburbs which have not been solved to anyone's satisfaction are aging and sprawl. Like the residential districts of the inner city, many suburbs are now old enough to be faced with real problems of blight, traffic congestion, and general deterioration of physical plant. These conditions, which are most acute in suburbs settled during the first automobile age—1910 to 1925—have forced people farther and farther out in their attempts to find more satisfactory living conditions. Rich and poor alike (but especially the latter) have tended to "jump" suburbia for the rural-urban fringe, where the pattern of the mosaic is changed for a system of beads along a string.

It may be that the hope for the future of the inner suburbs is to treat them realistically in the light of what they actually are—a part of the urbanized area of the city. But to "urbanize" the suburbs—to bring them more cultural facilities, apartment houses, public housing projects, properly planned commercial centers, and other appurtenances of the urban way of life will demand a different attitude on the part of their residents, whose ideology and attitudes to the city have so far proved a barrier to change in this direction. They are still holding out for "country living," while the true country is receding farther and farther from the visible horizon.

ELEMENTS OF THE FRINGE

Beyond the "urbanized areas" described above (the city and its suburbs) and in many parts of the country extending as far as the next urbanized area, lie the new living spaces called by social scientists the *rural-urban fringe*. This is the land between the cities and in the counties, formerly agricultural, which today has become a mixture of agriculture, residence, and industry, and is where the fastest population growth is taking place.

Views in the rural-urban fringe, with new subdivisions (*left*) and owner-built houses (*right*).

It can easily be imagined that "interurbia," as it has been called by the economist Richardson Wood, where land controls are weak and land prices are usually cheaper than in the suburbs, presents a picture of arbitrary development. One cannot find elsewhere so little relation between a reasonable use of land and its actual utilization, or so little observable relationship between the different uses. That there is a pattern of sorts is made clear in some detail in Part II, but this pattern, based upon known and predicted uses, has no rhyme or reason in terms of esthetic continuity or order. If we have called it in a very simplified way a pattern of beads along a string, this is because fringe development is tentacular, spreading out along existing highways and town roads, but thickening in places where subdivisions or industries have located in a congerie of developments. Open space exists, but it is often unusable open space, since new building along the roads cuts it off from any access by the public.

Among the more distinctive characteristics of these fringe areas the following may be noted:

(a) The population density is low, compared with the true suburb, but at the same time its recent rate of growth is higher.

(b) The movement to the fringe is a movement of families. Single persons are not attracted. Fringe dwellers are property owners rather than renters, but "ownership" consists of small down payments on easy terms. The families are on the whole larger and younger than the national average. Some of these factors have caused observers to characterize the fringe as "the poor man's suburbia" or as "blue collar country," the true suburb being primarily "white collar."

(c) The population generally contains a large proportion of "rural, non-farm," non-village types, that is, people who work in urban surroundings or in industry. There is a heavy dependence on nearby urban centers for specialized economic and social services.

(d) There is little regard for political boundaries. A comparison of actual land use and town lines reveals little in the way of conformity. Urban and agricultural uses are intermingled.

(e) Rarely is the rural-urban fringe dweller served by city water, and still more rarely by a sewerage system.

(f) Land values are extremely varied, but generally increasing rapidly.

The problems of the fringe are multiplying in the light of advancing technology and the change in leisure-time occupations. Many activities that the suburbs will not tolerate have found their way into these less restricted areas. Track-car racing, junk yards, automobile wrecking enterprises, gravel pits, outdoor movies, and other space-consuming activities, many of them noisy or otherwise objectionable, are to be found here in numbers. Together with uncontrolled commercial development along the country roads, these activities account in large measure for what the English *Architectural Review* ten years ago described as "the mess that is man-made America."

It is this landscape that inevitably becomes the main concern of the present study, largely because so little attention has been given it heretofore. In the last fifteen years the fringe has had some planning, through county agencies, Federal 701 programs, and the like, but very little from the point of view of design. Architects, on the whole, do not work in the fringe; highways, power- and pipelines cut through it like a knife through cheese; others find it convenient as a dumping ground. Nobody thinks of the apple orchards, wooded swales, or stream valleys which are continually being violated—nobody, that is, except a few thoughtful planners, soil conservationists, and wildlife authorities. The resources of the fringe are many, and while we try desperately to preserve a myrtle forest in Oregon or a redwood grove in California, the exploitation of more localized scenery goes on apace near the cities themselves. The nature of this exploitation will be analyzed in our discussions of low-density housing and of open space.

THE RURAL LANDSCAPE

Before the 1920s, when the urbanism of the United States was still limited to the classic metropolitan form and the highway network was as yet undeveloped, when shopping by farmers was done by mail-order or in the nearest agricultural market town, and when mass-distribution of agricultural products was confined to items which could not be spoiled in transit, it was possible to call the land outside the cities "rural," to find regional differences in ways of living and to speak of the United States as having an agricultural population in Jeffersonian terms. Although the cities had come to dominate American life after the Civil War and had produced the harvesters and other machines which revolutionized agricultural production, there were still strong vestiges of agrarianism in politics, in literature, and in the mores of American life.

Today, this ruralism has largely disappeared.

A definition of the rural areas of the United States would presumably be based on the characteristics of land occupied by farming and grazing, but this would scarcely be a guide to their location, since on the one hand these activities frequently impinge on suburbia (Long Island, New Jersey) or in other instances can more properly be described as wilderness (the sheep ranges of Idaho). They may not even have the appearance of farms—intensive chicken, turkey, or mushroom raising have little of the rural character of the old farmstead.

Physically, huge areas of the American landscape are still dominated by farming. The farmhouse and its outbuildings, fenced and surrounded by cultivated fields, merging in turn to those of the neighboring farm, may still be seen in every state of the Union, and in many states they are the dominant settlement pattern. The river curves through the valley, bordered by acres of golden grain or verdant pasture, and only the hilltops and inaccessible woody escarpments have no mark of cultivation. Wisconsin, Iowa, Pennsylvania, and Arkansas have huge areas like this, and in other states, with the exception of some of the very smallest in land area, they are still not hard to find.

But nearly all areas of the country outside the mountain and desert states have become or are becoming industrialized, although this process may not occupy a large percentage of the land. More important, even where farming dominates, new service industries have sprung up. The farmer no longer markets his produce or purchases his goods in the decaying rural town but in the city. Sometimes he even lives in the city or in a suburban home. Many "farmers" work on their farms part-time; indeed, the number of part-time may have already exceeded that of full-time farms, which is only another indication of the spread of urbanization over the countryside. The agricultural pattern has changed, and the isolated farmhouse, although it may be found in wide areas still, is no longer the symbol that it once was. Farm-city conflicts in state legislatures, reservations of formerly rural areas for the use of city dwellers, possibilities of sale to week-end or summer residents, rising taxes, and the "industrialization" of farming itself—all these and many more phenomena of modern life in which the farmer is involved have made the term "rural" so much less descriptive nowadays that we must use it with extreme caution. It can scarcely be applied anywhere today in its classical sense except in parts of the country which are predominantly agricultural and at the same time economically distressed.

Farm landscape in Somerset County, New Jersey, with creeping fringe development.

Where farming is dominant, the appearance of vast rural areas may change, too, every thirty or forty years. In our lifetime, nothing has altered so drastically as the former cotton belt of the Deep South. Erosion, depletion of the soil, and the advent of mechanization have forced the abandonment of the old unlamented sharecropping system in favor of a different agricultural economy based on grass, grain, and livestock. A broken topography and small-acreage farms made mechanization difficult in much of the Southeast's cotton belt just at the time when increased irrigation made cotton-growing on fertile western lands a profitable enterprise. The transition in the South is not complete and has caused dislocations of people and farms, but a new landscape is painfully being created there which is a more appropriate reflection of the changing economy of the South.

Every technological change in agriculture affects the rural landscape pattern significantly. Irrigation advances have been in large part responsible for the dramatic upswing in agricultural production in Florida, Arizona, and California, while new methods of canning and freezing vegetables account for landscape changes in Wisconsin and Minnesota. The movement of the eastern chrysanthemum industry to Florida was made possible not only by favorable growing conditions but by the discovery that the use of artificial light in the open air could control the flowering season and prolong it through most of the year. We can confidently expect increased agricultural production in many areas of the United States as a result of a speeded-up application of farming technology. This technological revolution has already doubled production in the last fifty years, on less land than in use half a century ago, and with not much more capital available now than at that time.

Since markets are increasingly important, we can also expect increased production in the regions adjacent to large cities. This may seem paradoxical at first glance, since we have all heard of farmers abandoning their land in the path of urbanization and selling farms at huge profits to subdividers when the time is ripe. But it seems to be true that "fewer and fewer farmers are producing more and more on less and less land" than formerly, and improved transportation near predominantly urban areas has made curious changes possible in agricultural life. To take but one example, milk can now be produced almost within the city limits by bringing the feed to the cows by truck. Fluid milk for consumption is perishable and requires controlled handling. It also loses no weight in processing. With new methods of feeding and easy access by truck, it may be cheaper in some instances to import the feed to the city rather than the milk itself. It is not surprising, therefore, to find dairy farming *increasing* in certain fast-growing counties near New York, and in Dairy Valley, California, since with the new techniques more cows can be accommodated on fewer acres.

The need for a rational plan to resolve conflicting and competing interests for farmland has been frequently discussed. Easements, outright purchase by the states, and agricultural zoning are some of the measures being advocated to keep farmland in production. Here, another less familiar argument can be used for the retention of existing farms, especially in the rural-urban fringe. While it is possible to be optimistic about the future of farming in general, provided long-haul transportation increasingly facilitates the movement of produce to every part of the country and to its ports, it would be unfortunate to have farms disappear entirely from areas near the big cities for another reason—that of amenity. In a recent newspaper survey of farm buildings near a medium-sized city in the East it was discovered that nearly all the barns were in a state of decay and either were about to fall down or be pulled down. It would be unfortunate to deny city children the sight of farm animals or of cultivated fields. Agricultural land can be thought of as a way of keeping country open, of preserving views, and of providing certain kinds of recreation in the fringe areas. These matters are discussed in Part V. Meanwhile, it may be salutary to quote a prescient author on the possibilities of rural amenity in the fringes of the cities:

> As one travels through the urban region, one will traverse open, breezy, 'horsy' suburbs, smart white gates and palings everywhere, good turf, a grand-stand shining pleasantly; gardening districts all set with gables and roses, holly hedges, and emerald lawns; pleasant homes among heathery moorlands and golf links, and river districts with gayly painted boat-houses peeping from the osiers. Then presently a gathering of houses closer together, and a promenade and a whiff of band and dresses, and then, perhaps, a little island of agriculture, hops, or strawberry gardens, fields of gray-plumed artichokes, white-painted orchard, or brightly neat poultry farm. Through the varied country the new wide roads will run, here cutting through a crest and there running like some colossal aqueduct across a valley, swarming always with a multitudinous traffic of bright, swift (and not necessarily ugly) mechanisms; and everywhere amid the fields and trees linking wires will stretch from pole to pole. Ever and again there will appear a cluster of cottages—cottages into which we shall presently look more closely—about some works or workings, works it may be with the smoky chimney of to-day replaced by a gayly painted wind-wheel or water-wheel to gather and store the force for the machinery; and ever and again will come a little town, with its cherished ancient church or cathedral, its school buildings and museums, its railway station, perhaps its fire station, its inns and restaurants, and with all the wires of the countryside converging to its offices. All that is pleasant and fair of our present country-side may conceivably still be there among the other things. There is no reason why the essential charm of the country should disappear; the new roads will not supersede the present high roads, which will still be necessary for horses and subsidiary traffic; and the lanes and hedges, the field paths and wild flowers, will still have their ample justification. A certain lack of solitude there may be perhaps, and . . .
>
> But I find my pen is running ahead, an imagination prone to realistic constructions is struggling to paint a picture altogether prematurely.*

The picture is still premature, although it was imagined sixty years ago by H. G. Wells in his extraordinary essay, "The Probable Diffusion of Great Cities." But it is not impossible of realization.

---

* H. G. Wells, *Anticipations of the Reaction of Mechanical and Scientific Progress upon Human Life and Thought* (New York and London, Harper and Brothers, 1902), pp. 68–70.

UNSETTLED COUNTRY

Once we were fighting the wilderness; now we can't have enough of it. Nibbled away by organized private groups, protected by government intervention in which some of the most famous names in recent American history have been involved, threatened by potential millions of nature-seeking tourists, the land that is left untamed has taken on new values and greater significance, as man-made America claims all the rest and advances here as well.

Wild country, unsettled, roamed by elk and bear, otter and swampfox, covered by stands of virgin timber or prairie grass, has become an item for immediate preservation in the United States. This is a delicate matter, since "preservation" is for the people, as well as for wildlife, natural resources, and natural scenery, and man has a way of intruding on the scene, spoiling the "wildness" with his presence, which nowadays involves trucks and cars, power boats, and even motels. Gone are the days when Thoreau advocated that each town should retain a piece of the wilderness on its boundaries—this cry has now, inevitably, become a demand for public recreational space in the form of intensively used parks. The population "explosion" has changed the whole picture of the wild and non-wild. Deer now nibble on the lawns of far-flung subdivisions, and once-remote mountain lakes in Colorado are ringed by cars with license plates from every state of the Union. The national parks and forests face the dilemma of maintaining "a state of nature" and at the same time admitting more and more people every year.

A look at the map showing the remaining wilderness areas in North America, defined as land more than five miles from a motorable road, railroad or navigable waterway, will show what has happened. While huge areas of nearly virgin wilderness exist in Northern Canada and Alaska, the largest single area not accessible in the United States proper is, ironically enough, the Nevada Proving Grounds of the Atomic Energy Commission. In the East the only wilderness areas are in northern Maine (much of this is forest owned by lumber companies), in the Adirondacks Forest Preserve, and in the swampy Everglades of Florida. And access by air has not been included in the calculation!

The map indicates that there are two kinds of wilderness in North America: a "frontier" type in the far north that is slowly being opened up for mineral resources, hydroelectric power, lumber, and defense purposes; and a "preserved" type which will suffer from encroachment if there are no strong controls over its use by man. The latter type is of significance in the United States proper.

Actually, and in spite of the fact that wild nature in its pure sense is very scarce indeed, the United States has more waste and unused land than one might suppose. Excluding the deserts and mountains of the west, the pattern of settlement in America includes within it a high proportion of unused acreage, from the vacant lot in a city street to the wooded hillsides beyond the city which are being held for future development. Almost any subdivision contains within it an unused or unusable piece of ground, and any country town will have cut-over scrubland, abandoned extractive

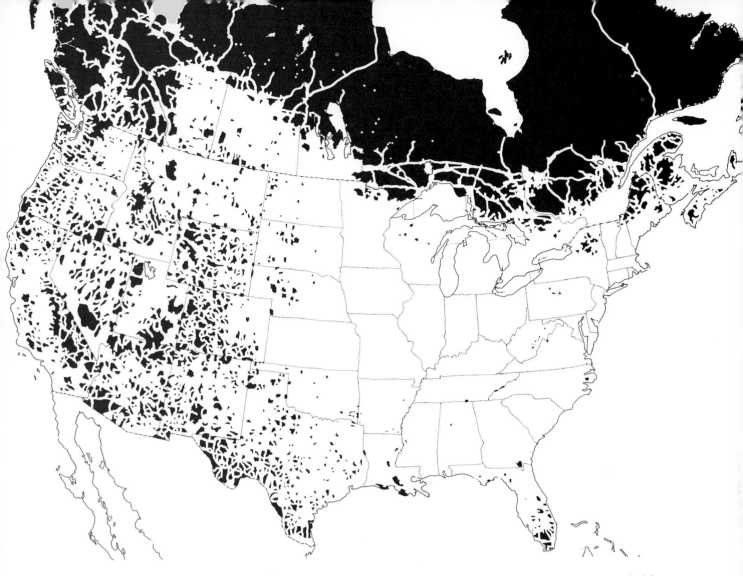

Remaining "wilderness" in North America: areas in black are more than 5 miles from the nearest railroad, highway, or navigable waterway.

gravel pits or flood plain along the river. In a crowded country such as Japan, or even in most European countries, some public or private use would be found for waste land; in America we have not yet felt the need for using all land ingeniously or for spending money for its upkeep.

As Dr. Marion Clawson has pointed out, the process of urbanization in the United States has been very wasteful of land, the average expanding city taking out of use as much land again as it actually occupies, in the form of vacant lots, rights of way and inaccessible parcels. The "leap-frogging" process of the subdivider contributes to this condition, as does the practice of holding land speculatively on the edges for future development. The contrast between our own settlement pattern and that of many European countries in which the cornfields or vineyards come up to the edge of the settled area is particularly striking.

Certainly, one of the ways of relieving pressure on the wilderness will have to be based on an expanded open space program nearer the main centers of population. While the old system of "custodian management" of our national parks and forests changes to the "intensive management" system to provide for more visitors, a parallel movement should be taking place in the states themselves, with this difference: while the national holdings must be protected from encroachment, the state and local inventory should be vastly augmented, especially in those states containing or adjacent to the larger urban regions. Two hundred new state parks with camping and other facilities in the midwest would do much to relieve the pressures on the Far West, and an extensive park reservation along the Appalachian Chain in parts of Vermont, Massachusetts, New York, Pennsylvania, West Virginia, Tennessee, and Georgia would provide a regional recreation space for the growing Atlantic Urban Region of the eastern seaboard, with its present population of forty million people.

Northwest Canadian wilderness: view on the Liard River.

These new reservations would not be wilderness, but they would go a long way toward relieving pressures on the truly wild, besides providing much-needed recreation space for our urbanized society. Although containing wildlife and vegetation, they would be part of a highly-organized network of recreation—urban and regional—

which we have not yet achieved in this country. In spite of the fact that the United States pioneered in the creation both of national parks and of the urban park system, the middle ground of regional recreation has not been given enough consideration. With our huge population increases and increasing mobility, the development of regional recreation resources for urban dwellers has become a prime necessity and it will not do any longer to point to unused open space on our state maps or congratulate ourselves on the small percentage of land actually occupied by urban settlement. As will be pointed out later, unused land is publicly useful only if it is made available and accessible, and future recreational space will have to be tied in with new highway programs, as some states are beginning to foresee in their acquisition policies, which now include recreational land tied in with a regional highway system. We should be considering ever-flowing belts of green from the city, through the suburbs, and into the rural-urban fringe, as an integrated part of our future settlement planning.

All this, and the wilderness too.

5. Beauty Spots

By describing the landscape in generic terms, one can reach certain conclusions about its form and variety. At the same time there are specific compositions which should not be ignored as lessons in the art of environmental design. Beautiful landscapes and townscapes in the classical sense of the term are to be found in all parts of the country, even though isolated and atypical. There are not enough of them to dominate and set the character of entire regions. The landscape of the James River, with its plantation-lined shores, the national parks and forests of Colorado, the Columbia River Valley, the Great Smokies, the towns of Nantucket, Charleston, and Savannah, the Vieux Carré of New Orleans, some rare subdivisions—one could make a very long list indeed of similar attractions which have disappeared, starting with the desecration by the railroad of the Hudson River Valley a hundred years ago. The regions dominated by a farming or settlement pattern so strong as to make a landscape congenial and harmonious are becoming fewer now in the United States, although they can still be found elsewhere. The Cotswold district of England, with its stone villages and pastured hillsides, bears few traces of its earlier flourishing sheep-raising economy, but is maintained without obvious change physically; in many parts of France, such as the Dordogne, where the influence of industrialization has not yet been felt, a harmonious town and village pattern prevails. A parallel can be found in the state of Vermont, where an earlier farming pattern and an intensely individualistic local culture persists, stamping a relatively large territory with a settlement pattern of white "villages" and pastured hilltops. If, as we have concluded elsewhere, such distinctiveness is maintained by economic stagnation or inertia, then it is obvious that such regional landscapes will be rare indeed. For the sake of preserving

some of these beauty spots, it is to be hoped that either the governments or an enlightened tourist industry (preferably both working together) will preserve chains or clusters of these villages in Vermont, Massachusetts, the Middle Atlantic states, in parts of the South, along the Ohio and Mississippi Rivers, in Arizona, and elsewhere; the change to a tourist and recreational economy should not be a haphazard affair, but needs strong organization. It should be the least destructive of economic bases under present-day conditions, requiring mainly the carefully planned "scenic" motorway, the addition of new roadside facilities for the tourist, and the conversion of existing buildings to new and compatible uses. Such enterprise has not yet gone much farther than the preservation of individual buildings or sections of towns; it is rare to find whole towns, like Nantucket and Deerfield, or a settlement pattern in a river valley, so treated.

This method of intensifying regional differences would require, as well as the use of preservation powers, the fostering of local customs and the revival of native industries. If this smacks of hothouse forcing and conjures up visions of tedious barn dancing or hoedowns, it should not be looked at too superciliously, nonetheless. We enjoy wine-pressing festivals on the Rhine, not only because they have a continuous tradition of five hundred years behind them, but also because they give pleasure to the eye, the ear, and the taste. In this way they can more comfortably be "justified" as tourist attractions, but revived traditions can be equally well justified if they are managed with care and skill. The examples of the colonial capital of Williamsburg, Virginia, of the Shaker village of Hancock, Massachusetts, and of Columbia, California (a Gold Rush town, now a state historic park), are only a hint of the many types of tourist attractions in the United States which have restored some facet of the American heritage and preserved it for our use.

Opposite page, left, Mount Washington, New Hampshire, one of the earliest American tourist attractions.

Right, City gate (still standing) of St. Augustine, Florida.

Opposite page, right, Thunder Cave on Mount Desert Island, Maine, now in Acadia National Park.

Right, The Giant Geyser, Yellowstone National Park, Wyoming.

Right, Ante-bellum Richmond, Virginia.

TWO VILLAGES

In Germany, where legislation restricting land use has existed from 1869, the more recent esthetic regulations are often referred to as "restrictions against disfigurement" —"disfigurement" being the creation of any positively ugly condition which would "offend the sensibilities of an esthetically intelligent observer." This law assumes that there are those who are esthetically intelligent and those who are not, which is at least realistic, although the distinction might not be recognized in American courts. In any case, the photograph above shows a successful attempt to avoid disfigurement of a German village by a new highway, in which its placing, the design of the double viaduct, and the character of the roadside resthouses shown beyond are all calculated to avoid disfigurement of the simple rural scene.

The aerial view on the left is of Old Deerfield Village, Massachusetts, where the later highway to the right of the village also acts as a bypass, avoiding widening of the main street. More has been done here to preserve the village itself, which is famous in American history. In fact, it is one of the rare examples of total preservation. Frank L. Boyden, Headmaster of Deerfield Academy (the playing fields are seen to the left), and who is celebrating his sixtieth year in residence, was able to interest many people in preserving the village, and especially Henry N. and Helen G. Flynt, whose Heritage Foundation has been sympathetically devoted to restoring the atmosphere of an earlier time, buying up many of the old houses not preserved for academic use.

Wherever such landscapes and townscapes exist, they should be jealously guarded, and, in cases where private enterprise or a changed economy cannot operate to preserve them, an Historic Preservation Agency of the federal government should be empowered to do so, since the present governmental agencies empowered to engage in preservation are restricted in the type of site they can acquire and the funds they can devote to this purpose. This agency does not now exist, but can be created if enough people will see the need for the perpetuation of the beautiful as well as the historical in the American scene.

6. The New Settlement Pattern

The cultural landscapes of America already described have their basis in new social and economic trends. If they have anything in common it is overlapping; they merge into one another, essentially reflecting differences only in their degree of urbanization or human settlement. It is this human influence emanating from the urban centers which gives the clue to future growth and which we must examine further in order to understand what is happening to man-made America.

Without presenting the reader with too detailed an economic or social analysis, it will be helpful at this stage to offer some recent thinking on the theoretical background of the man-made American region in order to reinforce the design suggestions which will be made in the following pages. The new form of the American community cannot yet be entirely foreseen, but sufficient evidence exists to show emerging differences from earlier patterns.

The dominant settlement pattern until roughly fifty years ago was the *metropolitan community* (city and suburbs, served by railroad) with secondary influences emanating from the *agricultural market town*. Industry, which had long since left the rural mill-dams for the cities with their new sources of labor and electric power, was still fairly well concentrated in an urban environment, although the *factory town* in the East and the *company town* in the South and the western mountain region could be called distinctive of the age.

What emerged hereafter, slowly taking advantage of a changing technological and economic system, was the regional city, or the *urban region,* as we prefer to call the stage of urbanization we have now entered. In Britain it is called the *conurbation.* This phenomenon has loosely been attributed to the rise of the automobile and truck, but it has other strong generators, as we shall see.

With 100 million Americans now living in these huge population clumps, the Standard Metropolitan Areas have joined, stretching out in vast complexes of houses, factories, highways, and commercial and institutional areas, and forming several easily-distinguished urban regions.

In an age of increasing interdependence, markets and production need close physical contact. A highly specialized producer can exist only where his product is available to a large number of people, since the amount sold to each individual is usually small. Ease of exchange means that distances between people must be reduced. A specialized society finds it more efficient to have the nation's population concentrated in a few areas or belts, rather than to have it scattered in widely spaced towns all over the country. These belts are areas of "high population potential" as the regional scientists call them; that is, areas in which any one person is relatively close to most of the other people on the continent. Manufacturing, intensive agriculture, and educational and cultural activities all tend to gravitate toward these areas.

The need for increased accessibility thus becomes the foremost factor in changing the environmental picture. But others, like shorter working hours, escape from city

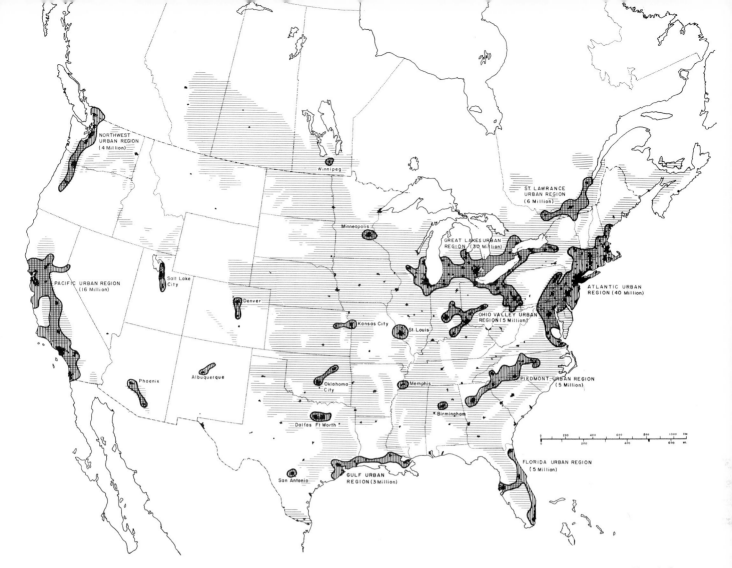

Major urban regions of North America: black indicates densely urbanized areas and dark crosshatching the areas of their immediate influence; horizontal shading shows the main agricultural areas.

conditions, and the new labor-saving devices are important. So are the spurring of new growth about existing established centers, "prestige" values of the Eastern Seaboard, the Chicago-Milwaukee area, and California, and the attractions of cheaper land outside the cities for group housing development. Technological change is implicit in the new pattern. Most activities become freer and freer from physical location restrictions with new inventions; lighter materials and miniaturization make transportation costs relatively less important; power supply is becoming wider and wider spread by pipeline and highly efficient coal-burning generator plants. Instead of raw materials, the human resource is becoming the most important locational factor in contrast to natural resources, and the human resource is most available in regions of great population concentration. The fringe dweller who loses his job in a carpet factory will turn around and drive forty miles in another direction from his home to find employment in an electronics plant, and the new employment opportunities, much more scattered than they were before the war, will often provide a part-time job for his wife after the children have reached high school age. Union security has also played its role in making home-buying safer for the factory worker on the fringe.

Under these circumstances, the desire to isolate population in new towns, or wishful thinking based on nostalgic longing for an earlier uncomplicated society, should not dominate our attitude toward the urban region. New approaches are in order. They are on their way, but old habits of thought persist. We are still searching for the optimum-size city on a scale far too small for the present-day facts of life. The economists can now tell us that any one function, such as power supply, police protection, secondary education, department store shopping, and so on, can have its own optimum-size region, determined by the economies and diseconomies of scale for this given function. One cannot simply add these up and arrive at the optimum-size city, since they are not additive but interdependent, and nowadays most of them demand a regional scale. Furthermore, every urban region is unique so far as its position and its productive base goes; for every kind of productive base, as well as for every individual relationship to outside resources and markets, the optimum size would be different.

Thus regional thinking will lie behind most of the suggestions made in the present study. We must now turn to some aspects of the internal structure of the urban region in order to illuminate the problems of its potential form and design.

Economists and geographers were the first to note the new trend, if we except the intuitive vision of the coming urban regions by H. G. Wells in 1902. Economists like N. S. B. Gras in the 1920s, turning their attention to what was still a metropolitan economy, began to notice the commercial dominance of the city over an area he termed the hinterland. Then it was discovered by the German geographer Walther Christaller and others that the cities were of different "intensity." In the retailing field, for instance, only certain cities merchandised expensive items. A "regional center" provided services to its immediate hinterland, but might have an extended trade area if it contained wholesale markets, a concentration of banking facilities, or certain institutions. Thus grew up the concept that the community had attained the dimensions of a region—a region different from the concept of a river valley (T.V.A.) or a historic-social indigenous culture, but "an area of any size throughout which accordant areal relationships between phenomena exist." This type of region, in the urban sense of the term, is a "nodal" region, which is "homogeneous with respect to internal structure or organization," as the late Harvard geographer Derwent Whittlesey put it.

The fully urbanized society which we have now attained requires a consideration of the entire land area of North America as being covered by overlapping fields of urban socio-economic influence, emanating from the major centers. A distinctive urban region may of course have several such foci.

There is a spatial structure to this phenomenon which has been described by the demographer Bogue. "On the average," he says, "as the distance from the metropolis increases, the number of persons per square mile decreases. With increasing distance, each square mile of land area supports steadily decreasing average amounts of retail trade, services, wholesale trade and manufacturing activities. [Other researchers have shown this to hold true for agriculture, whose intensity also decreases.] The effect of distance from the central business district does not cease to exist at the suburb, but continues throughout all distances."

The complex pattern which has evolved as a result of these socio-economic intensities has great variety within it. The spread of people over land is not even. There are places—towns and even whole counties—which predominantly contain only people: the dormitory suburbs. There are cities which are predominantly manufacturing districts: industrial satellites. There are areas which produce only crops, and there are those cities and towns which have the distinction of being regional centers, providing services to the hinterland—administrative, cultural, trade (wholesale and retail), financial, health services, and so on. But all these types fit the pattern of dominance and subdominance of regional centers—national, metropolitan, subordinate, and local—and the most striking aspect of these centers is their spacing or "constellation," with regional centers of a lower order actually being found about halfway between centers of a higher order. At the halfway point, where the influence of adjoining large centers is equally weak, a lower-order center can serve the area more efficiently for less specialized services.

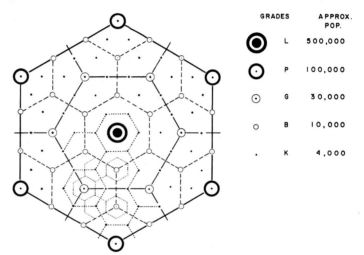

Theoretical location of regional centers, according to Christaller and Dickinson. Centers of lower order are spaced halfway between centers of higher orders; each center has its own hexagonal market area, with the market areas of the dominant centers including those of the subdominant ones.

GRADES		APPROX. POP.
◉	L	500,000
◯	P	100,000
◉	G	30,000
◦	B	10,000
·	K	4,000

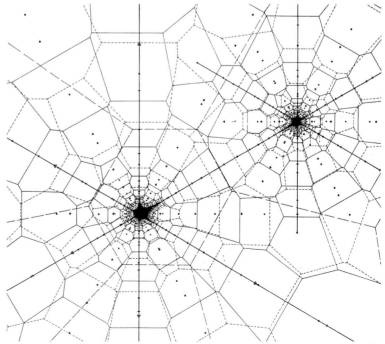

Hexagonal market areas, distorted by unequal population density, according to Isard. Major corridors of urban activity and wedges of open space are also apparent. The drawing represents a close theoretical approximation of the actual shape of an urban region.

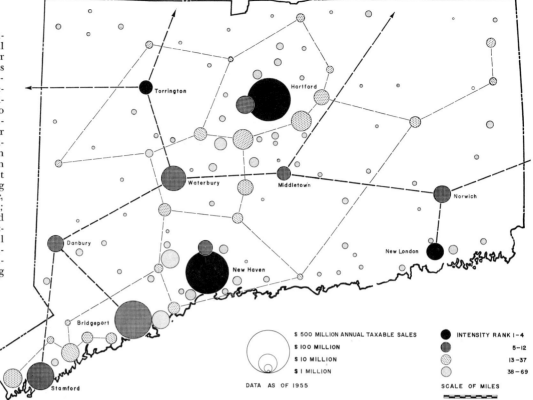

Spacing of retail centers in Connecticut in 1955, an empirical example of the regional center hierarchy. Size of the circles is proportionate to the sales volume, and their shading represents their "intensity rank," taking into account sales volume to population ratio, type, and diversification of sales. The four highest-ranking centers, accounting for somewhat more than 25% of all sales, are spaced, on the average, 37 miles apart. Eight intermediate centers, accounting for another 25% of all sales, are, on the average, 23 miles apart; 25 low-order centers are spaced about 14 miles apart, and account for another 25% of all sales; 132 towns classified as noncenters account for the remaining sales; their average spacing is 6 miles.

A few examples of this hierarchical pattern will serve to reinforce the concept of the urban region.

If we assume an even distribution of population over the land, we should have equally spaced centers of equal intensity covering hexagonal market areas. This diagram as developed by Christaller and Dickinson approximates reality in some parts of the Middle West, but in other parts of the country, especially in the Eastern Seaboard, the population densities are decidedly unequal and the urban areas are more closely spaced. The reason for this is that the concentrations of manufacturing and commerce in different-sized centers are unequal, and it is therefore logical that distribution is unequal, both of production facilities and population. The economist Walter Isard adapted the theoretical diagram (page 39), which has been used by Lösch and other location economists, to reflect this situation more accurately. His modified hexagonal pattern of market areas is distorted by higher population density near the metropolitan centers. In this adaptation, the hexagonal market areas decrease in size as we approach the central business district and population density rises. Isard omitted secondary centers along transport routes and other satellite centers in order not to make his diagram visually confusing.

To show how the principles of the regional hierarchy work in practice, we have made a case study of Connecticut, a highly urbanized state in the shadow of New York and a part of the Atlantic Urban Region.

The map of retail centers reveals two striking pieces of evidence: First, the intensity of a center depends not only on its size, but also on its location; isolated, distant

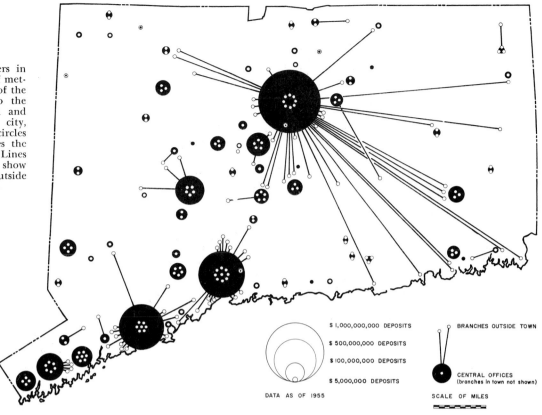

Location of banking centers in Connecticut, an example of metropolitan dominance. Size of the circles is proportionate to the total assets of commercial and savings banks in a given city, and the number of white circles within black ones indicates the number of institutions. Lines radiating from the circles show branch banks located outside each central city, as of 1955.

$ 1,000,000,000 DEPOSITS

$ 500,000,000 DEPOSITS

$ 100,000,000 DEPOSITS

$ 5,000,000 DEPOSITS

DATA AS OF 1955

BRANCHES OUTSIDE TOWN

CENTRAL OFFICES
(branches in town not shown)

SCALE OF MILES

centers can be small but very intensive; towns close in to the major centers are less intensive, many of their retail functions being taken care of by the dominant city. Second, centers of equal intensity are relatively evenly spaced. The accompanying map shows this phenomenon quite clearly for four different levels of intensity.

Another expression of urban dominance may be found in banking. The large circles of the cities show the combined assets of their banks, and the radiating lines with small circles show the location of branch offices. The latter clearly bring out the spheres of influence of the major centers. Most of the branches have grown up in the period since World War II, indicating rapid suburbanization.

For the expression of interaction between centers, long-distance telephone calls are an excellent measure. The map clearly shows the predominant orientation of Connecticut centers. There is a ring of "satellite" cities, nine altogether, whose greatest single number of calls goes to Hartford, the state capital; New Haven has four "satellites"; but these two cities are, in turn, primarily oriented to New York as their dominant center.

Regional scientists and human ecologists have recognized for several years now that the interaction between two centers of population depends largely on the size of these two centers and on the distance between them, and have been able to systematize this pattern of interaction by means of the "gravity model." The "gravity" pattern is clearly visible on the map of telephone calls—the larger the cities and the closer together they are, the greater the volume of communication between them, in this case telephone calls. Keeping population constant, some 83 per cent of the variation in telephone calls between cities on the map can be explained by distance alone.

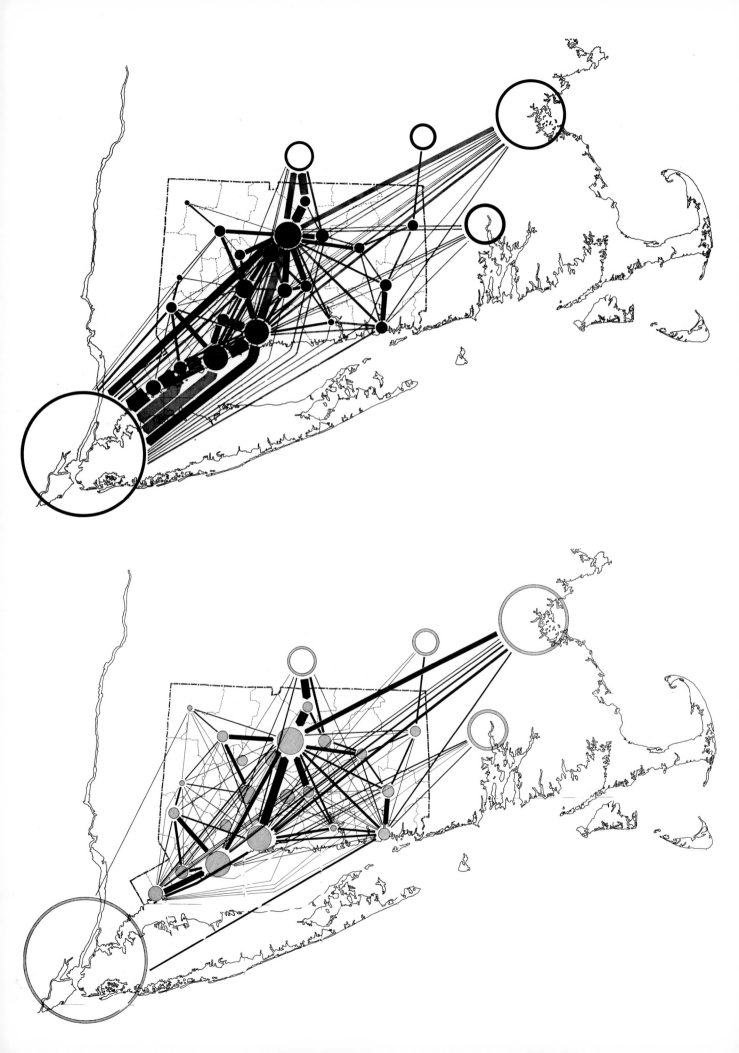

Telephone toll calls between 22 Connecticut centers and to 5 outside centers. The larger flow between any two Connecticut centers is shown on the map. The arrow points in the direction of the heavier flow. Extended local service calls are not included. The heaviest flow from any one center is shown in black, suggesting predominant orientation. The regression equation, relating the number of calls between any two centers to their respective populations and to the distance between them takes the form of $\log H \div P_1 P_2 = \log a - b (\log d)$, where H is the number of calls, P_1 and P_2 the number of inhabitants, a the intercept on the y axis, b the slope of the regression line, and d distance between the two centers. For the area in question, the value of $a = 2.756$ ($\pm$ .585 for 95% confidence limits), the value of $b = 2.357$ (.152 for 95% confidence limits), and the corellation coefficient $r = .91$. The expected number of calls between any two centers in the given area is thus $H_e = 2.76 (P_1 P_2 \div d^{2.36})$.

Deviations from the gravity pattern are charted on the second telephone call map. It shows all telephone-call volumes that are significantly greater than one would expect—variations that cannot be explained by population and distance, but are due to other factors, such as localized social and economic ties and the greater propensity of some social groups to interact. The interaction between Hartford, Connecticut, and Boston, Massachusetts, for example, is much greater than one would expect statistically, perhaps indicating a stronger homogeneity of "New England" or the linkage between insurance companies. In fact, not only Boston but Springfield, Worcester, and Providence as well show stronger than expected ties to major industrial cities in Connecticut, while New York stands out in relative isolation on the second map—having stronger than expected ties only to the small exurban community of Canaan and to New London—a center of advanced defense industry.

Trips to shop and trips to work display gravity patterns similar to the telephone calls, except that their fields of influence are more localized. Here the most striking phenomenon is the dispersal of "desire lines" of traffic, showing the deconcentrated activities of people living in the rural-urban fringe. Interestingly, the movement to work into many old industrial cities is now less strong than the out-commuting of their residents to new plants in the surrounding semi-rural towns. Social and recreational trips show the widest degree of dispersal, but they, too, can be fitted into consistent "gravity patterns" of their own.

The above examples give an indication of the dimensions of the urban region, with its overlapping zones of influence. They indicate that the self-contained settlement has vanished and that all new growth is based on an interdependence of parts and people.

What indications exist to show that the new settlement pattern can produce an agreeable landscape, conducive to the common good? We hear that it is already producing the anonymous man, without local allegiances or responsibilities, whose journeys to work and play are through scenery of unrelieved sameness, and whose home is at best a machine for living, without cultural significance or evidences of art—the house of the Mechanical Man.

> From the desert man has come;
> A new desert is his home.*

From W. H. Auden to the Angry Young Men the cry is the same; Lewis Mumford thinks he has found a new view of Hell in the "sprawling giantism" of the contemporary living pattern; others fulminate against the congestion, conformity, and confusion which new living habits seem to generate.

* "A. J. Ryder," untitled satirical poem, *New Statesman* (November 12, 1960), p. 757.

Volumes of telephone calls between 22 Connecticut centers and to 5 outside centers which are higher than those expected on the basis of probability, taking into account population and distance alone, as given by the above equation. Factors other than population and distance (such as close economic and social linkages, as well as the absence of extended local service) account for about 17% of the variation in the number of long-distance telephone calls between any two centers in the area. Raw data for 1957 courtesy of the Chief Statistician's Office, Southern New England Telephone Company.

All this is perhaps to look at the effect rather than the cause. Pictures of the horrors of our landscape are not difficult to obtain; we have included a few of our own with which to end this chapter. But the landscape we see is the result of our attitudes and actions, and although it may help to condition man's thinking and depress his spirit, there is nothing to prevent its changing for the better, except ignorance and inertia. With pressure from forward-looking action groups, a stroke of the President's pen would wipe out billboards along federally-aided highways, and local ordinances can clean up junk-yards or assure the replanting of disused gravel pits. The grey areas of the cities may take longer to improve, and subdivisions will record the blight of non-imagination in design until the common good is interpreted as putting man rather than the market at the center of our thinking. Yet there is no need for longer journeys to work if our highway system and our industrial sites are planned together and if we are willing to prevent the "fiscal mercantilism" of local property taxation from interfering with a sound land use policy.

As man moves from the relative isolation of the small, semi-dependent community to the new world of the urban continuum he must leave behind isolationist thinking as well. Luckily, it is not in man's nature to sink into anonymity, and, although his method of self-expression may now be taking either rebellious or negative forms among some sections of society, the wider strata of that society are beginning to face up to the problems of a living space that is used in common. The first signs of this will come through a government more responsive to the people's needs. Clarity of design will come through the substitution of order for urban chaos, and of action preceded by theory, which is the essence of planning. No one should imagine that this will be easy for Americans, but there is plenty of evidence that they desire the common good, and, as the political scientist Karl Deutsch has advised in his essay on Social Communication and the Metropolis, "ways will have to be found to let planners use the powers of the community to guide urban growth toward a clear and pleasing pattern of new and old landmarks where people can once again feel well-oriented, exhilarated and at home."

Trailer house

7. The Non-Beautiful

The American society produces waste, but unlike some other societies, does not often consume it.

New England town dump

Crates and cans

Abandoned truck near Detroit

Airplane dump

Nor does it repair the scars which disfigure the surroundings of towns.

Gravel pits, Woodbridge, N.J.

Nor does it count the cost of visual offense to the eye and outrage to the sensibilities produced by the lack of consideration for neighbors.

White Horse Tavern, Newport, R.I.

Cemetery

Trailer park and gravel pit

Nor does it consider any natural thing as an entity, as, for instance, a river, which demands consideration in its own right as an important element in the landscape.

The river flows down to the sea.

Roof as billboard

The American philosopher Josiah Royce was brought up in a rugged mining town in California, a community only six years older than himself. His message is particularly appropriate today, when millions of Americans are living in equally new communities—many of them just as raw and brash as Royce's early surroundings. "Here I speak of a matter," said he, "that in all our American communities has been until recently far too much neglected. Local pride ought above all to center, so far as the material objects are concerned, about the determination to give the surroundings of the community nobility, dignity, beauty. . . . We Americans spend far too much of our early strength and time upon injuring our landscapes, and far too little upon endeavoring to beautify our towns and cities."* Royce believed that no sacrifice was too great in order to achieve in our surroundings an expression of the worth a community attaches to its ideals.

In Jefferson's time, an interest in the arts marked one as a trifler and somehow suspect when it came to matters of business. In a letter to Madison in 1785 Jefferson made his position clear by saying that his enthusiasm for the arts was one "of which I am not ashamed, as its object is to improve the taste of my countrymen, to increase their reputation, to reconcile them to the respect of the world and procure them its praise." According to one of his biographers, Jefferson's thoughts on the environment ran thus: "Houses, grounds and towns should be planned with an eye to the effect made upon the human spirit by being continually surrounded with a maximum of beauty. Mean and hideous surroundings, in other words—surroundings that reflect a low, commonplace or eccentric taste—have a debasing and dehumanizing effect upon the spirit. Cultivation of the instinct of beauty, therefore, is a primary practical concern, not only of the moralist but of the statesman; and especially so under a form of government which makes no place for the tutelage of an aristocracy."†

Jefferson died in 1826.

Royce died in 1916.

How often do we have to be reminded?

---

* Josiah Royce, *Race Questions, Provincialism and Other American Problems* (New York, 1908), p. 68.

† Albert Jay Nock, *Jefferson* (New York, Harcourt, Brace & Co., 1926), p. 282.

Billboard alley

PART TWO

The Dwelling Group: The Esthetic of Low-Density Housing

1. The Growth of Low-Density Housing

2. The Morphology of the Urban Fringe
   The Distribution and Scale of Development
   The Location of Development
   Street Form and Arrangement of Units

3. Visual Principles of Small House Grouping
   Variety within Unity
   The Order of Pattern
   The Meaning of Curvature
   The Spacing Intervals
   Articulation of Groups
   Architectural Consistency
   Integration with the Environment
   Continuity of Land Form
   Modulation of Space
   Focal Elements
   Clarity of Orientation

THE GROUPING OF DWELLINGS is as old as man-made shelter. Yet, in the pre-industrial age, limitations built into the cultural fabric of society secured to a large extent the unity and visual dignity of the dwelling groupings. There was no place for monotony in a small community, growing by slow historical accretion. The primitive state of technology forced man to integrate his settlements closely with the natural environment. The limited choice of materials available in any one area resulted in an overall visual order, within which there was room enough for subtle individual variety. For example, the repetition of roof materials such as clay tile or straw dictated certain roof angles and provided a dominant order of shape, color, and texture. Climate and local materials, by dictating certain structural techniques and hence certain visual forms in one region also provided for significant differences between regions. Tightly knit groups of craftsmen, whose values were those of the entire community, guarded high standards of professional excellence. Committed participation in religious and social ritual gave everybody a measure of esthetic education within the deep stream of a given tradition. Capricious self-expression by the individual outside the visual discipline of his time and place was unthinkable. To quote from the editors of *Architectural Forum,* who did not much overstate the case, "before the industrial revolution man never created ugliness."

Possibilities of the new technology eventually gave man a freedom from age-old limitations and objectives. Site, climate, and local materials become fairly irrelevant in the face of the bulldozer, air conditioning, and mass-produced building elements. But even prior to these developments, the integrity of the building process itself was shattered as the designer-craftsman, powerless in the face of drastically new techniques and economic relationships, was eased out of decisions on design. Good building receded into the minority and housing for the market became the domain of real estate speculators and their moneylenders, whose single-minded efficiency was to maximize financial profit, at the expense of less tangible human or esthetic values. The result—the unbelievable congestion of the nineteenth-century urban slums—has been described too often to merit repetition.

The complexity of the new problems and the lack of built-in cultural restraints forced the public to impose upon builders external legal controls in the form of building codes, zoning ordinances, and subdivision regulations, as well as various property standards applied in an indirect way through government and private channels. All these gained in importance as the city burst from its high-density confines and began to spill over huge areas of formerly rural land, where urban dwellers were fleeing to find relief from noise, heat, dirt, darkness, and overcrowding by buying single-family houses, each on a little plot of land of its own. Some of the most flagrant abuses of the laissez faire system have been corrected, and undoubtedly the residential areas built under present-day planning controls are safer and healthier to live in. But their extremely low densities are raising new questions about the proper use of the landscape, and their visual design obviously lags far behind their utilitarian amenities.

In the past, the doctrine has been widely accepted in America that it is unconstitutional to use the police power of the community to accomplish purely esthetic objectives. The relativistic premise that esthetics are a matter of personal taste and not subject to objective evaluation has hampered not only the development of esthetic controls but also the adoption of comprehensive design ideas in large-scale housing and the refinement of public attitudes toward it as well. Being fed an overdose of heterogeneous visual stimuli, the public often has difficulty distinguishing between good and bad, and frequently does not seem to care very much.

On the scale of the macro-landscape, physical design obviously cannot be an individual prerogative. It must reflect the collective will and self-restraint of the community, as expressed through various avenues of social control, all of which can be used to elevate the esthetic standards of shelter in our society.

Foremost among them are the inner controls, the esthetic and social conscience of the cultural élite, in particular of those groups to whom land development is a matter of professional concern: architects, engineers, landscape architects, site planners, and enlightened developers. They can exercise their leadership through education and demonstration—producing examples of creative design which kindle the imagination of others, or at least stimulate imitation. It is their task to make the creation of significant form, of useful beauty, a deliberate goal of society in shaping its physical environment.

While no substitute for creativity, restrictions in the form of legal regulations are nevertheless essential to prevent malpractice. Zoning, subdivision, housing, and land development standards can all be written with a view toward beauty as well as safety and health. A long-overdue change in attitudes has been foreshadowed by the 1954 ruling of the U.S. Supreme Court which states that it is "within the power of the legislature to determine that the community should be beautiful as well as healthy, spacious as well as clean [Justice Douglas in *Berman* v. *Parker,* 348, U.S. 26]." The goal is not one of rigidly controlling style or design details, which makes architects rightfully indignant, but one of establishing a coherent overall image in the landscape.

There is also the force of the market mechanism which, under conditions of abundant supply, tends to make it more difficult to sell the drab, the dull, and the mediocre. Enlightened real estate interests have long realized that the permanence and beauty of a neighborhood "enhance resale values," and the problem may be one of giving the initial developer a vested interest in long-term returns. The sovereignty of an educated consumer must not be underestimated, but greater public and private financial inducements to good design should also be considered.

Finally, the development of industrial technology itself, along with its freedom from old-time restrictions, brings with it a new discipline of its own. Of course, ugly and exaggerated forms, such as automobile tailfins or grotesque house-trailer shapes can also be mass produced, but if the purity of technology, derived from its roots in physical laws, is maintained, then, in the words of Mies van der Rohe, "whenever technology reaches its real fulfillment, it transcends into architecture."

We will now explore some of the forces which give our low-density residential areas

their present form, and investigate the visual principles which could be applied
through the different avenues of control to improve this form in the future.

1. The Growth of Low-Density Housing

While the population of the United States doubled between 1910 and 1960, the
non-farm population increased almost three times, reflecting the magnitude of our
urban expansion. This expansion has gone through three distinct cycles. Up to the
turn of the century urban growth was very compact, but distributed throughout
many cities, large and small, dotted all over the country. The first decades of this
century witnessed some loss of compactness, as suburbs began to develop in the vicinity of major metropolitan areas, following trolley lines and commuter railroads.
With the widespread diffusion of the automobile, and the building boom following
World War II, urban growth ceased altogether to be compact, and scattered low-
density development set in, confined, however, even more to the immediate sphere
of influence of big metropolitan centers. Thus between 1950 and 1960 some 96 per
cent of the national population increase occurred in Standard Metropolitan Areas,
that is, in counties or groups of counties with at least one city of 50,000 inhabitants or
more. More than three-quarters of this increase occurred outside the administrative
boundaries of central cities, many of which have lost population. As was pointed out
earlier, the new low-density urban tissue is physically connecting adjacent urban areas
into multi-centered urban regions, a few of which may become hundreds of miles in
length.

Aside from the fact that rising living standards and diminishing household size require today almost one and one-half times as much housing per person as in 1910
(3.1 persons per dwelling unit in 1960 as against 4.5 in 1910), low density of development is the main reason why the physical expansion of cities over land has outstripped
the rapid growth of the urban population by far. It has been estimated that had the
densities prevalent in New York in 1860 been maintained today, the entire 1960
population of the metropolitan region, about 80 miles in diameter, could be accommodated within city limits, with some room to spare. As it is, the average density of
developed urban land within the New York metropolitan area dropped from 64,000
persons per square mile in 1860 to about 13,000 in 1960, as outlying areas were built
up. While the gross density of Manhattan fell from a high of over 100,000 persons per
square mile in 1910 to 77,000 in 1960, the densities of developed land in the outer
suburbs are in the order of 1,000 to 6,000 persons per square mile. In fact, the U.S.
Census now considers enumeration districts with a population density of 1,000 or
more per square mile (a mere 1.5 persons per acre) as "urbanized."

To understand the reasons for this development it is useful to recapitulate some
patterns apparent in the distribution of urban population in general. In any urbanized area, population density is highest near the center, and falls off toward the fringe,
rapidly at first, and more slowly as distance from the center increases (disregarding

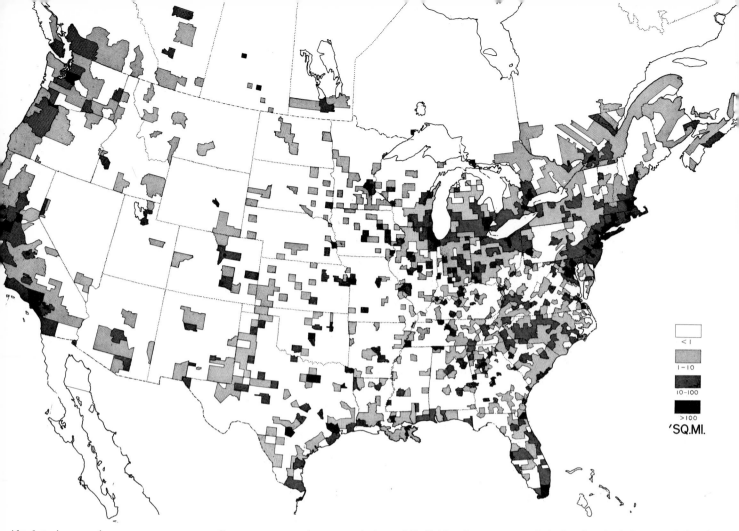

Absolute increase in persons per square mile, 1940 to 1950, by county (minor civil division for large counties), showing the influence of city clusters, fusing into urban regions. Regional concentrations are even more pronounced in 1950–1960, while many central cities show up in white.

secondary peaks).* A high rate of density decline away from the center shows that the city is compact. A low density gradient indicates that the city is more spread out. An urban area can thus expand in one of two ways: with the density gradient constant or increasing, peak density grows (predominantly vertical expansion); with the density gradient decreasing, peak density either remains constant or falls (lateral expansion). The first pattern prevailed in Europe and North America during the initial industrialization of the nineteenth century, while the second pattern—the decline of peak densities and a flatter spreading out of the population—has been typical of the twentieth century in most industrially advanced countries. The North American experience is merely a more extreme case of a general trend.

This trend has been explained primarily by technological innovations in intraurban transport. Colin Clark points out that if the cost of transportation within a city is high (say, if all circulation must be on foot,) high densities and a compact settlement necessarily result. As soon as transport costs are reduced by a new invention,

---

* Following Colin Clark, the equation relating density to distance from the center of a city takes the form of $y = Ae^{-bx}$, where y is the density of population in thousands per square mile at any point, x the distance in miles from the center, A the theoretical peak density at the center, b the "density gradient" characteristic of the given city, and $e = 2.718$ (the base of natural logarithms). The relationship applies only outside the central business district, which has little resident population.

such as rail transit or the automobile, the population is able to spread out and density drops. Only when no further reduction in transportation costs is feasible and expansion must continue does density tend to rise again. One can add that the automobile in particular reinforces this trend since it cannot be moved or stored in high-density areas without huge capital outlays for wide roadways, interchanges, and garages; the cheaper alternative, up to a point, is to spread out.

Internal circulation is more costly in a large city than in a small one. Therefore, on the whole, large cities tend to have higher densities than small ones. This relationship, is, however, by no means clear cut,* which suggests that other factors besides the costs of transportation affect density. For example, Lancaster, Pennsylvania, which is nearly two hundred times smaller than the urbanized area of New York, has the same population density, while major cities like Houston or Duluth are among the urbanized areas in the lowest density range. In North America, part of this variation is due to the age of the city, with large urbanized areas, over half of whose central city growth occurred in the nineteenth century, having, on the average, about 50 per cent higher densities than their counterparts in which most of the central city growth occurred in the automobile age. To some extent, the age explanation supports the theory that density depends upon the mode of intra-urban transport prevailing at the time the city was built. But at the same time it leads us to consider important non-economic factors such as custom, tradition, and accident. For example, the very low density of Duluth is partly the result of speculative over-platting in 1870–99 and 1910–29, which anticipated booms that were never realized and produced a scattered building pattern. A considerable portion of new construction around Philadelphia and Baltimore consists of attached row-houses, because these are a traditionally accepted form of housing in the area. On the West Coast, the Spanish tradition of enclosed yards allows for privacy on very small lots, which would be considered intolerable in New England with its open lawns.

Regional influences of tradition and custom are particularly pronounced in Europe, where density is even less dependent on city size than it is in North America. British and Belgian cities, regardless of size, have relatively low population densities (despite the fact that these countries are the most crowded ones); Dutch and West German cities show intermediate densities; while Paris and the cities of East Central Europe have traditionally shown very high densities.

Certainly, the British tradition is very much responsible for the low density of urban development in North America. From the days before 1830 stem some very

---

* Marion Clawson shows that the relationship between the size and the density of urbanized areas in the United States in 1950 followed the equation $y = 2.150 \ log \ x - 6.700$, with y persons per square mile and x the total population of the urbanized area. But the coefficient of correlation between the two variables is .42, which means that only 18 per cent of the variation in density can be explained by size. The low predictive value of this equation is partly due to an inadequate measurement of density, since urbanized areas, as defined by the U.S. Census in 1950, contained varying amounts of open land: particularly in smaller cities their line of demarcation switched back and forth between the actual edge of the built-up area and physically irrelevant political boundaries. The 1960 definition is physically even less accurate; but this does not detract from the essence of the argument in the text.

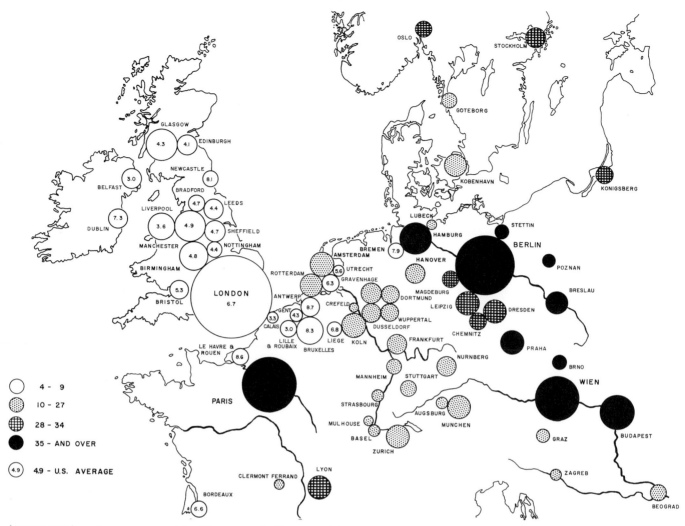

Average number of persons per residential structure in European cities, taken as an index of density varying independently of city size. Adapted from Goederitz, Rainer, and Hoffman.

persistent features of the American scene: the open lot; the town that is not a town but countryside; and the almost universal desire to live under one's own roof. Individualism, the pioneer spirit, a nostalgic esteem for the virtues of rural life, and the desire to rear children in a homogeneous social environment close to nature have often been cited among the reasons for preferring low density. Child-rearing, in fact, has been called the major institutional focus of the suburbs and the rural urban fringe, even though very low density offers unequivocal advantages only to children of a limited age group.

The preference for low density is in practice almost inseparably tied to the preference for home ownership. Among the emotional motives for ownership one finds family pride, the desire for independence and freedom of self-expression (gardening, entertaining, decorating, hobbies, pets), and the striving for prestige, recognition, security, and stability. Although theoretically the achievement of many of these goals does not necessarily require a detached house—one can own an apartment in a cooperative high-rise building, well insulated against sound and odors, with balconies and adequate green space for private and community use—it appears that a dwelling in a multi-family building does not give the resident a sufficient sense of identification and symbolic meaning. Besides, the only real choice for most people is between a detached house in a low-density area and obsolete, congested, and hygienically and esthetically inadequate quarters inside the city; the possibility of high-density living with suburban amenities has so far been rather academic, primarily because of cost.

Various studies as to whether it is "cheaper" to own a detached house or to rent in a high-density area have to date been inconclusive; they fail to take into account the actual amount of living space one purchases for an equal amount of money. With the existing relationship of land prices and construction costs, there is little doubt that in new structures the low-density resident gets many more square feet of shelter for his dollar than the in-city dweller. Although the same relationship does not necessarily exist in countries where other construction standards prevail, in the United States, where some 80 per cent of new single-family houses are light wooden-frame buildings, the construction cost of a dwelling unit in a high-rise structure, with its reinforced concrete frame, fireproof walls, and expensive mechanical equipment such as elevators can be as much as one and one-half to two times higher than that of a detached dwelling of the same size on the ground. Thus high-rise building becomes warranted only when land costs are sufficiently high, which they are not, except near the center of the city, so long as the opportunity to spread out exists. Low-rise garden-type apartments or attached row-houses could conceivably be more economical to build than either high-rise or single-family units, offering as they do savings from shorter utility lines, common walls, and a less extended construction site without the cost of elevators or scaffolding. But these savings are at present marginal, and do not overcome popular psychological objections rooted in a tradition that demands physical expression of individual ownership with ample space around one's dwelling. And entrepreneurs prefer to build housing for sale, since it offers a quick profit without long-term responsibilities.

In the past the major hurdle to ownership was the need for a large one-time capital investment, but since the '30s, federal policies to encourage and stabilize mortgage financing, in particular the amortized mortgage with a low down payment and regular monthly payments on principal and interest over a long term, have made ownership competitive with renting for the individual who lacks large savings. Ownership has been further encouraged by taxation policies which allow the owner to deduct interest and local property taxes from his income tax, an advantage which the renter does not have. Taken together, these measures have provided a very important impetus to lower residential densities: the proportion of U.S. families living in their own homes has increased from a post-depression low of 43 per cent in 1940 to 62 per cent in 1960. We have arrived at the unusual situation in which for many years almost nine out of ten new non-farm dwellings built in the United States have been single-family structures. From 1950 to 1956 the proportion of new dwellings in two- and multi-family structures was about 11 per cent and only between 1957 and 1960 did it rise to as much as 18 per cent of the total. For the sake of comparison, 40 per cent of the non-farm housing built in the 1920s in the United States was in two- and multi-family structures. In West Germany since World War II, this proportion was in excess of 60 per cent, and in the Soviet Union, exclusive of rural areas, around 70 per cent.

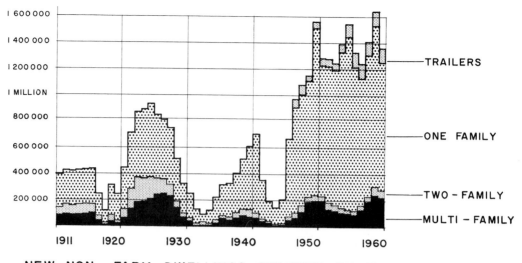

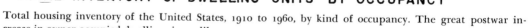

NEW NON - FARM DWELLINGS STARTED BY TYPE OF STRUCTURE

When the low-density urban areas grew: New non-farm dwellings started, by type, in the United States from 1910 to 1960. Bureau of Labor Statistics data for 1948–58 adjusted to conform to U.S. Census series.

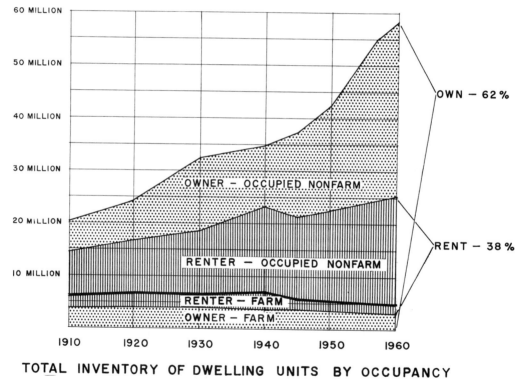

TOTAL INVENTORY OF DWELLING UNITS BY OCCUPANCY

Total housing inventory of the United States, 1910 to 1960, by kind of occupancy. The great postwar increase in owner-occupied dwellings is readily apparent.

Those who do select apartment living by choice in the United States today are mostly individuals and young couples who do not yet need a house, or older couples whose children have grown and who do not need a house any longer. The first group is on the move and does not expect to settle down for long; the second is tired of mowing lawns and shoveling snow. Another important group is professionals who are both mobile and in need of ready access to the downtown area. The largest number of renters are, of course, those who can only afford an apartment in an older building which has already amortized itself; about 2.5 per cent live in public housing, subject to a means test.

To summarize, the reasons for the low density of our new residential fabric are deep-seated and manifold. They include the "physics" of the urban structure as affected by the technological evolution, cultural values, and habits; the economics of the construction industry; fiscal policies of the government; the sociological composition of the population; and many other factors, including the existing pattern of land ownership and political pressures at the local level, which we will review later on. It is quite clear that the totality of these forces cannot be reversed at will, but at best only gradually modified.

However, some signs of modification are already apparent, as for example the recent increase in apartment construction, especially pronounced in large metropolitan areas like New York, which reverses a declining trend of some thirty years' duration. Some authorities, among them Miles Colean, state that this is indeed a new trend, not merely a short-term cycle. One of the reasons for it is the growing proportion of households in the 20 to 30 and over 65 age groups—those who commonly seek rental quarters. Another may be the diminishing amount of inexpensive land within a reasonable distance of the city core. Nevertheless, in the long view, the somewhat greater emphasis on apartment construction is an adjustment, a correction of an extreme situation, not necessarily the portent of a revolution in the total density pattern of the country.

Meanwhile there are a number of people who are advocating no less than such a radical change. Conservationists point out that low-density development is eating up too much agricultural land, and is destroying open space, or at least taking it out of reach of the average urbanite. Some planners argue that overextended utility and communication lines demanded by low density are costly and inefficient. Many architects feel that masses of single-family houses are inherently not conducive to good design—that interesting spatial compositions can only be achieved with large-scale building blocks. Finally, there are sociologists who feel that low density is unhealthy because it provides too few oportunities for interaction.

The conservationist argument appears to be quite convincing until one realizes that, as of 1950, urban areas occupied only 18 million acres out of a total of 1,904 million acres in the continental United States (excluding Alaska). Though no accurate statistics exist on how much land is actually converted to residential or even strictly urban use every year, estimates of conversion to all non-agricultural uses (including highways, airports, defense and watershed reservations) range from 1 million to 1.5 million acres annually in recent years.

If we assume for the sake of argument that in the future the average new dwelling will have a half-acre lot (an extreme and rather unlikely assumption), and if we further assume that net residential use will occupy 40 per cent of new urban areas, then, at a time when the 1960 population of 180 million doubles (somewhere around the year 2010), it will need 75 million additional acres of urban land. This is only 3.9 per cent of the land area of the 48 continental States, or 18 per cent of the area currently in use as cropland. Since obviously not all of the new urban land will be taken out of cropland, and since double the U.S. productivity of cropland has already been achieved in some densely settled European countries, the encroachment of urban use upon food supply does not seem to present a serious problem in the foreseeable future. Donald Bogue shows that up to 1956 the conversion of land to urban use has taken less than 5 per cent of the agricultural resources of the country and has been fully compensated for by reclamation. In fact, some Standard Metropolitan Areas with a rapidly growing population have gained rather than lost cropland.

While there seems to be plenty of land left in the overall picture, acute local problems of conflict between agricultural and urban use do exist. Donald A. Williams of the U.S. Soil Conservation Service states that "it is often the best agricultural lands that are being diverted to suburban development, highway growth and industrial expansion. They are usually the most desirable for such development because of topography, drainage and other natural features. These features contribute to cheaper construction and maintenance costs." Between 1940 and 1955, "one million acres of the best cropland in each of the states of Ohio, Indiana, and Texas have been withdrawn to nonagricultural uses." The situation has been most acute in California where urban growth in some areas has already consumed 15 to 20 per cent of the available supply of tillable land. Much of this cropland is exceptionally desirable because of its unique ability to grow high-quality citrus and other fruits, as well as winter vegetables at high yields and with the minimum amount of crop failure. One should add that in many areas the pressures of haphazard development inflate the valuation of land far beyond its agricultural earning capacity as a result of which land is held idle in anticipation of resale for urban uses.

What all this indicates is not that low-density urban use is taking too much land, but that it frequently takes it in places which may be wrong from the long-range viewpoint. This suggests regulation and direction, rather than limitation of the urban expansion. The problem, from the conservationist viewpoint, is where, not how much.

The same argument holds true for open space. Aside from the fact that with a half-acre density, some 90 per cent of the urban land not covered by buildings and pavements is practically open, proper planning can insure the intrusion of "wedges" or "fingers" of green space into the residential fabric. As for the access to completely open country, our hypothetical added population of 180 million, if accommodated at the half-acre net density, would fill a belt 2,500 miles long (this is roughly the combined length of the seven major urban regions of the U.S.) and only 50 miles wide. Even if this belt would have to widen in places to as many as 150 miles, access to completely open country on adequate freeways could be assured for any resident, with the round trip taking less than 10 per cent of a three-day weekend, which presumably will become standard much earlier than the year 2010.

The problem of transportation and utilities is more complex. Interestingly enough, it is raised as the main argument against low density by planners in the Soviet Union. But there it reflects, aside from the ideological preference of the regime for multi-family structures, the absence of individual transportation. Mass transit, if it is to be efficient, demands concentrated desire lines and cannot be made to work at low densities. Individual automobile transportation, by contrast, is inefficient if overly concentrated in time or in space, and works best when the desire lines of traffic are more or less equally dispersed in all directions. And in actuality the factories, shopping centers, churches, and schools in low-density areas tend to locate in a scattered pattern, which is rational from the viewpoint of minimizing traffic congestion. If a person lives, works, shops, and studies in the suburbs, his lines of transport may not really be overextended in terms of travel time, given the private automobile. Traffic studies tend to indicate that some 90 per cent of the trips to work in medium-size metropolitan areas are shorter than 20 minutes. But, admittedly, per capita automobile mileage rises in a geometric progression with decreasing density, and very often the only tangible increases in the family budget for people who move from the city to the outer suburbs are higher costs of operating the automobile and higher telephone bills.

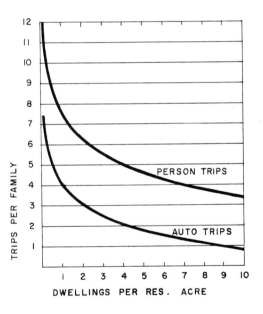

Increase in daily trips per family with decreasing density, based on conditions in the Chicago area. The graph shows all trips, regardless of origin or destination; the number of home-based trips is smaller. Source: Chicago Area Transportation Study.

The situation becomes worse if the low-density resident needs access to some specialized function of which there are only a few, and which is likely to be considerably farther removed from him than if he were to live in a high-density area. Such a specialized function can be an opera house, a bank headquarters, a high-class specialty shop, or any other use that requires a fairly central position in an urban business district. From the central business district, transportation lines to the outer suburbs may be overextended indeed, as far as travel time is concerned. Houston Wynn suggests that a central business district serving more than half a million people can hardly be effectively served by private automobile alone. Efficient public transit, with easy transfer to and from the automobile, seems to be one answer for very large urban agglomerations. Another, related answer may be that those needing frequent contact with the central business district should forego low-density living.

As far as utilities go, low densities have made use of such technological developments as cheap overhead electric and telephone wiring, bottled gas, drilled wells with automatic pumps for water supply, and septic tanks for sewage disposal. Under proper conditions, a house can therefore be fairly independent in terms of utility service. As densities increase, one can progressively centralize water supply, gas supply, sewage disposal, and eventually the supply of steam heat. This may be safer from the viewpoint of public health, and is more efficient from the viewpoint of conserving energy. However, taking into account the total magnitude of our energy consumption, the energy losses that result from lower residential densities are marginal indeed.

A much more important item is capital cost. As the size of the residential lot increases, its frontage becomes longer, and the construction cost of streets and utilities grows. For a detached house on a quarter-acre lot, this cost is roughly double what it would be for a row house on a 25 x 100-foot lot. However, as lot size increases from the quarter acre on, the cost of appurtenant street and utility construction does not rise in the same proportion. Rather, it grows at a decelerating rate. This is so, first, because in practice neither the setback (and hence the cost of connections) nor the lot frontage (and hence linear street costs) increase as fast as the lot area. Second, construction standards usually get lower as density gets lower. On lots beyond the quarter- to half-acre range, septic tanks can be substituted for sewers with a considerable saving when soil conditions permit, even though, admittedly, septic tanks are much less dependable than a sewerage system. Moreover, curbs and sidewalks can be progressively eliminated and cheaper types of pavement used, as density decreases. As a result, depending on community standards, street, driveway, and utility costs for a one-acre lot may not be significantly higher than those for a quarter-acre lot, remaining in the order of some 15 per cent of the cost of the medium-priced house.

In general, the provision of utilities for larger lot sizes is not a serious problem, unless the lot or group of lots is far removed from the existing utility network. The critical factor is not the lot size but the proximity of existing facilities. Compact development at fairly low densities, which does not leap-frog across vacant tracts, can be quite economical, whereas even a higher density cannot be economically supplied with utilities if the lines have to be extended over miles of empty land. Again, the problem can be solved by preventing haphazard, disorganized growth, not necessarily by enforcing higher densities.

With regard to overall municipal costs, which include the costs of development as well as the costs of municipal services, such as schools, police and fire protection, road maintenance and the like, a study by the Massachusetts Institute of Technology for the Urban Land Institute concluded that "density alone, when divorced from other variables, has relatively little effect on muncipal costs." In a more detailed and refined study, based on a purely hypothetical situation and released by the Federal Reserve Bank of Boston, Isard and Coughlin show that total annual municipal costs in a growing community would be lowest at a fairly high density (1/16-acre lots), somewhat higher for a very low density (one-acre lots) and highest for medium density (quarter-acre lots). Empirical investigations of municipal expenditures in areas of different lot size are not very conclusive, because each community is essentially unique in its combination of income distribution, level of services, the way it avails itself of the economies of scale for different functions, and many other factors which strongly affect municipal costs.

The esthetic argument of architectural design in low-density areas is less tangible, particularly since not too many examples of good small-house groupings exist. But the architects' argument that "nobody has done it yet" can be countered with equal fairness by the question, "how many really tried?" The design of building groups and ensembles, as distinct from individual structures, continues to be the weak point of American architecture, and most architects have shied away from trying to arrange the nearly identical plywood and plasterboard boxes that are dotting our landscape in a pattern that would be pleasing, livable, and imaginative. They have shied away, largely, because there is very little money for them in this field at present, because neither public nor private interests are willing to subsidize new pioneering efforts of the scale of Radburn or the Greenbelt towns, and finally, perhaps, because of a certain intellectual snobbery. The British *Architectural Review* has pointed out that the only good architecture built in the United States today is for the rich—be they individuals or corporations—rather than for the rank and file, in contrast to post-World War II Europe. And Dean Burnham Kelly of Cornell University states that "the combination of genuine design ability and a sensitive understanding of the housing industry is rare, and almost nowhere is it being taught."

Thus, physical design of mass residential development has to be done by persons who are not visually trained—businessmen, contractors, engineers, and administrators. The antipathy between architects and residential developers is quite mutual—while the former accuse the latter of lack of taste, the latter accuse the former of being expensive, impractical, unwilling to understand the public, and authoritarian in trying to impose preconceived personal design ideas. The National Association of Home Builders reports that only some 34 per cent of its members use the services of an architect. These services usually pertain to the design of the houses themselves—the employment of visually trained site planners and landscape architects to lay out the roads and house groupings in a subdivision appears to be even less frequent.

It is our contention that good design is not the prerogative of any one density or building scale. Attached row-houses, so often advocated by architects as a substitute for single-family units, can be even more dreary and chaotic if built in large masses, as many developments in Latin America conclusively prove. Meanwhile, if we accept the automobile and reduced opportunities for walking, many essential qualities of livability are associated with low density, no matter how bad its architectural expression. It has a redeeming proximity to nature and it seems to satisfy a basic social instinct for wanting to call one's shelter one's own. To be sure, the esthetic of low-density design is different in many ways from the esthetic of urban architecture.

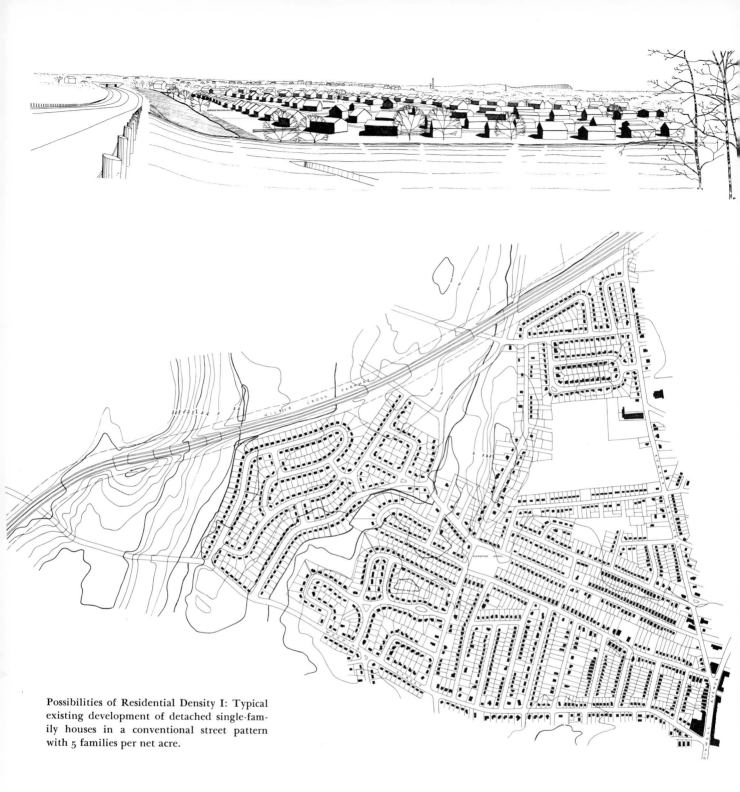

Possibilities of Residential Density I: Typical existing development of detached single-family houses in a conventional street pattern with 5 families per net acre.

Building masses are less important in defining space, and landscape elements assume a dominant role. There are the micro-elements of trees, shrubs, fences, and driveways to be considered as well as the macro-elements of total order of pattern, texture, and land form. These elements require new applications of esthetic analysis and new kinds of design sensitivity, some of which we shall attempt to develop as discussion proceeds.

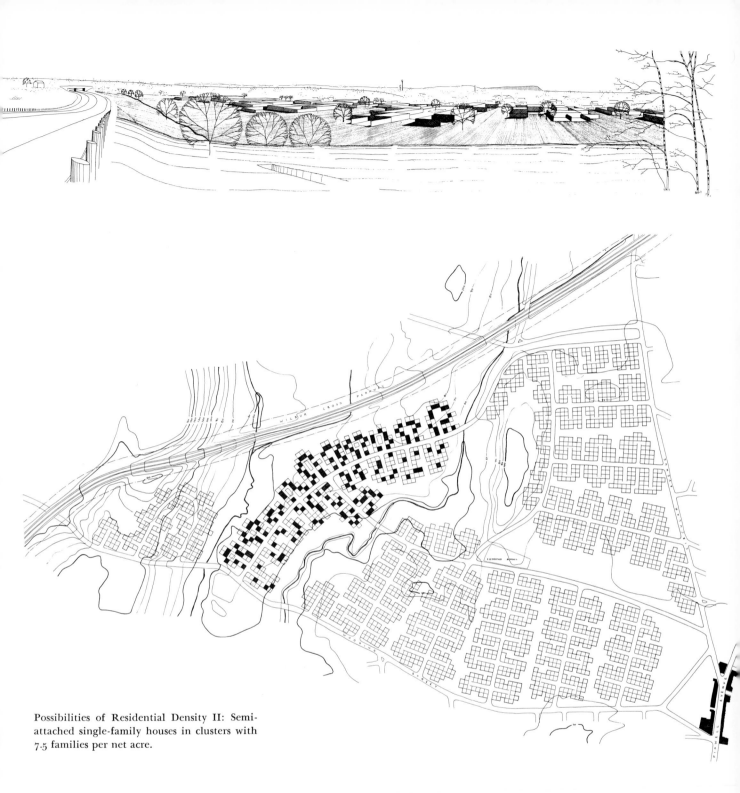

Possibilities of Residential Density II: Semi-
attached single-family houses in clusters with
7.5 families per net acre.

As to the final sociological question concerning reduced opportunities for interaction at low density, it must be granted that sociological theory has failed so far to
give us sufficiently firm conclusions with regard to the influence of alternate physical
planning arrangements on community life and the mental health of the individual.
This may be understandable in view of the complexity of the socio-psychological
forces of human association, attraction, and isolation, of group tastes and preferences,

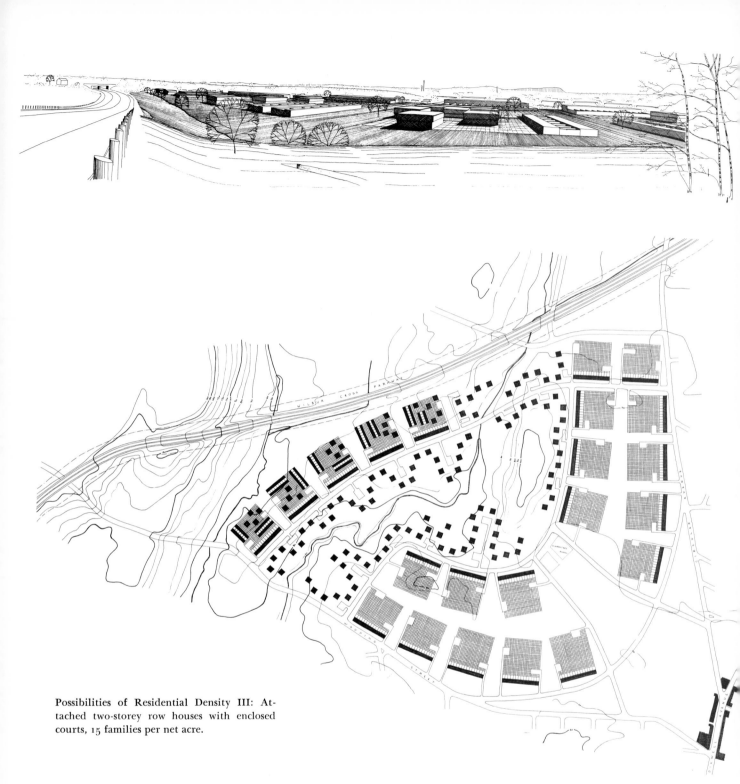

Possibilities of Residential Density III: Attached two-storey row houses with enclosed courts, 15 families per net acre.

as well as of the institutional arrangements that give them expression. It is plausible to assume that certain physical settings affect various individuals and groups differently. Can one safely say that the overexposure to stimuli of the congested city, or the underexposure of the low-density fringe, is better for everybody? It seems that only by maximizing the opportunities for free choice can an optimum balance be achieved. This requires, among other things, large-scale experimental residential developments

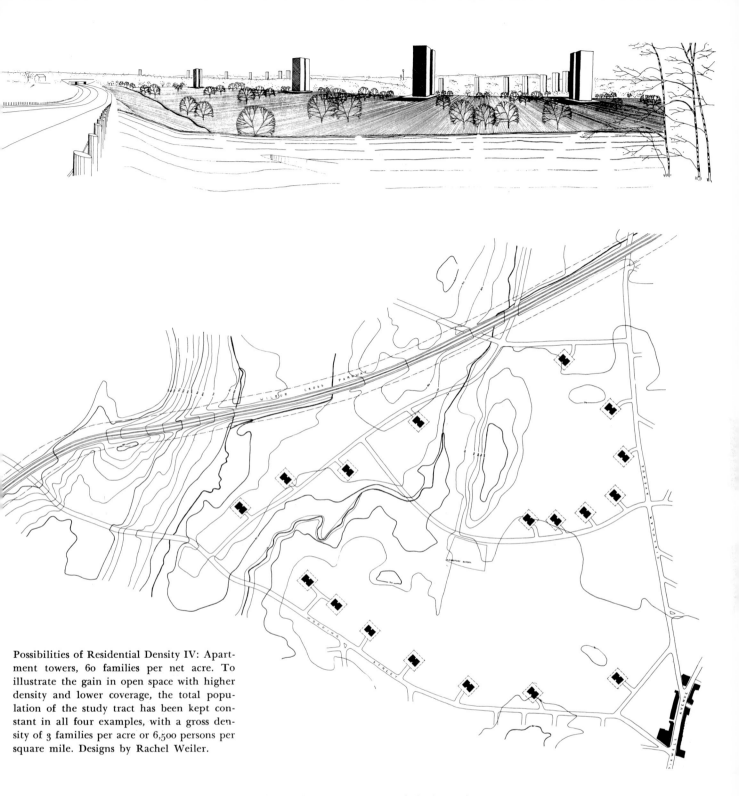

Possibilities of Residential Density IV: Apartment towers, 60 families per net acre. To illustrate the gain in open space with higher density and lower coverage, the total population of the study tract has been kept constant in all four examples, with a gross density of 3 families per acre or 6,500 persons per square mile. Designs by Rachel Weiler.

to test different combinations of density, coverage, and design, since the average person's imagination is too limited to prefer something he has never seen.

While such experiments would undoubtedly produce some better visual and social relationships—there certainly is room for improvement—it is doubtful that in the foreseeable future it would lead to a fundamentally different residential pattern. It may be true that people's reluctance to embrace the brillant utopia of Le Corbusier

or the "Radburn idea" so highly cherished by Lewis Mumford is due to what some
scholars call "the cultural lag." Nevertheless, it is hard to see how such a basic preference of so many people for low-density individual living can be dismissed by a
pluralistic society, especially if it can be made to work better. Rather, it seems, we
must envision a future in which a few of Le Corbusier's residential skyscrapers in the
middle of parks, some attached houses in the Radburn manner, and a great many individual dwellings of the American suburbia and rural-urban fringe will exist side
by side in a balanced urban setting. The problem again is not one of either/or, but
one of where and how. It is one of refining objective esthetic and functional planning
principles which can, with equal success, apply to a variety of physical settings for
society and help us determine what are the optimum density distributions under various conditions.

2. The Morphology of the Urban Fringe

The factors influencing the form of group residential development are numerous,
subtle, and complex, involving, as we have seen, the whole cultural fabric of society.
They are especially so in the rural-urban fringe, an area that is characterized by extreme heterogeneity, lack of clear dominance and orientation, and a continuing succession of uses in which elements of a receding ecological order exist side by side with
those of an advancing one. However obscure, these elements of order and the reasons
for existing forms must be understood if we wish to place design suggestions into a
realistic framework.

THE DISTRIBUTION AND SCALE OF DEVELOPMENT

As previously indicated, residences tend to cluster toward the node of any urban
area, and are spread farther and farther apart as one moves away from the center. Yet
this scatter around a nodal point, following as it does a "gravity" or "probability" pattern, is by no means uniform. Density tends to be higher along major radial arteries,
where ease of access is greatest, so that the shape of a spreading city is more or less
starlike. Along the prongs of this star one can find secondary density peaks—satellite
nodes—and, if major centers are located sufficiently close together, the prongs of their
stars join each other in a web that encloses diamond-shaped wedges of open land. This
idealized pattern is of course deformed in practice by major topographic obstacles—
ridges, swamps, bodies of water—and disrupted further by large non-residential uses
such as reservations, railroad yards, or industrial districts.

The population density map of central Connecticut shows a constellation of urban
areas that merge to form what can be called an urban continuum, and illustrates star
patterns deformed by topography. The correlation between density and distance from
a major center on this map is quite high—in the order of .82, which means that 67 per
cent of the variation in density can be explained by distance from a major center. On

The Gravity Pattern: residential density in central Connecticut, a simplified section of a 1951 density map. Each square represents 40 acres, or one quarter
mile square. The original map was prepared by a count of dwelling units from
aerial photographs. Together with the star-shaped pattern of the major cities, one
can discern the linear pattern of development along rural roads.

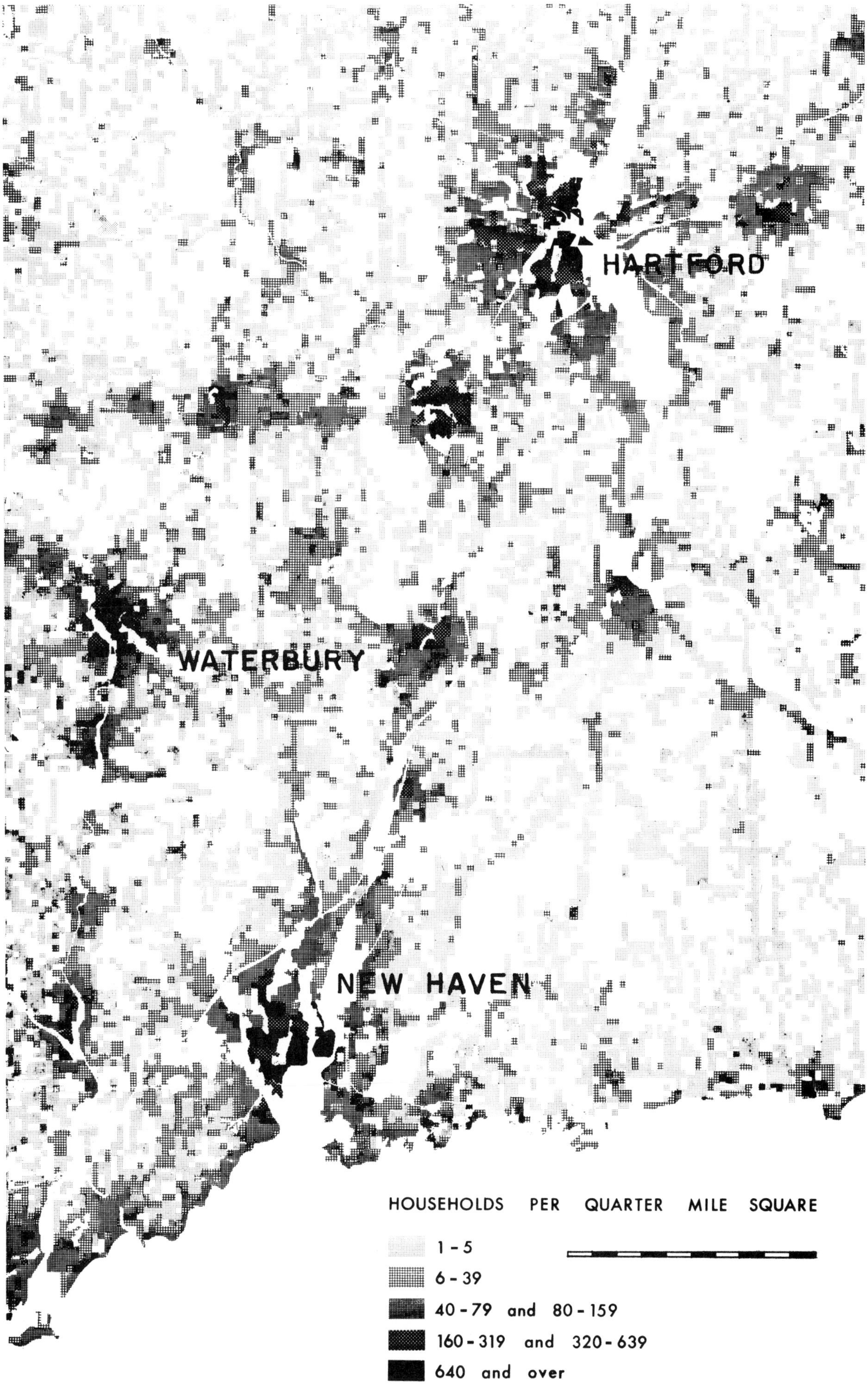

HARTFORD

WATERBURY

NEW HAVEN

HOUSEHOLDS PER QUARTER MILE SQUARE

1 - 5
6 - 39
40 - 79 and 80 - 159
160 - 319 and 320 - 639
640 and over

the negative side, the roughness of topography explains about 12 per cent of the variation in density. Thus, a house is unlikely to be located really "in the middle of
nowhere." Individuals in society being dependent on each other, a house is likely to
be located where its inhabitants will have reasonable access to most other persons.

To observe the structure of residential fringe development at close range, one
should enlarge the scale of the density map about 25 times and view a section of it,
so to say, under a microscope. This is done on the aerial photograph and the graphic
analysis that follows. The area selected for magnification is from a different region;

A "gravity pattern" of land use in the urban fringe: Passaic County, N.J.; *below,*
schematic map; *opposite page,* aerial photo of same area.

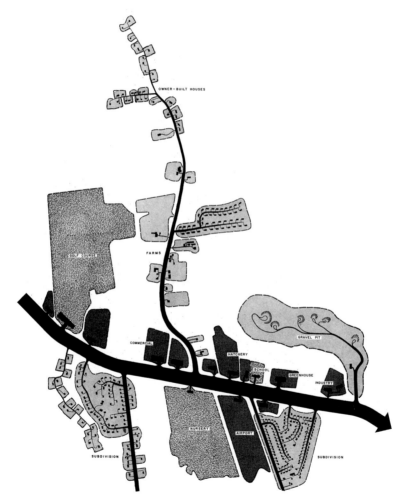

it represents some four and one-half square miles of land in Passaic County, New Jersey, about 20 air miles from Times Square, as it looked in 1954. Across the lower part of the photograph runs a radial highway—the four-lane route 504 from Paterson, with a daily volume of some 10,000 cars. Along it are located two major residential subdivisions with 140 and 70 houses, respectively, a private airport since subdivided for residence, a golf course with a fashionable country club, a large gravel pit with a concrete mixing plant, a major nursery, a commercial greenhouse and florist, a hatchery and agricultural implements warehouse, a school, library, grange, as well as typical elements of roadside commercial development, such as restaurants, groups of retail stores, real estate offices, a machine shop, and gasoline stations, all within one and one-half miles. Along the side road to the north, which carries much lighter traffic, one finds a large orchard and several farms, some of them still active, some of them developed into smaller subdivisions of 20 to 30 houses since the photograph was taken. As the side road ascends into the hills and branches out, group development ceases altogether and occasional individually built houses face directly on the road. A few such houses are also located off the main road, but they are not new. They date back to a time when the area was still rural; some of them are in disrepair, others are being converted to commercial use.

It can be seen that the physical form of the study area in our photograph reflects the superimposition of several characteristic spatial patterns in time. First there were the farms with their fairly regular pattern of oblong rectangles, defined by the farm roads and field boundaries, terminating at the foot of the wooded hills. Then the first urban influence came in the shape of the highway, cutting diagonally across this rectilinear pattern. It brought with it the golf course and the gravel pit, exploiting different aspects of the rolling alluvial land; the private airport, intensive agriculture in the form of the nurseries and the greenhouse, occasional residences, and a small school. The third wave of land use succession brought intensive residential subdivision, petering out with increased distance from the main highway, with commercial establishments along the spine to service the new population. While some uses from previous periods have been obliterated, others continue to coexist with the later ones, contributing both to the nostalgic charm and to the chaos of the area. The wooded hills and the rolling fields are still prominent in the view, but are partly obliterated by haphazard excavation, billboards, and commercial buildings along the main road. The silhouette of trees has often been replaced by a silhouette of wooden utility poles. The look of some of the subdivisions on denuded land is sterile, to say the least. Zoning, which came quite late in the picture, has merely confirmed the pattern of strip commercial development and established minimum lot sizes for new houses. One can add that in what might usher in the fourth period of succession the entire area will be cut in two pieces by a new interstate freeway, running north-south. Its location is determined by regional, not local considerations.

Perhaps the most striking aspect of the situation is the pervasiveness of the "gravity pattern," as it applies to intensity of use and scale of development. Land cannot be used without access, and the basic means of providing access is a road. Since new

The "gravity pattern" of small to medium-size residential subdivisions along radial roads near Hartford, Conn.

roads are costly, new development tends to grow first on the pre-existing rural net. The character of this growth will depend on the function of the road: the larger and more intensive the land use, the more it gravitates toward the large, heavily traveled route. While a small lane in the back country may have a farm and a few scattered houses, a strong artery will produce large subdivisions, or smaller but more intensive industrial and commercial uses. Only when frontage along the artery becomes largely developed do some of the major housing groups shift farther onto the side roads. The commercial uses, which generate as much as 15 times more traffic than residential land, stay on the main road. Through the spontaneous working of the market mechanism we thus get a general pattern that has some logic to it, unsightly as it may turn out to be in the landscape.

Relating the scale of circulation facilities to the scale of residential development in general we can see that developments of several thousand houses, such as the three Levittowns in the vicinity of New York, are directly related to regional or interstate freeways; large subdivisions of several hundred houses usually locate on conventional arterial highways on the outskirts of a metropolitan area. The country roads of Connecticut or Massachusetts typically generate small subdivisions of ten to 50 houses, with a few larger ones. Further out in the urban fringe are the owner-built houses on isolated lots, sometimes accessible by roads as yet unpaved.

The scale of residential development itself, highly important from the viewpoint of functional as well as esthetic planning, depends on factors other than transportation. For example, the scale of construction is smaller for higher-priced houses, for houses in areas with a rough topography, and for those in large acreage zones. On the other hand, the greater the size of the metropolitan area and the faster its rate of population growth, the larger the scale of construction. Many of these influences merely reflect the fact that the scale of construction depends on the size of the market to be satisfied, which largely shapes the organization of the building industry. A survey by the National Association of Home Builders among its members showed that the average number of houses built per builder in 1959 was 32 in New England and 45 in the Middle Atlantic and Great Lakes states, where population increase was moderate, as compared to 67 houses per builder annually in the South Atlantic states and 118 on the West Coast, where population growth was very rapid.

Average annual numbers of houses built per builder do not of course show us the extreme variation in the size of operation among individual members of the building industry. The survey quoted above found that 6 per cent of the builders built more than 250 units annually and were responsible for 43 per cent of the total housing volume constructed by NAHB members. At the other end of the scale, 50 per cent of the builders who built less than 20 units a year accounted for only 7.5 per cent of all the homes built. Though small builders are probably under-represented in this survey, the figures are nevertheless quite striking.

The extreme variation in the size of the building firm is partly explained by the fact that with present home-construction techniques the economies of scale in the industry are still not too sharply pronounced. While a large operator will realize savings from bulk purchase, greater mechanization, and standardization of work, the small builder has better supervision, greater flexibility, and less overhead cost. True mass production by prefabrication may have been hampered by custom and obsolete building codes, but probably more so by the fact that building materials and systems have not yet been adapted to fully industrialized assembly, and that savings from factory production can still be easily offset by increased cost of transporting the bulky prefabricated parts to the site. As a result, small operators are often able to compete with larger builders, especially when the local market is small.

But in spite of the numerous retarding forces, the scale of residential group development has been consistently growing in recent decades. Between 1949 and 1956 alone, the proportion of owner-built houses on individual lots has dropped from 34 per cent of all non-farm one-family units built to about 15 per cent, according to the Bureau of Labor Statistics.* By contrast, the proportion of houses built in large de-

* Aside from economic forces, such as the introduction of shell "finish-it-yourself" houses, this drop was due to tighter building code coverage and enforcement. Most codes do not permit a family to live in a tarpaper-capped basement waiting to save enough money to put up a superstructure.

velopments has more than doubled in the post-war period and accounts for an over-whelming part of the total. Prefabricated houses increased from some 6 per cent of the new house starts in 1950 to 12 per cent in 1960, reflecting the gradually expanding possibilities of industrialized manufacture. The latter have also been exploited by the house trailer or "mobile home" industry, which has been capturing between 6 and 8 per cent of the new housing market.

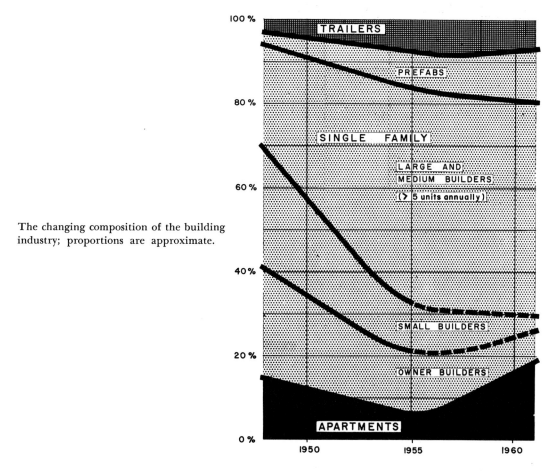

The changing composition of the building industry; proportions are approximate.

The gradual trend toward larger residential subdivisions has been encouraged by the large developer's ability to realize a substantial profit on the land as well as on the houses, and his opportunity to better control the site to suit his requirements. The largest developments are able to provide a complete set of community facilities, including a shopping center, as an integrated part of the whole. In the Levittowns, even schools have been built by the developer at no cost to the municipality. Developments of several hundred houses still can offer some common facilities such as playgrounds, a disposal system, or a group of local stores. By contrast, the only community facility a small subdivision of 10 to 50 houses can offer is a new street—a loop or cul-de-sac, and still smaller groups as well as individual houses locate as a rule on an existing road, which, quite often, ought not to be permitted to become a residential street, both in consideration of the resident's safety and of traffic capacity.

The point to be made here is not so much that small-scale development can be a greater burden for the community financially, but that it is much more difficult to control and to plan, both functionally and esthetically. Though sentimentalists may deplore the gradual departure of the small, individual builder, large-scale development and prefabrication clearly offer better opportunities for comprehensive planning and visual design; it is on these large operations that design leadership must be focused.

THE LOCATION OF DEVELOPMENT

Though the scale of residential developments and that of their access facilities are definitely related, relative accessibility to places of employment or shopping in itself is not the only consideration in the developer's selection of new residential sites. Recent studies, such as those of Alan M. Voorhees, have emphasized the impact of other factors, both physical and psychological, on the location of urban growth. Thus, the absence of sewer and water mains, large lot zoning, fragmented land ownership, speculative land holding, and high land cost will significantly retard development. By contrast, a picturesque landscape without serious topographic problems, the "prestige" of an area, and availability of good schools accelerate growth. It is well known that lakeshore frontage, for example, is among the first to be developed; as for prestige, communities considered "high prestige" are known to have grown twice as fast as the average, other conditions being equal.

The growing importance of the pyschological and esthetic factors in site selection has been made possible by the automobile. The rural-urban fringe generally possesses a rather closely meshed network of paved country roads, and since the automobile has made minor differences in distance unimportant, there is a tremendous area from which sites for development can be chosen. True, when the new areas have grown, the rural road network becomes inadequate to serve the greatly increased population, and accessibility becomes a problem, making necessary expensive street widening and reconstruction, which usually destroys the landscape amenities of the rural roads. But neither the developer nor the home buyer thinks far enough ahead to ultimate development, as long as the existing relationship of roads to population density is adequate.

The most important physical result of the great freedom of residential site selection has been the discontinuous pattern of development, known as "leapfrogging" or "sprawl," which is as characteristic of the urban fringe as the low net density of developed land. Just as premature subdivision leaving vacant lots in the wake of urban development was a scourge of the 1920s, the leapfrogging sprawl, on an immensely greater scale, leaving thousands of vacant acres within the urban fabric, has become the scourge of the '50s and '60s, even though some might argue that in the absence of a planned system of open space the haphazard vacant tracts do provide a reservoir of open land for the future.

Where the scale of development is small, leapfrogging typically takes the form of individual houses, strung in a bead along rural roads. Here, one is often confronted with a farmer who wishes to sell one or two lots from his farm acreage to complement his income. He is not concerned with selling any land that does not abut a public road, and is unwilling to give any thought to the future need for streets and a comprehensive development plan for the area. The buyer often wants to live in a rural atmosphere, but clinging of necessity to the road, he eventually blocks it off from the rural land. The road assumes a chaotic semi-urban character, and huge areas of open space in the interior are sealed off from access or view; the process becomes self-defeating.

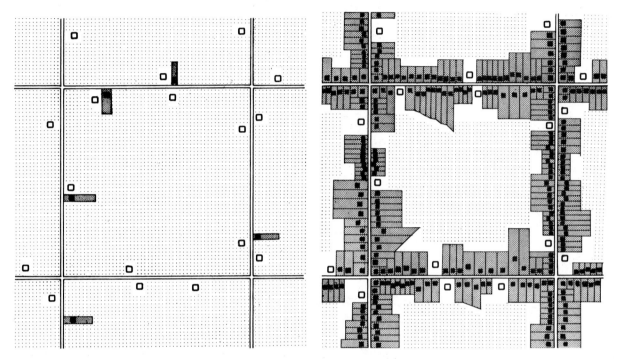

Stages of small-scale development in a rural area: *left,* original condition, open land—scattered farms; farmers begin to sell individual house sites along the roads; *right,* final problem stage, road frontage completely built up, open land in the interior of little use, road capacity sharply reduced. Example from the Lansing Tri-county Regional Planning Commission.

Where the scale of development is large, entire farm tracts are sold off for subdivision in a random, checkerboard pattern. The developer passes over land adjacent to existing built-up areas that may be too high-priced or otherwise unsuitable for his purposes, and seeks cheaper land further out that will enable him to sell houses at prices within the means of the income-group for which he is building.

Aside from individual preferences of present landowners to sell or not to sell, the inflation of land values near existing development is one of the principal reasons for discontinuous, scattered subdivision. As the area subjected to scattered development gets larger, the area of land overvalued in anticipation of development gets larger still, so that soon, despite thousands of empty acres between subdivisions, no land with an economically tolerable price tag is available within reasonable distance from the city. In a dramatic presentation of the land problem, the journal *House and Home* (August, 1960) showed that between 1950 and 1960 prices for residential land soared anywhere from 100 to 3,700 per cent (more than 300 per cent on the average), in contrast to the cost of materials and labor, which in the same period rose only 24

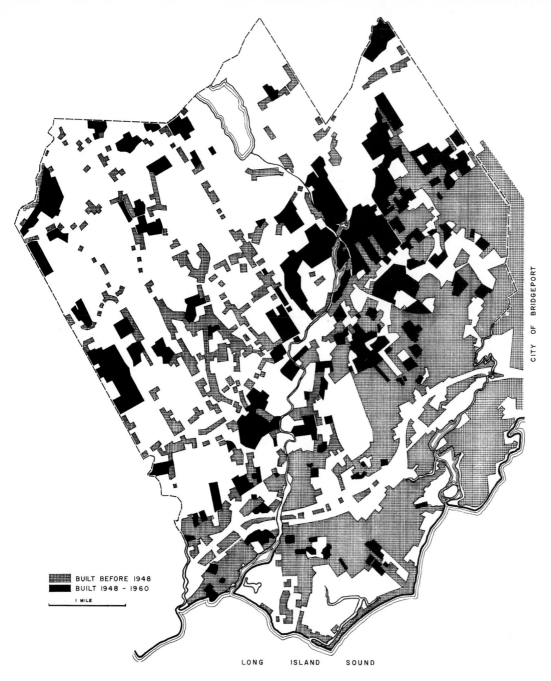

Patterns of sprawl: new subdivisions in the town of Fairfield, Conn., in relation to the built-up area.

BUILT BEFORE 1948
BUILT 1948 – 1960

1 MILE

CITY OF BRIDGEPORT

LONG ISLAND SOUND

per cent and 60 per cent, respectively. Speculatively inflated land prices have led residential builders to consider "shortage of suitable land" their worst headache. As indicated, the shortage is an economic, rather than a physical one: around San Jose, California, for example, where subdivisions are scattered over 200 square miles of fruit land, they actually occupy only 12 square miles, with 188 square miles left over in between; a similar pattern prevails in most other metropolitan areas.

A related source of the economic shortage of the land is fragmentation of ownership. With large-scale development the dominant trend, builders find it difficult to assemble tracts of adequate size near existing development, and have to go far out to find acreage that is for sale all in one piece.

While some individuals who happen to own land in the path of urban expansion are holding on to it in the expectation of astronomic profits (in 1960 a very common

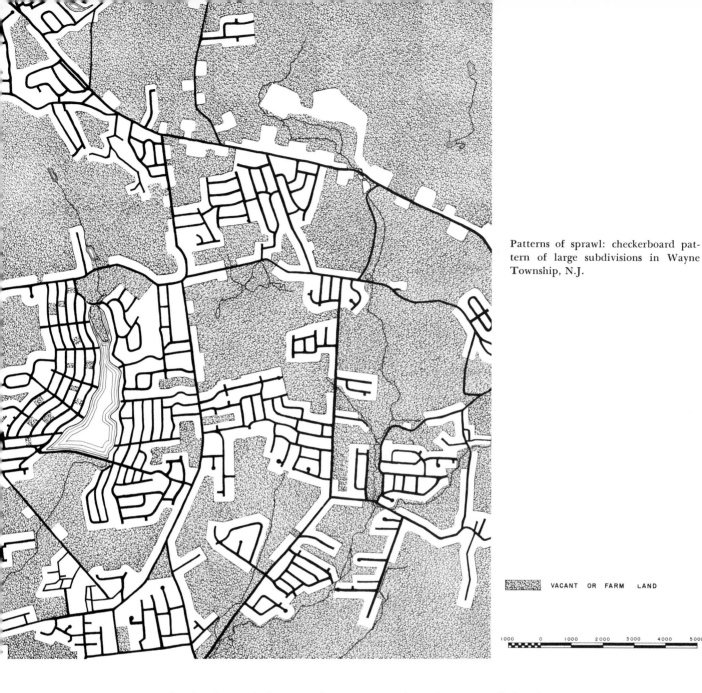

Patterns of sprawl: checkerboard pattern of large subdivisions in Wayne Township, N.J.

VACANT OR FARM LAND

1000   0   1000   2000   3000   4000   5000
                                          FEET

occurrence was for land worth $200 to $500 an acre in a farm to sell for $3,000 to $30,000 an acre for single-family development, depending on permitted lot size), the resulting scattering of urban development results in major economic inefficiencies and social costs, not to speak of the esthetic desecration of the landscape. The cost of land has accounted for an increasing proportion of the dollar spent on new housing: 19 per cent in 1960 as against 12 per cent in 1950, according to *House and Home*. The extension of municipal services and utilities into scattered outlying areas is grossly inefficient and puts an additional burden on the home owner. As an alternative, he has to accept a lower level of services. Travel time and transportation costs also increase appreciably in the aggregate.

Scattered development makes a mockery of planning for ordered, livable and efficient communities, and its chaos often contains the seeds of future blight on a scale that may dwarf the blight problems of present-day central cities. Thus, while many a good thing can be said about moderately low densities of developed land, little can be said for scattered development. It does provide "open space," but this open space is chaotic in its location, socially unusable and legally unprotected against future encroachment. The inflated land prices that accompany scattered development may force builders, occasionally, to go into apartment house and other higher-density construction nearer to urban centers, so that to a limited extent "sprawl" has a self-correcting instrument built into it; but surely more dependable means of controlling discontinuous development ought to be available.

So far, alternate means of control have been rather weak, and many are still in the experimental stage. One technique is to zone areas contiguous to existing development (to streets, water, and sewers) for moderate lot size, while outlying areas, not ripe for development from the planning standpoint, are zoned for very large lots on a deliberately temporary basis, with a view toward changing this zoning as soon as the construction of municipal services reaches the outlying areas. This is often the most realistic solution, but it is not free from administrative difficulties, and it can lead to inefficient land use patterns, if the "large" lot size is not in reality large enough to discourage development completely. In this case, a heterogeneous mixture of large and small lots can be left in the wake of "staged" zoning.

Another method is to confine development by means of municipal utility extension. This can work only if established lot sizes are sufficiently small to make public sewers mandatory, and if the scale of development is sufficiently small to make the construction of private disposal plants in freestanding subdivisions uneconomic.

A third method has involved Planning Board designation of "low priority areas" as part of subdivision control. In these areas, construction is subject to a schedule which permits only a specified proportion of houses in a subdivision to be completed in any one year. This recently introduced method has not gained the favor of real estate circles, since it makes uneconomic construction practices mandatory: the added cost of inefficient construction is merely passed along to the consumer; it is not high enough to discourage building.

The fourth method is the use of information and persuasion. The Indianapolis Metropolitan Planning Commission, for example, has carefully mapped all land it considers ripe for development which is located between the fingers and islands of existing subdivisions. There is enough land in this area to take care of that particular city's needs for the next 35 years. By encouraging the construction of trunk sewer lines in this area and by public-relations techniques the Commission hopes to concentrate development there, rather than in the outlying farm reserve area, for which it favors 10-acre zoning.

It would appear that to cope effectively with the problem of haphazard location of residential development new legal tools are needed. The most plausible one, which has worked successfully in Scandinavia and other parts of Europe, is the authority for municipal or regional public agencies to "go into the real estate business" in suburban and rural fringe areas (as redevelopment agencies in American cities have done) and assemble large-scale reserves of development land, which could be sold or leased to investors under proper planning and design controls. The first step in this direction was the legislation proposed by the Kennedy administration in March 1961 (which never passed Congress) to create a Land Bank and to authorize loans and grants to localities to help acquire land for future public or private development. Indispensable as such an approach is for the future, particularly in areas where land prices are still relatively low, it cannot be of much immediate help in areas where land prices are high. In fact, the increased demand would drive them still higher.

To discourage speculation in vacant land, a far-reaching revamping of the present tax system appears necessary. Since the increase in value of vacant land results from the activities of society rather than from those of the land owner special taxation of land profits has been held justified by many theorists. Unlike the case with other commodities, added taxation of land does not decrease its supply. So far, however, American policies have indirectly encouraged land speculation: for local taxes, undeveloped land is typically assessed farther below market value than other real estate. On the Federal level, profits from land sale are taxed liberally, like any other capital gain. The constitutionality of differential tax rates deliberately designed to reduce profits from the sale of land may be open to question in some states, but this approach also has been successfully tested abroad.

A related new legal tool should be region-wide or state-wide density control and the establishment of "development districts" of different priority on top of existing zoning and subdivision controls. Because the police power is delegated by the states to the municipalities under the American system, the obstacles to the states' taking back some of the zoning power from the municipalities would be primarily political rather than legal. But nothing short of a comprehensive, scheduled density control on a region-wide basis, with some areas "frozen" against development for extended periods of time, and with inequalities of local taxation evened out by region-wide taxation, could clear the present mess of a multitude of fragmented and conflicting municipal development policies.

Another necessary and less drastic innovation would be the compilation of detailed statistics on land by the Federal government. The market price of land is an expression of the expectation of its future economic productivity, and the need for data that would help gauge future supply and demand more accurately than a broker's, developer's or speculator's hunch is acute. An accurate land-use census of metropolitan areas every five years, including undeveloped, subdivided, and developed areas seems quite feasible with present-day aerial photogrammetry techniques. It is a standing joke among land economists that more facts are known about the marketing of a single agricultural commodity—peanuts—than about the marketing of land.

A combination of approaches—public land reserves, new methods of real estate taxation, regionwide density and development scheduling controls, together with more accurate data on land use and land consumption, could ultimately lead to more effective land planning policies that would insure more compact urban development with plenty of deliberately planned, not accidental open space.

STREET FORM AND ARRANGEMENT OF UNITS

Next to the confused alternation of developed and undeveloped tracts, a confused street system within the developed areas is another characteristic of the rural-urban fringe. In the past, when houses were constructed on an individual basis or in small groups, the subdivision of land was usually done in very large tracts by speculators who let their surveyor stake out street and lot lines, sold off the parcels, and let the municipality install pavement and utilities. The large-tract subdivision provided a firm overall framework into which individual houses were fitted; the compactness of urban growth insured a modicum of coordination with existing street net, unimaginative as it may have been.

The major drawback of this system was speculative overplatting; the city often found itself with miles of empty streets on which expensive utilities had been installed but without the accompanying houses. By the end of the Depression, American cities found themselves burdened with an estimated 15 million prematurely subdivided lots, frequently tax delinquent and useless because of poor design. To discourage speculation in badly planned land development, the policy of subdivision regulation was devised to put the burden of installing street improvements and other community facilities on the developer, by means of binding municipal specifications. Today, the three processes of land purchase, house construction, and street improvement are no longer divorced, but usually united in the hands of the same entrepreneur.

This latter system gears land platting closer to the demand of the market, but at the same time it inevitably introduces the small and medium-size subdivision in areas where the scale of housing construction is not large. Thus, the overall street network is planned and built in little pieces, which creates a real problem when growth is dispersed and the small subdivisions are widely scattered. Subdivision regulations naturally require the provision of proper connections to future streets, but where the future streets are going to be located is the developer's guess, and his own street layout will be strongly influenced by the accidental shape of his property. When the pieces of the jigsaw puzzle of miscellaneous scattered and random-shaped subdivisions are eventually fitted together, the resultant street network can become a labyrinth of utter confusion. In the western states, the rectilinear grid of section line roads provides some overall order of orientation, but in those regions where the underlying network of rural roads is irregular, orientation is totally obscured for anybody but the native.

The problem could be solved if the municipality would establish precisely and in advance all rights of way for future streets on land that is ripe for development. The legal tools to do this (at no cost to the community) exist in the form of the Master Plan and the Official Map. Superficially it would seem that a complete map of future streets would be the first product expected of a city planning agency worthy of its name; in reality, planning authorities in the U.S. are very reluctant to pin down precisely a complete future street network, although this is often done in Europe. The argument is that for an efficient utilization of land the street system has to bear

Street system shaped by property lines on flat land in New Jersey. Note stub ends of streets "for future expansion."

Street system shaped by property lines and rugged topography in the highlands of San Mateo, Calif. Actually, quite an agreeable pattern, if most of the openness of the area could be preserved.

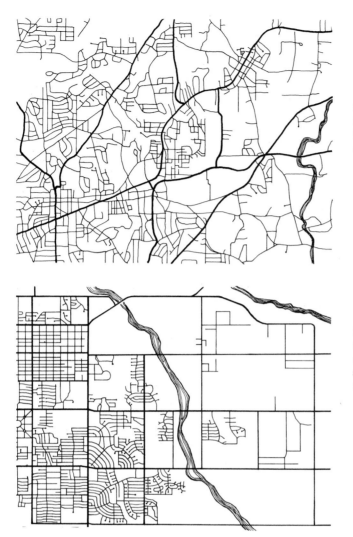

Confused suburban street system, resulting from the accretion of small subdivisions around an irregular rural road net. The example is near Atlanta, Ga.

Some order introduced into the street pattern by means of a rectilinear super-grid of section line roads in Tucson, Ariz. The closer spacing of streets in the second example is the result of smaller lot sizes.

some relationship to the property lines of the parcels to be developed, and one can never predict in advance which particular parcels of land will be assembled for development. Other arguments are that a detailed map of future streets would be too inflexible, and that the money and qualified manpower to undertake such a project thoroughly are not around, anyway. The most that some advanced planning agencies do is to reserve land in advance for freeways and major arterial streets, to save on future acquisition costs and prevent the tearing down of brand-new development in the path of road construction, a condition that is not infrequent in this country.

A compromise solution for introducing order and clear orientation into the residential street net might be as follows: the county or the municipality should plan and reserve adequate rights of way for a *super-grid* of future *arterial* and *collector streets,* leaving it up to the developers to fill in the interstices with local service streets. The basic super-grid, with landscaped buffers included in the rights of way, would have controlled access, permitting the entry of local streets, but not of private driveways. A clear expression of the functional street hierachy and delineation of residential house groups would thus be achieved.

As to the form and design of the streets themselves, they are now governed to some extent by subdivision regulations, which do define—at least theoretically—a hierarchy of street types (local, collector, arterial) and specify the engineering standards for them. These include specifications for materials, as well as such items of geometric design as width, maximum curvature, maximum grades, minimum distances between curves and intersections, maximum length of block, angles of intersecting streets, curb radii, and turn-arounds. It is clear that this type of standard, concerned primarily with safety of operation, still leaves the designer a great deal of freedom: he can lay out a rectilinear grid, a free-form curvilinear plan, or a loop system and remain within the limits of the law.

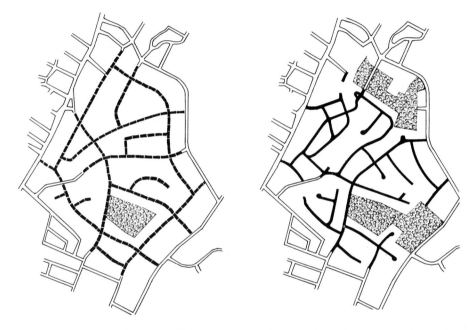

An attempt to plan future streets by persuasion, presented as an achievement of "planning in action" by a local planning agency. *Left,* street plan as suggested by the Planning Board of a New England town in 1952; *right,* final design completed in 1960, after consultations between the planning board and the developers. The proposal does not have much conceptual clarity, but the final result is still weaker, and raises the question as to whether any planning was necessary to achieve it.

Meanwhile, we all know from observation that street form has changed considerably in the past thirty years, basically from the rectilinear grid to the curvilinear plan. This change has been effected through indirect controls, for which the Federal Housing Administration has in large degree been responsible. The reasons for the change have been healthy and necessary, even though the curvilinear layout has often been misused.

The traditional rectilinear "gridiron" street plan, despised by avant-garde planners of the 1930s, and used almost exclusively by American real estate developers up to that time, has, objectively speaking, many things to say for itself. It provides a strong visual order, clarity of orientation, flexibility of circulation (one-way streets) and spatial organization (green squares), and flexible density and land use. But the rectilinear plan does have its defects, particularly in residential areas: it conflicts with a hilly terrain; it has difficulty accepting diagonals; it encourages through traffic; provides excess street capacity at low density while creating too many conflict points at intersections; finally, it becomes monotonous if overly large and undifferentiated.

As street networks began to approach their present size, and traffic its present volumes and speeds, planners began to look for a functional, not merely geometric, street system that would differentiate between different kinds of traffic, eliminate points of conflict and unnecessary street area, define comprehensible, undisturbed areas for living, and fit the streets to natural topography. Briefly, elements of the "functional" street plan are: different design standards for streets intended to carry different traffic volumes at different speeds; local streets, designed to serve only the abutting properties, laid out as loops and cul-de-sacs; long blocks or perhaps even super-blocks with interior pedestrian movement; a limited number of access points to major streets; and employment of three-legged T-intersections, which have only three theoretical traffic conflict points as compared with sixteen in a four-legged inter-section, and have the added advantage of built-in right-of-way assignment. Such "limited access" subdivision design has been demonstrated to reduce right-angle automobile collisions as much as seven times. It cuts down the paved street area considerably and provides a more livable environment—at the expense of some in-directness of movement. Some of these features, particularly if coupled with the need of conforming to a hilly terrain, suggest curvilinear street layout, which can offer the added benefits of reducing speeds on residential streets and creating visual interest. But straight streets can also be fitted into a "limited access" design.

The functional street plan, in its most consistent and radical form, was first employed by Clarence Stein and Henry Wright in Radburn in 1928. The venture failed commercially because of the Depression and did not exercise any immediate influence on speculative land development, but with the New Deal the federal government began to participate in promoting sound land planning practices. In 1934 the Federal Housing Administration was organized to provide mortgage insurance to local banks for loans on privately-built housing: to make sure that the housing was marketable and that risks were kept down, insurance was made conditional on detailed construction standards, and pamphlets were issued suggesting desirable street patterns, under such titles as "Planning Profitable Neighborhoods" and "Successful Subdivisions."

The suggestions did not go as far as advocating the Radburn "superblock" or Elbert Peets' consistent loop design, but concentrated on eliminating the most flagrant violations of safety and economy in plan, with a heavy emphasis on T-intersections and curvilinear adaptations of the street grid. Largely responsible for the latter was Seward Mott, a landscape architect then with the Land Planning Section of FHA, who may have drawn his inspiration from Olmsted's plan for Riverside of 1869 or Forest Hills Gardens of 1911.

Although the proportion of FHA-insured housing construction is not very high (in 1950–1960 it has ranged between 17 and 36 per cent of all private non-farm housing starts), the planning proposals put forth by the agency have found wide-spread acceptance. Many of the suggestions were sound and had a salutary effect in improving the standards of real estate developers—well known as a "tough" group. At the same time, some of the ideas, meant essentially as illustrations of principles, ossified into misapplied rules and clichés, used without meaning or purpose. After

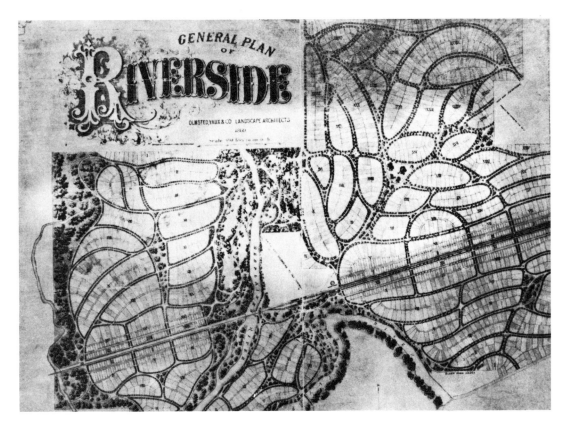

Two predecessors of present-day curvilinear subdivisions: *above,* a section from Olmsted's plan for Riverside, Illinois, 1869; *below,* suggested subdivision design by the firm of Pitkin and Mott, published in 1936 by the Federal Housing Administration in one of its early brochures, "Planning Neighborhoods for Small Houses."

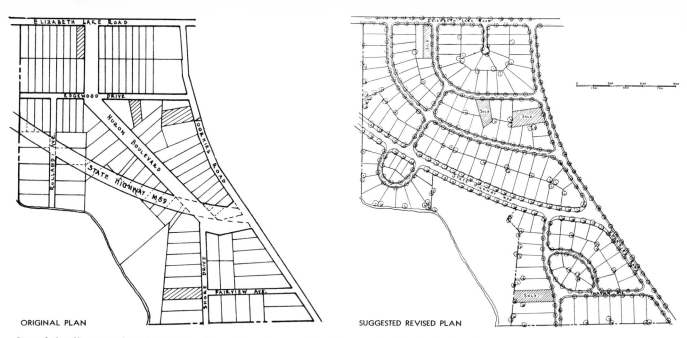

ORIGINAL PLAN

SUGGESTED REVISED PLAN

One of the diagrams that changed the face of American residential areas: "original plan" and "suggested revised plan" from FHA's 1938 brochure, "Planning Profitable Neighborhoods." The drawings indicate the elementary malpractices FHA had to contend with in its early days, and how much it was able to achieve.

World War II and up to the late '50s, land planning ideas were not further developed either on the federal or on the private level, as a result of which most of the postwar residential development became a scaleless mass of uninspired design exercises in asphalt and concrete, safer to be sure, and more efficient, but not much more interesting or less arbitrary than the patterns they replaced.

Also responsible for the monotonous design of today's subdivisions are the existing zoning regulations. The thinking that underlies most present-day zoning ordinances dates back to the early '20s, when individual lot development was still predominant. Coverage, density and location requirements are typically specified in terms of uniform setback lines, uniform side yard, rear yard, and lot size regulations which are all drawn with reference to the individual lot and not to the entire subdivision, the actual building "block" of our residential pattern today. The position of the house on the lot is so rigidly pinned down that there is very little opportunity to design open spaces and house groups for the subdivision as a whole. The Radburn plan, with its pooling of some front yard and side yard space to form an interior park, and with its mixture of house types, could not be duplicated under most zoning ordinances. The uniform location of houses on the lots suggested by the zoning ordinances has inhibited the developer's imagination even in areas where the wording of the law permits greater freedom than he has dared to exercise.

The overall image and the visual character of a residential area is of course decisively influenced by its zoned density. Because of the relatively inflexible position of the house on the lot, lot size and lot frontage alone determine the feeling of spaciousness—or lack of spaciousness—that results. Not without FHA influence, the evolution of the lot size paralleled the evolution of land platting concepts. In the beginning of the century, the traditional 25- or 30 x 100-foot lot, or 1/17 to 1/14 of an acre, was predominant in single- and two-family house developments on the outskirts of urban areas. It meant dark, slot-like sideyards and could provide no space for off-street automobile storage. Today, 60 x 100 feet or 1/7 of an acre is usually considered the absolute acceptable minimum for detached houses, and a quarter-acre may come close to being typical in many suburban developments, though considerable regional and local variations exist: in the New York-New Jersey-Connecticut metropolitan region, average lot size for new one-family houses had reached a half-acre by 1960. Larger lots are frequent and are advocated as desirable by many planners. Surveys undertaken by real-estate men and independent researchers tend to show that quarter-acre to one-acre lots are what most buyers generally desire. Zoning provisions specifying up to five-acre minimum residential lot sizes have been upheld as reasonable by the courts, and ten-acre zoning is in force in some semi-rural areas.

The actual distribution of these lot sizes remains obscure. What proportion of the new building is located on what size lots, where are the different sizes predominating, and on what factors does their location depend? How much land is consumed, on the average, by the new residential development? Unfortunately, as we pointed out, there is no agency in the United States, public or private, that has collected this data on a systematic, countrywide basis. As part of this study, inquiries on the subject were sent out to 70 planning agencies in different parts of the country. Useful replies were received from 20 of these agencies, and some of the results are tabulated below:

PLACE	PERIOD COVERED	LOTS RECORDED	MEAN SIZE (IN SQ. FT.)	Small below 9,999	Medium 10,000– 39,999	Large 40,000 and more
Western areas:						
Los Angeles County (unincorp. territory)	1959	25,982	ca. 14,000	.....	.....	.....
Santa Barbara Co.	1956–1959	....	ca. 22,000	60 %	13 %	26 %
Pima County, Ariz. (including Tucson)	1954–1959	28,278*	15,560	83.9%	11.7%	4.4%
Midwestern areas:						
Minneapolis-St. Paul Metro Area (6 counties)	1950–1958	71,024	12,300	.....	.....	.....
Lansing, Mich. (city)	1958–1959	....	ca. 16,000	50 %	45 %	5 %
Southern areas:						
Durham County, N.C. (part only)	1955–60	226***	38,563	1 %	62 %	37 %
Middle Atlantic areas:						
Allegheny County, Pa.	1958–1960	16,779	9,614	57 %	42 %	1 %
Broome County, N.Y.	1950–1958	8,599	ca. 11,500	75 % ca.	20 % ca.	5 %
Delaware County, Pa.	1951–1958	28,234**	ca. 12,200	65.5%	28.3%	6.2%
Lebanon County, Pa.	1958–1960	1,126	ca. 13,000	74 % ca.	25 % ca.	1 %
New York-New Jersey-Connecticut metropolitan region:						
11 counties	1958–1960	36,778	22,120	35 %	56 %	9 %
New England towns:						
Canton, Mass.	1959	244	ca. 20,100	13 %	86 % ca.	1 %
Guilford, Conn.	1955–1960	522*	ca. 24,000	16 %	56.5%	31.5%
West Hartford, Conn.	1959–1960	454	21,108	18.7%	80.6%	0.7%
Windsor, Conn.	1954–1960	....	ca. 24,000	6.0%	93.0%	1.0%

NOTES: * — Building permits issued, rather than lots approved.

    ** — Includes 34% attached dwellings on lots smaller than 5,000 sq. ft.

    *** — Subdivided lots sold in sample area 25 square miles.

The figures in the table are fragmentary and do not lend themselves to any statistical analysis of nationwide validity. But, for the areas listed, they would tend to show an average lot size of some 14,600 square feet. This average reflects the occurrence of relatively few very large lots, and to retain a proper perspective one must realize that some 70 per cent of the newly developed lots in the political divisions considered are still smaller than 10,000 sq. ft. The proportion of these small lots ranges from about 90 per cent in California to less than 10 per cent in some Connecticut towns. They are typically located on flat ground in the valleys, in areas of high land value. Large lots are traditionally associated with lower land values, a hilly topography, and high incomes—and, sure enough, according to our table, we find them principally concentrated in the hills of Connecticut and Westchester, and in the mountains of Santa Barbara County in California. Whereas the typical density distribution is that of a great many small lots and a few large ones, some of the communities listed exhibit a strong concentration of medium-size lots, with a few very large or very small ones.

A few other remarks pertinent to our table are in order. For relatively small geographic divisions, average lot size fluctuates rather erratically from year to year, due to the incidence of large-tract development in various zoning districts. Therefore, an attempt was made to get totals for longer periods than a year whenever possible. Lot sizes increased rapidly soon after World War II, but since the mid-'50s the rate of increase has slowed down in many areas. A shortcoming of the table is that it represents, with few exceptions, lots approved for subdivision, not building permits issued. Thus, individually developed lots are not included, and large lots may be over-represented in some cases since house construction on large lots often lags several years behind subdivision; small lots are usually built on quite soon.

It was not possible to include in the table services provided to the lots. All small lots and some of the medium-size ones have both water and sewerage. Those larger than a half-acre generally depend on septic tanks. Allegheny County, with 94 per cent of the lots smaller than 20,000 square feet provides sewerage for 95 per cent of its new lots; but the proportion served by septic tanks has been increasing. In Delaware County the proportion increased from 9 per cent in 1951 to 40 per cent in 1958. This trend is due not only to larger lot sizes but also to more scattered development. Lots with individual water supply represent a rather small minority; this practice is now actively discouraged by FHA.

Lot size recorded in building permit and subdivision statistics essentially reflects the zoning limits in areas where development occurs. This minimum, in turn, is set by the interplay of real estate considerations (economic demand for land), political citizen pressure (community preferences concerning visual and socio-economic character), and technical planning principles. The latter have mostly to do with the quality of the land: whether bedrock makes utility installation prohibitive in cost; whether a high water table can be a hazard to health; whether the steepness of natural slopes will prevent reasonable street grades; whether the soil is sufficiently absorptive to permit installation of tile fields for septic tanks, and if so, of what size. These are the factors which force large-acreage zoning in spite of the developers' inclinations.

It should be borne in mind, however, that actual lot size as provided by the developer does not rigidly follow the minimum set by zoning. In some instances variances permitting lots smaller than the legal minimum are granted, but the usual practice is for developers to exceed the zoned minimum, to fit the lot layout to the shape of the property or to topography, or because of public health standards, or of market demand. Studies by the Regional Plan Association indicate that in the New York region the average excess of actual lot size over the legal minimum ranges from eight per cent of the minimum zoned size for very large lots to 80 per cent for small lots. The proportions vary rather erratically from county to county.

Quite often, however, large lot sizes result from reasons that have little to do with the design of the lot itself, with site considerations, or with market demand. The principal one among them is an attempt on the part of the community to slow down its rate of growth through excessive zoning requirements. The hope is that lower density will result in lower expenses for schools, sewerage, and other public facilities, or at least will postpone the need for major capital investment in these fields. To what extent large acreage zoning can in fact result in lower per capita community costs is, as we have pointed out, open to question. Reduced municipal costs at low density can be illusory, if they impose a higher burden of indirect costs on the homeowner or

Average lot size in subdivisions approved 1950–1960: trends in suburban counties around New York and in the Minneapolis–St. Paul metropolitan area. Regional Plan Association and Twin Cities Metropolitan Planning Commission.

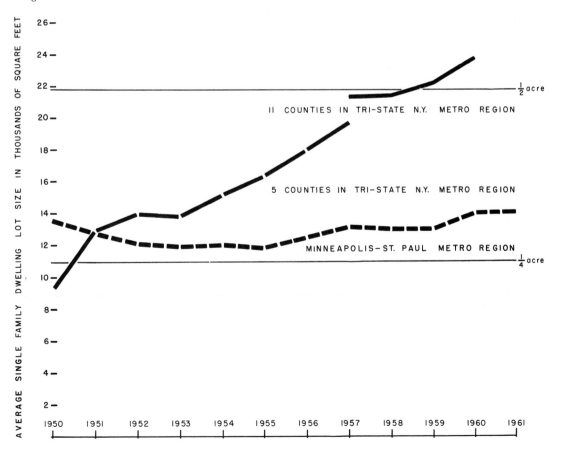

on neighboring communities. Nor does large lot size guarantee that public sewer and water facilities will not eventually be needed, if the pressure of population and rising land values is strong.

It can be said in conclusion that an equitable, region-wide distribution of the costs of municipal growth and the institution of region-wide legal devices to effect the staging of growth would cut down considerably on large lot sizes in areas where they are not functionally justified. At the same time, new zoning techniques must be introduced which will permit gain in openness and spaciousness through more efficient site design, rather than through increased lot size. Some of these techniques are already being tested, under such names as "designed residential districts," "averaging out of zoning," "clustering regulations," "dwellings per acre ratio," "open space bonuses," and so on. Under adequate safeguards, New York State law permits municipalities to allow greater density in one part of the tract and a pool of open space in another, provided the average density remains the same as under conventional zoning. Similar provisions have been adopted by other states. Various types of special permits are being devised to allow variation in side yards, setbacks, as well as the mixing of dwelling types, and thus to eliminate the sterility of identical house-to-site relationships on hundreds upon hundreds of acres. With adequate performance standards and with competent design teams working on the development as well as the municipal review and approval of the plans, the emerging techniques offer considerable hope for the future. It should be emphasized that there are still many areas —particularly on the West Coast with its high land prices—where excessively high rather than excessively low densities of detached houses are a major problem. Here, new site design methods and the introduction of new house types which would eliminate the fragmentation of open space typical of the conventional layout are especially needed.

Typical Suburban Densities I: lot size 5,000 square feet, net density about 8 families per acre, net coverage about 30%, land cost about $40,000 per acre. Lakewood–Long Beach area in Los Angeles County.

Typical Suburban Densities II: lot size 7,500 square feet, net density about 6 families per acre, net coverage about 17%. Port Charlotte, Fla.

Typical Suburban Densities III: lot size 10,000 square feet, net density about 4 families per acre, net coverage about 12% (note two-storey design). The golf course in the center was purchased by the municipality at a cost of $8,200 per acre. West Hartford, Conn.

Typical Suburban Densities IV: lot size 20,000 square feet, net density 2 families per acre, net coverage about 8%. Fairfield, Connecticut.

3. Visual Principles of Small House Grouping

Even a casual inspection of new housing in the rural-urban fringe tends to reveal two basic esthetic faults: first, the opposite tendencies toward monotony or chaos in the arrangement of the individual units themselves, and second, a lack of any harmony between the house groups and the overall natural or man-made setting. Thus, taking a clue from freeway esthetics, we have good reason to speak of "internal" and "external" harmony in subdivision layout. The internal harmony here means consistent relation of the units to each other in a pattern that provides variety within an overall unity. The external harmony means integrating the house groups with their natural and cultural environment. The formal devices which can be used to achieve these two ends are paramount among the esthetic factors to be investigated.

VARIETY WITHIN UNITY

The unity of varity grows essentially out of a complex order, out of a hierarchically-related superposition of orders, perhaps. A very simple, mechanistic order, such as that of a gridiron street plan, is conducive to monotony. Absence of order or regularity, quite obviously, equals chaos. But when we superimpose upon the simple gridiron plan even a rudimentary variation *in the third dimension,* already we can create the beginnings of unity within variety. Complex orders with well-integrated hierarchical relationships, those sometimes referred to as "organic" (such as the structural order of a tree), will give us the best esthetic results. It is therefore not in vain that sculptors and engineer-architects lately have been taking a studious look at the structural orders of nature. Though morphological analogies with nature should be used with caution in the planning field, the principle of "order within an order" is worth remembering, since it enables us to play variations on a theme. And the principle of a hierarchical superposition of orders certainly holds a lesson for us when nature is solving its own locational problems; as for instance, when it determines the optimum spacing of different plants in an ecological community.

THE ORDER OF PATTERN

Taking first the visual problem of small house arrangement, we must seek a basic order within which to start introducing variety, and the first that comes to mind is the order of pattern. We should not be deterred by the fact that in its entirety, this pattern can only be seen from the air. One may be quite aware of it if one stands between the houses, without having to visualize the total plan.

The geometric order of a pattern is set by the shape of its component parts, just as the texture of a fabric is set by its weave. Hexagons demand a hexagonal pattern.

Triangles demand a triangular pattern. Circles and other non-directional shapes can lend themselves to various free arrangements. And rectangles, which most of our single-family houses reveal in their plans, demand a rectilinear pattern. Rectangles, set at odd angles to each other create violent visual conflicts at corners and produce the impression of disorder and confusion. These tenets are subject to substantial modifications when we come to spacing and small angles (to be dealt with in due course), but for the time being we may accept them at face value.

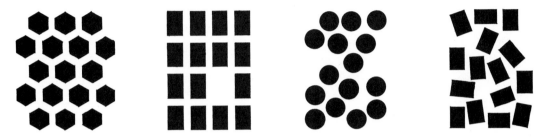

Hexagons demand a hexagonal pattern; rectangles demand a rectilinear pattern; circles can be freely arranged; but if closely spaced rectangles are freely arranged, chaos results.

In arranging single-family houses, we are dealing essentially with rectilinear volumes, and we must be concerned that the spaces between them, if relatively narrow, should be rectilinear, not angular. But this does not mean that the space between the house and the street pavement must be rectilinear, for the pavement is flat and does not define space as strongly as a house. Contrary to what one reads in many subdivision manuals, there is no esthetic reason why the house should be placed parallel to the street line, so long as the houses themselves are arranged in an orderly system. If the order of houses is naturally rectilinear, and the desirable street pattern under given conditions happens to be curvilinear, we can play these two orders against each other and achieve interesting visual compositions. They can also be functionally appropriate, for there is usually one orientation that is best for the houses on any particular site, and turning houses with an identical plan at different angles to conform to the street orientation inevitably leads to poor exposure to sun, wind, or view for some of the units. Independent alignment of house and street allows us to give optimum orientation to all houses and optimum landscape treatment for all streets. A "sawtooth" effect of house façades can be much richer and varied than the traditional flat line of façades, and maintain a firmer order of pattern. Also, if properly handled, it can permit more privacy between the houses and more distant views from the houses onto the street.

THE MEANING OF CURVATURE

Unless houses are very widely spaced, they and not the street pavement are the dominant definers of space. Therefore, in the design of house groups one should ideally think first of siting the houses, and second about a street alignment to serve them. The latter, as we know, can be straight or curvilinear. What are the esthetic uses of the two forms?

The traditional rectilinear grid may have been monotonous, but at least it had a rudimentary order of pattern, as above in Flushing, N.Y.

The new curvilinear grid is hardly less monotonous, and has lost the last vestiges of order and clarity of orientation, as below in Nassau County, N.Y.

A consistent order: rectilinear house arrangement on rectilinear semi-loop streets. A site plan study—never realized—prepared by Skidmore, Owings, and Merrill for Air Force Academy housing.

An inconsistent order: rectangular houses arranged in circles. The functional shortcomings of the plan with regard to traffic and privacy are also apparent.

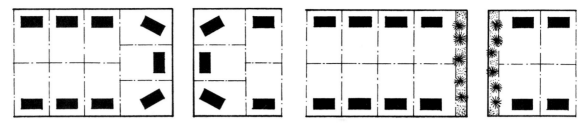

A frequent violation of the order of pattern: the corner lot (*left*), and suggested improvement (*right*).

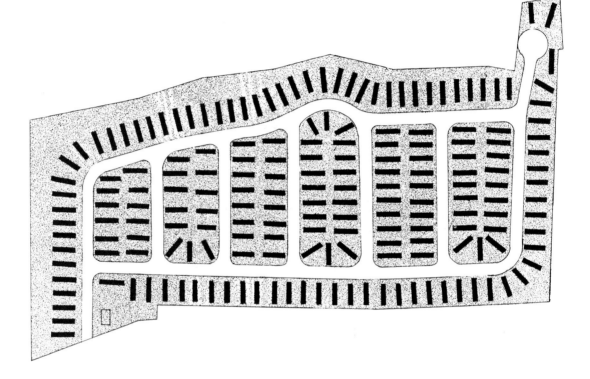

The order of pattern as applied to trailer park design. An existing trailer park in which monotony prevails (*above*), and an improved design with unity of order and variety of open spaces (*below*), as suggested by Earl Rush.

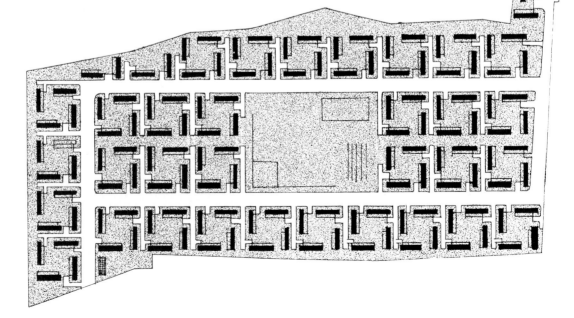

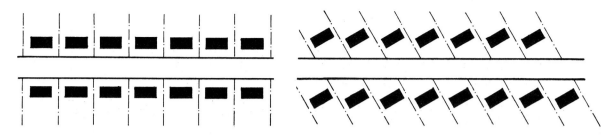

The conventional parallel arrangement of houses and street is satisfactory if not too long (*left*), but independent alignment with "sawtooth" effect (*right*) can often be better.

Flat row of façades versus independent alignment of house and street.

A street can be straight if it reads as a rectilinear space in its own right, that is, if it is relatively short and bounded by strong rectilinear masses along the sides. It should be straight if it offers a vista or is oriented toward some landmark at the end. Finally, it should be straight if it is a major artery, the progress along which is in itself a substitute for a visible feature at the end. Some of these three requirements are usually fulfilled in high-density urban areas.

Not so in suburban or semi-rural areas. There, first of all, major arteries should not be permitted to double as residential streets, so that this reason for a street being straight does not apply. Then, unless the suburban street is quite short, like the cul-de-sacs of Radburn, single-family houses, low and widely spaced, do not allow it to read as a rectangular enclosure in its own right. If it does not read as an enclosure, it will probably offer a vista, but very likely a vista to nowhere. To close a vista that shows nothing, we can introduce curvature. Highway esthetics will show us that curvature stops an unnecessarily long view, and provides interest by displaying the outer side of the road.

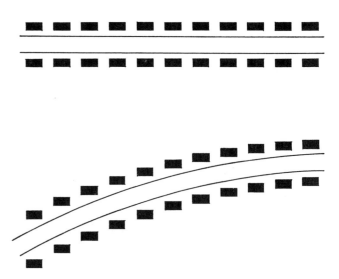

Long residential street with single-family houses: (*above*) neither space, nor axis, nor artery; hence, not justified. To close the vista, curvature can be introduced (*below*).

It should be made clear that to close a vista, the curvature of a street does not have to be sharp. Just one degree of curvature* (roughly a 6,000-foot radius) effectively closes the view along a 50-foot-wide street within 1,200 to 1,800 feet, depending on the viewpoint; that is, within twelve to eighteen houses on 100-foot lots. In practice, of course, the curvature on curvilinear street layouts is much sharper than that, with radii ranging from 200 to 1,000 feet. These sharp curvatures can have a reason—adaptation of fairly narrow blocks, their width set by the lot size, to a difficult topography—or they can be completely arbitrary—such as those in flat terrain, where they are sometimes explained by the need to discourage excessive vehicular speeds.

* Degree of curvature is the angle enclosed by a 100-foot arc.

When we deal with sharply curving streets, the "law" about rectilinear units, closely spaced, demanding a rectilinear arrangement, holds true. But when the curvature is slight, houses can be placed parallel to the street and gently curve with it. The deviation from a rectilinear order in any single space between two houses is then so small that it is not visually obtrusive.

Gently curving the pattern of the houses in conformity with curving contours of the land can be both pleasant and economical, since straight streets in undulating topography can result in added expenses for extra foundation and grading work. Fully aware of the fact that the ancient Greeks planned straight streets even in very hilly terrain, and that Olmsted located a curvilinear pattern on completely flat ground, one would nevertheless tend to suggest two desirable principles. On very flat ground, curvature in residential streets should, if it is to be introduced at all, be only as flat as necessary to close an uninteresting vista—see, for example, the major streets at Radburn or Chandigarh. But it should be borne in mind that the planning requirements of limited access, no through traffic, and T-intersections can be fulfilled

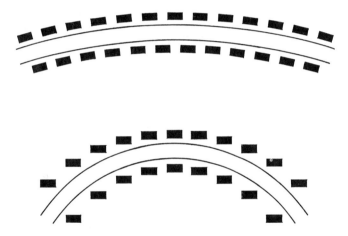

Flat street curvature (*above*): houses can curve together with street. Sharp street curvature (*below*): rectilinear order may govern.

with a modified discontinuous rectangular grid, a device that has not been used as much as it warrants. With relatively short streets reading as enclosed rectilinear spaces, monotony can be avoided.

In undulating topography, curvilinear street designs can be very appropriate. But unless the curvature is rather flat, independent alignment of house and street should be considered to prevent angular conflicts between units.

The Spacing Intervals

The question of angular conflicts—when they occur and when they can be disregarded—leads us to the subject of spacing intervals. In the following chapter we shall see that one country lane poses few problems of organizing space, whereas two

Geometric order of houses coordinated with the geometry of the terrain: the units on flat ground are arranged in a rectilinear order; the units on a curving slope (a public housing project in this instance) curve gently with the curving slope of the hill. An expressive visual pattern in the macro-landscape is achieved. Note the importance of the green wedge and the factory for the visual accent and separation.

broad ribbons of freeway pavement do pose an esthetic problem because they interact to create a space of their own. Similarly, one isolated house in the landscape does not create a space by itself—the space is molded by topography and vegetation. But when two or more units are sufficiently close to be perceived in one view, they begin to pose problems of arrangement between themselves.

Buildings of substantial size, such as row houses or apartments, can enclose well-defined, "positive" architectural spaces that can be proportioned and arranged to create an urban atmosphere. Detached single-family units are much weaker definers of space, so that the main esthetic reliance has to be on their overall pattern and on landscaping elements. Nevertheless, they do modulate space, even if the space is largely freely floating or "negative," rather than firmly defined. Three distinct spatial situations can be singled out, depending on how far apart the units are set.

The first situation occurs when two houses are placed very close together—let us say when the distance between the units is shorter than their width. The resulting space is visually unpleasant, reading as a constricted slot, an "interval" rather than a positive, useful area. While the days of the four- to six-foot slot between houses are largely gone (FHA requires that the sum of side yards be at least 15 per cent of the lot width and not less than 10 feet, and most zoning ordinances have comparable

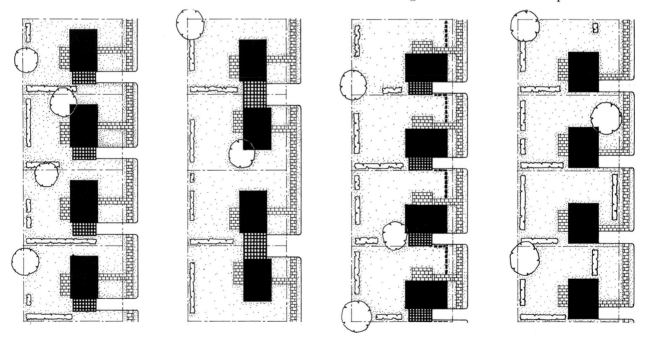

A. Conventional plan with narrow side yards. *B*. One solution: pool side-yard space, eliminating one side yard by attaching garages. *C*. Another solution: face gable end toward street; place house off-center on lot; make magnified "side yard" the outdoor living area, screening it from the street. *D*. A third solution: reduce the length of the house (and lot coverage) by erecting a two-storey house.

provisions), narrow side yards out of character with the openness of single-family development still remain an insistent esthetic problem. In practical land planning terms, a narrow side yard, unless it accommodates an apron for the garage, is an under-utilized, largely wasted area—its only purpose is to insulate the house from its neighbor.

The desire to achieve wider side yards was an important motive in the drive for wider lots, but increasing lot frontage is probably the most expensive way to achieve satisfactory side-yard relationships. At least three more imaginative and less costly al-

The narrow side yard: an esthetic problem.

ternatives are available: pooling side yards by attaching pairs of dwellings, preferably through their garages; placing the house off-center on the lot with the narrow side facing the street; reducing lot coverage by erecting a two-story house.

Any one of the three solutions can create the impression of greater spaciousness and more harmonious area relationships without increasing the width or the size of the lot. The important point in using these devices is to resist the temptation—because of the greater apparent openness—to cut the size of the lot and thus end up where we started. For small lots—narrower than 60 or 70 feet—none of these remedies can offer much help. Where lots have to be so narrow because of high land cost, the only esthetically correct solution is to abandon the attempt to express the houses as detached units and express them for what they visually are—a string of attached dwellings, without any side yards.

It is incongruous to pretend that these dwellings on 40-foot lots are "detached houses." Visually, they read as a row and should be expressed as such, with the narrow slots between them eliminated, at a considerable saving in land and construction costs.

A second distinct relationship between detached dwellings occurs when they are spaced fairly widely apart, when the distance between the houses is greater than their width, or even than their length. This open arrangement, in general, is satisfactory, and in keeping with the intended spaciousness of single-family development. With this intermediate spacing, a firm geometric relationship between the units still has to be maintained, since the units visually affect each other quite strongly, particularly in open terrain. Unfortunately, the order of pattern in this instance is all too often disregarded by developers, so that standing between the houses one sees them, even through the foil of trees, as a set of disjointed planes turned at haphazard angles to each other. This confusion is often compounded by discordant roof shapes and color schemes.

No order of pattern: each house turned at a different angle to every other house; even with moderately wide spacing the enclosed spaces are visually disturbing.

Only when the distances between houses become very large—the third situation—can the order of pattern be disregarded, since the units cease to form a pattern and are each perceived individually. This is generally the case in wooded, hilly terrain with lot sizes of two acres or larger. The tree growth in this case serves as the unifying design element and conceals nearby houses, creating an atmosphere of seclusion and privacy. In such very low density areas one rarely sees more than three or four houses at a time. Buildings seen in the distance through trees seem less intrusive in the landscape and can be freely arranged, regardless of their shape or relationship to other units.

ARTICULATION OF GROUPS

While proper spacing intervals in an ordered pattern can create harmonious relationships between units, they cannot, in and of themselves, prevent monotony unless the houses are so far apart that a visible pattern does not exist. Monotony arises from a very large number of units spaced at identical intervals. The way to combat it without destroying order is to reduce the number of units perceived in any one view, to create sub-groups within the overall pattern. This separation of visually comprehensible groups can be achieved by fairly conventional devices, such as the short street or the cul-de-sac, or by methods which so far have received less attention, such as the varying setback line and the cluster.

The varying setback is the easier to achieve under present zoning regulations, if the lots are sufficiently deep. By pulling back from the building line groups of three to five houses, a progression of wider and narrower spaces in the street can be created to give a more distinct identification to the individual units, which begin to read as "one out of three" or "one out of five," rather than "one out of an indefinite number." The varying setback should be used with the utmost caution in the case of individual units, since a random line of façades can all too easily result in complete chaos, especially when the units are closely spaced.

A more radical approach to articulating separate house groups is the "cluster." In this case, not only is the setback varied, creating lateral enclosed spaces along the street, but distances between houses are also increased at certain intervals, permitting the landscape beyond the houses to merge with the street every so often. In practice, this means that lot size—or at least, lot frontage—is reduced, and the land thus gained is left around groups of houses as permanent open space. While the overall density within the development remains the same as in conventional design, a greater feeling of openness is created and more of the landscape is left in its natural state.

The cluster idea, which has been on the drawing boards in planning schools since the early '50s,* did not gain national publicity until 1959, when it suddenly broke through in several widely separated parts of the United States. This belated and hesitant recognition is due to several practical difficulties First of all, reducing the lot size in order to gain open space around groups of lots is illegal under most existing zoning statutes, and legislation permitting the "averaging" of density or "gross density control" (instead of net lot size control) and "planned residential districts" that allow a flexible house location is only gradually being introduced by progressive

* See "City Planning at Yale" No. 1. Graduate Program in City Planning, Yale University, New Haven (1954).

Varying the setback line to achieve visual enclosures along the street; a design suggested by architect V. J. Kostka. By articulating groups, houses that would otherwise form an undifferentiated line are given a greater identity.

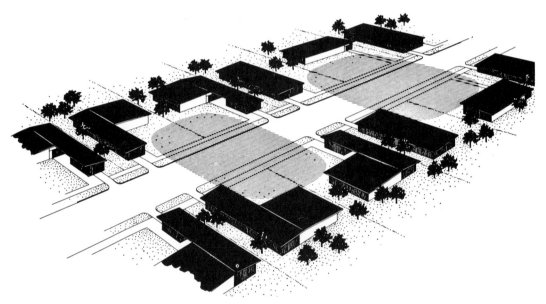

Another approach to a varying setback, creating friendly and intimate outdoor spaces along a street; design by Anshen and Allen, architects.

planning agencies in some states and municipalities. Unless the houses in a cluster are to be attached, the principle can work only in areas of really low density (say, two families per acre or less), since even in a cluster one would not want to advocate too close a spacing of free-standing houses. Furthermore, clusters create some problems of a psychological nature. In an undifferentiated line of houses, each family possesses to some extent the anonymity of a horizontal apartment house. In a cluster, a small group of families who may have no reason at all to belong together are singled out and brought into physical proximity, a condition that is resented by some home-owners. A consistent cluster design would pool the garages or carports of the several houses into one "car harbor" to exploit the advantages of a compact paved area. This also conflicts with the desire for individuality and for having direct access from car

The practical advantages of a cluster design:

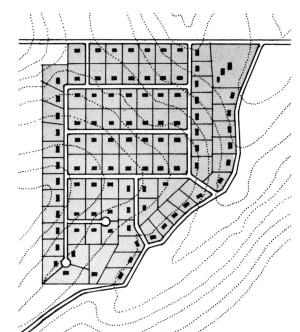

Rectilinear plan, 94 lots, 12,000 feet of streets and utilities.

Curvilinear plan, 94 lots, 11,600 feet of streets and utilities.

Cluster plan, 94 lots, 6,000 feet of streets and utilities.

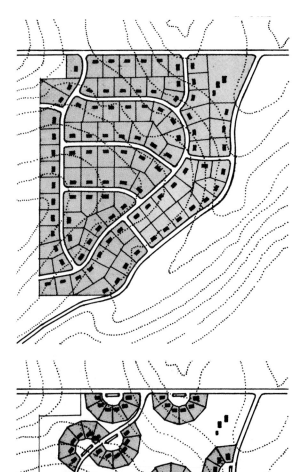

Lot size in the first two cases is 50,000 square feet; in the third case, lot size is reduced to 30,000 square feet, with some 44 acres left open. Design by Myron X. Feld, planning engineer, from *The American City*.

to kitchen in any weather. Moreover, the maintenance of the common open spaces is often cited as a problem. A municipality would generally hesitate to maintain these areas, which are not really public. It is often suggested that the open space be held in corporate ownership by the residents of the subdivision, but this solution presupposes an unusual amount of cooperative neighborhood spirit, and can probably work well only if the open space is an extension of a common with some focal community facility such as a golf course, a swimming pool, or a marina. Under ordinary conditions, the simpler solution is to run property lines across the open space creating, in effect, very deep and irregular lots. Finally, there is the problem of insuring that the open spaces between clusters remain permanently open, and are not sold for development at some future date.

In spite of these difficulties, the cluster principle offers some practical as well as visual advantages. It reduces cost by cutting the length of streets and utilities, by reducing the amount of earthwork and site preparation, and by allowing flexibility to preserve natural features. Finally, it provides informal play areas for children of different ages. In view of this, it deserves to gain at least a limited popularity.

A further esthetic advantage of the cluster principle is that it allows one, under certain conditions, to digress from a regular geometry of rectilinear relationships between units, and to arrange them with the informal ease demanded by some landscapes. In closely-knit architectural spaces, when separate houses do not read as isolated objects but rather as parts of a common space enclosure, the free geometry

Even though planting is sorely lacking in this scheme and the street layout leaves much to be desired, the superiority of this cluster-type plan over comparable conventional low-cost developments is evident. Notable are the firm geometric relationships between units and the pooling of open space; a World War II National Housing Agency development near Vancouver, Washington.

(*Left*) The principle of loop streets and a firm yet rich geometric order of pattern are incorporated in this cluster-type neighborhood plan by Gonul Tankut, 1954. To eliminate problems of communal open-space maintenance, it is suggested that all areas except the parking bays and tot-lots be individually owned.

(*Below*) The collector street is unencumbered with houses and permits full enjoyment of the landscape; the free-form landscape design is played against the firm geometry of the clusters, which are freed from it to some extent only in two cases. One of the structures in each group is the common garage. Design by Lewis Roscoe, 1959.

of light oblique angles can be not only visually permissible, but even quite desirable, as witnessed by the house-to-house relationships in medieval villages and towns. Usually, however, the prerequisite for such a free arrangement is some physical connection between the units—in the form of garden walls, hedges or screens. In summary, the requirement for a rectilinear order in a plan for rectilinear houses, which we have strongly emphasized in this chapter, holds true primarily for intermediate distances between detached units; it can be dispensed with not only on very large lots, but also in very tight clusters, provided that, in the latter case, the irregular space enclosures are carefully studied and designed.

A British example of detached houses in a cluster, arranged in a free order and tied together by serpentine garden walls. The communal auto court with access to individual garages gives the group an urban atmosphere, which is played against the openness of the surrounding wooded landscape. The development, at Coombe Hill, Kingston, Surrey, was designed by architect Patrick Gwynne.

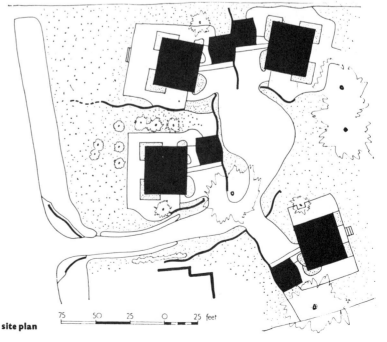

75   50   25   0   25 feet

site plan

ARCHITECTURAL CONSISTENCY

So far, we have discussed the individual houses as rectangles in plan, or as abstract volumes in space. In reality, these volumes possess a distinct shape, determined by their height, their roof design, and their massing. The five basic combinations of silhouette and mass typical of American builders' practice are the single-storey house with a flat roof, the single-storey house with a lightly pitched roof (often termed the "ranch type"), the single-storey house with rooms on the attic level ("Cape Cod"), the split level, and the two-storey house. To avoid a chaotic appearance, it is imperative that in any group which the eye sees in one view, some order and consistency be maintained with regard to these architectural characteristics. Flat roofs and pitched roofs and different kinds of gables cannot be mixed indiscriminately, and a consistent cornice line is no less important than a consistent arrangement of setbacks from the street. Variation can be introduced between groups, but identity should be maintained within.

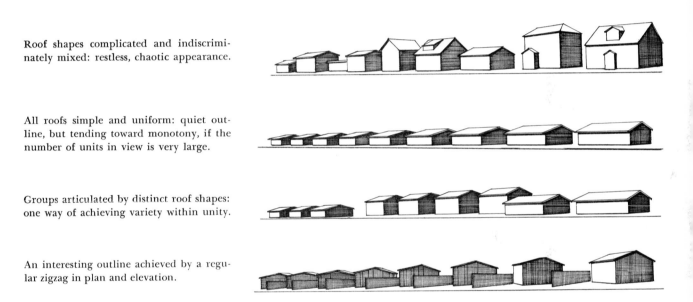

Roof shapes complicated and indiscriminately mixed: restless, chaotic appearance.

All roofs simple and uniform: quiet outline, but tending toward monotony, if the number of units in view is very large.

Groups articulated by distinct roof shapes: one way of achieving variety within unity.

An interesting outline achieved by a regular zigzag in plan and elevation.

The roof line particularly is to be watched on sloping streets: it is very important that the houses along the street "march" up or down the hill in equal and not irregular steps. If pitched roofs are used, it is advantageous for the gable end to face the street: this minimizes the visual conflict between the slope of the roofs and the slope of the ground, as the direction of both slopes becomes parallel. Roofs of similar pitch should naturally be chosen for any two rows of houses on a sloping street, and if the roof pitch echoes the slope of the ground to some extent, harmonious relationships can more easily result. In a flat landscape, steep gable ends can sometimes be interesting by their contrast. On the side of a hill, a flat roof angle can pick up the dominant rhythm of the ground.

Houses and roof lines ascending a slope in an irregular manner; even in this open, ½-acre lot development the rhythm of the gables should be much stronger.

Houses ascend the hill in regular steps, but their roofs slope the wrong way, creating a harsh relationship with the slope of the ground; a subdivision near Seattle.

A roof line that successfully echoes the dominant slope of the ground: house near Atlanta; subdivision designed by Finch and Barnes, architects.

The present-day scale of residential construction, which makes it realistic to consider the street not as an accidental accumulation of individual houses but as a deliberately designed group ensemble (an opportunity, alas, rarely seized by builders), allows us to go one step further and to treat the roofscape of new development as a designed texture in the macro-landscape. Single-family houses being low, there is very often an elevation of the ground from which the total pattern of the development can be appreciated, and in fact such outlooks in residential areas are just as desirable as the vantage points on freeways, from which the highway can look at it-

A view over the roofs of Levittown, Pa.; distant views over Levittown roofs are quite pleasant, but the broken roof planes in the foreground confuse the picture.

self. In the confined, domestic scale of residential streets, a long view is very refreshing, and care should be taken that the sight is worthwhile. To this end, the order of pattern in the location of the buildings, an orderly rhythm of roof angles, and the texture and color of roof materials can all contribute, but very often adding trees or tall structures is essential to provide contrast and relief.

The need for boldness and simplicity of outline, for design through large-scale, distinctive arrangements of units—not through a confused agglomeration of details—is especially noticeable in the massing and the façades of typical American speculatively built houses. Houses in a group—be it a row, a court, a cul-de-sac or a cluster—

Flat roofscape in a flat valley in Marin County, California: mountains provide a pleasing backdrop, but vertical elements, such as tall trees, are definitely needed, as shown in the drawing.

cannot relate to each other harmoniously unless they have some strong recurrent elements in common. Aside from the pitch of the roof, the roof line, and the roof ridge, which we have emphasized, these unifying elements are the floor line (where the foundation ends and the wall begins), the sill line or lines (if there are high and low windows), and the head line (either door or ceiling height). Further basic elements are vertical modules (the spacing of columns, panels, windows), the choice of exterior materials, and their color. Keeping the general order of these elements consistent, variety can be introduced by interchanging parts without destroying the visual logic of the whole group.

The difficulty with the average speculatively-built American house is that it is not even consistent within itself; hence little relationship with the neighboring structure can be established. Typically, its horizontal elements do not line up: the sills of the living room, kitchen, bathroom, and bedroom windows are all of a different height (established in part by interior requirements), and door heads do not line up with window heads. The roof is usually broken up into several planes, often with projecting dormers of various shapes, and the façades may also have meaningless projections. If the house has pretentions, it may feature an exhibit of assorted building materials on its exterior—brick, permastone, wood siding, asphalt shingles, plastic awnings, and so on. Occasional exhortations in the professional press notwithstanding, builders seem slow to learn that simplicity is a virtue, that windows should line up and that one just cannot use more than two basic materials on the exterior of one house.

Roof planes can be broken in long buildings, such as row houses, to prevent monotony, but the detached house is too small for any but the simplest roof shape; broken roof planes create a disturbing busy effect.

A strong social pressure behind this visual confusion seems to be a misguided effort on the part of the home-buying public to achieve variety and individuality. This pressure acts not only through the housing market, but also through the informal and formal instruments that regulate it. Among the latter one finds deed restrictions and covenants as well as such esthetic legislation as the "no look-alike" ordinances of

Scarsdale, New Rochelle, or White Plains in New York. These ordinances prohibit the erection of a building if it is substantially similar to any neighboring building in more than three of such measurable respects as roof height, roof pitch, length of the roof ridge, width of the house, location of windows, garages and gables. Such an approach, more often unwritten than explicit, encourages architectural confusion and forces the builder, who works from standard plans, into contortions which are ridiculous and at the same time obvious violations of the intent of the regulation. Some esthetic ordinances, such as that of Eastchester, N.Y., come closer to the heart of the matter by prohibiting both excessive similarity and excessive dissimilarity, but again the preoccupation with façade dimensions of individual units misses the basic point of large-scale group relationships.

The way to achieve variety is not in pretending that standardized units are not standardized, but rather in striving toward unique arrangements of units and toward a distinct relationship to the natural landscape, which is always unique, even though never afraid of standardization (a tree, covered with thousands of nearly identical leaves, is a thing of beauty). A measure of similarity between buildings is essential to make them look like parts of a larger design: a house should be similar to other houses in its group with regard to characteristic proportions, materials and shapes. Variations between standardized units in a group can be limited to interchangeable modular elements (openings and solids, reflecting different variations of a basic plan), the color and texture of panels, the design of outside enclosures such as fenced-in patios, porches

The confusion of unrelated, self-conscious house shapes in a Virginia subdivision.

In contrast is the relatively dignified quiet of a street of look-alike houses in Levittown, Pa. The smaller setback and the curve, both confining the space of the street, also help.

The homeowners' reaction to standardized design: examples of "folk art" in Levittown, Pa.

and carports. But each group of houses can differ in the way the house shapes are used to form a composition, in the way the group relates to the ground form and to clusters of vegetation; in a rich geometric order each "look-alike" house will have a distinct relationship to every other house. Focal points should likewise be chosen in relation to groups, not to individual houses. The eye becomes irritated by monotonously petty devices of self-conscious individualism, but delights in recognizing repeated form, and moves along with its rhythm to points of significant emphasis.

Variations between house groups can be achieved by the use of house types (the split-level group, the two-storey group), roof shape (the flat roof group and the steep gable group), exterior materials (the shingle group and the brick group), the dominating focal element (the group with the oak tree, the group around a meadow, the

group with the rock outcrop, the group around a pond), as well as the general architectural style, carrying the personal imprint of the designer. Conversely, one can
state that if houses are essentially dissimilar, if each is designed by a different architect
for an individual client, they should not be placed in a group, but rather spaced
widely apart out of sight of each other, on three- or five-acre lots. Otherwise, the subdivision can become a horrible museum of different cults of contemporary architecture.

INTEGRATION WITH THE ENVIRONMENT

Although wide differences in taste will continue to exist in the architectural design
of houses, appreciation of the natural landscape seems to be an esthetic area in which
a consensus can more easily be reached. Much of the movement out of the city seems
to be motivated by the desire of people to be closer to trees, meadows, ponds, and
brooks, but it is exactly these things that are very often destroyed in the process of
subdividing. While committed to providing adequate landscaped spaces in the redevelopment of old city slums at enormous expense, our municipalities are, by de-
fault, permitting the construction of hundreds of square miles of new residential
areas, which, sound as they may be in their elementary structural and public health
standards, are lacking in environmental esthetic features that produce handsome and
enduring neighborhoods. Because of the relatively weak imprint of man-made elements at low density, a neighborhood of detached houses cannot be successful unless
the houses and their natural environment are molded into one integral form. The
point here is not one of architectural philosophy, of whether a house should be
designed to blend with the landscape, or be placed in deliberate juxtaposition to it.
The essential requirement is that, whether by conformity or by contrast, a relationship be achieved which respects the character and individuality of the site, and preserves and expresses the green setting that called low density into being.

CONTINUITY OF LAND FORM

The first item to be considered in relating house groups to their environment is
preserving the natural continuity of the land form. In the typical detached house
development, only some 15 to 35 per cent of the land is covered by pavements and
buildings; the natural surface of the earth remains the dominant feature. Hence, the
contour and the character of the raw land should be allowed a decisive role in the
arrangement of man-made elements. The geometric order of pattern, randomly superimposed upon the site in the initial stage of design, should then be molded by the
land form just as iron particles are arranged by a magnet along its lines of force. It is
this interaction between geometry and nature that gives the house group amenity,
interest, and life.

The placement of houses and streets should disturb the natural topography as little
as possible, and to the extent that grades have to be changed, they should be reconstructed to approximate the natural flow of the land form. Present-day heavy equipment, capable of moving huge quantities of earth at low cost, is all too often care-
lessly used to violate the landscape; but with proper sensitivity and forethought, the

scrapers and bulldozers can be used to undertake some extra earth-moving for purely esthetic purposes so that where large earthworks are indispensable, their scars are healed and sculptured into pleasing forms.

In locating streets for detached houses, many principles of highway esthetics discussed in Part III apply on a smaller scale: streets should follow ridges and swales; they should not straddle hills perpendicularly to contours, but rather at an oblique angle; they should avoid rollercoaster, broken back, and other discontinuous profiles. Spirals and other refinements of the horizontal alignment are unnecessary, but a clear decision should be made whether the street system is being designed in a "natural" curvilinear style simulating a country road, or whether it represents a modified rectilinear grid. In the first instance, straight lines should definitely be avoided, and in the second emphasized. Unfortunately, most current designs are a thoughtless mixture of the two idioms. Topography is too often considered a nuisance complicating drainage requirements and increasing cost—not an asset, to be enhanced by a fitting street line.

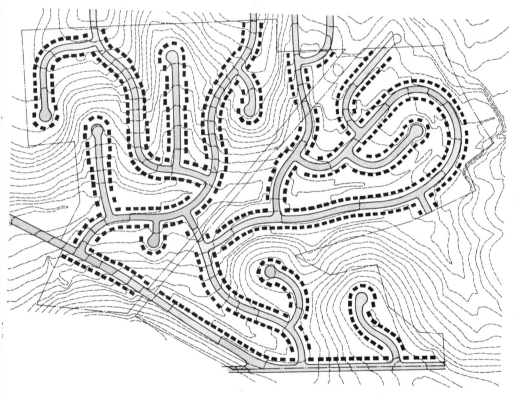

A curvilinear street plan closely fitted to a rough topography: note how streets follow ridges and swales, and how contours are crossed at oblique angles. Insufficient expression of the valley, however, can be questioned, and so can the uniformity of the parallel house-to-street relationship. Design by Community Planning Services, Inc., Pittsburgh.

In order to stimulate sensitivity to the topography by administrative action, it can be recommended that the process of subdivision review should require the mandatory submission of contour plans at two-foot intervals (the usual present requirement, which is often waived, being for 5-foot intervals); moreover, in difficult topography, submission of accurately constructed foreshortened perspective drawings of the contours of the site showing the relationship to proposed development could be required. A much wider use of earth removal regulations is also to be recommended.

Such regulations make significant amounts of excavation illegal without the approval of the local planning agency. Sometimes, as in California, their main purpose is to prevent erosion and nuisance from dust, but in many cases these regulations are esthetic in intent, designed to prevent the mutilation of the landscape by thoughtless grading and unsightly borrow pits, and requiring the replacement of a specified amount of topsoil after excavation.

Two examples of poorly fitted streets: (*above*) the long tangent running perpendicularly to fairly steep contours is too harsh, and creates an unsightly street perspective; (*below*) the better, oblique street-to-contour relationship is spoiled by the small S-curve, which appears weak and unnecessary. Examples are from typical subdivisions in Connecticut.

The grading of man-made slopes between detached houses should be continuous, with edges generously rounded to blend imperceptibly into the natural sculpture of the ground. The transition in grade from lot to street should be gradual, not forced. Even more than in freeway roadside design, gentle slopes are important. A minimum slope of about one per cent is needed for grass-covered areas to insure proper drainage of surface water. But the maximum slope should not exceed 25 per cent, or one vertical unit on four horizontal units. Slopes as steep as one on three need unsightly diversion ditches to prevent erosion, while one on two or 50 per cent slopes invite children to slide and are difficult to mow. Special planting of ground cover or shrubs, which visually expresses the break in the continuity of the land form, is one way of dealing with steep slopes when they are unavoidable. On very flat sites, interest can deliberately be created by mounds of excavated material, but here, too, the effect should not be overdone by unfittingly steep slopes.

The limitation on the steepness of slopes in subdivisions establishes a definite relationship between the spacing of houses (lot size) and the steepness of the terrain. If a house is to be placed on a flat pad, rather than built into the incline of a hill, quarter-acre lots generally should not be planned on natural slopes steeper than ten per cent, while 15 per cent slopes require at least half-acre lots. Still steeper terrain often needs special treatment, such as the use of retaining walls.

Though one cannot condemn retaining walls in principle—for when expertly designed, they can become interesting landscape features—the average retaining wall in American subdivisions is ugly, and unnecessarily destroys the continuity of the land form. Cribbing, often used in conjunction with street construction through rugged terrain, is particularly obnoxious. A sound retaining wall is expensive—it requires considerable structural strength, a deep foundation, careful provision for drainage, a sensitive fit into the curving form of the ground, and an interesting material for surface texture—not painted cinder block. Therefore, the best solution is to avoid retaining walls whenever possible in low- to medium-cost development. In fact, a sound policy of esthetic controls may require the prohibition of retaining walls in

Gently rolling base plane of the ground unnecessarily violated by a series of small and confused retaining walls. Unsightly basements make for a poor transition between the ground and the living level of the houses.

areas where developers are tempted to use them unnecessarily. Such a regulation, coupled with maximum slope limitations, could go a long way toward insuring continuity of land form in developments with a mildly rolling terrain.

On steeper sites, a major problem—and a frequent reason for retaining walls—is the intersection between the house and the ground. If a house cannot be placed on a flat

Example of a clean articulation between house and ground—note cantilevered entrance platform with shadow joint and terrace. The terrace is supported by a wall of stone slabs excavated on the site. General Electric model residence, built to FHA minimum standards for a low-cost house, designed by Walter Harris, architect, with John Simonds, landscape architect.

pad, the angle between the floor level and the ground creates an unfortunate lopsided or sliding effect. The architectural devices used to obviate this condition are either a deliberate articulation of the basement level as a support quite distinct from the upper part of the house (say, by cantilevering the upper level), or various terracing arrangements with retaining walls. An artificial landscape of terraces quite obviously is one in which rules about the continuity of rolling natural land forms no longer apply. In this case, the important task is to integrate the retaining structures with the houses: the natural ground surface becomes visually subordinate.

The terraced landscape: in structure and in material, retaining walls are part of the houses; examples from a speculatively-built development in New Haven (*above*) and a model settlement of prefabricated houses at Veitingergasse near Vienna (*below*). The Vienna development, designed by Professor Roland Rainer and Carl Aubock, was built in 1954 at the suggestion of the U.S. Economic Mission to Austria.

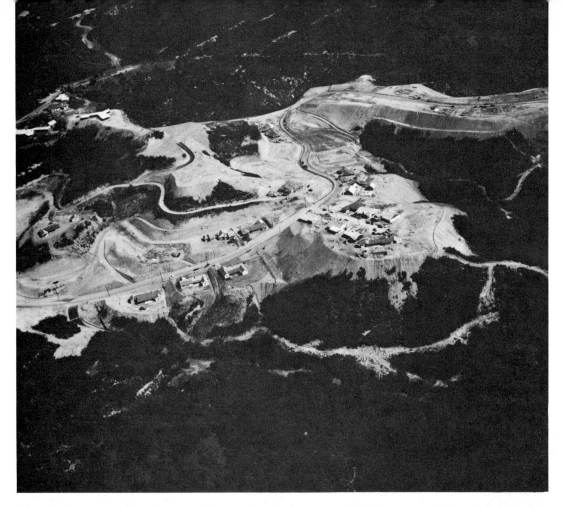

Terracing in the Santa Monica mountains near Los Angeles. An artificial landscape of this scale requires particularly careful three-dimensional study; the fees of an engineer-sculptor-landscape architect team would amount to a small fraction of the earth-moving cost.

MODULATION OF SPACE

A desert can be beautiful because of the flowing continuity of its ground forms alone. This is scarcely the kind of beauty one would like to see in a residential environment—though many developers come close to providing their buyers with the "desert look" in areas previously lush and green. They justify the ruthless destruction of the natural vegetation by the argument that planting can always be replaced. But it takes nature decades to duplicate what man can destroy in a few minutes, and many present-day houses will become obsolete by the time the new planting around them is full-grown. Compared with the time and effort involved in landscaping a site from scratch, the cost of preserving the existing assets of the site is negligible: some forethought in design and some care during construction is all it takes. Besides, more often than not, the existing growth will be more fitting—both ecologically and visually—than any artificial landscaping. The latter becomes essential only if the site is bare.

Provision of fairly large lot sizes (or better yet, smaller lots in clusters) and careful restriction of cut and fill operations alone will do much to preserve the natural flora in a residential development. Reducing standards for curbs and street grades, for storm drainage and sidewalks in low-density areas, can further help the "rural look." In addition, an increasing number of subdivision regulations—for example, most of those in Massachusetts—contain paragraphs requiring the developer to show "due regard for all natural features, such as large trees, natural groves, water courses, scenic points, historic spots and similar community assets which, if preserved, will add attractiveness and value to the subdivision."

Many subdivision regulations qualify the paragraph concerning conservation of natural features by the phrase "if required by the Planning Board," but some go beyond generalities about "due regard for large trees and particularly attractive natural groves" and specify in detail a minimum number of trees per lot to be preserved or planted, or else require all trees above a certain size (say, 10″ caliper or more), to be preserved, unless they are within 10 feet of a proposed building, or in the street right of way. For these purposes, a detailed plan showing existing and proposed planting on the site is required by the municipal planning agency.

Attractive as such strongly worded requirements sound, they are at times difficult to implement because of their rigidity—in submitting a subdivision plat for approval, a developer does not know in advance the final location and design of his houses. Therefore, many professionals feel that conservation of the natural growth and adaptation of developments to natural terrain can best be handled through administrative review, and not through detailed and complicated specifications, meant to apply across the board. The success of administrative review, of course, depends on the presence of talented and vigilant design personnel in the office engaged in subdivision approval. Since this advice cannot always be had at the municipal level, the desirable solution is to concentrate subdivision review at the county or regional level, where a competent team of landscape architects and site planners can be assembled to revise developers' plans in accordance with region-wide standards and a region-wide master plan. Such an approach could help to eliminate local differences in standards and in enforcement, and insure a uniformly high level of conservation practices in land development, particularly if encouraged by federal aid and a firm national policy.

Aside from simply providing relief from the dreariness of bare houses on bare ground, planting, whether natural or man-placed, serves the additional purpose of defining and organizing space in low-density development. If a clearing in the woods is used as the site for a subdivision, the wall of trees behind the houses—and not the houses themselves—defines the space of the street. If selective cutting and thinning is used to create an umbrella effect above the houses and the street, again it is the umbrella and not the houses beneath it that dominate the view. If the landscape is a rich one of alternating meadows, hedges, and small groves, the houses have to be placed carefully to accent—not negate—the succession of natural spaces created by vegetation and topography. If the site is bare and trees are planted along the street at some standard interval—such as 60 feet—then it is the row of street trees that will eventually dominate the development. Preserved natural vegetation or large-scale artificial planting thus unifies the whole development site; prevents it from falling apart into a haphazard agglomeration of individual garden plots; and gives it depth, character, scale, and an overall order in a progression of large spaces, into which the order of the housing units and their individual gardens will fit.

This overall order clearly should not be left to chance, but should be consciously designed by a competent landscape architect, who will use a variety of formal devices at his disposal. He can use the rhythm of thin and tall trees to create a vertical screen effect, and play it against low-slung horizontal houses. He can take free-standing large trees or small groves and use them as anchors in space, around which float open meadows, and which, in turn, serve as the base plane for houses. He can take trees which lend themselves to creation of a wall effect, such as hemlocks or spruce and other evergreens, and build a geometric pattern of green walls to reinforce the geometric order of houses on a flat site. Of course, none of these devices have to be purely ornamental

In a northern or southern climate, a residential trailer park can be saved from drabness by preserving dense original vegetation. Examples in Springfield, Mass., and Bonita Springs, Fla.

—they can, and often should, be designed to double as screens, windbreaks, noise buffers, as erosion control devices, or simply to provide shade.

Both the practical necessity of planting and the visual reason for organizing space remain just as important at the scale of the individual lot. The prevailing stereotype for landscaping individual lots is foundation planting under the windows and a few scattered shrubs in the middle of the lawn. Functionally, this kind of planting is use-

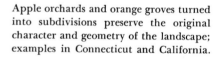

Apple orchards and orange groves turned into subdivisions preserve the original character and geometry of the landscape; examples in Connecticut and California.

Open, rolling pasture and densely wooded landscape give character to fairly expensive subdivisions.

less, and visually it negates rather than defines space. A shrub in the middle of a lawn destroys the continuity of the lawn; shrubs along a foundation create a two-dimensional picture-postcard effect that may be good for real estate advertisements, but in fact clutter up the house and give no feeling of depth or enclosure. Conceived to cover up high Victorian foundations at a time when the hot-air furnace was invented, foundation planting is incompatible with the horizontality of most present-day houses. Although sound professional advice has been condemning this practice for decades, it still persists, perhaps as an easy way to market miscellaneous nursery stock.

Fully grown foundation planting forms the impenetrable jungle around Sleeping Beauty's Castle.

The numerous manuals on how to landscape a residential lot stress the idea that the garden is an outdoor extension of the house, to be viewed primarily from within, and to be designed for living. The builder's conception of a house as a box, enclosed within itself, placed in the middle of a slick expanse of carefully mowed lawn is, of course, the opposite of this idea. Not that free-standing volumes of houses set on a smooth green base plane cannot be good-looking; but outdoor living requirements of American families being what they are, such slickness, fit for an exhibition, can rarely be maintained for long. Some enclosure or separation becomes essential to screen the view of the neighbors; to hide unsightly necessities such as the drying yard (if any), garbage bins, and the incinerator; to create auxiliary outdoor spaces such as the dooryard, the dining terrace, or patio; to protect one's gardening efforts from pets; to define play areas for children; and so on.

"The benefits experienced by breathing air unconfined by close streets of houses, and uncontaminated by the smoke of chimneys; the cheerful aspect of vegetation; the singing of birds in their season; the enlivening effect of finding ourselves unpent-up by buildings, and in comparatively unlimited space, are felt by most people. But these enjoyments are greatly increased by the possession of a garden, in which taste and fancy can be exercised by continually forming new and beautiful scenes."

J. C. Loudon, *The Villa Gardener*, 1850.

While detailed landscape development of the lot is clearly up to the owner rather than the builder, the latter should nevertheless provide an overall landscaping order, into which the individual do-it-yourself efforts will harmoniously fit. As a counterpoint to a long horizontal house, three small birches in a cluster are infinitely more useful than any number of randomly placed shrubs. Even a modest hedge in front of a fairly narrow front-yard is infinitely more effective than any amount of foundation planting, at the far end of an overly-large front yard. Such a hedge can become *the* element which unifies the street, and behind it all sorts of individual gardening exercises can go on without hurting the overall view of the development. Natural scrub-growth, selectively pruned, can sometimes be preserved along lot lines to provide the visual privacy that all home-buyers appear to seek, but very few actually get. In fact, terminating the view from the house by a strong wall of planting along the rear lot line—preferably by preserving existing growth—is one of the best landscape contributions a builder-developer can make.

Planting, of course, is not the only way to provide privacy and enclosure. The desire for enclosure and definition of space leads some owners to erect lightweight fences, trellises, and screens along lot lines, often designed to carry trained or self-clinging plants. Substantial fences, however, are very often prohibited by fire regulations or by esthetic covenants on the ground that they destroy the continuity of the front lawn, which they do. However, as Bernard F. Spring suggests: "The outdoor space around the house is being used more and more intensively for family activities. This, in turn, leads to a desire for screening outdoor activities from public view. Most of our current site planning and landscaping practice allows neighbors and passers-by to see such activities. This is no more satisfactory than having the indoor living areas on display. Rational site design, in which screening achieved by walls and landscaping plays as important a part in the total picture as the house itself, may eventually give an entirely new appearance to our neighborhoods."

In a survey of attitudes toward lot privacy conducted among residents of detached structures by the New Haven City Plan Commission, it was found that almost two-thirds of the sample wanted "a yard with shrubbery around the edges and perhaps some fences to give privacy, but open in small places to the neighbors." About one-third desired a lot "almost totally enclosed with wall or shrubbery for complete privacy," and less than one-tenth wanted "a yard mostly open to the neighbors, with shrubbery around the house." The desire for privacy and enclosure was found to be rising with rising income. Oddly enough, the desire for enclosed rear yards was combined with a desire for large setbacks from the street, even at the expense of the rear yard, despite the fact that 30 per cent of the respondents could think of no use for the front yard and 50 per cent listed "esthetic" use. But the significant fact is that overwhelming demand seemed to be for a type of landscape treatment which is still rare in the East, despite its growing popularity in California or Arizona.

The completely enclosed lot (perhaps with a shallow open front lawn), even though it poses some structural and safety problems, could portend drastic changes in subdivision design: the return to small lot sizes of 4,000 to 6,000 square feet (a 40 x 60 rear yard can be quite adequate for an average family, if none of it is used as a buffer from neighbors), the abandonment of the free-standing house concept (since all houses would be attached through their fences and walls), and a new, much more urban image of the street, in which planting would again become subordinate to the solid, low-slung wall of houses flanking the right-of-way. This kind of development would suit many architects, who are trying to promote various "patio house" schemes, as well as those planners who see the danger of lower and lower residential densities and the total reliance on the automobile that they portend. Aside from custom and public taste, the problem of screening and privacy is largely one of cost: to the extent that the price of land is low, a great deal of space around the house, with some natural planting left, is the cheapest way to purchase privacy; but when land prices rise, smaller lots with fences or even masonry walls may become the more economical solution.

So far we have discussed the positive elements that can organize and define space between detached houses in residential developments. But there are also negative elements, which destroy the continuity of space, and in fact become major and rather obnoxious eye sores. The main ones are billboards and utility poles with overhead wiring. The problem of billboards is discussed in connection with highways and commercial development, since in most cases they are prohibited by zoning law in new residential areas and continue to deface only some older residential districts in central cities, or rural communities without zoning. The problem of overhead wiring, however, is most insistent even in communities with the most up-to-date planning and zoning regulations.

Attempts at enclosure: a rustic fence in New England and hedges around rear yards in Seattle; note the close, domestic scale of the rear yards and the alley which could, with a little extra width, be the access street to the houses. The width of most existing suburban streets is grossly exaggerated, and out of scale with single-storey, detached houses.

The heavy and clumsy wooden utility poles are a sufficient visual nuisance themselves, but if one considers that they are often out of plumb (especially on curvilinear streets, where guy wires do not help much), that their crossarms seem haphazardly

Openness and enclosure: (*above*) the base plane of an immaculate lawn, pleasantly accented by pine trees, in a Florida development—the outdoor space is purely ornamental; (*below*) walled enclosures for privacy in an Arizona development—a somewhat tenuous compromise between the open-lot concept and the enclosed-patio concept. The spaces between the walled enclosures serve little functional or visual purpose.

aligned, that they often carry heavy transformers (which help them look drunken), that wire and cable of different diameter hung from them sag in differing curves, that feeder lines to houses shoot off from them at all sorts of angles without any visual discipline, then the ugliness of these temporary-looking makeshifts becomes extreme.

Photographs from an advertisement by Eichler Homes for "outdoor living" in fully enclosed yards in California: the inner terrace and the outside view of the street façade may set the tone for similar designs in other parts of the country.

The detrimental effect of wooden utility poles on the residential street has, of course, long been recognized, and many developers are striving to locate their power

A wooden utility pole with overhead wiring: the major eyesore in residential developments.

and telephone lines in an easement along the rear lot line, while lighting the street from unobtrusive metal standards with underground cable service. This solution, while it helps the street, does not help the part of the property where all the "outdoor living" takes place, and in either location wires can and do interfere with trees. In some European countries, power and telephone wires are hung from metal stanchions attached to houses; this eliminates unsightly feeder lines and the conflict with trees, but such a solution requires masonry construction and legal concepts of access to private property different from those in North America.

The only radical solution to the problem is, of course, underground wiring. This, in North America, has been customary only in high-density urban areas. But during the 1950s a number of utility companies, such as the Public Service Company of New Jersey, undertook development work leading to designs that can be used to provide underground service to residences in low-density areas. These designs feature direct burial of primary and secondary service cable and pad-mounted transformer vaults for each 4 to 6 houses on the ground. In fact, according to *Electrical World,* 78 per cent of the major U.S. utilities were offering underground wiring in new subdivisions by 1960—provided that the developer paid the added cost of the installation. This cost ranges anywhere from $200 to $1,500 per house, so that cases of actual installation are very few and far between. For example, a proposal by the utility to install underground wiring in Levittown, N.J., was rejected by the developer. On the other hand, residents of an exclusive 118-lot residential community near Seattle have organized a local improvement district to put all their utility lines underground, assessing themselves at $1,000 per house, with the utility company putting up another $300 per house. Costs can be kept toward the lower end of the range if the scale of construction is large, if the soil and the site permit the use of modern high-speed trenching equipment, and if the anticipated power consumption per household is high. There are still some unsolved technical problems, such as whether telephone and power cable can be laid in the same trench, or the possible inflexibility of the installation in case of rising demand for power. On the other hand, underground service has its practical advantages—safety and dependability during storms, and much lower maintenance costs; these have been recognized by some maintenance-conscious telephone companies, which offer underground wiring free of charge.

Clearly, the main obstacle to wider use of underground wiring is cost. While one cannot expect many individual developers to place themselves at a competitive disadvantage by raising the cost of their houses by some three to five per cent, this percentage does not seem to be excessive if all developments in an area are required by law to provide underground wiring. From the standpoint of total community appearance, the improvement would be well worth the sacrifice. An alternate solution would be region-wide regulations requiring underground wiring, which would allow

Large-scale towers of a high-voltage transmission line, set in an easement of adequate dimensions, do not conflict with residential development. If well designed, they add interest and accent.

the utilities to absorb the costs through increased power and telephone rates. The utilities' rates are based on their capital investment, so that aside from their reluctance to submit to additional public controls and to raise rates, this would not be a losing proposition for them. Technological advance is constantly reducing the cost of power production, and a nation as affluent as ours can certainly afford to divert some of the resources that become free in this way to the furtherance of civic beauty.

It is the low-voltage lines on wooden poles, serving the consumer, that ruin his immediate environment. The paraphernalia cluttering the backyards is bad enough, but when wires are added the ugliness and confusion spreads.

FOCAL ELEMENTS

The monotony of much present-day residential detached-house development results from the evenness of its texture. Neither a firmer order of pattern nor a more sensitive continuity of the land form will help here, unless the even texture of one-family houses is broken up, in proper places, by contrasting elements which attract attention and become landmarks, or focal points. A landmark lifts a considerable area around itself out of anonymity, giving it identity and visual structure. There can, and should be, a whole hierarchy of focal points organizing the residential texture, starting from small accents in a street or block, proceeding to the subdivision and then to the neighborhood and community level.

Among the elements that can be used to create focus, natural features of the landscape are foremost. Bodies of water are a unique asset, and the subdivision should be carefully designed to preserve streams, rivers, waterfalls, ponds, and lakes. Difficulties do arise here in areas where septic tanks and tile fields are the method of sewage disposal, for the streams can easily be contaminated by seeping sewage effluent; also, the changed surface runoff conditions can cause flooding and erosion during storms, while in fair weather the streams may run dry because of a change in watertable. All these conditions can be foreseen and prevented by a thorough engineering study in the design stage. Unfortunately, the usual expedient among developers is to *pipe* the stream, to save time and trouble. The correct solution involves reserving a buffer strip of proper width (some 50 to 100 feet or more on each side of the stream), in which natural conditions and natural growth are preserved so that the stream can be left

An eroded stream in the middle of a subdivision, on its way to becoming a drainage ditch through denuded land.

to operate in its own way; proper precautions against flooding or drastic changes in watertable must also be taken. If carried out consistently, these precautions will often lead to a comprehensive scheme of public acquisition of stream valleys and their headwaters as part of a park and open space program, an undertaking now being pursued by such cities as Hartford. The argument that stream preservation is a public responsibility and should not be left to private developers alone has considerable merit. The Maryland-National Capital Park and Planning Commission for example, as part of its plan to preserve the Henson Creek Valley, has been revising subdivision plats to eliminate construction within 800 feet of the stream.

A stream with the wooded growth around it carefully preserved is a major asset that gives character and value to the neighborhood.

Subdivision around a lake (*photos at left, plan at right*): a nondescript swamp by the roadside, instead of being filled in, was excavated to create a lake which became an intimate and pleasant focal point for a subdivision that would otherwise not be above the average. Tanglewood development in Cheshire, Conn., designed by the office of Bradford Tilney, architect.

SCALE

0 25' 50' 75' 100' 125' 150' 175' 200'

CONTOUR INTERVAL 2 FEET

Among features that are less costly to preserve one can list rock outcrops, large glacial boulders, and stone walls, which can sensitively be incorporated into a subdivision design as sculptural elements. Remaining farm structures, such as barns, can be remodeled for community or private use, or at least their ruins or foundations can be left intact as picturesque or historic features. They can all help to ameliorate the frequent sterility of a brand-new development.

Preservation of natural features leads to the question of preserving public open space in subdivisions, since properly designed open space can become a permanent and important focal point even in residential areas of very low density. Even very small open spaces designed as part of the street system are of great visual importance. A 12- to 20-foot grass mall in the middle of a street entering the subdivision, although unnecessary for traffic purposes can be a pleasant ornamental accent, which also helps orientation. Even the stereotype circle in the middle of a cul-de-sac turn-around, and the just as stereotype "eyebrow" on a sharp turn of the street should not be overlooked as an accent, although municipalities do not always favor them because of maintenance problems. The more significant the open space the better; it is regrettable that the open square or "the village green" is a design device completely forgotten in modern subdivisions.

Original features of the landscape preserved: fieldstone walls enclosing a public playground, and a pond in a former pasture preserved on a private lot.

Aside from the need for small ornamental open spaces, subdivisions also need playgrounds—more than is commonly assumed. In areas of higher population density and smaller lots, elementary schools with their new large playgrounds are spaced fairly close together to serve the optimum number of pupils. In areas of large lot size the schools are spaced correspondingly farther apart—too far to meet the maximum walking distance of the child. Thus, in many suburban areas with half-acre-lots or larger, one finds children playing baseball and other games in the streets—just as in the downtown slums—while children who live on smaller lots use their school playgrounds. The solution for the very low density areas seems to be to provide numerous small (one- to two-acre) unsupervised play areas spaced closely enough to be within easy walking distance of all homes. These play areas, the need for which few subdividers realize, can also be treated as focal points around which a subdivision can be designed. If one adds the requirements of ornamental open space, playgrounds, protective areas around streams and other natural features, scenic outlooks and green buffer strips along major arteries (to be dealt with later) the public open space requirements in low-density areas become considerable.

Seemingly the simplest way to acquire this open space is acquisition by the community in advance of development. In the case of the larger spaces, such as stream valleys, this is often difficult financially, and in case of the smaller spaces difficulties also arise because location cannot be pinpointed exactly in advance of development. An increasing number of municipalities, therefore, have included requirements for dedication of open space by the developer to the community in their subdivision regulations. For example, 18 out of 33 ordinances in the Minneapolis-St. Paul metropolitan area require some sort of public land dedication. Some ordinances relate this requirement to the master plan for parks; others qualify it by the statement "if required by the Planning Board" and set a maximum percentage of land that the Planning Board can demand from a developer; still others require a mandatory minimum from any developer (the areas to be dedicated range between 3 per cent and 12 per cent of the subdivision). Since in small subdivisions dedication of a fixed percentage may not be practical (the areas may be too small and of little use), some municipalities accept payments in lieu of dedication, though these have been ruled illegal in certain states, such as New York. Clearly, the tools for open-space acquisition through mandatory dedication by developers need further refinement, but an even more urgent need is to enforce uniformity of standards at the regional or state level so that the more backward municipalities are pulled up to the level of the advanced ones. At the same time, new legal and design techniques, such as clustering, will often obviate the need for public dedication of scenic spots, and keep them in private hands subject to development controls. A recent trend involves developers designing expensive subdivisions around golf courses and country clubs, in which case the golf course becomes a "village green" held in communal ownership by the residents. Preservation of open spaces may seem costly to the developer at times, but the cost of the land thus sacrificed has often been more than offset by the enhanced value which accrued to the development as a whole. The increased value of building sites due to the proximity of park and recreational areas is by now well-documented.

Public open space has been historically one of the most permanent focal points a community can have. Generations of buildings have been built and torn down while the squares and parks have remained, in spite of intrusions and defacements. In addition, however, buildings differing in character from the repetitive one-family house are needed as focal points in low-density development. These are the community facilities, public and private; schools, libraries, community centers, municipal structures for fire and police protection; churches, clubs, groups of stores; and recreation facilities such as marinas, swimming pools, and skating rinks. Many of these can be

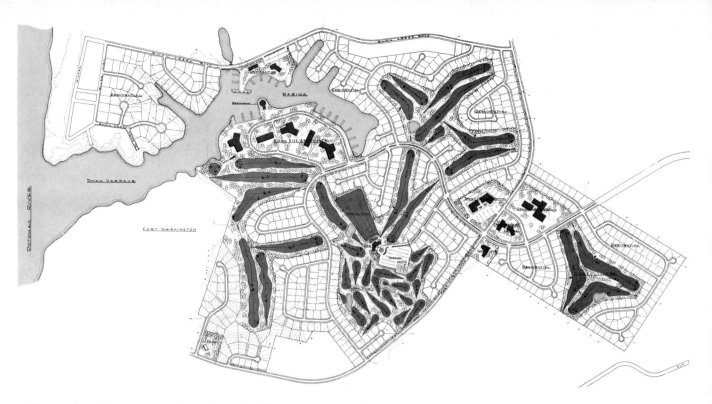

A "prestige" subdivision planned around semi-public open spaces—golf courses and a marina. "Tantallon," development on the Potomac River in Prince George's County, Md., about 13 miles south of Washington.

integrated in an architecturally coherent center, rather than scattered haphazardly among subdivisions. Although churches and schools are often the only architect-designed buildings in the urban fringe as far as the eye can see, their siting is not always visually advantageous. The tradition of placing a church on a prominent, preferably elevated site with vistas oriented toward it has been too frequently abandoned in favor of tucking it away at some intersection, like the corner drugstore, where neither its design nor its symbolic meaning is made visually effective. To a lesser extent this holds true for schools. Their location in plan often appears purely "functional," two-dimensional, without any consideration for the relief of the ground, of vistas, perspectives, or the overall composition of the residential texture in the macro-landscape. To the extent that elevated sites (sometimes difficult for residential construction) are not pre-empted by water towers, radio relay stations, and similar technological uses, they should be reserved for buildings of civic significance, which would provide visual accent to the sea of houses below. These esthetic considerations have their proper place in the land-use plan of the municipality.

Apart from community or institutional structures to introduce variety and interest into the flat skyline of low-density development, apartment houses can sometimes be a useful device. In the past, the market for apartments in the urban fringe has been extremely limited, and low land values ruled high-rise construction out of the picture. But, as the low-density areas mature and their social composition changes, and as they become more accessible to the center by freeways (or, perhaps, in the largest metropolitan regions, by high-speed automated rail service), one can expect apartment buildings to rise near suburban shopping, community, or office centers, near freeway interchanges, and near auto-to-rail transfer points in greater numbers

Two examples of subdivisions grouped around public open space in Delaware County, Pa.: (*above*) Highmeadow, U-loop street layout with lots of 20,000 square feet; (*below*) Lawrence Park, conventional street layout with lots of 8,000 square feet.

Community facilities provided by a developer in Port Charlotte, Fla.: a church, a swimming pool, and a marina.

than before. An important esthetic aspect to consider here is the conflict in scale between one-family houses and apartment blocks. To obviate this, proper buffer strips of open space should be introduced; the two should not be mixed on either side of the same street. Using design devices of this type, even high-rise apartments can be good neighbors to single-family subdivisions (though not to individual houses), and can greatly enrich the no-man's-land of the urban fringe by giving it focus, interest, and drama, as well as a greater feeling of urbanity.

CLARITY OF ORIENTATION

Having considered the order of pattern, the articulation of groups and their architectural consistency, the continuity and modulation of land form and space, and finally the need for focal elements, we now come to consider an overall system which will give our residential fabric coherence, unity, and structure on a regional scale. We find this system in a supergrid of arterial streets and a supergrid of green space. As already shown, a confused street system in which anybody but the native gets lost soon after leaving the exit ramp of the freeway (particularly at night) is one salient result of our unplanned urban growth. By contrast, few things delight foreign visitors to New York more than the ease of orientation in Manhattan. One would certainly not advocate recreating Manhattan's 22 square miles of rectilinear grid on thousands and thousands of square miles of urban America, but an easily comprehensible pattern, be it orthogonal or radio-concentric, without confusing deformations is important for the basic supergrid of arterial thoroughfares.

The arterials and feeder roads from new freeways which open up residential territory for development should be built in advance of that development, or at least their rights of way should be reserved by means of the official map or a similar device, so that the existing rural road network would not be burdened by the kinds of traffic and the kinds of development for which it was not made. This task of building a comprehensive feeder network to the major urban and interurban freeways—the skeleton of the future urban tissue—is beyond the means of countries and municipalities as a rule, and should be carried out as a federal-state program, in cooperation with regional or county planning agencies, and in conjunction with freeway construction. It would help to tie the freeways closely to the future urban fabric, and would make their future traffic loads much more predictable.

Apartments in the Urban Fringe: public housing in Greenwich, Conn.; a geometric order fitted into a rolling topography; density, 10 families per net acre.

Apartments in the Urban Fringe (*pho tos at left; plan at upper right*): gar den apartments well integrated with rough, wooded site with lakes, formerl a watershed reservation; density, 1 families per net acre.

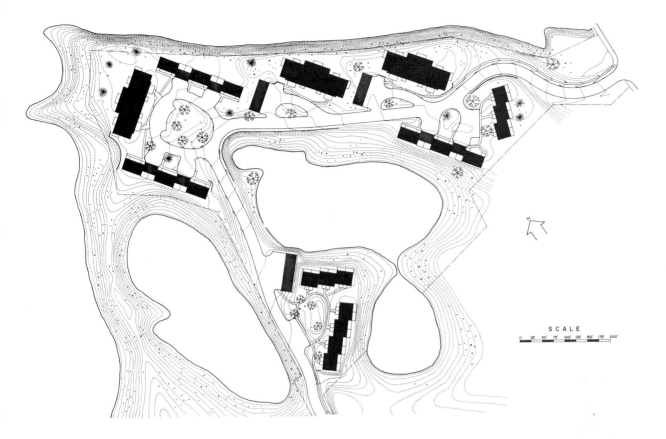

SCALE

0 25' 50' 75' 100' 125' 150' 175' 200'

The next problem; and a very important one, is to express with absolute clarity the functional hierarchy of the circulation system. In the urban fringe today, a 20-foot wide pavement of a winding country road often carries arterial volumes, while a 60-foot boulevard-like pavement leads to a subdivision of a dozen homes. The circulation network, basically, includes four levels of facility: the freeway; the arterial street; the collector street; and the land service street.

While the sole function of the freeway is to carry traffic (hence its limited access), and the sole function of the land service street is to provide access to properties, the arterial and collector streets perform, as a rule, mixed functions. This should be discouraged for visual as well as practical reasons. The principle of partially limiting access should be applied to primary and secondary arterials, so that private driveways, for instance, would be prohibited from entering streets designed to carry more than a specified volume of traffic, and even collector streets could enter these arteries only at specified intervals. Instead of being flanked by two strings of commercial development, a limited-access main street would be flanked by rows of evergreens comprising its buffer belt, and commercial development would be grouped in commercial clusters or plazas. Even if costly, limitation of access should be imposed on many existing rural roads, to prevent their being blighted by string commercial or residential de-

A typical conflict in scale between 2-storey walkup apartments and one-family houses on quarter-acre lots.

Unarticulated urban growth: random agglomeration of subdivisions on Long Island.

velopment. This type of development would be accommodated on land-service loops and spurs extending from the arterials.

Along with much stricter control of access to surface streets and roads, particularly to those built on new right-of-way tying freeways to new residential development, should go a much sharper differentiation of their design standards, especially of their right-of-way width. Today, the right-of-way width for most streets, whether local, collector, or secondary arterial, generally varies between 50 and 80 feet (as specified in subdivision regulations), and the differences are not enough to be visually meaningful. Generally, the width of local streets is over-designed, while arterials do not have a sufficiently wide right-of-way to allow for adequate landscaping and buffer zones. While the right-of-way of small residential access streets can be reduced to 40 feet or even less, to bring them down to a domestic scale, the right-of-way for arterial streets should be extended to some 200 feet, to provide for adequate roadside planting areas. Thus, both the width of the right-of-way and the degree to which access is limited would clearly identify the functional importance of a given street.

Attempt at articulation through geometry, roads and open spaces: Levittown, Pa.

Considerable importance in the above discussion must be attached to protective green buffer belts, both for practical reasons of controlling noise, fumes, and haphazard traffic access, and for the esthetic reason of clearly identifying the hierarchy of the street system. Green buffers, essentially, are slots which separate incompatible elements, whether their incompatibility be functional or visual. They are a form of open space that is not nearly as much used as it should be. Aside from separating residential development from freeways, and from primary and secondary arterials, green buffers should be used around industrial and commercial development, around parking lots and other land-consuming facilities. Minimum standards are difficult to specify, since they depend on the size of the use to be enclosed or separated, but we can scarcely visualize an effective densely planted buffer narrower than 30 to 50 feet. Desirably, they should be much wider in many cases—perhaps as wide as a meadow, or as wide as a lake, on the other side of which a visually or functionally incompatible use is located. Some form of open-space separation between uses should, in any case, be made mandatory by every municipal zoning or subdivision ordinance. One of the

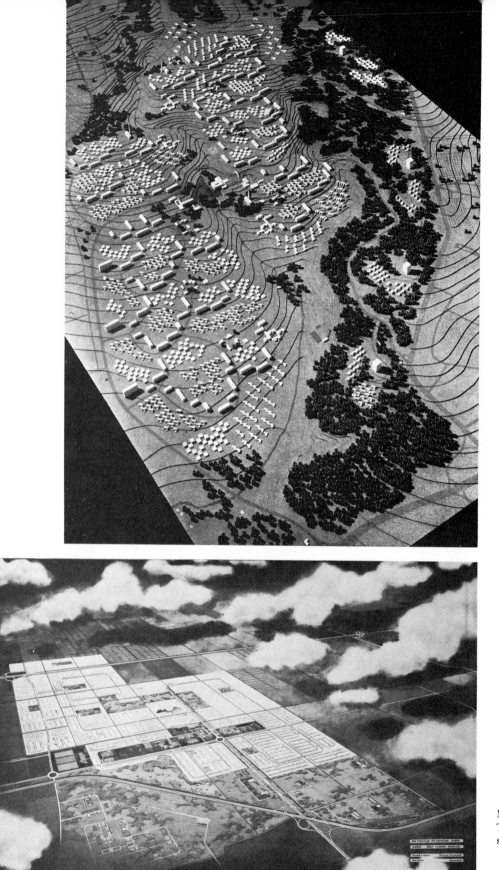

Experiments in the design of the macro-landscape.

A community for 13,000 people ⬝ Kassel, Germany; winning de⬝ for a competition, by Ingo Sch⬝

New town plan for Davistown, F⬝ Tunnard and Harris, planning c⬝ sultants.

Apartment development on the Island of Kulosaari, Finland; Helsinki City Planning Commission.

few communities that so far actually has initiated a systematic program for the acquisition of green buffers is Oak Park, Michigan, which has installed 3.3 miles of buffer strips eight to 150 feet wide in the period from 1952 to 1960.

In the system of circulation arteries and their attendant areas of access and non-access, and in the system of public open space, whether it be based on river valleys, hilltops, parkway access to scenic areas, or any of the other approaches discussed in Part V, the planner-designer of low-density urban areas possesses two very strong tools for shaping the urban fabric, and creating an overall planned network, into which the spontaneous activities of private individuals will logically take their place with a sufficient degree of freedom and personal choice. Consistently designed, the two systems of highest activity (traffic) and lowest activity (open space) will provide for a visually articulated and comprehensible urban fabric.

From then on, the problem of civic design in the macro-landscape is a question of partnership between the public designer (the planner) and the private designer (the developer, architect, and landscape architect). Together, they must solve such questions of macro-landscape design as the proper ratio of man-made texture to open spaces; ways of confining a texture (whether by a hill, by a valley, or by breaking it up); the spatial delineation between foreground and background; the needed spacing to achieve visual demarcation; the needed background to unify a residential texture; the treatment of a hill silhouette; the creation of man-made focal points. To do these things effectively, they must be imbued with the principles of order of pattern, continuity, separation, and accent which we have now described.

The low-density region spreading around its high-density core: New York and environs from an altitude of 35,000 feet.

PART THREE

The Paved Ribbon: The Esthetic of Freeway Design

1. The Development of Freeway Form
   A Historical Note
   The Formal Approach
   Vision in Motion

2. The Internal Harmony of the Freeway
   Continuity of Alignment
   Three-Dimensional Coordination
   Harmony of Enclosed Areas

3. The External Harmony of the Freeway
   Integration with the Macro-Environment
   Integration with the Micro-Environment
   Definition of Elements
   Focus, Interest, and Drama

THE AMERICAN PUBLIC thinks of the United States highway network as a necessary convenience, but it rarely gives the visual design of its high-speed roads much thought. Only in matters of location, when personal properties or particular community assets are threatened by highway plans do sections of the public come near a real concern over the difference a highway can make in the environment, and they breathe a sigh of relief if, as occasionally happens, public pressure forces an alternate route (which may or may not be as good in the long run as the Highway Department's original suggestion).

Actually, there are always alternative possibilities, and the designers have usually foreseen most of them before the route of the highway becomes public knowledge. The route that the designers and the public tend to overlook is the route that respects esthetic values—that which considers the highway as a work of art, not merely of utility. The purpose of the present discussion is to make highway esthetics intelligible to more people. Equipped with the means of esthetic recognition (what is good and what is bad) as they travel our growing mileage of limited access highways, they will soon find that a truckload of trees and shrubs does not make a beautiful highway, and that many of our newest super-roads leave much to be desired.

The driver in this case is the consumer, and consumers have a right to know what they are getting—in safety and convenience, primarily, but in the proper use of the landscape as well. Properly informed, local public and planning groups could turn their energies from blanket opposition to this or that inevitable new freeway toward demanding higher visual standards for the facility, so that it could become an all-around community asset.

The highway as a cultural asset is long overdue for consideration in the United States. With few exceptions, all the really inspiring rights of way, from the Via Appia to the Blue Ridge Parkway, contain strong esthetic elements which produce extraordinary scenic beauty. Every day we are missing opportunities to bring this beauty into our daily lives, an increasing proportion of which is spent on the highway—going to work, going to play, shopping or going to school. Who knows? Familiarity with the mediocre, dull, or downright ugly in our travels may in future be as detrimental to the American spirit as the in-city slums which we are now all committed to remove.

1. The Development of Freeway Form

The joy of floating freely over the waves of the landscape was probably first experienced by man on horseback. He could dive into valleys, emerge on the crests of hills, seek the cool meadows of the forest, or shoot straight through the sunlit plains.

The railroad sacrificed this primitive freedom to speed and efficiency. The rider became a spectator, not a participant in the drama. He was shown a man-made cross-section of the surface of the earth through the window. Only with the arrival of the automobile was man ready to recapture the experience of rapid, three-dimensional movement in free-wheel travel up and down hills.

But the automobile required continuous ribbons of pavement on which to move, and the resulting highway network conspicuously altered the face of the earth. The reception the automobile received was, accordingly, a mixed one. While most people apparently desire to travel by motor car, a vocal minority has been decrying it for disrupting established patterns of settlement and for conflicting with traditional architectural forms, not to mention the usual complaints about frustrating traffic congestion.

Partisans of rail transit argue that it can carry 20 times more people per unit of road width than a limited access highway (assuming an occupancy of one person per automobile). And one must concede that the railroad has a permanent place in compact urban concentrations. But in our expanding, differentiated society, all too many functions are of necessity widely separated. For a dispersed pattern of travel desires, and intermediate travel distances, the relative flexibility of the automobile seems essential. As for possible individual air transportation, its extreme flexibility makes it even more vulnerable to congestion than the motor car. Psychologically, the automobile seems to satisfy a human urge to control one's destiny in movement, and, according to Patrick Horsbrugh, "an instinct for awareness of what is coming in the direction of sight."

A HISTORICAL NOTE

Within and between our urban regions of today, the automobile has demanded roads capable of moving huge volumes of traffic at high speed. The answer was the freeway or motorway, known in Europe as the *Autobahn, autostrada,* or *autoroute.* Such a road can move something like three times the number of cars, at twice the speed and with a five times lower accident rate than a comparable conventional highway. The freeway is defined by three essential properties:

> The two opposing streams of traffic are separated by a *median divider.*
> *Access is limited* to interchanges with proper merging and diverging lanes.
> All *intersections are separated* in different levels, eliminating crossing maneuvers and turns against the traffic stream.

High speeds demand a lot of room for stops or turns, which explains the tremendous scale of the freeway: a simple cloverleaf interchange takes about 40 acres of land. This scale has brought up completely new problems of visual organization of macrospaces in the landscape. And, interestingly enough, the three inventions which characterize the freeway had their early origins to a large degree in the field of urban esthetics.

Twin roadways separated by a strip of greenery were used on city boulevards before the automobile was invented. Commonwealth Avenue in Boston is an example. Overpasses to separate incompatible kinds of traffic were used by Olmsted in 1858 in New York's Central Park. And the first public "limited access" road in the United States, the Bronx River Parkway north of New York City, was conceived in 1906, when there were only 105,000 automobiles registered in the whole country. In fact, this motor parkway was an incidental feature in a comprehensive scheme of conservation, reclamation, and park development, triggered by the need to protect animals in the Bronx Zoo from water pollution.

The 15-mile Bronx River Parkway, begun in 1916 and opened to traffic piecemeal between 1921 and 1924, anticipated many features of today's freeways. To the extent that the road traversed an elongated park, abutting private property owners had no right of access. Where it followed the river valley, intersecting streets crossed it conveniently on bridges, with special ramps provided for exit and entrance. The winding, freeflowing alignment was eminently fitted to the topography. Its maximum

The Avus in Berlin, completed in 1919, a prototype of modern freeways.

A typical parkway of the 1920s in Westchester County, N.Y.

curvature permitted safe speeds up to 35 miles per hour—ample at a time when average speeds on rural roads did not exceed 25 mph. The consulting landscape architect, Herman Merkel, conceived of the entire road as two ribbons of pavement, designed independently and located at different levels and with a variable distance between each other when necessary, to achieve the best possible blending with the terrain. Unfortunately, he was overruled by the Bronx River Parkway Commissioners, who favored one undivided roadway, and only two divided sections were eventually built.

Nevertheless, the success of park development in the Bronx River Valley was such that, beginning in 1923, a newly created Westchester County Park Commission embarked on a $90 million program of park acquisition and parkway construction. It was followed by the Long Island State Park Commission in 1926, and by the City of New York in 1929, so that by 1934 some 114 miles of parkways were completed in Queens, Nassau, and Westchester counties. The Federal government built the 17-mile Mount Vernon Parkway in 1929–32. Although all of these roads, except sections of the Taconic Parkway in Westchester, were undivided and had occasional intersections at grade, private access was eliminated and a gently undulating alignment, lavishly landscaped, was a prime feature of their design.

Advanced developments on highways not conceived of as recreational were slower to come. The Du Pont highway in Delaware, built in 1924, was probably the first divided all-purpose road in America; a "super-highway" from Detroit to Pontiac followed in 1925: its 70-foot wide central mall carried the tracks of an interurban trolley. Yet these and other divided all-purpose highways that followed, unlike the parkway, had no grade-separated intersections, and abutting property owners had unlimited right of access. In 1928, the first cloverleaf interchange was built near Woodbridge, New Jersey, but it was an isolated traffic improvement, located at the intersection of two conventional roads subject to commercial roadside blight.

By that time, commercial roadside blight was reaching incredible proportions in the United States. On a road between Newark and Trenton, for example, a distance of 47 miles, 300 gasoline stations, 472 billboards, 440 other commercial uses, and 165 intersections were counted in the mid-'30s. In downtown areas, traffic congestion was so great that cars capable of 80-mile-an-hour speeds were slowed down to eight, six, or even three miles an hour. Thirty to forty thousand people were being killed on the highways each year—a rate eight times higher than on some contemporary freeways. Clearly, the concepts of the "parkway" and the "superhighway" had to be fused, to achieve a road designed in the nature of motor travel. An attempt to do this was the Lake Shore Drive in Chicago, built in 1933 to feed the downtown area. Yet, a comprehensive network of urban freeways (the term freeway was coined in 1930 by Edward M. Bassett) was still some three decades away.

In Europe, meanwhile, the concept of the road devoted exclusively to motor travel had been developed on a theoretical level since pre-World War I days. In 1906, the French engineer Eugene Hénard published a tract on "Intersections having superposed roadways," in which he proposed the cloverleaf as a prototype of intersections

World's first cloverleaf interchange near Woodbridge, N.J., built in 1928.

Meadowbrook Causeway to Jones Beach on Long Island, the first fully-divided, limited-access highway in America, opened in 1934. The continuous, curvilinear form is in the tradition of earlier, undivided parkways around New York.

designed for continuous flow. And in 1913 in Berlin, a private group went ahead to embody the new principles in an experimental speedway, the Avus. Delayed by war, the Avus (*Automobil-Verkerhrs-und-Übungsstrasse*) was opened to traffic in 1919. It was a four-lane divided highway with limited access and no grade crossings, which ran straight as an arrow for six miles through the Grünewald forest.

Following the completion of the Avus and throughout the '20s, heated debates in the professional press were going on for and against "motor only" highways. But, like many of the revolutionary architectural and city planning ideas of the '20s, the new highway schemes remained on paper for many years. The only exception was in Italy, where a privately financed network of motor roads began to develop, mostly in the vicinity of Milan, between 1922 and 1930. But travel on these roads was quite meager, reaching only 1,000 to 1,500 vehicles daily in the later '30s. Since toll charges could not even pay for interest on borrowed capital, the Italian government took over the *autostrade* in 1933 and built the stretches Florence-Viareggio and Genova-Serravale as free roads. The latter traversed rugged mountain terrain through numerous tunnels, but other than that, the early *autostrade* were of little visual interest. They were all undivided, mostly two lanes wide, and had occasional grade separations. Like the New York parkways of the time, they have to be considered as the predecessors of the modern freeway. Their construction was terminated in 1937, at which time their length totaled 318 miles.

Conditions were different in industrially advanced Germany, the birthplace of the automobile. There, agitation for a comprehensive freeway network was mounting throughout the '20s. Two groups were largely responsible for it, the *Stufa* or "Society for the Study of Motor Road Construction," founded in 1924, and the *Hafraba*, or "Association for the Motor Road Hanseatic Cities Frankfurt-Basel," founded in 1926. These and related organizations did a huge amount of research and many design studies; yet, no actual construction took place because of legal roadblocks to private toll financing. The only physical result of the agitation was a 12-mile undivided motor road from Cologne to Bonn, built in 1930–32.

In 1933, however, when the advent of the National Socialists to power made a large-scale freeway program politically useful for unemployment relief, national prestige, and military strategy, the ground was well prepared, and construction commenced immediately, in September of the same year. In May, 1935, the first section of the *Autobahn* between Frankfurt and Darmstadt, which followed the early *Hafraba* plans, was opened to traffic. By the end of 1941, when war gradually forced further work to be abandoned, 2,326 miles of *Autobahnen* were in operation (some 340 miles of these had only one roadway completed), and 1,467 more miles were in various stages of construction.

The *Autobahnen* were the first real freeways in Europe—access was fully limited, there were no intersections at grade under any conditions, and the two roadways were separated by a median strip 13 feet wide. Most of the mileage had heavy-duty concrete pavement, adequate shoulders, and, in moderately flat terrain, the design speed was 100 miles per hour, with a maximum grade of four per cent and a minimum curve radius of 6,500 feet. Average daily traffic volumes reached 6,000 to 8,000 vehicles, even though the *Autobahnen* bypassed built-up urban areas, having been designed primarily for medium-distance interurban movement.

Following the German tradition of high regard for native landscape values, which was incorporated into the ideology of the new regime, strong emphasis was placed on considering the freeway as a work of art and relating it positively to the surrounding landscape. This was largely achieved without artificial planting by careful grading and well-thought-out alignment, fitted to the sculpture of the land forms. Sections of visually unpleasant alignment were widely criticized in the professional press, and highway esthetics became a respectable topic among engineers.

The German freeway example did not go unheeded, and shortly before World War II a number of countries went ahead on a small scale with similar road projects of their own. In 1937, Belgium began to work on the *Autoroute* Brussels-Ostende; in 1938, France on the *Autoroute de l'Ouest* near Paris; and Holland on 40 miles of freeways near Den Haag; in 1939, Czechoslovakia on an east-west *dálnice,* the construction of which was abandoned after the war. All of these projects generally followed the German standards for cross-section, profile, curvature and limitation of access. In South America, *Avenida General Paz,* a circumferential parkway around Buenos Aires, was built in 1937.

Meanwhile, in the United States the first road to conform fully to freeway standards was a five-mile section of the Meadowbrook Parkway to Jones Beach on Long Island, opened to traffic by Robert Moses in October, 1934, seven months prior to the first German *Autobahn.* Soon, other projects by Robert Moses followed, which radically transformed the face of New York: Grand Central Parkway from the Triboro Bridge to the World's Fair site in Flushing, 1936; the West Side Highway and adjoining Henry Hudson Parkway into Manhattan, 1936–38; the Whitestone Bridge and Parkway, 1939; finally, 32 miles of the Belt Parkway around Brooklyn and Queens, 1940. The newer parkways in New York and on Long Island had a right-of-way up to 400 feet wide and 9- to 12-foot wide medians; the concrete pavement was colored with carbon black, and had contrasting white curbs and acceleration lanes. Billboards were prohibited within 500 feet of the right-of-way.

In Connecticut, construction began in 1934 on the Merritt Parkway, the first 17 miles of which were opened in June, 1938. This was a road frankly designed to move passenger traffic, and the acquisition of a 300-foot "park" strip was largely a legal device to get full control of access. Though the road traversed a semi-rural area, technical standards were much lower than on the German freeways of the time: design speed varied between 50 and 60 miles per hour, maximum grade was eight per cent, minimum radius only 800 feet; the median was 22 feet wide, but narrowed down to nothing under overpasses. The visual shape of the roadbed itself, 84 per cent of which was laid out on straight lines, and only the remainder on short curves, was a step back from the continuous curvature of the New York and Virginia parkways. Nevertheless, lavish and sensitive landscaping, careful grading and the inherent beauty of the countryside made up for some of the defects. During its first year of full operation, in 1940, the parkway carried an average of 20,000 cars daily. With foresight, the twin roadways were placed off-center in the right-of-way, to allow for future expansion.

The first freeway on the West Coast and the first to employ acceleration lanes at ramps was the Arroyo Seco Freeway in Los Angeles, opened in 1940. In the fall of the same year, 160 miles of the Pennsylvania Turnpike were opened. Catering largely to truck traffic, it had a narrow, 10-foot median, paved in part, a maximum grade of

three per cent, a minimum radius of 950 feet and a speed limit of 70 miles an hour. Laid out on the right-of-way of an abandoned railroad and utilizing old tunnels through the Allegheny Mountains, its appearance was stark and left much to be desired. Yet, in many respects, it was the Pennsylvania Turnpike rather than the rich experience of the earlier parkways that set the example for the postwar boom in toll highways. All in all, some 330 miles of full freeway-type roads were open to traffic in the United States by the end of 1940. Undoubtedly, there were many obstacles to comprehensive freeway development: one was the legal difficulty of limiting access to a public thoroughfare. New York and Rhode Island led the way in enacting legislation to enable access control in 1937; California, Connecticut, Maine, and West Virginia followed in 1939. But by 1950 only 30 states had adopted such legislation. Another obstacle was political: as late as 1941 the Information Chief of the Public Roads Administration stated that "it would be wholly unreasonable to assume that an imitation of the German superhighway would equally serve our purpose." Nevertheless, by 1944 the freeway concept gained sufficient acceptance for Congress to direct the designation of a "National System of Interstate and Defense Highways," to be developed to freeway standards. Yet no additional monies were appropriated for this purpose. To overcome this third obstacle, the States reverted to highway financing by independent public authorities with bonds sold to private financial institutions and issued against the revenues to be derived from tolls.

Though adequate design was sometimes restricted by the conservatism of the private investor, the new administrative arrangement inaugurated a ten-year era of booming toll highway construction. The emphasis was on facilities for mixed traffic, rather than parkways. Between 1947 and 1957, more than 3,000 miles of toll freeways were built in 19 states. But few of these roads, although safe and efficient, have achieved visual distinction.

Still, several projects of the two decades between 1940 and 1960 deserve special mention. The Pentagon network in Virginia, built during the war in conjunction with the Defense Department, and designed by Joseph Barnett, was interesting because of its involved system of directional ramps, and careful employment of spiral transition curves. The Baltimore-Washington Parkway, a section of which was built by the Bureau of Public Roads as a demonstration project in 1953, is outstanding because of its employment of free-flowing continuous curvature, a liberal median of varying width, and highly successful integration with the landscape. Similar principles were used by some of the better consulting firms on sections of the New York Thruway, probably the best looking of the all-purpose toll roads, built at the same time. Freeways on the West Coast are particularly notable for the clean design of some bold engineering structures. A number of refined principles of cross-section and alignment were incorporated into the design of the Garden State Parkway, by Clarke and Rapuano, designers of the early Westchester parkways. No less exciting are the Palisades Interstate Parkway and some postwar parkways on Long Island, where Clarence C. Coombs was landscape architect. Undoubtedly the most beautiful and dramatic freeway in the United States to date is the northern section of the Taconic Parkway designed between 1940 and 1950 by Charles J. Baker of the New York State Department of Public Works.

section of the Merritt–Wilbur Cross Parkway in Connecticut (completed 1940), an important early work of freeway design. Well known ⸱r its rich and sensitive landscaping, the road nevertheless cannot conceal the kinks in its alignment, composed of short curves and long ₋raight lines.

Divided highways with fully limited access, four or more lanes wide, completed or under construction in Europe as of 1960. Freeway network in operation about 3,400 miles.

Unprecedented possibilities for freeway development were offered by Congress, when in passing the Highway Act of 1956 it provided for financing the 41,000-mile network of Interstate and Defense Highways, thus boosting the construction rate of freeways to more than 2,000 miles annually.

Accelerated freeway development has not been limited to the United States. Since about 1955 construction has been renewed vigorously in West Germany, Austria, Italy, Belgium, and the Netherlands. The first urban freeway in Europe was opened to traffic in 1958 in West Berlin. Large new freeways have been built in Canada, Britain, and Japan, and some construction has been taking place in Argentina, Brazil, Denmark, France, Mexico, Portugal, Sweden, and Venezuela. Even Czechoslovakia and Hungary are thinking of building freeways again, and Yugoslavia has built a 530-mile undivided *Autoput* with limited access from Ljubljana to Belgrade. The Soviet Union opened its first freeway—a section of the Moscow Outer Ring—in 1960. The leadership in highway esthetics was picked up by West Germany, and the new Aschaffenburg-Nürnberg *Autobahn*, laid out on a continuously curving alignment, is undoubtedly the most beautiful and "complete" freeway in Europe so far.

In spite of a number of impressive accomplishments in the United States, one has

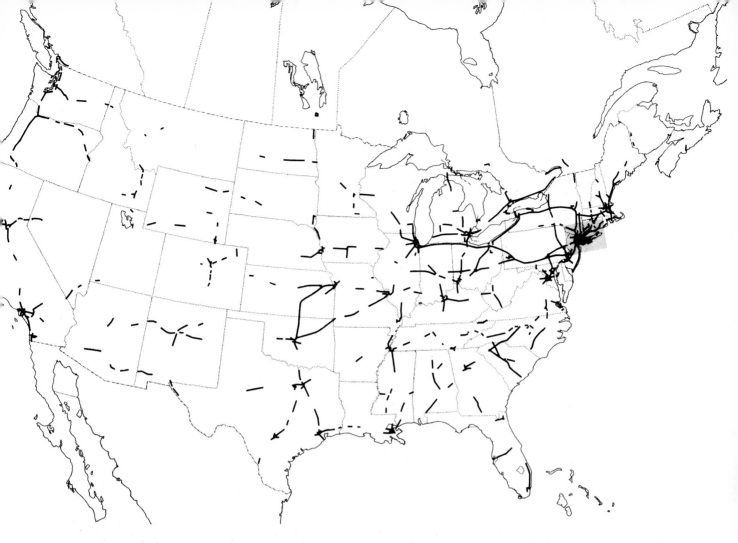

Divided highways with fully limited access, four or more lanes wide, completed or under construction in North America as of 1960. Freeway network in operation about 10,000 miles. For enlargement of New York area see p. 274.

to concede that only a small fraction of our freeways have achieved unqualified esthetic distinction. With the exception of parkways, most freeways are still considered as little more than utilitarian travel channels. Even though the federal government pays 90 per cent of the cost of the new Interstate system, federal authorities have so far failed to impose on the states a sufficient amount of the available leadership, taste, and skill, so as to make the Interstate system a national monument of enduring beauty. And there is to be found in America a definite lack of concern with the esthetic theory of highways.

THE FORMAL APPROACH

The highway can be conveniently analyzed in three basic aspects of *structure, function,* and *form.* The structural aspect, involving soil mechanics and the resistance of pavements, has obviously received the thorough attention of the engineering profession. Intensive research is being carried on about function: about the characteristics of the traffic stream, about safety, maintenance, and location. These two directions of inquiry, that is, structure and function, have led to adequate specifications for materials and geometric standards for design. Surely, both are guides to the development of form. But form as such has merited only scanty attention. The practice has been to pay lip service to "pleasing appearance" and relegate it to a footnote in engineering handbooks.*

The independent study of form is unnecessary in the case of some tools, which operate at the threshhold of technological possibility. The form of a jet plane or a rocket evolves almost entirely from a rigorous expression of function by mathematical means. The highway, by contrast, very much like a piece of architecture or industrial design, lies in an order of precision where scientifically determined functional limitations leave the designer considerable freedom to give the object intuitively a more refined and unique expression, beyond the bare minima of utilitarian standards. The moving eye perceives the form of the highway not as an engineering problem, but as an esthetic entity, a piece of sculpture or architecture, built of earth, asphalt, concrete, steel, shrubs, and trees. The highway is seen before it can be traveled upon—being seen is an integral part of its purpose. Hence the importance of the formal or visual approach.

As early as the 1930s German highway engineers took considerable pains to determine what qualities constitute the visual appeal of the highway. Most of this work was published between 1934 and 1943 in *Die Strasse,* then the official organ of the German highway engineering profession. These early studies can be divided into two categories: those dealing with the relationship of the highway to the landscape, and those concerned with the visual quality of the alignment of the roadway itself, regardless of its setting. The two categories had been established by Fritz Heller in a short paper in which he developed the theory of the external and the internal harmonies of the highway.

Heller's paper, published in January, 1938, seems to have had little influence outside Germany. In the United States, considerable stress has been laid by various research committees on the need for "fitting" the right-of-way to the topography. Led by the Bureau of Public Roads, the American Society of Landscape Architects, and the Highway Research Board, this movement has been by no means sterile, even though the recommendations have not been followed by many states. But as such the term "external harmony" has never been used by American road builders, for the esthetic value of its complement, the "internal harmony," does not seem to have been appreciated or understood.

The Committee on Roadside Development of the Highway Research Board, while stressing the need to integrate utility, safety, beauty, and economy in a "complete highway," made no mention in its 1944 report of the intrinsic esthetic merit of the geometry of the alignment itself, seen merely as an abstract ribbon in space—a merit that does not derive any of its qualities from the relationship with the surroundings. Only in considering the pros and cons of the "tangent" (straight) and the "spline" (curvilinear) alignment has American thought approached the concept of "internal

---

* Of 910 articles in the Proceedings of the Highway Research Board in the past 20 years, only eight deal with the esthetic aspects of form. 579 deal with structure, 250 with function, and 73 with administration. The proportion of articles on administration is increasing; of those on esthetics, decreasing.

harmony." We shall deal with both of these concepts in the discussion that follows. But first we should recapitulate some of the principles of vision that apply when the observer is moving.

VISION IN MOTION

To know the abilities and limitations of the eye is obviously important for the highway designer since, at his scale, he works close to the threshholds of human vision, where the very survival of his clients is at stake. He has to plan consciously their progress through a multidimensional world of space, time, and energy. The range of psycho-physiological data on vision collected by scientists is wide indeed, and our present purpose will be served by singling out briefly a few of the relevant principles.

Seeing depends on light energy. While the eye can adapt itself to an amazing range of luminant energy, the basis of seeing at any level of illumination is a reasonable contrast in brightness or hue. In full daylight, brightness differences of two to four per cent can just be discriminated. At dusk, the contrast has to be as much as 60 to 70 per cent. Excessive contrast produces glare.

The brightness of colors as seen also depends on the sensitivity of the eye to rays of different wave lengths: with equal lighting, the yellows and greens appear many times brighter than reds and blues. As luminance decreases, the ends of the spectrum begin to lose their color until all differences in hue are lost, and the eye sees only differences in brightness: this is the basis of night seeing by silhouette.

Seeing takes time. Visual responses are not instantaneous. It may take the eye one-tenth to three-tenths of a second to fixate, and unless the eye and the object are in a relatively fixed position with respect to each other, the eye does not see. At most, it can discern twelve separate images per second. It takes about a second to change focus, from the speedometer on the dashboard to some detail on the road ahead, and reaction time is commonly assumed by drivers' manuals to be three-quarters of a second. These are appreciable magnitudes if we remember that at 60 miles an hour the observer is moving 88 feet per second.

To the driver everything around him is moving. Nearby objects move most rapidly, so that closely spaced verticals on a railing, for example, completely disappear from sight, and shrubs become just a blur. Objects in the medium distance can be observed only for a short time, and an opportunity missed never returns on the same trip. Only distant objects, the sky or the silhouette of the horizon, have any degree of permanence and can be observed at leisure.

Seeing is limited in space. The size of the minimum visible object is limited by the size of the cones and rods in the retinal mosaic of the eye, and by the presence of holes between them. For a person with normal visual acuity (so-called 20/20 vision) to discriminate detail under average lighting conditions, the object has to subtend a visual angle of at least one minute. This means 3.5 inches at a distance of 1,000 feet. The threshold for lines is finer than that—the minimum angle may be as small as 4 seconds, if lighting conditions are ideal. But such visual acuity is exceptional. Experiments with highway signs have shown that for most people to read an unfamiliar name at a distance of 1,000 feet, the letters have to be at least 18 inches high. This may appear large, but actually it corresponds to eighteen thousandths of an inch at reading distance on a desk. While driving, the observer, focusing one to two thousand feet ahead, is constantly called upon to orient himself in this order of magnitude. A car at 1,800 feet has the size of a pinhead at 18 inches.

Limited in its ability to discriminate detail, the eye is also limited in the scope of its visual field. Looking straight ahead while standing, man can be aware of what happens in a field that is somewhat more than 180° sideways, about 69° up and 76° down. But the most sensitive part of the retina, the fovea, can only encompass an angle of 2.5 degrees. The peripheral parts of the retina give little detail. Moreover, peripheral vision, and with it the total visual field, diminishes, as the eye concentrates on smaller detail. The visual field can thus be only expressed in relative terms, and, depending on the stimulus employed, it may vary from the large area described above to a small circle around the fixation point.

In a short study of "Human Limitations in Automobile Driving," published in 1937 and still a minor classic, J. R. Hamilton and Louis L. Thurstone have derived from the general principles of vision five propositions directly applicable to highway design. These can be summarized as follows:

AS SPEED INCREASES, CONCENTRATION INCREASES.

The attention of a person standing idly is dispersed. As speed increases, the number of things to be seen and attended to increases proportionately. It becomes more and more dangerous to observe irrelevant objects, and concentration becomes fixed on the approaching ribbon of the road. It follows that, while offering the driver variety, the highway designer cannot distract him from watching the road. If any objects of interest are to be shown, the road must aim the eye. Planes perpendicular to the road are prominent; parallel ones are not.

AS SPEED INCREASES, THE POINT OF CONCENTRATION RECEDES.

The eyes are feeling their way ahead of the wheels. They are trying to allow the driver sufficient warning distance for emergencies. Their focusing point at 25 miles an hour lies approximately 600 feet ahead on the road. This distance is increasing with every increase in speed. At 45 miles an hour the fixation point lies some 1,200 feet ahead, at 65 miles an hour as far as 2,000 feet. It follows that anything to be brought to the driver's attention must not only lie on the axis of vision but must also be of a scale sufficiently large to be recognized at long distance.

AS SPEED INCREASES, PERIPHERAL VISION DIMINISHES.

It was pointed out earlier that the total visual field shrinks as the eye concentrates on smaller detail. At 25 miles an hour the eye encompasses a total horizontal angle of about 100 degrees. At 45 miles an hour this narrows down to about 65 degrees, and above 60 miles an hour the angle is less than 40 degrees. This restriction, called "tunnel vision" by some, is similar to the kind of perceptual restriction used for inducing

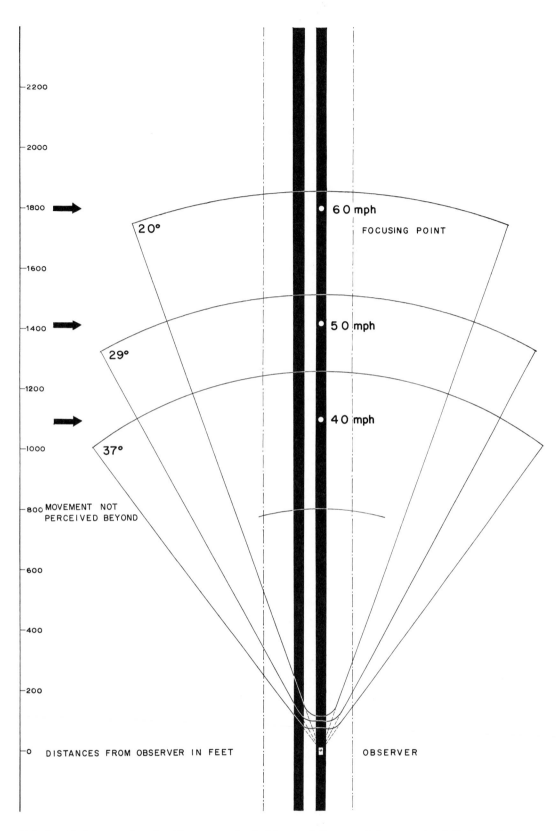

Relationship between focusing distance, angle of vision, and distance of foreground detail at speeds of 40 mph, 50 mph, and 60 mph.

hypnosis and sleep. It follows that unless the point of concentration is made to move around laterally by means of a curvilinear layout of the road, driving along an uneventful highway may become as hypnotic as gazing into a crystal ball. Elements to the side must be quiet, subdued, calculated to be perceived semi-consciously in the blurred field of peripheral vision, in order not to annoy. The main features are reserved for the axis of vision.

AS SPEED INCREASES, FOREGROUND DETAIL BEGINS TO FADE.

Since rapidly moving objects cannot be perceived separately, the driver does not see clearly except at some distance. At 40 miles an hour the earliest point of clear vision is about 80 feet away. Foreground detail is greatly diminished at 50 miles an hour, and its perception is negligible beyond 60 miles an hour. Only detail beyond 110 feet can be discerned at that speed. But from the previous discussion we can deduce that beyond some 1,400 feet the eye cannot discern detail because it becomes too small. Thus, only within an angle of 40° and at a distance between 110 and 1,400 feet is vision really adequate at 60 miles an hour—an interval that is traversed in less than 15 seconds. It follows that emphasis on elaborate detail is meaningless for the driver— only large, simple shapes are meaningfully perceived—the geometry of the paved ribbon, the total sculpture of the land forms, areas, textures, edges, silhouettes.

AS SPEED INCREASES, SPACE PERCEPTION BECOMES IMPAIRED.

Space and motion are perceived indirectly, with the help of memory, by relative changes in the size and position of objects. Looking straight ahead at long distance, these changes are so small that one cannot tell whether a car is coming or going except by indirect cues such as its position in the left lane. The movement of objects, traveling parallel and close to the axis of vision, cannot be discerned beyond some 800 feet. As speed increases, the time interval between discerning the movement of an object and coming abreast of it shrinks. Besides, accustomed to high speed, the observer gradually becomes "velocitated" and underestimates his own speed. It follows that the fewer clues the highway offers for judging one's own speed, the more likely is the driver to lose judgment of space and motion. While very narrow lateral restrictions are dangerous and visually disruptive, some variation in lateral enclosure is indispensable to keep the driver in touch with reality.

Added to all this must be some very important differences between what the eye sees on a conventional two-lane road, versus a multi-lane freeway. If we take as our visual frame the windshield of a standard 1960 model American automobile, assume a horizontal visual angle of 100 degrees, which corresponds to the slow speed of 25 miles an hour, and a straight road with uniform tree growth some 30 feet high and properly set back on the roadside, then a driver 5 feet 8 inches tall gets visual impressions indicated on the sketches that follow. Percentage figures show the approximate proportion of visual field occupied by sky, roadside, and roadbed.

Two-lane road: Sky   10%
                Roadside   82%
                Roadbed   8%

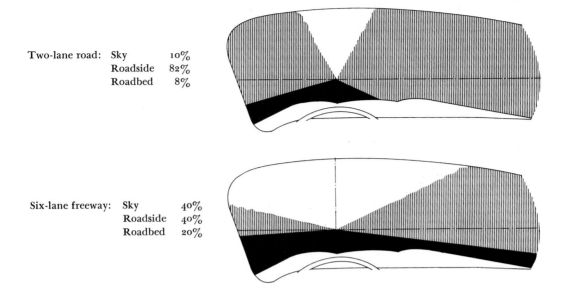

Six-lane freeway: Sky   40%
                   Roadside   40%
                   Roadbed   20%

If we reduce the visual field of the freeway to 45 degrees, which corresponds to a speed of 60 miles an hour, the proportions change as follows:

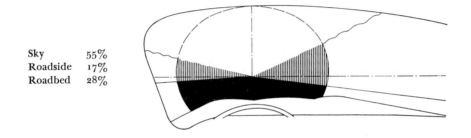

Sky   55%
Roadside   17%
Roadbed   28%

Roughly speaking, on a six-lane freeway at high speeds, the sky occupies over one-half of the visual field, the roadbed almost one-third, and the roadside the remaining sixth. If the roadside is flat and does not rise above the horizon, it shrinks to a tiny five per cent of the visual field, and the sky and the pavement dominate the view completely. Naturally, the driver's head is not rigidly attached to the automobile, and if no special dangers are present he does glance sideways occasionally, becoming aware of a broader visual field than that previously discussed. This holds true even more for passengers, though their predominant direction of vision is forward. While one could correct the above figures statistically for the frequency of sideways glances, the important point is that the essence of the argument holds true.

It follows that the visual space of the conventional road, like that of an urban street, is fully defined by its walls, be they made of buildings, trees, or billboards, as the case may be, and by the gaps in these walls—the lawns and the scenery beyond. The pavement is no more important than the floor in a picture gallery.

A six-lane freeway by contrast lays bare before the observer a flat surface some 120 feet wide. This surface becomes the most prominent element seen and, except in high-density urban areas, the two separate ribbons of pavement define the visual space of the road. While the builder of a conventional road has had little opportunity to modulate its space other than by planting trees and establishing setback lines, the designer of a divided freeway possesses, in the very interplay of the two undulating ribbons of pavement, a basic tool of spatial expression. This new condition requires much greater effort and subtlety. Anyone could think of planting two rows of chestnuts along a dull, open country road, and anybody could enjoy their shade after they were fully grown. Two rows of chestnuts, planted with sufficient setbacks to be safe for cars out of control, would in general mean very little on a modern freeway. Instead, the designer has to treat the twin ribbons of pavement as a sculptural form in its own right.

The problem today is how to recapture the appeal of the road ribbon on a completely new scale: the Carquinez Straits interchange and the nine-million-cubic-yard cut dwarfing the hillside village of Valona in California.

This form, taken as a plastic abstraction, derives its beauty from four elements: first, from the harmonious rhythm of its curves—their form, their scale, and their coordination in three dimensions; second, from the proportions of the shapes it encloses as seen from the driver's seat—those that the varying median strip forms in perspective and those between the horizon and the pavement; third, from the way the paved ribbon "sits" in the total sculpture of the landscape—the way it clings to hills, jumps over valleys, winds along bodies of water, or pierces steep rock barriers; fourth, from the vistas it offers the traveler—broad panoramas from hilltops, dramatic industrial complexes, memorable landmarks, broad expanses of water. (These, in general, cannot be moved to suit the highway, but the highway can be oriented to bring them into view.)

To use the terminology we have introduced earlier, the first two sources of beauty derive from the internal harmony, the second two from the external harmony of the freeway. Both are equally important, though perhaps the internal harmony should take precedence over the external. For the intrinsic flaws in the design of an object cannot be eradicated by the beauty of its setting—an ugly house in a beautiful garden still remains ugly. Faulty grading and ugly structures can be screened out by trees, but no amount of planting can screen out an ugly alignment of the pavement itself, which the driver is compelled to see constantly, on and on. Hence the importance of the internal harmony—the fundamental approach, as contrasted with the cosmetic approach, post-factum "beautification" of the roadside.

2. The Internal Harmony of the Freeway

To the eye of the moving observer, the highway slab and its shoulder form an unwinding ribbon of parallel lines, swinging and changing into various horizontal and inclined planes, standing out in stark white or black against the soft, warm colors of the landscape. As it turns and changes direction, as it rises and falls over hills and valleys, as it diverges to accept a stream or pulls together to enter a city, the paved ribbon assumes qualities of an abstract composition in space, which gains in richness because it is not only passively seen but actively traversed by the driver, who experiences visual as well as kinesthetic sensations of tilting, turning, dropping, and climbing. "It is like sculpture and dance together," an enthusiastic interviewee told Kevin Lynch.

Certain forms of sculpture, built of steel rods or plastic strips, exhibit a visual quality reminiscent of the paved ribbon. Such forms are significant owing to the plastic harmony of their flowing lines. This same plastic harmony applies to the geometry of the freeway. Its esthetic, apart from its setting, lies in organizing the component parts of the alignment in a continuous, free-flowing three-dimensional line, property proportioned and consistent in scale.

CONTINUITY OF ALIGNMENT

Aside from the sculptural analogy, continuity is inherent in the job the highway does. The landscape is essentially wavy and undulating. The path of the vehicle is, in essence, also a continuous curve, with turning radii ranging from infinity on straight lines to whatever may be the minimum radius at a given speed. The momentum of a

Plastic continuity in space: *Tripartite Unity* by Max Bill

The tangent and the curve: Route Europe 5 in the Main River Valley.

vehicle precludes any sudden or abrupt change in its vertical or horizontal direction. It follows that an ideal alignment in the landscape logically would be a continuous curve, with constant, gradual, and smooth changes of direction.

Such a complex and irregular three-dimensional curve, however, would seem to be somewhat difficult to analyze and to build. Therefore, for the purposes of design, a highway is broken down into a horizontal *plan* and a vertical *profile*. Plan and profile are, in turn, broken down into *tangents* or straight lines, and *curves* of simple geometric form that can be easily calculated and staked out. It is this design procedure that often results in a discontinuous alignment, where individual pieces of what should be a flowing ribbon are evident separately. This condition is visually annoying and can even result in erratic traffic behavior. A continuous alignment, by contrast, is one in which the commencements and terminations of the individual curves and tangents cannot be noticed by the eye. To see what makes up such an alignment, we shall discuss its components one by one.

THE CONTINUITY OF HORIZONTAL FORM

In the horizontal plane, a highway alignment is made up of three geometric components: the straight line, the circular arc, and the transition curve.

Historically, the tangent or straight line is the most common element of alignment on deliberately planned roads since Roman days. It is easiest to lay out, and is the shortest distance between two points. It is justified in very flat terrain or where the predominant man-made landscape pattern—such as a street grid—is rectilinear. It provides clear orientation, but at the same time, unless it is aimed at some landmark, it is esthetically uninteresting, since it is totally predictable; it is monotonous and fatiguing, since the view is completely static; it encourages excessive speeds, since the driver tries to "get it over with." The radius of a straight line is infinite, and seen in perspective a straight line remains a straight line.

RADIUS = ∞

The Tangent.

The second most common element of horizontal alignment is the circular arc. It is also easy to lay out, and appears to be the logical way to turn. It is interesting because it brings more roadside into view, because it shows the driver a changing panorama and arouses a sense of anticipation for what is beyond. A curve encourages attention and a steady hold on the steering wheel. At the same time, the curving roadside provides much better optical guidance, since it is seen ahead, rather than peripherally. A circular arc has a constant radius; seen in perspective the circular arc appears as an ellipse.

RADIUS = CONST.

The Circular Arc.

Neither the tangent nor the circular arc, taken in themselves, pose any problems of continuity. The problem arises when the two are joined, when the infinite radius of a straight line suddenly changes to a finite and relatively short radius of a circular curve. Visually, such an abrupt break appears harsh and unmeditated. The trained eye can always spot the point at which the circular arc begins for some distance ahead. This is so since the straight line, with zero curvature, touches the circle, which appears as an ellipse with a continuously changing curvature, at a point where this curvature appears the sharpest. Conversely, driving out of a circular arc onto a tangent, one feels one is making a detour and wishes one could cut the corner. Perspective foreshortening from a viewpoint only some four feet above ground accentuates discontinuities of alignment and, in spite of the huge scale of the curves, makes them visually very disturbing.

The Tangent and the Circular Arc.

Moreover, the vehicle itself cannot change the direction of travel abruptly: the steering wheel is turned gradually, rather than with a sudden jerk. As it is being turned, the vehicle describes a path with curvature changing gradually from zero on the straight line to the constant curvature of a given circular arc.

The functional need to soften the transition between the tangent and the circular arc has been known to engineers since the days of the railroad. Trains would derail if there was no provision for gradual development of radial acceleration. In highway practice, however, the pavement is usually sufficiently wide so that every vehicle can choose its own transition path without running off the road. A highway transition curve designed according to the laws of the physics of motion would thus represent a design refinement, but not an absolute necessity.

The Tangent and the Spiral Transition.

Still, on sharper curves such a refinement is sometimes warranted. The geometric form usually employed in highway transition curves is the clothoid, better known as the spiral or Euler's spiral. It is a curve whose radius between two finite points ranges from zero to infinity. It approximates very closely the natural transition path of the vehicle and is fairly easy to stake out. In perspective, it appears as a line with gradually changing curvature which connects the straight line smoothly with the apparent ellipse of the circle. Functionally, it is used to achieve gradual development of radial acceleration, or side thrust; gradual introduction of superelevation runoff;* and gradual widening of the pavement when necessary.

* Superelevation is the banking of pavement on curves, to counteract centrifugal forces. Superelevation runoff is the gradual buildup of this cross-slope from the normal crowned section, usually by raising the outer edge of the pavement.

The difficulty with the functional approach is that different formulas suggested to calculate the minimum length of spiral on the basis of radial acceleration all contain a factor C, an arbitrarily assumed constant indicating the "comfort" involved. Degrees of "comfort" actually selected by drivers vary over a wide range. Besides, distances needed to attain a reasonably "comfortable" change of radial acceleration are often so short as to become visually insignificant. In America, as a result, the distance required to attain the superelevation runoff is used to govern the length of spiral on flatter curves. This second factor is even less determinate than the first one. One standard suggests that the superelevation runoff should not be traversed by the driver in less than two seconds. But the recognized guide to American highway practice, the American Association of State Highway Officials' *Policy on Geometric Design* acknowledges that ultimately "the appearance aspect of superelevation runoff largely governs its length."

This being the case, it seems that a frankly esthetic approach to transition curves is justified, with their length determined not by pseudo-utilitarian minima, but rather by what is visually necessary to achieve a generous, free-flowing continuity of alignment. When entering a curve from a tangent, the driver perceives its sharpness by the distance in which the roadway bends out of sight in front of him. If it turns away abruptly, the exaggeration of curvature in perspective not only is ugly but may frighten the driver into unnecessary braking. A gradual reduction of the distance in which the pavement is seen ahead promotes visual continuity and uniform operation.

Without going deeper into the question of exactly how fast the roadway should bend out of sight at the beginning of a curve to preserve a visual continuity of alignment, we could perhaps state, as a rule of thumb, that a pleasing relationship would result if the lengths of spiral to circular arc to spiral were to relate in a proportion of 1:2:1, rather than something like 1:7:1 or less, as often results from current American standards, if spirals are used at all.* While spirals of the latter order are of little visual significance in perspective, spirals that are too long (longer than the circular arc they connect with) can be visually displeasing, since they create the impression of a sharp bend in the middle of the curve.

Besides connecting tangents to circular arcs, spirals are sometimes used to connect adjacent circular arcs to each other, if the radius of one is more than 1.5 times the other, or if they turn in opposite directions. This can create pleasing visual effects. In fact, Hans Lorenz, who was experimenting with long transition curves as far back as 1940 on the then proposed Breslau-Vienna *Autobahn,* made the next logical step in suggesting that the spiral should be used as an independent design element in its own right, next to the tangent and the circular arc. Its length would then be determined by the need to accomplish a visually significant turn—generally greater than three degrees. The result could be a freeway without any straight sections whatsoever. The American answer to this is that long spirals are undesirable since steering conditions on them are not constant, in contrast to the circle and the straight line. One can argue, however, that even a straight road always requires small compensating steering

---

* About half the states in the United States occasionally employ spiral transitions. In Germany spirals were used on freeways in the early '30s, then dropped as functionally unnecessary, then reintroduced again on esthetic grounds.

Curve with and without spiral transition. The sharp "corners" at the juncture of curve and straight line in the top view are quite obvious from the driver's seat.

adjustments. One does not just set the wheel and let it go. Though no scientific studies have yet been made of the completed sections of the Aschaffenburg-Nürnberg *Autobahn,* designed by Lorenz with only arcs and spirals, its operating characteristics appear to be excellent.

THE CONTINUITY OF HORIZONTAL SCALE

In discussing the length of spiral transitions we have actually digressed from the subject of continuity of horizontal form, and have entered the realm of scale. A straight line in itself has no scale. But when a straight line has to change direction and is thus interrupted by a curve, the question immediately arises: How long should that curve be to preserve visual continuity? A curve may be fairly flat and nicely transitioned, but if it is too short it will still appear as an unnatural kink in the road. Curiously enough, the question of "how long" is seldom discussed in engineering handbooks, which are preoccupied with answering the question: How sharp can a curve be to be safe?

The maximum sharpness of a curve is, of course, technically very important, and depends, essentially, on the comfortable side friction between pavement and tires at a given speed, and on the maximum safe superelevation of pavement under local climate and traffic conditions. Friction and superelevation together counteract the centrifugal force that tends to throw a turning vehicle off the road. With the design speed and the superelevation given, the minimum radius of a curve is fixed: it is, for example, 1640 feet for a speed of 70 miles an hour (superelevation eight per cent, friction factor 0.12).

A turning radius of 1640 feet is, quite obviously, rather sharp, even if safe. In most cases, the designer would tend to choose a flatter (hence longer) curve with a less steep superelevation. This is where esthetics comes in. What length of curve to choose for what change of direction, provided we are not required to hold to the minimum radius?

Let us say we have a change of direction of fifteen degrees between two straight lines. If we hold to our minimum radius, we come up with a curve that is only 429 feet long, and it looks, of course, ridiculously short. The same curve can be made a mile long, if we choose a radius of 20,000 feet. The angle between tangents still remains fifteen degrees, but the feeling the curve creates is completely different. And the larger we make the radius, the longer the arc will be, keeping the angle between tangents constant.*

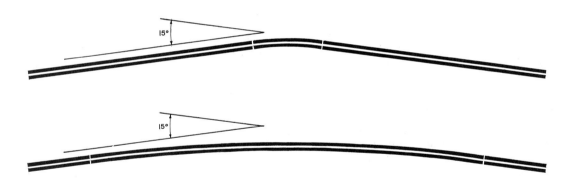

Angle constant—different radii.

The rule is generally recognized that smaller angles should have longer radii, but few more specific recommendations exist, with the result that too many curves on our freeways are too short for the turn they are accomplishing. The difficulty with a very short curve is that from a distance it looks like an arbitrary kink in the road. When

---

* Radius, length of arc, and angle between tangents are in a fixed relationship to each other, expressed in the formula $L = 0.01745 \triangle R$, with L (length) and R (radius) in feet and $\triangle$ (angle) in degrees. We may note for future discussion that the ratio $\frac{L}{R}$ equals 0.01745 delta, and is thus merely another measure for the angle between tangents.

Discontinuous and continuous alignment in the Catskills and on Long Island.

the driver comes to it, it looks like nothing at all, for the eye is focusing far ahead where the road is straight again. Sometimes, the driver never notices a short curve— an indication that the designer has failed to utilize the advantages of curvilinear alignment.

Since at high speeds the driver looks some 1,000 to 2,000 feet ahead, it seems that a curve ought to be at least that long to be visually significant while the driver is on it. Systematic observation by several visually trained individuals on a Connecticut free- way indicated that curves shorter than 1,000 feet were generally experienced as "too short." German 1942 geometric standards established 300 meters (984 feet) as an absolute minimum for length of curve.

On the graph below, angles between tangents are plotted against radii, and the resulting hyperbolas are lines of equal length of circular curve. The 1,000-foot length is shown as a suggested minimum for freeways, and the area between 1,500 and 5,500 feet is shaded as the desirable range for the length of simple circular curves on free- ways. Curves more than a mile long are seldom practical due to topographic restric- tions—unless they are compound curves, which can be as long as two or three miles.

Striving for longer and hence flatter curves, one can, naturally, go overboard and make the radius so large that the curve will be hardly distinguishable from a straight line. What is then the longest reasonable radius? The Germans have used radii up to 9,000 meters (29,520 feet), while the Bureau of Public Roads used a radius of 85,943 feet near Greenbelt, Md. The first of these curves, 3,540 feet long and enclosing an

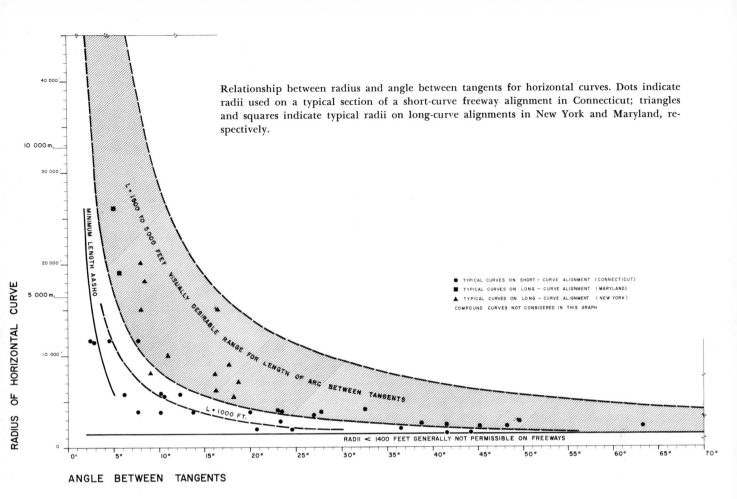

Relationship between radius and angle between tangents for horizontal curves. Dots indicate radii used on a typical section of a short-curve freeway alignment in Connecticut; triangles and squares indicate typical radii on long-curve alignments in New York and Maryland, respectively.

● TYPICAL CURVES ON SHORT — CURVE ALIGNMENT (CONNECTICUT)
■ TYPICAL CURVES ON LONG — CURVE ALIGNMENT (MARYLAND)
▲ TYPICAL CURVES ON LONG — CURVE ALIGNMENT (NEW YORK)
COMPOUND CURVES NOT CONSIDERED IN THIS GRAPH

RADIUS OF HORIZONTAL CURVE (vertical axis)

MINIMUM LENGTH AASHO

L = 1500 TO 5000 FEET VISUALLY DESIRABLE RANGE FOR LENGTH OF ARC BETWEEN TANGENTS

L = 1000 FT.

RADII < 1400 FEET GENERALLY NOT PERMISSIBLE ON FREEWAYS

ANGLE BETWEEN TANGENTS (horizontal axis)

angle of nearly seven degrees, still reads very well in the landscape, while the second, 4,300 feet long with an angle of nearly three degrees, is somewhat less obvious. Hans Lorenz points out that curves generally cease to be visually significant if the *visible* part of the curve accomplishes a turn of two degrees or less. A 50,000-foot radius would thus require a visible length of roadway of at least 1,750 feet. Within this distance, the deflection from a straight line would be only 7.6 feet. In practice, no horizontal curves with angles between tangents smaller than three degrees probably should be used; depending on how far ahead the road can be seen, the maximum radius for most conditions lies somewhere between 10,000 and 100,000 feet.

Another way to approach the scale of horizontal curves is to compare their length with that of the tangents. Most widely used in America is the long tangent—short curve alignment:

Long Tangent—Short Curve Alignment.

Typically, it consists of straight sections one to three or more miles long, connected by curves 1,500 feet long or so, with 2,000- to 12,000-foot radii. From our definition of continuity, this is the epitome of discontinuous alignment, for every curve and every tangent is clearly seen as a separate thing Curves usually make up less than one-fifth of such an alignment.

The main argument for it has been that long straight sections are necessary on two-lane roads to attain proper sight distances for passing. This does not always hold true, for if there is enough room for flat curves (radii in the order of 20,000 feet), proper passing sight distances can be attained on them. On divided highways, passing sight distance is of no consequence, and the only reason for the use of long tangents here is probably the force of habit. Curves are no more expensive to build than straight sections, and the little extra effort in design is well worth the improvement. Somehow the fact is often overlooked that if the angle between two tangents is given, a flat curve will result in a shorter and more direct alignment than a sharper one. More weighty functional arguments against the short curve—long tangent alignment are that curves at the end of long tangents are accident-prone and that long straight sections produce monotony. On these grounds, it appears logical to increase the length of curves to such a degree that they surpass by far the length of the tangents they connect. We thus arrive at the long curve—short tangent alignment:

Long Curve—Short Tangent Alignment.

For this design, not a straight line but rather a flat curve is taken as the basic unit of alignment. For example, the basis for the geometric design of the Garden State Parkway was a curve with a radius of 15,000 feet, and these long curves were connected by short tangents, 220 to 2,300 feet in length. Other advanced designs feature curves with 6,000- to 20,000-foot radii, and only about one-third to one-fifth of such an alignment consists of straight sections. The latter are not meant to read as tangents visually, in perspective, but rather to appear as a part of a continuous compound curve. This type of layout often goes under the name of "spline"* alignment.

The only esthetic problem of the long curve–short tangent alignment is that unless the radii are very long—which is often not permitted by topography and other restrictions—the points of connection between circular curves and tangents still retain all the visual faults we have discussed previously. Hence, spiral transitions have to be introduced. Now, if the tangents are as short as "spline" alignment requires them to be and spiral transitions are made as long as we recommend them to be, then often very little room is left for the tangent. So we make the next logical step and arrive at the continuous curvilinear alignment:

Continuous Curvilinear Alignment.

* The spline is a drafting instrument—a flexible rule to draw irregular curves.

This consists of long, flat circular curves, simple and compound, connected by fairly long spiral transitions, with about two-thirds of the alignment on circular arcs, and one-third on spirals. This would approach the ideal we postulated at the outset of our discussion of continuity, and reviewed in describing the treatment of spirals by Hans Lorenz.

Discarding the traditional, discontinuous tangent-and-curve alignment in favor of the new continuous curvilinear alignment naturally requires a radical break with accepted procedures of design. The old procedure was to use given topographic controls to establish the basic tangents, and then connect them with circular arcs. The new procedure would be to use given topographic controls to establish the basic circular arcs, as flat and as long as practicable, and then join them with suitable transition curves. The tangent is thus eliminated as a dominant element of design. Needless to say, the pure arcs and spirals alignment should not be taken as a dogma, for there will always be room for tangents in cities, or in an absolutely flat landscape, where curvature could look arbitrary and contrived.

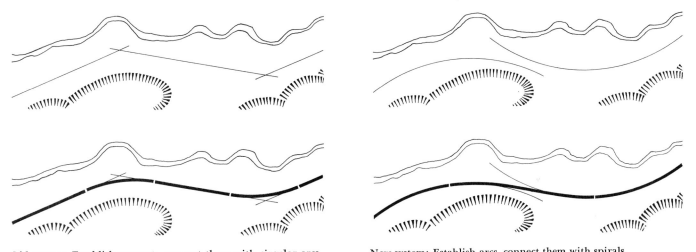

Old system: Establish tangents, connect them with circular arcs.   New system: Establish arcs, connect them with spirals.

The continuity of alignment can be expressed and studied graphically and mathematically by means of the curvature diagram, or $\frac{1}{R}$ graph. The method is simple and easy to visualize. One merely plots the center line of the highway along the horizontal axis of the graph, and the value one divided by radius along the perpendicular axis. In such a diagram, the tangent appears as a straight line on the horizontal axis. A circular curve appears as a straight line parallel to the axis, but at a distance $\frac{1}{R}$ from it, up or down, depending on whether it is a right or left turn. The spiral appears as a sloping straight line, connecting the two. In essence, the $\frac{1}{R}$ diagram shows the second derivative of the highway curvature, which represents, among other things, the movement of the steering wheel. Areas enclosed between the $\frac{1}{R}$ line and the horizontal axis show $\frac{L}{R}$, that is, are proportional to the angle between tangents. On the illustrations that follow curvature diagrams are shown for 10-mile stretches of four characteristic kinds of horizontal alignment.

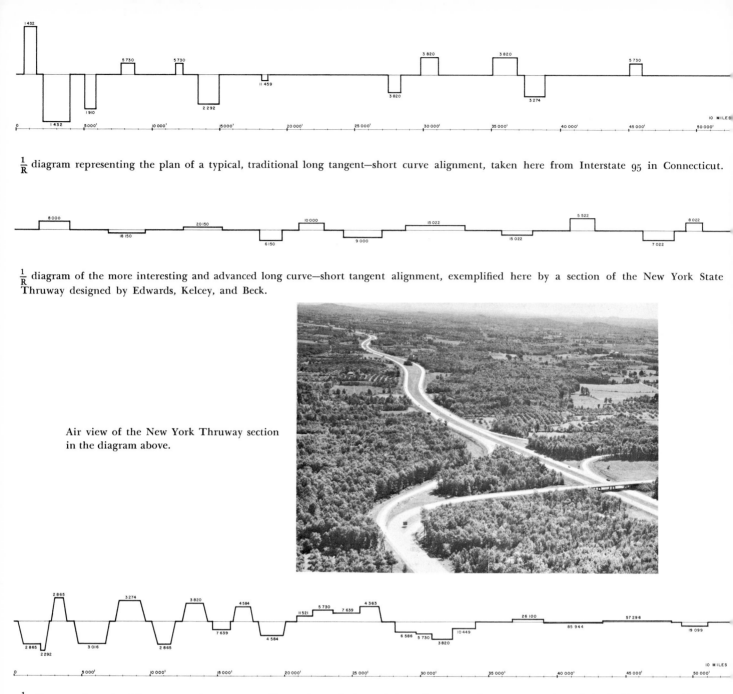

$\frac{1}{R}$ diagram representing the plan of a typical, traditional long tangent—short curve alignment, taken here from Interstate 95 in Connecticut.

$\frac{1}{R}$ diagram of the more interesting and advanced long curve—short tangent alignment, exemplified here by a section of the New York State Thruway designed by Edwards, Kelcey, and Beck.

Air view of the New York Thruway section in the diagram above.

$\frac{1}{R}$ diagram of a refined long curve—short tangent alignment, employing spirals and compound curves: a section of the Baltimore–Washington Parkway, designed by the Bureau of Public Roads.

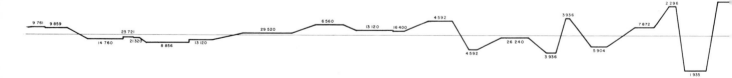

$\frac{1}{R}$ diagram of a continuous curvilinear alignment—the ultimate in geometric design. No tangents are used, just circular arcs and connecting spirals. A section of the Aschaffenburg–Nürnberg *Autobahn* designed under the direction of Hans Lorenz.

To relate the size of circular and spiral curves to the angles between tangents and to the straight sections of the road in a visually correct way, it is of course not enough

Air view of *Autobahn* section in bottom diagram on opposite page.

to make them merely as long as possible. It is important that the whole "flow of thought" in the design of the road be continuous. If we enter a city, for example, it is important to build up the curves gradually from very long and flat ones to sharper and shorter ones, until we reach the climax of the downtown interchanges. Continuity of the design process will prevent us from introducing a sudden turn, the im-

With sufficiently long radii, proper sight distances can be achieved even on two-lane roads with curvilinear alignment. The example shown, beautifully fitted to the topography, is in southern Ohio.

pendence of which has not been indicated visually for miles. It will prevent us from putting a tangent between two turns in the same direction, for it is incomprehensible to the driver why a turn should be interrupted by a straight line, only to be continued later. It will allow us to build what the engineer calls a "directional" alignment—without detours—but within the curvilinear medium.

THE CONTINUITY OF VERTICAL FORM

In the vertical plane, or in profile, the highway is made up of two geometric components: the inclined straight line, which is called the grade, and the vertical curve, which can be either a crest curve (hill) or a sag curve (valley).

The Grade

A road is seldom completely level; usually it has at least a slight incline along its axis, and this grade is measured in per cent. A five per cent grade means that the road rises or falls five units in every 100 units of its length. The steepness of grade is limited by functional considerations. Trucks are not powerful enough to negotiate steep grades without substantial reduction of speed, and therefore on freeways where truck traffic is present maximum grades are usually limited to three per cent. For passenger cars, up to eight per cent is allowable, if icing conditions can be controlled. If the pavement has curbs, minimum grades should not become smaller than 0.5 per cent or 0.3 per cent to facilitate drainage.

From the esthetic viewpoint, grades provide variety and drama. The field of vision is restricted on upgrades; with a lower horizon line the sky and the roadbed dominate the view. On downgrades, by contrast, a high horizon line permits a sweeping view of the countryside and of the road ahead. Visually, grades flatter than about 0.8 per cent usually appear to be level. Grades one per cent to three per cent are quite obvious as flat grades, whereas those from four per cent to eight per cent appear rather steep and dramatic, particularly when an upgrade is seen across a valley. However, the perception of grades is relative and what counts most is the change in grade, rather than the incline with respect to a horizontal plane.

In the selection of a route conflicts can arise between the requirements of efficient operation and dramatic interest.* Though one cannot assign a monetary value to the esthetic appeal of a grade and weigh it against such things as the economics of truck operation, it is possible to select several designs which are economically tolerable and then choose the one with the greatest visual appeal. The use of electronic computers now enables the engineer to investigate the costs and benefits of many more alternate alignments with much greater precision than formerly. This advance should be exploited for the sake of beauty.

---

* This is illustrated by a section of the Salzburg-Vienna freeway near Lake Mondsee in Austria. Designed under the Nazis with landscape considerations primarily in view, it rose to the crest of a mountain. When the Austrians resumed construction in 1955, they applied American cost-benefit methods, and discovered that a long detour around the mountain would be more economical in the end. The old alignment was abandoned and the freeway follows the more efficient route.

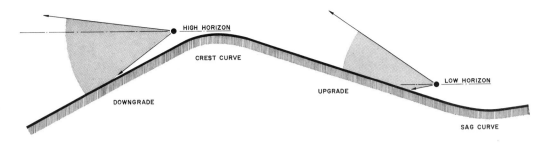

The profile: Upgrade, low horizon, restricted view; downgrade, high horizon, large view.

The Vertical Curve

Two different grades are connected by means of a vertical curve, either a crest or a sag. The geometric form employed as a rule in vertical curves is the parabola. The grade on a parabolic curve has a constant rate of change, and the curve is easy to design since vertical offsets from the tangent vary as the square of the horizontal distance from the curve end. In a way, a parabola also serves as its own transition, though in the order of magnitude of highway vertical curves the differences between it and the circular arc are quite negligible. A number of authorities, while designing vertical curves as parabolas, speak of them as if they were circular arcs. We shall do the same, to simplify matters and to maintain comparability with the discussion of horizontal curves.

In the vertical plane we also have two tangents which form an angle between each other, except that it is quite small and is now measured in per cent of grade, not in degrees.* And we have essentially the same problem to solve: what length of curve (i.e., what radius) to select for a given change in grade?

The two functional controls that govern the minimum length of vertical highway curves are stopping sight distance for crest curves, and headlight sight distances for sag curves. Drainage and vertical impact (on sag curves) have also to be considered. On the basis of these, AASHO recommends, for a design speed of 70 miles an hour, a minimum vertical radius of 14,000 feet for sag curves and 24,000 feet for crest curves. The radii for slower speeds are shorter, reaching 5,000 feet.

Still we can see that the angles of vertical curves are about ten times smaller and the radii about three times longer than those for horizontal curves. Such a flat curvature poses neither functional nor visual problems of continuity at the point of change from tangent to curve, and hence we do not have to worry about transitional spirals in the vertical plane. They are almost never used in practice, even though some British authorities have advocated them. Continuity in vertical form is not a problem. Continuity in the scale of vertical curves, however, is very much a problem, and we shall turn to it presently.

* When a 3% upgrade joins a 3% downgrade, the angle is 3°30′. In most cases, vertical angles between tangents on freeways are smaller than that. They are expressed by the algebraic difference (3%−(−3%)=6%) between the two grades which, divided by 100, is the tangent of the angle. Vertical curvature in American practice is measured by a value K, which is horizontal distance in which a change of grade is achieved divided by the change of grade in per cent. For small angles K multiplied by 100 equals radius of the vertical circle that approximately corresponds to the parabola.

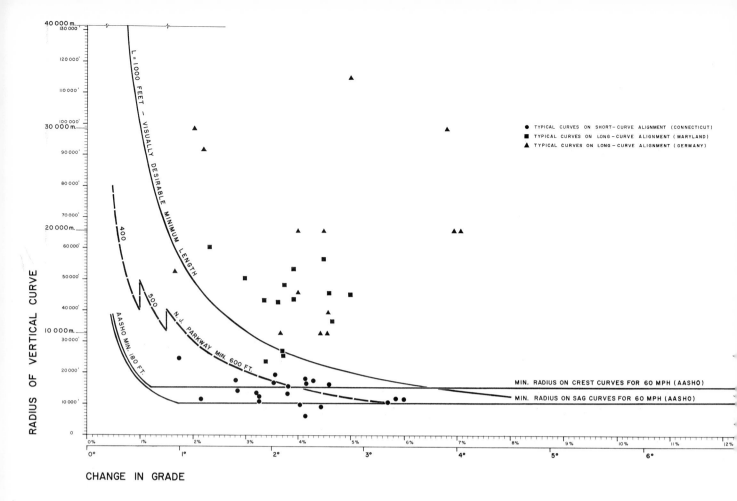

Relationship between radius and angle between tangents for vertical curves. Dots indicate radii used on a typical section of a short-curve freeway alignment, where minimum vertical radius for sags and crests is applied throughout regardless of the length of the curve; triangles and squares indicate typical vertical radii used on sample long-curve alignments.

THE CONTINUITY OF VERTICAL SCALE

Minimum lengths of vertical curve that result from the application of minimum radii are quite short—they range from 200 feet to 900 feet on sag curves for differences in grade between one per cent and six per cent. Such short vertical curves, while functionally adequate, are visually entirely out of scale on the freeway. While the eye does not notice small grades in themselves, it is very sensitive to even the smallest changes of grade. These appear as unnatural "breaks" in profile, if they are too short. From a distance, an alignment with minimal vertical curves looks as if it were made of a series of rigid boards, lined up one after the other at different angles, up and down.

The standard practice on freeways with a conventional long-tangent short-curve plan is to employ long tangents and short curves in profile as well, making the vertical curves as short as the functional standards will permit, with a deleterious effect on esthetic continuity. While the choice of curves that are visually too short has no rational explanation in the horizontal plane, short vertical curves can be rationalized on the grounds that they save cut and fill. This may be true in some cases. But since the landscape is essentially wavy, it appears that a curvilinear vertical alignment would on the whole fit it better and more economically than long straight grades. If

Transition of a 2% downgrade to a 3% upgrade effected by the minimum curve for 70 mph. The curve is 700 feet long, vertical radius about 14,000 feet.

Transition of a 2% downgrade to a 3% upgrade effected by a liberal curve 3,000 feet long, vertical radius about 60,000 feet.

sufficient care is exercised in the location, longer vertical curves do not have to be more expensive. Naturally, their radii have to be related to the profile of the topography, and in gently rolling terrain long vertical curves are especially pleasing. The Baltimore-Washington Parkway or the Aschaffenburg-Nürnberg *Autobahn,* for example, successfully use sag curves 1,500 to 3,000 feet long, which is often two to three times more than would be required by minimum utilitarian standards.

Crest curves, or hills, do not pose the esthetic problems that sag curves do if they are so high that the road terminates visually on the horizon line at the crest. Their minimum lengths are as much as one and one-half times larger than those of sag curves. Still, the stopping sight distance (600 feet at 70 miles an hour) beyond which the driver does not see while going over the crest visually often appears quite precarious, even though it is functionally safe. Some high-speed freeways, like the New York State Thruway, adopt a minimum sight distance of 1,000 feet throughout, which results in gentler crest curves and brings them more into scale with the very long and flat sag curves that one would like to advocate.

In summary, to achieve continuity in profile, vertical curves should be made much longer than minimum standards require. This is particularly important in the case of sag curves and small changes of grade, where perspective foreshortening is acute. Pursuing this tendency to minimize tangents in profile, we arrive at the *continuous curvilinear alignment* in the vertical plane. While curves may make up, in moderately hilly terrain, some 25 per cent of the conventional vertical alignment, they can make up, under comparable circumstances, as much as 50 per cent of the curvilinear vertical alignment. This means, essentially, reducing the *number* of vertical curves and increasing the *length* of the remaining ones more than twice. Compound vertical curves form, of course, a natural part of such an alignment. Vertical curves can perfectly well touch each other, and do not require tangents or spirals in between.

By employing the principle of a continuous, curvilinear profile, a number of visual faults in vertical alignment are automatically excluded:

Short tangent between two sag curves, a "board effect," particularly bad on bridges, which should curve together with the roadway.

Short "hump," usually occasioned by the attempt to save on fill at the approaches to a short bridge, a situation frequent in flat topography.

Short "break" in grade; a small crest, with the road visible after the crest.

THREE-DIMENSIONAL COORDINATION

Continuity in plan and continuity in profile will lead to continuity in three dimensions only if the vertical and horizontal elements are carefully coordinated. For the purpose of analysis, we have talked so far about the tangent and the horizontal curve as if they were level in profile.

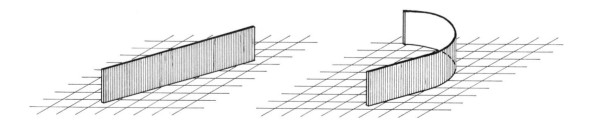

We have discussed the grade and the vertical curve as if they were straight in plan.

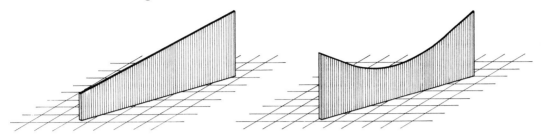

All four combinations are actually encountered in practice, and to give a tangent some smooth curvature either vertically or horizontally is one of the easiest ways to improve its appearance. Still, the crest or sag on tangent remains a two-dimensional curve, just like a level horizontal curve.

Not so a horizontal curve that is superimposed on a steady grade. The grade does not tilt it, but rather, pulls it up, and the result is a three-dimensional curve called the screw curve:

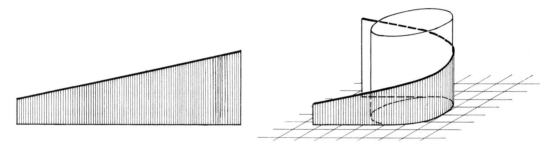

Mathematically, a screw curve is a line with a steady pitch, wrapped around a cylinder. In our case, the cylinder does not have to be round, it can have the shape of a transition curve in plan. The three-dimensional quality of the screw curve can be visualized from the fact that tangents, drawn to it at any two points, do not intersect. A three-dimensional curve exists only in volume, and can be represented in planes only by means of its projections.

When a horizontal curve is superimposed on a vertical curve, the result is a three-dimensional curve called the helix:

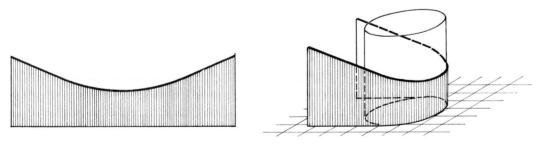

Mathematically, a helix is a line with a constantly varying pitch, wrapped around a cylinder. Again, in our case the cylinder can be partly circular and partly transitional in plan. The line with the constantly varying pitch is our vertical parabola.

The latter does not quite produce a mathematically correct helix, but in our order of magnitudes it approaches it within some one-fifth per cent.

Horizontal curvature combined with vertical curvature of similar length. Examples of helical three-dimensional curves on a parkway and a freeway.

F. W. Cron points out that "most of the awkwardness of the highway arises from failure to visualize the road in three dimensions in the planning stage." The sculptural images of the screw and the helix can help us overcome this deficiency. Being three-dimensional, they are properly in the nature of the highway, which is a three-dimensional construction. They can become the *two basic building blocks* of a continuous, sculptural alignment, as contrasted with traditional design where short and long vertical and horizontal elements overlap at random. Level horizontal curves, straight vertical curves, or even level or inclined tangents can naturally be added to the helix and the screw, when conditions require.

But the important point is the essential *unity of plan and profile,* which the three-dimensional curve expresses best. It can therefore help us formulate some basic rules of coordination:

(a) A generous alignment in one plane does not associate itself with small and frequent adjustments in the other. Although technically the minimum length of sag vertical curves, for example, is much shorter than that of horizontal curves—they are occasionally as much as ten times shorter in practice—visually, they should be similar in length. Hence, the length of vertical curves—and grades, for that matter—should not be determined abstractly, but rather influenced by the length of the horizontal elements on which they are superimposed.

(*Above*) Short sag on long horizontal curve; (*below*) long sag on long horizontal curve.

(b) While the scale of vertical and horizontal elements should be related, they should not commence and terminate simultaneously. Fritz Heller points out that the eye may find it disturbing when the vertical and horizontal alignments change at the same time, since any irregularities at this point will be emphasized in perspective and be cumulative in effect. Desirably, horizontal curvature should always "lead" vertical curvature somewhat, and should remain appreciably (but not too much) longer than the latter. This overlapping will permit smooth and gradual changes between the individual elements of the alignment, and promote safety through optical guidance. For, as AASHO states, sharp horizontal curvature at the crest or at the low point of a vertical curve is dangerous and undesirable.

(c) Elements of the plan should generally coincide with those of the profile not only with respect to length, but also with respect to location. The rule suggested by

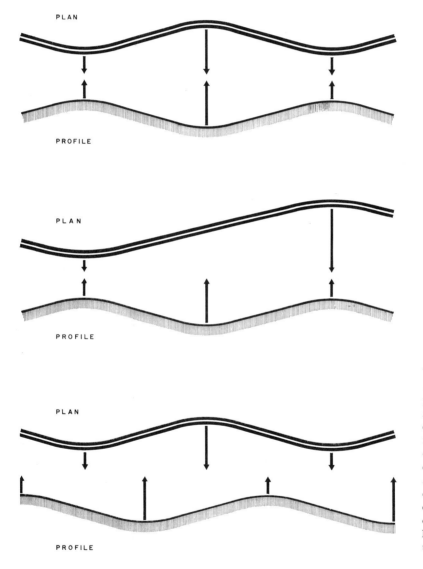

The classic case of coordination between vertical and horizontal alignment: the vertices of horizontal and vertical curves coincide, creating a rich effect of three-dimensional S-curves, composed of convex and concave helixes.

A legitimate case of coordination: one phase is skipped in the horizontal plane, but vertices still coincide. The long tangent in plan is softened by vertical curvature.

Weak coordination: vertical alignment is shifted half a phase with respect to horizontal alignment, vertices coincide with points of inflection. Note that superelevation in this case occurs on grade, while crests and sags have normal crowned section; in the first case, superelevation occurs on crests and sags, while grades have normal crowned section.

Hans Lorenz is that the vertex or turning point of a vertical curve should coincide roughly with the vertex of the horizontal curve. At times the vertices may be shifted as much as one-quarter of a phase, but a shift of one-half a phase results in an ugly situation where the vertical curve lies at the beginning of the horizontal curve, creating the impression of a sharp angle. This effect can be ameliorated, as Hugo Koester points out, with the use of very generous radii and with spiral transitions in the horizontal plane.

(d) The three rules above seem to suggest a fourth, generalized one, that, on a well-coordinated alignment, every movement of the vehicle along a foreseeable section of the paved ribbon should be subject to description in one unequivocal three-dimensional term, and should not consist of a series of small movements within a large one. One hesitates to suggest any standards for "*maximum* sight distance," but the term may nevertheless be a useful one.

The point is that a classic case of malcoordination between vertical and horizontal alignment is the rhythm of crests and sags on a tangent, allowing the driver to see the road appear and disappear in front of him for quite a distance. Many arguments have been raised against this "hidden dip" or "rollercoaster" profile, which does not prevent it from being built on supposedly modern freeways, from Oregon to North Carolina. The remedy for the "rollercoaster" is, of course, if the hills should not be leveled, to introduce some horizontal curvature, which will prevent the crest-after-the-next-one from being seen. In effect, this means setting a limit on sight distance, so that the driver can concentrate visually on the movement he is about to perform now. This increases attention and anticipation, which are indispensable to esthetic enjoyment.

One could go into other, more subtle aspects of coordination between plan and profile, and discuss the curious optical effects that arise from certain combinations of vertical and horizontal curvature, where dips look like turns or vice versa. But not all of these are yet well explored and understood, and a deeper investigation should be properly the subject of a more specialized study. For our purpose, the four principles of coordination, set forth above, cover fairly completely the most obvious situations.

A typical case of poorly coordinated alignment: the horizontal curve performs a sweeping turn (5,500 feet long) while the vertical alignment jumps nervously up and down (vertical curves 400 to 500 feet long). Note how the freeway appears to be a foreign body in the landscape.

Another frequent condition: short sag at the beginning of a major horizontal curve; the abrupt transition from straight line to curve is accentuated in perspective and an unpleasant "sideways turn" effect results.

It is quite clear that a dignified design of a free-flowing, continuous, and well-coordinated alignment cannot happen by chance—it requires thorough preliminary study from the visual, and not merely the functional, viewpoint. Strangely enough, even such a simple device as the perspective drawing has found little application in highway design. The perspectives employed are usually impressionistic drawings or photo-montages used exclusively for public relations, not for technical studies. They are not precise enough to reveal the subtleties of alignment. As an alternative, some 25 years ago, Victor von Ranke developed a mathematically accurate and quite simple method of foreshortened perspective construction, by means of which fairly long sections of alignment can be studied graphically.*

* Victor von Ranke: *Perspektive im Ingenieurbau insbesondere im Strassenbau*. Bauverlag Gmbh, Wiesbaden, 1956. 141 pages.

Visually disjointed arcs and tangents (*above*) versus a continuous, coordinated ribbon (*below*).

The $\frac{1}{R}$ diagram, which we have mentioned earlier, used in conjunction with the profile, is another very useful method of study. The experienced designer can visualize from it certain recurrent situations, and the less familiar ones can be singled out for study in perspective. Complicated or otherwise visually critical sections of freeways, particularly in urban areas, definitely warrant study in model form. So far, these have not been very widely used, either. A state design engineer is reported to have remarked: "Hell, models are too much trouble. If we come to a difficult three-dimensional curve, we take a sheet of paper, bend it like this, look at it, and if it looks right, go ahead and do it." Much more reliable representation can, of course, be achieved with large-scale paper or clay models, where details like superelevation can be precisely represented and photographed. Experiments which have been undertaken at MIT involve taking movies of a model with a camera mounted on rollers to simulate the position of the vehicle. Though some of these methods may be costly and time-consuming initially, a backlog of prototype situations can be built up with their help, to be referred to when comparable conditions arise. On the whole, three-dimensional study methods can hardly be dispensed with, if the esthetic significance of the highway is to be recognized.

HARMONY OF ENCLOSED AREAS

In discussing vision on freeways we have mentioned the unprecedented width of their roadbed. The stark, desertlike impact of a 120-foot-wide roadbed can be broken up and softened by independent alignment of the two roadways, separated by a wide median strip of variable width with natural growth. The AASHO Standards for the National System of Interstate and Defense Highways state that "divided highways should be designed as two separate one-way roads to take advantage of terrain and other conditions for safe and relaxed driving, economy, and pleasing appearance." The Geometric Standards of the State of New York expand on this directive by requiring that the separate roadways be placed at different levels whenever practical, that parallel roadways and hence a constant median width be avoided as "wearisome and monotonous," and that the median in rural areas be at least 36, but desirably 100 to 250 feet wide, with frequent variations. No other states have such advanced standards at present, though New Jersey has used a median up to 400 feet wide on its Garden State Parkway.

Wide medians can very well be defended on several functional grounds. Medians some 50 feet wide are desirable to minimize headlight glare. With an increase beyond that, reduction of headlight glare is not very significant. F. W. Hurd points out that an increase in median width up to 50 feet substantially reduces "crossed median" accidents and head-on collisions. Still, even 80-foot-wide medians are being crossed by cars out of control and, from the viewpoint of safety, adequate recovery distance is far superior to any existing type of physical barrier. Wide medians also appear desirable to reduce the effect of heavy volumes on lateral vehicle placement, and generally lessen the psychological strain produced by oncoming traffic. Wide medians can reduce the amount of earthwork during construction, thus permitting a much better landscape fit and minimizing the cost of the freeway where land is cheap.

Variation in width does not necessarily occur on wide medians—sometimes restricted conditions make it necessary to reduce, let us say, a 24-foot traversible median down to a six-foot paved strip with a guide rail barrier. Esthetically, any change in the width of the median presents a somewhat ticklish situation which can look either the world's best or the world's worst. The driver is insistently aware of the shape of the area enclosed by the two roadways as it appears in perspective, and hence these shapes have to be thoughtfully studied and designed.

The first rule that could be suggested from the visual standpoint is that medians which are not much wider than the one-way pavement and its shoulder (say 36 feet) should never be narrowed except at the entrance to large urban areas. Though a constant median may be a little monotonous, it invariably looks right as long as the two roadways appear to belong together. When entering a bridge, the visually correct solution is to carry the two roadways on a pair of parallel bridges, and not squeeze them together on one, if the median cannot be economically carried across the bridge.

There is no objection to widening a narrow median, if several other rules are adhered to. The widening, no matter how gradual, should never occur on a tangent. The place to change the width of the median is the horizontal curve. It permits widening—or, if need be, narrowing—the median in an elegant sweep. When differences in grade are involved, the vertical separation of the roadways should be commenced and terminated unobtrusively at a sag or a crest curve common to both roadways. The widening of the median and the vertical separation, if any, of the roadways should be sufficiently long to be visually meaningful.

Even a modest widening of the median in a curve, which preserves the original tree growth, is a welcome relief on the freeway; but sections like this one near Cleveland on the Ohio Turnpike are still an exception rather than the rule.

When the median divider becomes wider than the one-way roadways that enclose it, the freeway no longer reads as a divided band, but rather as two separate bands, loosely belonging together. In this case, parallel alignment loses its justification, and

A wide median and independent roadways are of little esthetic value when the alignment of the roadways is discontinuous and the grading does not blend with the topography. Merely separating the freeway lanes from each other does not automatically produce a good-looking road.

The George Washington Parkway (*above*) and the Baltimore–Washington Parkway (*below*) show a superb handling of the variable median, achieved by a carefully studied interplay of two curvilinear roadways.

Successful handling of a variable median on the Palisades Interstate Parkway: (*above*) at the Bardonia interchange; (*below*) approaching a stream in the Bear Mountains.

a freely varying median is the solution. While constant median width begins to look arbitrary and in conflict with the landscape, the importance of horizontal curves for achieving changes in median width still remains fully intact, as does the need for some coincidence of vertical curves on the two roadways. The need for some awareness of one roadway in relation to the other also remains, lest one roadway begin to look as though it has lost its companion and has started to wander aimlessly in the landscape. Other than that, possibilities for enclosing different shapes by the twin ribbons as seen in perspective become so rich and varied that no real rules can be formulated. We enter the realm of purely esthetic expression, where only the designer's intuition, experience and careful perspective studies will lead us to harmonious proportions and pleasant shapes.

Refined functional beauty of the alignment, following the principles of continuity and harmony, undoubtedly results in greater safety. It is, of course, not easy to prove this proposition statistically, because of the complex nature of accident causation and of insufficient data. Nevertheless, the following table, intended merely as an illustration, is quite revealing.

NAME OF FREEWAY	1957–58 FATALITIES PER 100 MILLION VEHICLE MILES	ESTHETIC CHARACTER	OTHER PERTINENT FEATURES
Garden State Parkway	1.15	Excellent	Passenger cars only
New York Thruway	1.40	Good	
Maine Turnpike	1.85	Monotonous	
Taconic Parkway (divided part)	1.90	Excellent	Passenger cars only
New Jersey Turnpike	2.20	Monotonous	
Merritt Parkway	2.50	Good	Obsolete design, passenger cars only
Ohio Turnpike	3.15	Fairly good	
Massachusetts Turnpike	3.25	Fairly good	
Florida Turnpike	3.30	Monotonous	
Indiana Turnpike	3.60	Monotonous	
Pennsylvania Turnpike	4.70	Monotonous	Narrow median
Oklahoma Turnpike	6.25	Monotonous	
Kansas Turnpike	7.00	Monotonous	

To establish a conclusive proof of the relationship between the visual qualities of the alignment and accidents or fatalities, it would be necessary to isolate the esthetic factor by eliminating influences such as traffic volume and traffic stream characteristics, manner of operation, degree of law enforcement, and technical design faults. Moreover, it would be necessary to establish objective, quantitative criteria of the visual character of the alignment. This seems quite possible. For example, one could establish an index of "curvilinear continuity" by dividing the proportion of the road that is on curves by the number of curves. A completely straight alignment would have the index zero, but one with many short curves would also have a low index.*

* Characteristic indices (per cent of curvilinear alignment per curve for 10-mile sections of highway) are as follows: Merritt Parkway, 1.0 (long tangents, short curves); Connecticut Turnpike, 2.1 (long tangents, short curves); Hutchinson River Parkway, ca. 3.0 (continuous curvature, but short radii); N.Y. Thruway, 4.4 (long curves, short tangents); Baltimore-Washington Parkway, 5.3 (long curves, short tangents with spirals); Aschaffenburg-Nürnberg *Autobahn,* 11.1 (continuous curvilinear alignment with spirals).

A point-marking system could be devised for such things as grading standards or cross-section design. If it is necessary to prove that beauty can pay off, such computation would seem quite worthwhile.

3. The External Harmony of the Freeway

The eye of the moving observer inevitably relates the unfolding three-dimensional ribbon of pavement to the landscape to which it clings. Though the roadside may occupy only a fraction of the driver's visual field at high speeds, this fraction is important because of its heterogeneity. The sky above is relatively uniform. The eye focuses on the road and flows along with the uniform flow of parallel lines. It is the roadside, entering from the periphery of vision, which causes a kind of visual friction by intruding into the quiet universe of highway slab and sky. Whether this friction is annoying or enjoyable depends on the relationship of the highway to its environment. Moreover, the freeway does not belong to the road-user exclusively—it strongly affects everybody in its surroundings. Hence, not only from the economic but also from the esthetic standpoint, we must evaluate "road-user" as well as "non-user" benefits and losses.

INTEGRATION WITH THE MACRO-ENVIRONMENT

A freeway cannot be esthetically satisfying unless it is designed to belong where it is put, and not to look like a foreign body in the landscape or city-scape. To give the freeway a sense of permanence and belonging, the planner must sense a relevant order in its environment, and inscribe the new element into the existing order. If the freeway itself establishes by far the dominant order, existing patterns in its neighborhood must be modified to respect the freeway.

THE NATURAL ORDER

The most frequent order in the environment is that of the terrain, as it was molded by geological forces. Though seemingly erratic, the geometry of the terrain possesses an inner logic which offers many avenues for alignment location. A freeway can follow swales, valleys and rivers in the most natural and poetic way, as many old and new roads in America do. Or, alternatively, it can follow ridges, watersheds, and plateaus, crossing valleys on tall viaducts. The latter approach has been employed on many freeways in Europe. Both have validity—the former offers the driver a sense of security and enclosure, the latter treats him to vistas and the thrill of soaring high over the obstacles of the world.

Rivers, lakefronts, valleys, and strong hillsides definitely demand that the highway be placed in a parallel relationship, reinforcing the existing situation. If a watercourse has to be crossed, on the other hand, this should occur, visually, at the narrowest spot and in the shortest possible, that is, perpendicular, distance. The crossing of substantial watercourses at an oblique angle or in a wide spot appears arbitrary and hence ugly.

Ridges can also be paralleled, but more often they have to be crossed. Unless it is done in a tunnel, the crossing of ridges should never be perpendicular. Instead of cutting the hill on a straight line, the correctly placed road should swing sideways at an oblique angle and in a gradual, sweeping curve seek out a saddle in the ridge, then deepen the natural saddle, if necessary. An undulating or nearly flat and not very directional topography leaves a great deal of freedom for location. But still greater

The highway encounters a stream: the imaginative approach.

Integration with the landscape: Massachusetts Turnpike along Greenwater Lake.

Integration with the landscape: New York Thruway along the Mohawk River.

Integration with the landscape: Northern State Parkway ascends a hill and enters a forest on a gentle S-curve, firmly hugging the land form.

subtlety is required in sensing and exploiting even slight changes in the sculptural order of the landscape to relate the freeway to them, and not to cut across them indiscriminately.

One must also remember that the freeway possesses great visual strength, which does not tolerate a petty and timid adjustment to every minor element in the topog-

Lack of integration with the landscape.

The ultimate harmony of art and nature: Taconic State Parkway.

raphy. The paved ribbon should neither destroy the landscape nor be hidden in the landscape. Rather, it should accentuate its character by a firm, yet sensitive, alignment. In addition to the usual questions about proper land-use relationship, the questions to be asked about how the freeway relates to the landscape are somewhat like these: Does it flow along the river smoothly, hug the slope naturally, climb the hill in a convincing way? Does it grasp the mountain firmly, jump the valley decisively? Or does it, on the contrary, climb a ridge needlessly, descend into a valley thoughtlessly, violate a lake brutally, cut up the landscape violently? Or is it simply trite?

Whatever the relationship, it must be visually conclusive—the road must be *here*—rather than arbitrary, when it could with equal success be here *or* there.

The passage of a highway through forest is not dissimilar from passage through hills. A straight slash is harsh and unsympathetic. By winding the freeway through the forest, visual continuity is preserved, and the driver can constantly enjoy the winding wall of trees from new angles.

Integration with the natural order involves not only the formal but also the structural order of the landscape. The action of sun, wind, and water has sculptured the surface of the earth into very definite patterns, determined by the laws of physics to a very subtle point. Any ignorant and arbitrary intrusion of man into this realm tends to be rectified by nature. Surface drainage is one such highly complex phenomenon, where every unenlightened interference with the nature's own ways often becomes not only ugly but hazardous and expensive. Streams of water should be tinkered with as little as possible, and a sufficient buffer zone should be left between them and the road to permit them to operate in their own way and to allow the vegetation along them to be preserved. A violated brook can take revenge.

Natural rock strata are always to be considered and used to the best visual advantage in rock cuts. Exposed rock formations give the driver the same sense of reality and permanence that exposed structure can give the observer of architecture. Besides, driving through a succession of rock cuts can become the experience of a living geological museum, sharpening a person's awareness of how his planet was built. Rock carefully cut along natural strata and natural faults can bring forth the most exciting sculptural forms, aside from eliminating "fallen rock zones." In finishing such rock cuts, the contractor with the pneumatic drill should be assisted by an expert geologist and a sculptor.

The language of rock formations along a freeway.

Man-Made Order

The most insistent man-made order in the macro-landscape is the pattern of streets and roads. Whenever a street pattern is regular and dense, it is imperative to tie in the freeway so that it runs parallel or perpendicular to the dominant pattern. Crossing a gridiron street pattern with a freeway diagonally or, worse yet, on a curve, is extremely disturbing. Frequent crossovers and underpasses at oblique angles to the

The alignment respects the order of the street pattern, but curves at the ends begin to create visual conflicts.

Winding the freeway through a rectilinear street grid creates numerous visual difficulties; a completely straight alignment may seem preferable in such a case.

An attempt to frame the order of secondary streets to fit the order of the freeway: Alameda County, Cal.

center line are most annoying, and so are odd-shaped or triangular lots created by the intersection of a curving or diagonal freeway with a gridiron street system. Also, when leaving the freeway, the driver is very likely to lose orientation, since he cannot mentally relate the direction of the freeway to that of the surrounding streets. In sparsely settled areas, however, isolated and widely spaced oblique crossings of the freeway are not objectionable and can, on the contrary, add to it an air of dynamic excitement.

A regular, rectilinear street grid paralleled by the freeway results in unobtrusive, perpendicular overpasses at regular intervals.

Closely spaced, irregular overpasses going in all directions can effectively ruin the visual space of the freeway.

An imaginative integration of the freeway with the topography under congested urban conditions; to the right are waterfront piers: Interstate 278 in Brooklyn, N.Y.

Another strong man-made order in the landscape is that of the railroad. Again, to arrive at a conclusive relationship parallelism or perpendicularity is almost essential. Odd angular or irregular spaces left between railroad and freeway are most unsatisfactory both from the viewpoint of esthetics and land-use planning. Though proximity between freeway and railroad in built-up areas can be a cheaper solution because of depressed land values, it poses difficult esthetic problems at interchanges. From a purely ideal viewpoint, unless it is possible to integrate railroad and freeway in one, or almost one, physical body (c.f., elevated structure, or tracks in the median strip), or unless the space between railroad and freeway can be made dominant by accommodating a natural feature, such as a stream, a wide separation of railroad and freeway is desirable. The reason is their visual competition, and the fact that freeway interchanges and the different curvature requirements of railroad and freeway produce bulges and annoying odd spaces between the two. Unless the wide separation is ruled out by some strong considerations of the total architecture of the urban landscape, the distance of some 2,000 feet, suggested as desirable by the National Industrial Zoning Committee, may be as good as any. The strongest objection should be raised against any freeway jumping back and forth across railroad tracks. Violence is done to the inherent order of both, and the result is a visual mess of huge, clumsy viaducts rising and falling at oblique angles that, to say the least, is poor public relations for the Highway Department.

Examples of the freeway in harmony and in conflict with a rail line.

Somewhat related to the problem of the railroad is that of other industrial transmission systems, involving substantial rights-of-way or physical plants. Gas and oil
pipelines, with their easements and clearings, are quite prominent in a wooded landscape. Their accommodation on a right-of-way parallel and adjacent to the freeway
(such as has been tried in Westchester County) seems a satisfactory solution esthetically, and efficient in terms of land use. Large power transmission lines, on the contrary, seem overpowering and distracting when they parallel a highway. Their presence in a parallel position resembles that of a fence, destroying the continuity of
space. Similarly, hitting a high-tension line head-on, as it were, when it crosses the
freeway perpendicularly is somewhat painful. An angular relationship of a high-
tension line and a freeway seems most satisfactory since, because of the large scale involved, a dynamic effect of floating through space results. And, in fact, the independence of high-tension lines from the predominant direction of transportation channels
makes angular crossings of freeway and power line a prevalent condition.

The relationship between the paved ribbon and buildings outside the right-of-way
is not simple. Long, low buildings close to the road look best when parallel. Walls
at right angles are much better seen, but they can be too harsh, and their screening with planting can be advantageous. Angular relationships between the paved
ribbon and nearby buildings, though more difficult than parallel ones, can sometimes
work out well if the distance from the road is sufficiently large and if the building
reads as a freely floating element, related to its site, but independent of the freeway,
preferably on elevated ground. The relationship of tall urban structures to the freeway should be the subject of a separate study, since here we are not primarily concerned with high-density urban situations.

SOME PLANNING PRINCIPLES

Our main point in discussing the relationship of the freeway to an urbanized landscape is the same as for the countryside: it must not be visually arbitrary. It must
visibly become an integral part of a visible pattern, simple, generous, and strong. The
scale of the freeway is so huge and its visual direction so powerful that it cannot be
pushed around and twisted by miscellaneous urban obstacles.

This visual respect for the freeway is something few planners and even fewer lay-
men have, trying as they do to keep the road out of somebody's backyard. The chaotic
relationship of many of our freeways to their urban environment is a direct out-
growth of our planning practices. Thus, when a new freeway is conceived, a line is
usually put on paper: picking up a heavily traveled street here, missing some existing
buildings there, following the invisible desire lines of existing traffic for maximum
use, and evading some likewise invisible property lines of existing real estate for
minimum cost.

Yet a freeway is, first of all, not a line, just as a building is not a dot. It is a band
100, 300, perhaps 500 feet wide, a space in fact which may be as wide as the eye can
see. Second, close adherence to desire lines on an urban scale, when we are talking

about moving the freeway a fraction of mile right or left, is marginal. Third, the street pattern is historically far more permanent that that of the buildings. Today, it happens that a freeway is bent out of its way to miss a supposedly important building which, three years later, is pulled down anyway as part of private or public redevelopment. The obstacle is gone but the detour will remain for decades, promising to make the freeway obsolete functionally long before it becomes obsolete structurally.

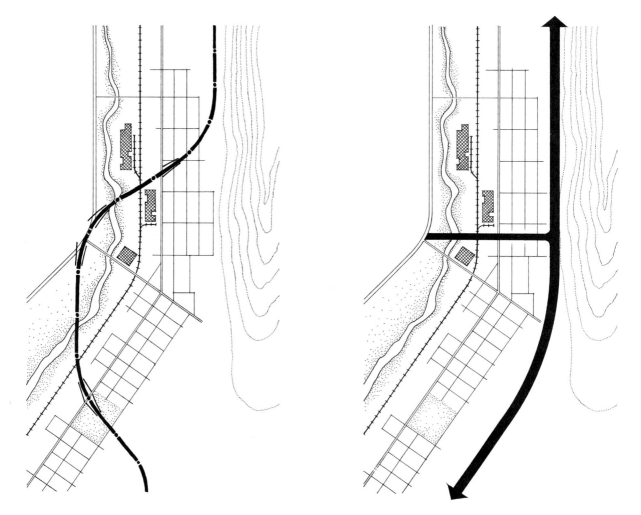

The freeway conceived of as a line (*left*). The freeway conceived of as a space (*right*).

In locating new freeways, we deal essentially with three sets of considerations: traffic planning, land use planning, and their visual or physical synthesis. Since the former two influence the latter decisively, we may briefly restate their underlying principles.

From the standpoint of traffic planning, a freeway is an artery for moving people and goods. Hence, it should be located where people want to go. The traffic planner connects the origins and destinations of all present and estimated future trips in an area with straight lines called desire lines, groups these into clusters or "traffic corridors," and then assigns the resulting estimated traffic volumes to the existing and the planned traffic facilities in the area. The estimated traffic volumes give him a clue as to what traffic capacity the new facility should have. Since most destinations are likely to be near the center of any given area of activity, the traffic planner naturally tries to locate his new facility as close to this center as possible.

A land use planner, by contrast, is primarily concerned not with traffic corridors, but with the inner organization of the areas that generate traffic, and with the relationships of these areas to each other. Recognizing the freeway as a means of communication longitudinally, he sees it as a barrier—transversely. Such a barrier disrupts the inner organization of any area of activity. Hence, a land use planner's rule is that a freeway should never cut across any homogeneous areas of activity—be they residential neighborhoods, parks, industrial areas, or business districts. One can readily see that there is some objective incompatibility between the ideal demands of traffic planning and land use planning. The city planner tries to locate the freeway as a barrier between areas of different land use, while the traffic engineer rightly argues that located outside the areas of activity the freeway will carry little traffic and be of little use.

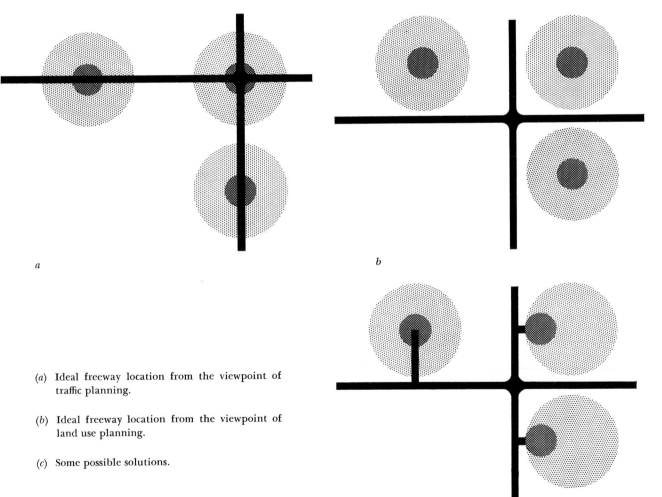

a

b

(*a*) Ideal freeway location from the viewpoint of traffic planning.

(*b*) Ideal freeway location from the viewpoint of land use planning.

(*c*) Some possible solutions.

c

There is no simple solution to the contradiction, except comprehensive thinking and esthetics. Comprehensive thinking means that the solution of traffic and land use planning problems should be vested in one mind—if not an individual mind, then a planning team. Such a team could arrive at a number of valid compromises:

Restructuring the community to fit the freeway by means of redevelopment.

Leaving the community intact, but providing new lateral feeder roads as part of the freeway improvement.

Sacrificing some parts of the community or some freeway efficiency.

Quite often, one area of present homogeneous use can be made into two areas which will survive separately; and conversely, some indirect freeway alignment may be of little practical consequence.

The question is essentially that of integration with the social environment. Parts of it can be dealt with on economic, psychological, and other scientific grounds, but ultimately, we are up against social values and, since we are dealing with physical objects, visual values. No matter what selfish motives are involved, citizen opposition to a new facility will seldom be on the grounds of efficiency unless direct financial loss is involved. It usually boils down to esthetic judgments (nuisance or amenity), no matter how misguided they may happen to be. And, if different sets of rational criteria are in conflict, the esthetic sense of the designer offers the only ground for valid decision. Speaking in less abstract terms, with proper public relations a visually strong solution that is also sensitively worked out in detail—the freeway as an integrated thing of beauty—will have a better chance to "kindle men's hearts," enlist citizen support, and minimize the friction of the freeway with its social environment.

INTEGRATION WITH THE MICRO-ENVIRONMENT

Integration with the order of the macro-environment is very important in the overall location of the freeway, but its effect on the public is by no means immediate or obvious. The public, however, is directly aware of embankments, bridges, planting, and a multitude of other design details that the road-user can see from the window of his car, or the non-user from the window of his home. All these involve integration with the immediate or micro-environment of the freeway.

CONTINUITY OF CROSS-SECTION

Continuity is inherent in the function of the freeway, which is designed for continuous flow, in contrast, let us say, to the staccato movement of a streetcar in a downtown section, or a pedestrian in a shopping mall. Discontinuous, chopped-up space along the freeway is visually annoying, and therefore the concept of continuity applies not only longitudinally—to the plan and the profile of the road—but also applies transversely—to its cross-section. Visual continuity of the paved ribbon with the adjacent grass surfaces of the roadside is one of the most obvious sources of pleasure that the highway can afford. Steep embankments and side slopes, by contrast, immediately make the highway look like a foreign body in the landscape.

Though brutal 1 on 1 cuts, as in the upper view, are a thing of the past, gentle 1 on 3 or flatter slopes have not yet been generally adopted and if so, only for lower cuts and fills.

The argument for gentle slopes and a continuous cross-section is functional as well as esthetic, as is evident from two examples of landslides and erosion on a new freeway; both views show standard 1 on 2 slopes. Mechanized mowing can be performed only on slopes 1 on 3 or flatter.

To quote the 1944 Report of the National Interregional Highway Committee: "Flattened slopes of excavation and embankment and well-rounded cross-sectional contour are essential to prevent soil erosion and to minimize the risks of injury and damage when vehicles accidentally . . . leave the roadway. They are needful also to mold the highway into the terrain and to make it a harmonious feature of the natural landscape. The flattened side-slopes will favor the growth of vegetation . . . and remove the cause of much troublesome clogging of the drainage system. The easier slopes can be mowed by machine . . . and the streamlined contours of cut banks will reduce snow drifting and facilitate machine methods of snow removal. Design for utility and economy is found to go hand in hand with sound landscape design."

Though the value of flat side-slopes has thus been long recognized, and the side-slopes on American freeways are getting flatter, they still have a way to go. Desirable side-slopes depend, in general, on the predominant steepness of natural terrain and on the height of cut or fill. In rugged, hilly terrain, when the embankments in question are perhaps several hundred feet high, nobody will advocate that embankments should be flattened beyond the angle of slope necessary for stability. Likewise, deep rock cuts naturally require steep angles. But, in gentle topography and particularly

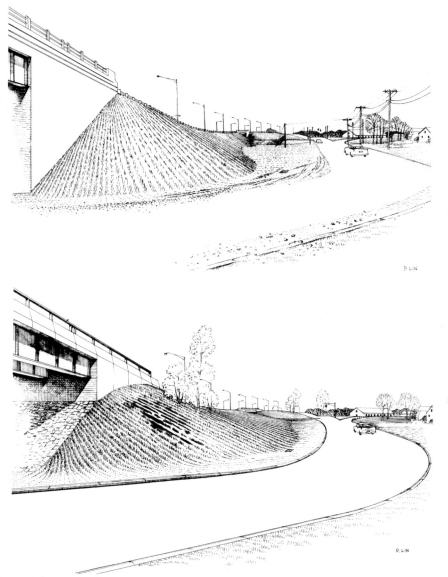

Example of a standard 1 on 2 slope on a 20-foot high embankment, which creates a gloomy wall effect and renders the extensive open space below meaningless.

Suggested improvement with a flatter slope provides continuity between the freeway and the surrounding landscape. An alternate solution could be to pack the leftover space in the upper picture with very dense planting which would obscure the embankment.

On very high cuts and fills, steep slopes cannot be objected to. The view shows the Redwood Freeway approach to the Golden Gate Bridge, here under construction (1955); the terracing prevents slides.

in suburban locations, gentle slopes on cuts and fills up to 20 or 25 feet high are a "must," esthetically. Slopes about that height are a frequent and insistent problem because 20 feet is about the vertical pavement-to-pavement distance on overpasses and underpasses. Graded to a standard 1 on 2 or 50 per cent slope, a 20-foot-high embankment looks definitely like a visual barrier, almost a wall. To blend naturally with the space of the surrounding topography, its slope should be flattened to 1 on 3 or even, if possible, 1 on 4. Though such a solution would involve 14 per cent to 28 per cent more earthwork, the added expense seems justified, since it would be limited primarily to suburban locations and areas near interchanges, where the continuity of lateral space is of the utmost importance.

On cuts and fills higher or deeper than 25 feet, one on two slopes do not seem visually objectionable, for they are in scale with the dominant dimension of the earthwork, which is expressed unequivocally as a man-made thing. But the lower the slope, the flatter it should be. Embankments up to perhaps 12 feet high or even more should be given a slope as flat as 1:4 or 1:6. In this case, it is possible to dispense with the guide rail, for cars out of control coming down such a slope will not overturn. A guide rail, besides being expensive to install and maintain, and besides doing damage to the car it prevents from running off the road, is visually objectionable as a space barrier. It negates the continuity of highway and landscape, and in cases where its installation at the outside edge of the roadway cannot be avoided, it should be as low as possible and should not obstruct lateral view. The three-cable guide rail is in this respect preferable to the solid types.

Minor cuts and fills, graded to flat slopes, can be blended into the landscape so naturally that they will not be recognized for what they are. The table below gives some of the more advanced standards for low cuts and fills on freeways. The rounding and warping of the edges of cut or filled slopes is also very important. This should be done smoothly and generously, to preserve the natural flow of the landforms, and to provide the proper drainage without erosion.

SLOPE	HEIGHT AND SITUATION	STATE OR AGENCY
1 on 6	up to 3 feet fill	State of New York
(17%)	up to 4 feet cut	State of Ohio
	up to 5 feet fill, or 3 feet cut	Garden State Parkway
	up to 8 feet fill	State of Connecticut
	up to 12 feet fill—desirable	(authors)
1 on 4	up to 5 feet cut or fill	German Federal Republic
(25%)	up to 10 feet fill	State of Ohio
	3 to 10 feet fill	State of New York
	5 to 12 feet fill, 3 to 6 feet cut	Garden State Parkway
	12 to 20 feet fill, 0 to 10 feet cut—desirable	(authors)
1 on 3	5 to 10 feet cut or fill	German Federal Republic
(33%)	8 to 12 feet cut	State of Ohio
	6 to 25 feet cut	Garden State Parkway
	10 to 25 feet cut desirable	(authors)

The AASHO Policy on Geometric Design states that "a uniform slope through a cut or fill section often results in a formal or stilted appearance. This can be softened

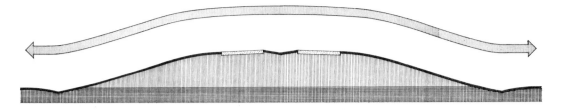

Continuity of space preserved in cross-section (*above*). Space visually chopped up (*below*).

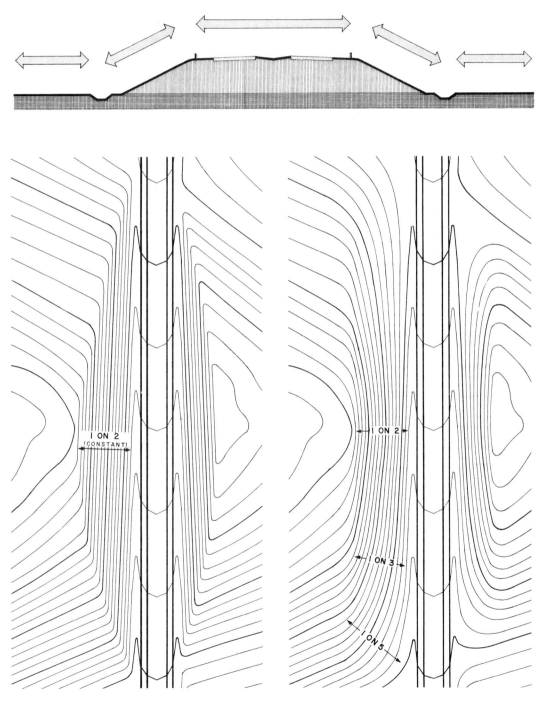

Slope treatment resulting from the application of a standard cross-section versus one worked out with a contour plan. Angle of slope is kept constant in the first case. In the second case, the width of the slope is kept constant, but its angle varies.

by flattening the slopes on the ends where cut or fill is light, and gradually steepening it toward the controlling maximum slope on the heavier portion of the cut or fill. On short cut or fill sections the result may be one of continuous longitudinal rounding, whereas on sections of substantial length the effect will be one of funneling. The transitioning of side-slopes is especially effective at ends of cuts when combined with an increased lateral offset of the drainage channel and a widened shoulder.''

Unfortunately, this authoritative advice is seldom heeded. The reason is that the somewhat complex variation of cross-section suggested is difficult to achieve, if one works merely with cross-sections, as most American highway design offices still do. Cross-sections alone are inadequate for any but the simplest topography and grading

Removing a residual piece of rock between the freeway and a natural slope can lead to smoother land-scape design and can open up vistas which are otherwise obscured.

design. For any refined sculpturing of the land masses, plans with horizontal contours have to be used. Instead of taking vertical cross-sections every 50 to 100 feet, horizontal cross-sections are employed, in this case spaced usually at two-foot intervals and represented by contours. Aside from giving superior esthetic results, this method has several technical advantages. Unless the topography is very simple, a contour map allows a much more precise determination of the amount of earthwork involved, and a much more confident drainage design; it eliminates duplication from surveying and is much simpler to work from in the field, since the contractor deals just with one basic set of plans, on which all information is included, not with three. Finally, it can be geared to electronic machine methods of computation. Its only drawback seems to be that some contractors are not accustomed to reading contour maps.

While working with cross-sections makes the engineer think necessarily in terms of digging a ditch, working with contours helps to make him think in terms of molding the landscape. Making man-made slopes conform to the character of the natural ones in the area and a liberal rounding of slope edges are automatically part of such an approach. Another part of it is not to confine excavation too closely to the standard cross-section, but occasionally go out of the way and remove mounds of earth or pieces of rock which remain sitting between the road and a natural slope. Sometimes these mounds can be improved without removal, by extensive flattening and rounding, so they will look like a small natural hill, rather than a shattered fragment, crying for compassion, of what used to be a large hill. The removal or flattening of such marginal mounds can be a substitute—though admittedly partial and sometimes more expensive—for separate borrow pits which hurt the landscape.

A very important element of integration with the landscape is highway planting. Policies on planting differ greatly between individual states. The State of New York, for example, with some of the most advanced design standards in the country, specifies that "no planting will be provided" on its Interstate System. In fact, the beautiful Taconic Parkway has very little man-placed planting along its dramatic and well-landscaped alignment. By contrast, the State of Connecticut, whose richly planted Merritt Parkway is also renowned, spent large sums of money as late as 1958 on planting the Connecticut Turnpike, establishing this operation as a major public relations effort. Aside from design philosophy, climate obviously plays an important role. The very effective planting on the slopes of some Los Angeles freeways is maintained only at the cost of continuous watering in the dry season.

It should be clear at the outset that, aside from visual appeal, planting can serve a number of functional purposes, such as erosion control, snow control, control of headlight glare, and optical guidance. Experiments with certain shrubs (Rosa multiflora) have shown that planting can be used as a deceleration barrier, to catch vehicles that have jumped the road without damaging them. Yet planting can also be a hazard: Albert Camus was one among many victims who have died when their automobiles struck a roadside tree.

Highway planting thus should not be viewed in isolation, as a nurseryman's hobby. Rather, it should help to integrate the freeway, a man-made tool that has an inherent

Lessons of the English garden landscape, applied here to create a setting for the modern freeway: a view along the Taconic Parkway in New York

functional order, with the surrounding natural order of the countryside. This can best be achieved by selective cutting and thinning of the existing growth, carefully preserving all those specimens that are visually or functionally valuable. For purely esthetic purposes man-placed planting should be used with restraint, only where indispensable for visual accent, enclosure, or relief. Of course, one can use planting to hide faulty grading or unsightly bridge abutments, but these situations should not be allowed to arise in the first place.

A nineteenth-century garden landscape: the Muskau Park on the Neisse River

In selecting plant material for the roadside, trees, shrubs, and grasses native to the area may well be used. Ornamental garden plants—unless as hardy as the common daylily of our waysides—are misplaced in the highway landscape and soon die. While shoulders, medians, and drainage areas have to be closely cropped, the native plant communities should be allowed to perpetuate or establish themselves on the remaining parts of the right-of-way, pleasing the eye with wildflowers, berry-bearing shrubs, and fall color, saving on maintenance cost and avoiding the incongruous slickness of urban-type lawns amidst fields and forests. In building up indigenous plant communities, the changed conditions have naturally to be taken into account. Quite often it can happen that trees carefully protected from heavy construction equipment have died because excavation lowered the water table or because their roots became exposed. Thus the goal should always be restoration of natural conditions, but within a new, man-made framework.

From the earlier discussion of vision it appears that individual plants on the roadside do not read as significant entities at high speeds. What is perceived are areas, textures, silhouettes, the contrast of large masses and voids, openness and enclosure, an oversized flowing assymetry of shapes, constantly changing as the driver goes by. Patrick Horsbrugh shows that there are many lessons which the highway designer can learn from the English garden landscape: casual continuity, sensitivity to land form, skillful use of existing objects, architectural as well as natural. This suggests that the grouping of trees in clumps on large open meadows, the opening of views toward lakes and streams, the use of hedges or strings of forest, are all in the nature of the highway landscape, but that symmetrical compositions are rarely compatible.

The intentions were probably monumental, but the result? Symmetrical planting on freeways.

A flat, widely open highway tends to be monotonous. Enclosure heightens interest and anticipation. It is the immediate proximity to nature that makes driving on small country roads so delightful: the feeling of foliage overhead, of grass right next to the wheels, of fields, hedges, and trees almost within reach, or, to use our statistical terms, the fact that the roadside occupies as much as 80 per cent of one's field of vision. To approach this kind of sensation on the freeway one has to bring the natural growth as close to the pavement as possible, preferably on both sides of the one-way roadway, whenever the median is wide enough.

Unfortunately, this "as close as possible" is not too close, since the shoulder and drainage swale must always be kept clear of obstructions, and sight distance may require further setbacks on curves. To prevent fatal "struck tree" accidents, large trees should be set back from the pavement perhaps as much as 80 feet in flat terrain. Such a wide swath of open land will of necessity lead to boredom, even with an interesting alignment. Looking for situations to bring large trees close to the pavement with safety we find the upward slope, where the bank of earth itself will prevent a car out of control from ascending to the trees, and where a feeling of enclosure can be created, a feeling of actually going through and under the trees. Sometimes, if an existing stand of trees looks particularly valuable, there should be no objection to protecting it with a guide rail, particularly on a downward slope. The overwhelming scale of the trees can dwarf the guide rail so that it may become fairly insignificant. The guide rail is objectionable and destroys the continuity of space when there is nothing immediately behind it, when grass continues on the other side. It is in these instances that gentle slopes should be used instead, slopes that can naturally blend into wide meadows on flat ground. We can thus arrive at a natural succession of openness and enclosure: where steepness is accentuated vertically and flatness is expanded horizontally, planting reinforces the sculpture of the terrain.

Dense stands of evergreens can shield highway neighbors from traffic noise, while protecting the traveler from the ugliness of other people's backyards. Thick hedges give excellent optical guidance on curves, and afford protection from headlight glare. Tree silhouette should be considered on hilltops, as well as the clearing of growth to open views. The clearing of undergrowth in a stand that is regular and where trees are fairly widely spaced can lead to a very pleasant continuity, in which the space of the freeway and the interior of the forest visually merge into one. In arid areas, various textural effects can be substituted for planting, such as the use of cobbles and pebbles instead of grass, as suggested by Geraldine Scott.

Opportunities for the use of artistic talent are innumerable, and perhaps the thing to guard against most is a standardized and hence half-hearted application of rules. One of these requires every bridge abutment to have its cluster of bushes. But bushes do not grow out of bridge abutments, and every once in a while it is pleasant to see an overpass without bushes around it. Another rule requires a hedge in the median on every curve, but the sight of feeble sprouts sticking out of the grass where the median is not wide enough to support a hedge is most pathetic. Mounds of earth, wooden baffles, or light steel structures of cable and wire to support creeping plants

Alternation of openness and enclosure on the Taconic Parkway.

Examples of artificial landscaping on the Merritt Parkway. The scale of the planting in this case is somewhat too small to be appreciated at high speeds; it was planned in a more leisurely era.

can be more satisfactory and more interesting solutions. In landscaping, more than in the other fields, nothing should be done with preconceived thought, and everything should grow out of the natural, technical, and visual conditions of the situation.

The Integrity of Lateral Spaces

Integration of the freeway with its immediate environment requires that the continuity of significant spaces which the highway intersects be preserved. Occasionally, of course, one wants to use the freeway as a deliberate barrier, say, between a residential and an industrial zone. But more often, it is important not to cut the existing valley, park, residential neighborhood, or industrial area into two pieces.

In rural areas, the continuity of large, open lateral spaces usually can be maintained with a sensitive development of the cross-section, by means of flat slopes, generously rounded and blending into the natural forms of the land, as previously described. Proximity of the pavement to the original level of the ground serves to make the freeway unobtrusive. But in thickly settled areas, where frequent grade-separated crossings are necessary and where there simply is not enough room for very gentle slopes on embankments, preserving the integrity of lateral space is an acute problem. Community opposition to a new freeway very often stems from its anticipated barrier effect, commonly likened to that of a "Chinese wall."

This leads us to the much belabored question of "over or under," that is, whether to carry the freeway in a cut under an existing street system or over it on a succession of embankments and bridges. From the viewpoint of the highway user, an elevated freeway is of course esthetically more desirable, because of the views it offers the traveler. But from the viewpoint of the non-user, an elevated structure, no matter how graceful, disrupts the continuity of lateral spaces if it is put into an urban, essentially pedestrian, scale. An esthetic choice has to be made, therefore, as to which space should be made dominant, and which subordinate. If the lateral spaces are of little visual value—such as in large industrial and warehousing areas—there may be little objection to an elevated design. The elevated structure can well fit the huge technological scale of gasometers, oil tanks, blast furnaces, and large plants. But in high-density urban areas, be they residential, commercial, or institutional, where the continuity and integrity of intimate pedestrian spaces is vital, an elevated freeway is out of the question.

Depressed urban freeways, esthetically least obtrusive, have also a number of functional advantages: the slopes of the cut screen traffic noise and headlight glare more effectively than any other device. Depressed design results in better traffic operation, since visibility on ramps is increased, and gravity acts *against* speed on deceleration lanes while acting *with* speed on acceleration lanes. The cost of a depressed freeway is sometimes higher because of the need to relocate utilities, but this sacrifice is usually warranted for the sake of preserving the integrity of important urban and suburban street spaces. The only real argument against depressed freeways in settled areas can be that of drainage, when the water table is high and cannot be lowered by

(*Above, left and right*) Short pieces of embankment between two bridges look incongruous and obstruct lateral space; a continuous bridge would be far superior. (*Below, left and right*) Supports should be few and widely spaced; better a few heavy piers than a forest of thin columns

gravity. One would hardly advocate the widespread operation of freeways under continuous pumping.

Evidence suggests that esthetic objections against elevated structures in relatively intimate urban spaces—the barrier effect, the obstruction of light and air, the undefined and often useless spaces below, which can be a source of nuisance—are strongly shared by the public at large. This is reflected in frequent depreciation of property values along elevated structures. The state of New Jersey found it worthwhile to commit $12,000,000 of its own funds to pay for the added cost of depressing an interstate freeway through a residential area, for which the federal government favored an elevated design.

In cases when there is no alternative to an elevated solution—visual obstruction of the lateral space, be it a valley, a park, or a street—must still be minimized, as indicated by our illustrations.

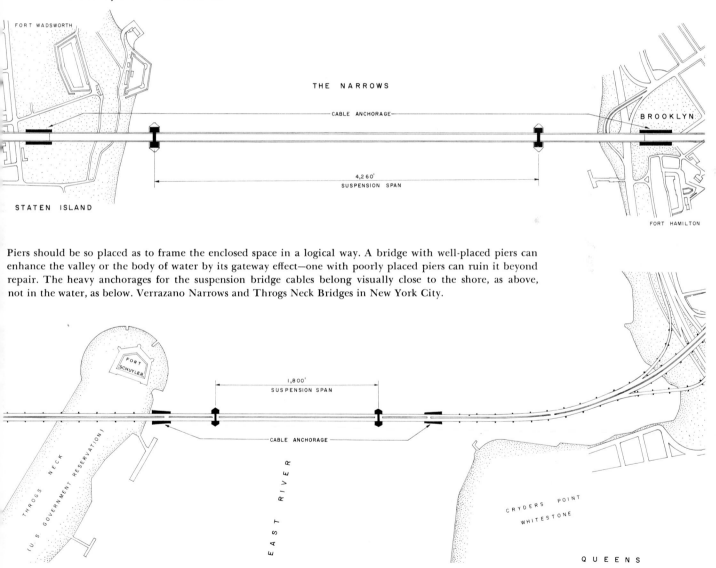

Piers should be so placed as to frame the enclosed space in a logical way. A bridge with well-placed piers can enhance the valley or the body of water by its gateway effect—one with poorly placed piers can ruin it beyond repair. The heavy anchorages for the suspension bridge cables belong visually close to the shore, as above, not in the water, as below. Verrazano Narrows and Throgs Neck Bridges in New York City.

A bridge must not interrupt the continuity of the highway ribbon. It should curve if the highway curves; it should be split if the highway is split. (*Left*) Bixby Creek Bridge, with curved roadbed and superelevation, in California; (*above*) the Mohawk River Bridge on Interstate Route 502 in New York; both are examples of successful solutions.

In general, the location which allows the bridge to be as short as possible is visually the correct one. The long drive over water on the Nyack–Tarrytown bridge (*above*), placed for administrative reasons at the widest point in the Hudson River, is visually stimulating, but the bridge by no means enhances Tappan Zee. Contrast that with the effect of the simple and unpretentious bridge over Willamette River (*below*) on Interstate Route 5 in Oregon.

The unity of the structural system must be preserved throughout the bridge. Only on very large bridges is the use of two (but not more) structural systems visually convincing—one for the approaches and one for the main span. Continuity of structure emphasizes, among other things, the continuity of the roadway. The worst offender in this case is the overhead cantilever truss—called by the famous bridge designer David B. Steinman the Ugly Duckling among bridges—more to be tolerated than admired. The cantilever arch, though usually more expensive, is a far more elegant solution for comparable span conditions, as evidenced by these photographs.

One must realize that these esthetic principles do not always go hand in hand with the cheapest solution. In particular, structural economy does not always mean financial economy. A clumsy design that uses more steel than necessary may be cheaper to calculate and to erect than a sophisticated design. Many short spans are usually cheaper than a few long spans, since a column is the cheapest thing to build, a span the most expensive. Likewise, an earth embankment is usually cheaper than a viaduct. To build a long bridge consisting of a hodgepodge of every structural system in the book—girder, truss, cantilever, suspension span—may be cheaper than to stick to the dignity of one structural system throughout. But the result is visually disastrous. In functional design, engineers have long decided in favor of the best solution, rather than the cheapest one. Why not so in visual design?

DEFINITION OF ELEMENTS

Within an overall, flowing continuity of the longitudinal and lateral spaces of the freeway, separate physical elements have to be sharply defined or articulated, to give, by means of contrast, a clear structure to the visual environment. Continuity of space should not be confused with fuzzy and undefined transitions between elements, such as a dirty border where macadam gradually blends with a grass shoulder. Such a condition can be picturesque on a haphazardly aligned country road, but it cannot be tolerated on the precision-conscious multilane freeway.

ARTICULATION IN THE MICRO-LANDSCAPE

On the micro-scale, articulation starts with a clear definition of the component parts of the freeway, namely the pavement slab, the shoulder, the median divider, the side slopes, and accessory structures, such as overpasses and retaining walls. The need for clean definition is by no means purely esthetic; it is of paramount functional importance, for the driver's first task is to identify his road surface and avoid striking other objects. To provide the needed definition, the designer can use color, texture, and relief.

The first to be defined is, of course, the pavement slab. It must stand out clearly against the background of the adjacent surfaces and be sharply delineated, so that its edges are obvious day and night, in good and bad weather. The shoulder should read in strong contrast to the traveled way, as a safety and emergency area not to be used as a traffic lane. Acceleration and deceleration lanes must, again, be sharply articulated as separate entities.

Perhaps the most common, yet the worst imaginable way to articulate these elements is to pave the traveled way, the shoulder and the entrance and exit lanes with the same type of asphalt surface, and then paint on it various stripes—solid white, dashed white, or yellow. When the paint begins to fade and the edges of the macadam begin to crumble, "articulation" is complete. Even elaborate signs saying in effect, "the right lane is not a lane but the shoulder," do not help. Desirably, the articulation must, of course, be built structurally into the pavement.

An example of a convincing way to define the travel path is the broad, white, mountable curb, corrugated if necessary. It provides contrast in texture, contrast in relief (since it is raised), contrast in color (if the pavement has a darker shade), and gives a very precise definition to the grass edge. The shoulder beyond such a curb can be asphalt—it will never be confused with a travel lane. Unfortunately, curbs conflict with drainage requirements on freeways, and flat pavement cross-sections are in predominant use today. This does not mean that built-in demarcation of the pavement is precluded.

A very satisfactory solution has been adopted in West Germany. Two strips of highly reflective white concrete, each about two feet wide, are laid on the base course and the asphalt pavement is placed between them. They are flush with the pavement, yet they give the traveled lanes a very clear definition. Unlike the narrow painted white lines, proper to city streets, they are in scale with the freeway. The shoulder, if paved, is in turn delimited by a flush stone border, which permits drainage yet prevents crumbling at the edges.

Non-roadway areas, such as narrow medians, traffic control islands, or shoulders in selected locations provide many opportunities for a visually interesting treatment contrasting with the pavement. Here, texture- or color-rich materials, such as granite block, brick, various types of slag block, perforated block, or corrugated concrete can provide welcome relief. For there is hardly anything drearier than a narrow median, paved with the same material as the travel lane.

The restful color and soft texture of grass contrast excellently with the pavement, and make grass visually the best material for shoulders. It has been shown that if shoulder use is not too frequent and the climate not arid, turf can be established and maintained on soil-aggregate materials compacted for stability and having considerable shear value. Unseeded and unpaved shoulders, made simply of gravel and soil, are visually most objectionable. Their dusty, ragged, trash-collecting edges are the antithesis of articulation.

A sea of asphalt—no articulation except by paint.

Attempts at articulation through texture and materials.

If the current selection of materials does not leave enough room for a rich and visually convincing definition of highway elements, this should be a reason for more experiment and research in the building materials and highway accessories industries. Essentially, one would like to get rid of applied paint, of delineating reflectors perched on metal sticks along the road, and even of lamp posts which confuse the visual space of the freeway: a less obtrusive method of illumination ought to be invented. Meanwhile, the standard shapes of lamp posts could be made more elegant.

Low-level lighting fixtures built into the railing of the Manahawkin Bay Bridge in New Jersey. Developed for better illumination in fog, t̲ device has considerable esthetic potential, since there are no poles to destroy the visual continuity of the bridge.

An important problem of articulation is presented by overpass structures. Adequate setbacks are required to let these structures read as clean, precisely defined elements with an existence of their own, set clearly apart both from the highway slab and from the flow of the surrounding landscape. Fortunately, research has established that objects too close to the roadway cause lateral displacement of vehicles, since drivers shy away from them. This led to the design of open structures with an unobstructed view, letting through not merely the roadway, but the entire space confined by it and the side slopes. Even though this results in considerably higher cost per structure, the open design is now generally adopted.

The construction of overpasses should be desirably standardized and their silhouette made as thin as possible, so that they give, as Sylvia Crowe put it, "the minimum sense of interruption to the road." Overpasses on freeways are so frequent and repetitive that the less they are noticed the better. In this, they differ from large

The open design of overpasses (like the above on the Massachusetts Turnpike) would have been considered extravagant 20 years ago. The bridge is almost three times as long as would be needed merely to span the roadway. Yet the design provides, psychologically, for an unobstructed flow of space. The articulation between the bridge and the natural rock formation is most sensitive. Had the abutment been perched on the edge of the rock, an unsightly conflict would have resulted.

bridges, which cannot help being landmarks. Any attempt at applied ornamentation —apart from interesting surface treatment—is incongruous and distracting. Often repeated, it can become a visual disaster.

The color of the paint is an important point to consider on steel elements in bridges, as well as on other accessory steel structures. Highly reflective colors such as aluminum look very distracting, very dark colors look harsh and somber. Green is much more sympathetic, though the possibility of using primary colors such as red and yellow should not be ruled out. Fortunately, the use of pastel shades has not been tried on highway structures so far.

Unusual overpass designs, even if successful such as the above bridge near Wuppertal, should be the exception rather than the rule. They can serve as isolated accents or landmarks, but a quick succession of diverse shapes can easily result in chaos.

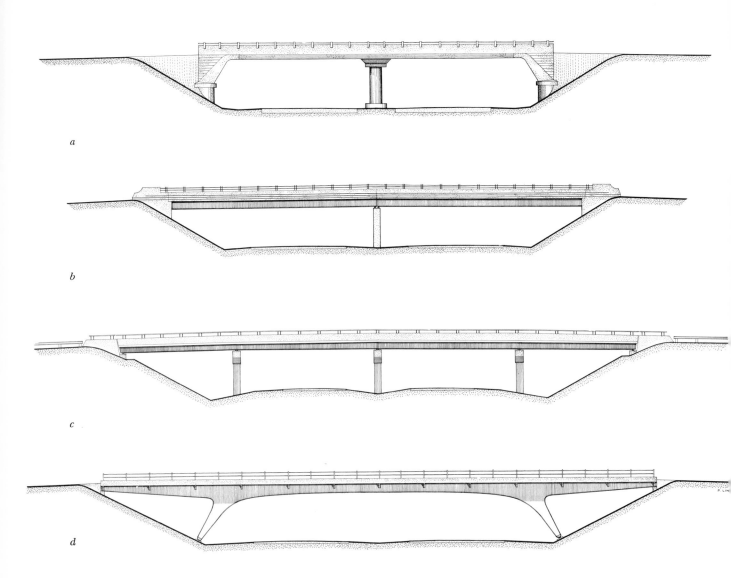

Four standard overpass designs: (*a*) London–Birmingham Motorway (1957), (*b*) Connecticut Turnpike (1957), (*c*) Maine Turnpike (1948), and (*d*) an award-winning design from a competition by the American Institute of Steel Construction, using high-strength steel (1960). The lighter and cleaner the silhouette, the better the design. The complicated formwork of the British motorway design appears anachronistic.

The lightness of silhouette is important not only from the viewpoint of those traveling under the overpass. A heavy parapet, which contributes a great deal to clumsiness, is objectionable from the point of view of those traveling on the bridge. On small or large bridges, heavy railings and parapets restrict the traveler's field of vision precisely where, in the nature of the case, it should be expanded. The driver—unless he is driving a bus or a truck—is robbed of some of the most breathtaking panoramas, of the excitement of floating high over cities or rivers. With all the proper respect for withstanding possible lateral impact loads from trucks about to jump from the bridge, the railings should be designed for maximum visibility. With the driver's eye level 4 feet or less above pavement in modern automobiles, the concrete parapet should not be higher than 2 feet. A completely open steel railing sufficiently strong to withstand lateral impact is preferable, of course.

(*Opposite page*) Sections through typical bridge railings on freeways in New York, California, New Jersey, and Connecticut. Visibility is calculated on the basis of what the driver would see under the horizon line if there were no railing. Railings have to withstand high lateral impact loads from cars out of control, and it can be seen that the transparency of a railing is inversely related to its resistance to lateral loads. But more effort is needed to design a railing with high visibility which would still be able to withstand lateral loads substantially in excess of the required minimum. See also the design on page 249.

NEW YORK

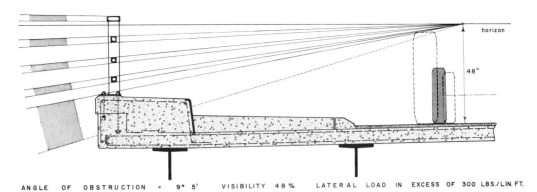

ANGLE OF OBSTRUCTION = 9° 5'   VISIBILITY 48%   LATERAL LOAD IN EXCESS OF 300 LBS./LIN. FT.

CALIFORNIA

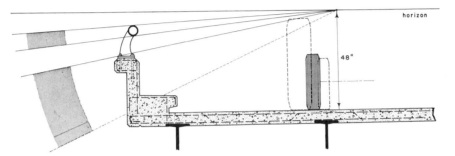

ANGLE OF OBSTRUCTION = 18° 10'   VISIBILITY 38%   LATERAL LOAD IN EXCESS OF 300 LBS./LIN. FT.

NEW JERSEY

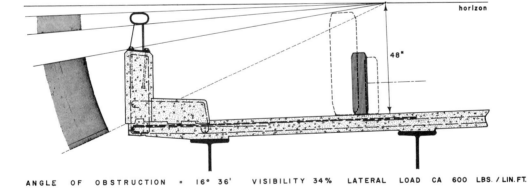

ANGLE OF OBSTRUCTION = 16° 36'   VISIBILITY 34%   LATERAL LOAD CA 600 LBS. / LIN. FT.

CONNECTICUT

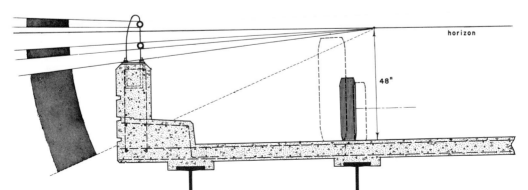

ANGLE OF OBSTRUCTION = 19° 36'   VISIBILITY 25%   LATERAL LOAD CA 1000 LBS. / LIN. FT.

Articulation of bridge supports on overpasses is likewise important: the visual obstruction they present when seen from an oblique angle should be minimized. The supports should let the bridge read as a light and airy overpass, not a dark basement that the car has to enter every now and then. Existing designs usually take four characteristic shapes:

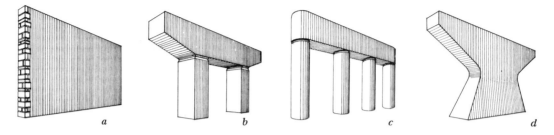

a   *b*   *c*   *d*

(*a*) Thin wall; (*b*) bent with square columns; (*c*) bent with round columns; (*d*) T-type cantilevered support.

Type *a* is suitable for flat arches cast integrally with the wall; otherwise it appears too restrictive of sight. Type *b* is satisfactory, if the number of columns is kept to a minimum. Cantilevering the ends of the bent, as in the picture above, is very successful in this respect. It also creates a dynamic feeling and interesting shadow effects. Type *c* is popular since round columns are cheap (cardboard pipe formwork) and produce slightly less visual obstruction than square ones. But the rectilinear beam which the columns carry can be visually in conflict with them, even if cantilevered. Without cantilever, the support looks static and uninteresting, and too many round columns are no better than too many square ones. Though fairly heavy in cross section, type *d* does not present the busy pattern of multicolumn bents, and has so far offered some of the most pleasing solutions for perpendicular as well as skewed overpasses.

The involved overpass system of a multi-level interchange can best be carried by round columns, to minimize visual constriction and confusion, so long as the bridge decks are designed as plates.

The special place for the single round column is an overpass crossing a freeway on a very skewed angle. Being nondirectional, it quiets the sharp conflict with the square abutments. If the overpass is long enough to need several supports, the single round column can be used with great visual advantage.

Openness (*above*) versus enclosure (*below*): the feeling of descending into a dark basement when entering an underpass should be minimized.

Attention to articulation in bridge detailing should go fairly far, to insure a consistent architectural expression of construction joints, expansion joints, form imprints, and so on. Today it frequently happens that a meaningless ornamental shadow line appears in one place and the construction joint it could have matched is a foot away. Since the facing of concrete with natural stone is expensive and restricted to special urban or parkway locations, attention should be paid to developing richer concrete surfaces. The rubbed finish, commonly employed, deprives the concrete surface of whatever character it had when it came out of the forms. A negative esthetic result is achieved at great expense. When metal or some other uninteresting formwork is used, the concrete should either be left as is (after obvious faults have been repaired) or else given a sandblasted or other tooled finish, to bring out the pattern of exposed aggregate. Alternatively, narrow wood planking or other interesting formwork can be used to produce a rich pattern of form imprints; no finish is necessary in this case.

A superior bridge railing design, with horizontal members inclined at different degrees to permit maximum view; the design was discontinued by the State of Connecticut in favor of the heavy railing shown on page 245.

Two situations showing cleanly articulated design (*upper photos*) versus meaningless attempts at ornamentation (*lower photos*). Both esthetics and economics have suffered.

(*opposite page*) A rich surface created by the form imprint of narrow vertical wood planks.

A final note on the articulation of structure must concern retaining walls. They are often another example of confused transition between natural and man-made elements, being haphazardly designed to fit the line at which ground contours terminate. To be visually convincing, a retaining wall must read as an independent structure in its own right, not as a section through an irregularly cut slope. It must consist of firm geometric elements, reaching the profile of the bank it supports either in one big sweep, or in a succession of firm rectilinear steps. Where feasible, it should be placed at the top rather than the bottom of the slope, to give the freeway more breathing space.

ARTICULATION OF THE MACRO-LANDSCAPE

The elements in a given visual space have to be clearly defined on the macro-scale as well as the micro-scale. The freeway must be given enough room to live a life of its own, without infringing on adjacent uses and structures, and without being infringed upon by them. Just as, on a small scale, a slot and a shadow line must be provided where steel and concrete are about to touch each other, and a still larger space between a bridge pier and a rock formation, so on a large scale a "slot" must be provided between the freeway and an adjacent subdivision, or between the freeway and a shopping center. A "slot" or green space, in this case, will prevent visual friction and conflict between the two adjacent uses. A lake, a river, a factory, or a skyscraper must all be set back from the freeway a sufficient distance for respect.

The need for this type of articulation is functional as well as visual. The freeway generates noises, fumes, headlight glare at night—all nuisance factors, particularly in residential areas. To save on right-of-way acquisition, highway departments occasionally let houses stand in an impermissible proximity to the freeway—only to receive later from the owners complaints about headlight glare in bedrooms or car wrecks in the backyard. Several statistical studies of the actual nuisance value of a limited access highway exist. One, which attacked the problem strictly with regard to noise, determined that, at a distance of 300 feet from the pavement, passenger cars at 55 miles an hour are approximately as loud as an acceptable background noise for a residential area. Accelerating trucks, however, were found to be four times as loud. A study of the attitudes of residents toward highways, carried out in Westchester County, indicates that within 100 feet of a parkway, 54 per cent of the sample considered it a nuisance. This percentage fell to 35 per cent at 100 to 200 feet, 18 per cent at 200 to 300 feet, and was 4 per cent at distances greater than 300 feet. Assessment of the parkway as a convenience rose from 27 per cent at the less-than-100-foot distance to 50 per cent at 100 to 200 feet, to 63 per cent at 200 to 300 feet, and to 75 per cent at distances of 300 feet or over. It has been also found that property values in Westchester county increased more in areas adjacent to a parkway than in areas away from it, a development attributed to the presence of at least some landscaped open space along the Westchester roads. A study of freeway influence on market value in California, where rights-of-way are extremely narrow and no landscape strip exists, found that houses on lots adjacent to freeways experienced a small one to two per cent depression in market

A distance of 60 feet from the shoulder edge to the right-of-way fence gives the impression of driving through the backyards of private houses.

A distance of 100 feet from the shoulder edge to the right-of-way line is adequate to let the housing development recede into the background, although more screen planting would have been helpful in this case.

value. Only those houses adjacent to a freeway which were farthest removed from the right-of-way fence could experience an occasional rise in market value. A concomitant opinion poll revealed that 46 per cent of those asked would not buy a home adjacent to a freeway again, against 40 per cent of those who would.

The contrast between a 150-foot-wide (view A) and a 40-foot-wide (view B) protective strip on the outside of entrance and exit ramps. The points from which the photographs were taken are shown on the plan (*opposite page*). The four houses on the right-hand side and the drive leading to them should have been removed as part of the right-of-way acquisition.

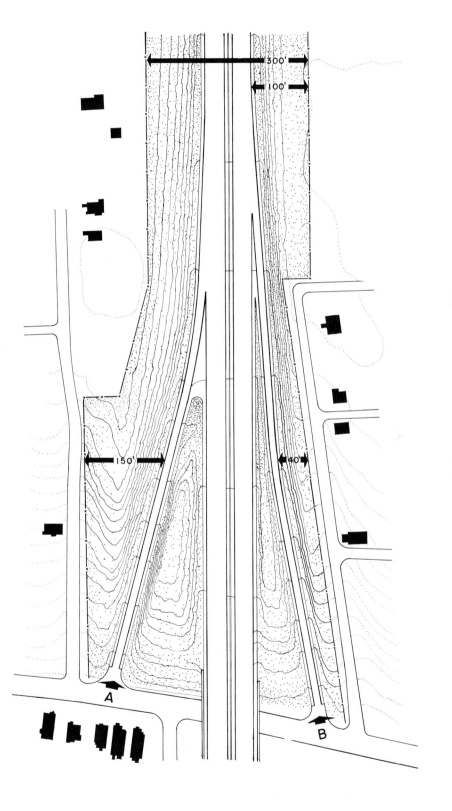

A freeway in a park strip (Meadowbrook Parkway on Long Island), a beautiful example of articulation between the highway and residential development. Note how the park strip breeds compatible adjacent uses: school, playgrounds, and water supply installations.

Considering the totality of highway functions, a protective greenbelt is just as much a part of the freeway as shoulders and a guide rail. This fact has been fairly widely recognized, but standards for adjacent-use setback from the freeway vary widely. AASHO Standards for the Interstate System suggest that the right-of-way should be wide, but go on to specify merely 150 feet as a minimum for four-lane roads. With a suggested minimum median of 36 feet, this leaves only 21 feet for a protective strip along the sides of the road. The State of New York, while suggesting medians 100 to 250 feet wide, specifies that the right-of-way line should be only 10 feet from the edge of the rounded side-slope. Connecticut specifies a right-of-way line not closer than 75 feet from the outer pavement edge, and for the more important freeways, a minimum right-of-way of 300 feet. This standard is widely adopted. Westchester County, in its "General Principles of Thoroughfare Planning," calls for a desirable overall width of 400 feet, which would leave about 150 feet on each side of the shoulders for a landscaped reservation.

From the visual standpoint, such a width appears to be a desirable minimum to set off adjacent uses from the freeway effectively. Anything below 100 feet is seen to be grossly inadequate, since it allows adjacent uses to encroach upon the visual space of the freeway. A 300-foot-wide right-of-way could thus be termed an absolute minimum, and 400 feet a desirable minimum, to be widened wherever the median divider exceeds 36 feet in width or wherever other conditions so require. In the case of wide medians or wide open areas between traffic lanes at interchanges, a wide greenbelt is especially important, because of the lopsided and illogical view that results when an open area on the left of the travel path is unbalanced by close encroachment on the right. A freeway in this case is more isolated from its other half than from land uses alien to itself. Another important point is that the right-of-way line should not indiscriminately follow a fixed distance from the center line. The average right-of-

Another excellent example of articulation in the macrolandscape, this in a high-density urban environment (Bronx River Parkway).

A less generous solution, but still visually satisfy-ing: Southern State Parkway on Long Island, air and ground views. Dense tree planting makes up for the narrowness of the right-of-way.

way width should be approximated by following existing hedges, walls, forest edges, and other physical property lines wherever these exist, even if this requires the acquisition of odd parcels of additional land.

It should be quite obvious that, unless the freeway passes through a densely wooded area, the traveler can see a considerable distance beyond the right-of-way, where his eye can be hurt by all kinds of visual nuisances outside the highway property line.

By far the greatest eyesores are, of course, billboards and other advertising signs. Located, in practice, beyond a 50- to 100-foot-wide protective strip of the right-of-way, they have to be huge in order to be read at 60 or 70 miles and hour, and garish to attract attention. Thus they destroy the continuity of the visual space of the freeway, they violate the integrity of prominent natural features such as hills or rock outcrops where they are located for maximum visibility, they distract the driver's attention while irritating him with irrelevant information, and, particularly in urban areas where official directional signs are closely spaced, they create visual confusion by interfering with the official signs.

Enlightened public resentment against the ruination of the landscape by various forms of outdoor advertising has led to some limited control over signs along highways in the United States. About half the states prohibit commercial signs near intersections, a few forbid signs at curves or signs with flashing illumination. Massachusetts permits nonaccessory signs only in business areas, and requires that those larger than 12 by 25 feet (the standard size "poster panel") be set back 300 feet from the road. Oregon requires a minimum spacing of 500 feet between signs (one billboard every six seconds or so). Only Hawaii, Alaska, and Puerto Rico have an effective ban on billboards along state highways.

Local county and town zoning has so far achieved more than statewide controls. Several important arterial roads in California, Colorado, Wisconsin, Tennessee, Virginia, and other states are effectively protected through county zoning. Residential zones established by towns also protect many miles of highways, particularly in the East. This kind of scattered protection, however, is inadequate for freeways because of their regional character and because local zoning can be fairly easily amended under concentrated political pressure. The protection through town zoning of the Merritt Parkway in Connecticut, for example, began to break down after 20 years.

The case for banning all advertising along freeways is, of course, even stronger than that for controlling advertising along ordinary roads. Adjacent property owners have no right of access, so why should an exception be made for "visual access" to the freeway? Advertising here is clearly a parasitic use, living off a public investment without rendering a public service; the argument that billboards reduce monotony or that they offer free space for different safety and educational campaigns is really most tenuous, since both ends could be better achieved without the esthetic annihilation of the landscape. It would appear that in a democratic society, the function of advertising is to inform those seeking information, rather than to impose the messages of a minority upon a captive audience without regard to values by which the community lives. Information in the direct interest of the traveling public—about food, automotive services, overnight accommodations, or local attractions—can be provided in the form of booklet directories, such as those issued by the Ohio Turnpike Commission, or in the form of outdoor directories at information sites, suggested by the Bureau of Public Roads, where much more information at less physical and esthetic cost can be given to a standing motorist, in contrast to one driving at 70 miles an hour.

Unfortunately, state initiative in controlling advertising along freeways has been very slow. Among the pioneers were New York, where state statutes prohibit billboards within 500 feet of the right-of-way of parkways and the Thruway, and Maine, where the same standard was applied to the Maine Turnpike. As a result, Congress moved to control advertising along interstate highways, for which the federal government pays 90 per cent of the cost. Strong controls, however, were defeated on the grounds that they infringe upon the states' rights. The bill finally adopted after severe fighting is the Federal-Aid Highway Act of 1958, which declares it "to be a national policy that the erection and maintenance of outdoor advertising signs, displays, and devices within six hundred and sixty feet of the edge of the right-of-way and visible from the main-traveled way of all portions of the Interstate System . . . should be regulated, consistent with national standards." The federal government will pay 90.5 per cent instead of 90 per cent of the cost of all interstate highways that are so controlled.

The National Standards, promulgated on November 10, 1958, apply only to those sections of Interstate Highways for which the entire right-of-way was acquired after July 1, 1956. This would mean roughly two-thirds of the ultimate mileage. Moreover, industrial and commercial areas as well as areas subject to municipal zoning are allowed to be excluded from the controlled areas. The worst and most dangerous concentrations of signs (commercial areas are usually in the vicinity of interchanges) can thus be allowed to flourish unchecked. Other than that, the National Standards in essence provide as follows:

Advertising of a general nature is prohibited within the 660-foot-wide protected area on each side of the right-of-way, but some types of commercial signs are permitted: (a) Signs advertising activities being conducted on the premises are permitted, and can be of any number or size. Only if they are farther than 50 feet from the advertised activity or if they state that the property is for sale or lease is their size limited to 150 square feet. There also cannot be more than one "for sale" sign facing the traffic on the same property. (b) Signs within 12 miles of advertised activities and signs "in the specific interest of the traveling public" are also permitted, subject to certain limitations.

No such signs can be located within 2 miles before or 1,000 feet after an interchange, in controlled areas, to eliminate competition with official signs. In an area between two and five miles ahead of an interchange not more than six such signs can be placed. Still further away, the number of signs should not exceed one per mile. In no case should they be spaced closer than 1,000 feet, and their size is limited to 150 square feet throughout. This is less than half the area of a standard billboard, and a

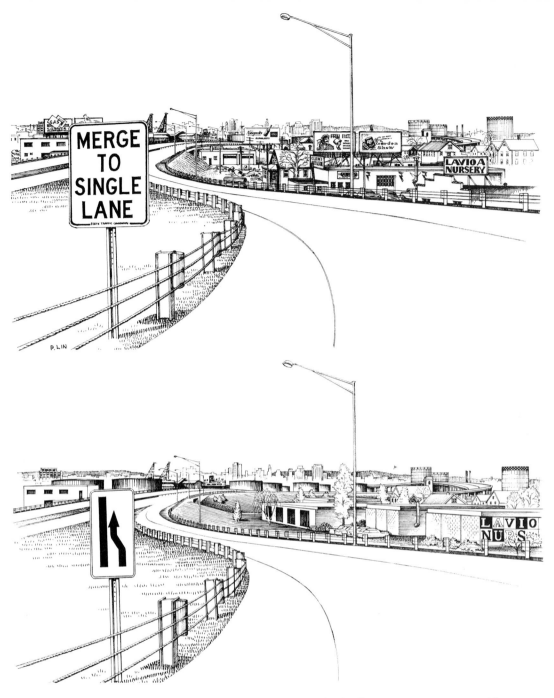

(*Above*) The entrance to a city cluttered up with billboards and miscellaneous structures encroaching upon the visual space of the freeway. (*Below*) A suggestion for improvement, which could be achieved by proper setback, building bulk, and advertising controls.

minimum for readability. Competition among eligible businesses for the relatively few signs that are permitted can be eliminated, if an informational site is provided. Any number of signs within 12 miles of advertised activities and those "in the specific interest of the traveling public," limited to 12 square feet in size (ample for the standing motorist) can then be placed on panels at these informational sites, which are carefully screened from the main traffic by planting and announced by standard official signs. No advertising is permitted within 12 miles of the information site except on-premise signs and those for activities which are within 12 miles of the freeway but more than 12 miles from the information site. All permitted commercial

The precision of technology and the beauty of nature—steel, concrete, rocks, pine trees—contrast sharply with human carelessness: overhead wiring, refuse bins, arrogantly placed billboards, and a parking lot indiscriminately cut into the hillslope to reveal permanently the bare subsoil. A case for "visual control zones" along freeways.

Even very well-designed advertising scarcely improves the highway: an entrance to Rome before a billboard control ordinance went into effect.

signs are subject to a number of provisions concerning illumination, movement, and interference with official signs.

The National Standards are a valiant attempt to restrict advertising along Interstate freeways without eliminating it, and, as the first federal legislation relative to advertising control, they should be viewed with full respect. It is to be regretted that three years after the adoption of the National Standards only sixteen states have entered into agreement with the Bureau of Public Roads regarding sign control.*

Ideally, a fuller control would be obviously desirable. First, coverage should be extended to all freeways and expressways, not just to sections of interstate routes. Second, the protected area should be extended to something like 1,000 feet on both sides of the roadway, to prevent extra-high structures from being erected in the distance to catch the motorist's eye. Controls should be just as stringent in municipal areas as in the open country, and they should be retroactive. Third, all commercial signs outside information sites should ideally be prohibited, with the exception of on-premise signs which ought to be limited in size, density, and method of illumination. Finally, within the visual control zone of the freeway the states could require all local utilities to be put underground, enforce regulations with respect to the removal of vegetation and topsoil, demand high standards for building setbacks, curbs, pavements, etc. Special interchange control districts could regulate the siting, traffic

In the United States the need for advertising control is the greatest precisely in the spots where its present likelihood is the least: in commercial areas near freeway interchanges.

* As of January, 1962, these were Connecticut, Delaware, Hawaii, Kentucky, Maine, Maryland, Nebraska, New York, North Dakota, Ohio, Oregon, Pennsylvania, Vermont, Washington, West Virginia, and Wisconsin. In addition, Virginia and New Hampshire have enacted laws which also provide for the control of outdoor advertising in areas adjacent to the interstate system. Some other states control billboards along certain designated—not necessarily interstate—freeways, but not on a comprehensive basis.

Official American traffic signs have been often accused—with considerable justice—of being unnecessarily complicated in shape and design, and of using too many words instead of symbols. Above, an elegant German freeway sign, which does not have to spell out "deer crossing." Below, a most recent highway marker, which uses three signs to convey one message. Most traffic signs are produced without the benefit of professional graphic designers.

circulation and appearance of restaurant, motel, and gas station areas on freeway approaches, to prevent the disorder of rapid and haphazard developments. Approaching the freeway from an existing community, one would feel it immediately to be a spine of orderliness and beauty in an otherwise chaotic environment. There would be an opportunity for the high visual standards of the freeway control zone to become contagious and to spread deeper into the local community on local initiative.

There should be no hesitation to acquire easements and development rights within the visual control zone to preserve interesting views, desirable tree growth, or important landmarks. Marginal condemnation could be used to set up organized commercial districts on state-owned land, rented out to concessionaires, thus redeeming part of the highway cost. For, as Franklin D. Roosevelt pointed out in his 1944 message on interregional highways, "why should the hazard of engineering give one private citizen an enormous profit? If there is to be an unearned profit, why should it not accrue to the government, state or federal, or both?"

FOCUS, INTEREST, AND DRAMA

When all our requirements for continuity, integrity, and articulation are taken care of, the freeway will be pleasant, fitting, and clean. It will have some dynamic variety, but it still may be somewhat dull. It will lack an element that pulls any artistic composition together: the element of focus, accent, or dramatic surprise. In the nature of the case, this element cannot lie in the ribbon of the pavement, which is always the same; it has to be pulled in from the outer environment. It can be a subordinate focal point—a landmark, or a climax: a destination.

Landmarks are a part of travel from times immemorial; we measure our progress by them. They give us articulation along the axis of travel. They are a source of surprise to the stranger, and a source of anticipation and identification to one familiar with the road. They have to be dominant and isolated, lest they negate each other through competition. They are the things remembered after a trip. The importance of proper orientation when traveling can hardly be argued, and a clearly recognizable structure of the macro-landscape is essential for that purpose.

A group of fifteen senior architecture students were given ten minutes to list spontaneously the things they remembered from recent trips along a familiar parkway. Among the objects listed we find: two industrial plants—the only ones visible from the road; an open valley with a distant view—contrasting with the "green corridor" feeling of the rest of the road; "Red Barn" restaurant—then the only one visible (can anyone remember a restaurant from a roadside commercial strip?); a water tank on a hill; colorful rock outcrops, and several steep hills. The hills, often explicitly contrasted with the blandness of such roads as the New Jersey Turnpike, and the large factory in a valley were listed most frequently, supporting the old truism about perception being achieved through contrast.

The opposition of low (right near the water) and high (on top of a ridge), of light (on a meadow) and dark (under trees), of wide and narrow, close and far, smooth and rough, thin and thick, are basic means of shaping interesting spatial progressions

As the perspective changes from close to distant, as visual edges converge and recede, the driver experiences a dynamic succession of spatial experiences which keep interest and attention alive. The views are on the Taconic Parkway.

and eliminating monotony. Physiologically speaking, overcoming monotony means inducing the driver to exercise his eye-muscles, to focus on close objects and on distant ones, to shift his eyes right and left scanning the view instead of staring straight ahead into infinity. When sections of tangent alignment are relieved by long stretches of gradually meandering alignment, the vanishing point, static in the first case, begins to move across the landscape. Since the eye looks in the direction the wheels are pointing, the continuation of the sight-line on a tangent beyond a curve is a logical place to locate prominent landmarks. These can be large, simple industrial shapes, like water towers, or they can be deliberately placed pieces of giant sculpture. The axis of vision, so important in the Renaissance, has been forgotten in modern decades, and here is a chance to restore its full validity. Curving alignment provides an opportunity to observe not only outside structures, but the freeway structures themselves, which would not be visible to the driver if the alignment were straight. A long S-curve on the approach to a bridge can permit the driver to get a glimpse of the structure before driving over it. Features like this, sculptured on the extra-human scale of the freeway in the macro-landscape, would attract attention in quite a different way from advertising signs. Huge in scale and abstract, they would not require

The most ordinary structures—a water tower, a hospital—can become prominent landmarks, if located at an elevation in the line of sight of oncoming traffic. They help the driver to orient himself and to measure his progress.

the driver to strain his eyes reading a lettered message at a substantial angle off the road, thus taking his attention away from driving. Spaced very infrequently at choice locations, they would not destroy the continuity of the landscape by a staccato intrusion of alien two-dimensional objects, as billboards do.

Aside from viewing objects, such as dams, towers, gasometers, or radio telescopes, changes in the direction of the alignment give the driver an opportunity to look at panoramas, and the freeway should be deliberately designed to exploit such views. The point is not primarily one of selective cutting of trees on the roadside, which would permit the driver to see a view through his side window. This can be both dangerous—since it detracts attention from the road—and uncomfortable—since such a view can only be seen for a second. Rather, the point is to let the road aim the eye, and show the driver the desired view *in front* of him, not sideways. Unlike hori-

The best way to display a bridge as a landmark is to give it a curvilinear approach. Approached on a straight line, even a major bridge goes unnoticed.

zontal curves, which are primarily suited to show the driver single objects and which do not distract his attention after he has entered the curve (he is looking at them while approaching the curve on a tangent), vertical crest curves are most suitable for panoramic views—of the ocean, of a hilly landscape, or of a level plain, seen from the artificial hill of an overpass. Dramatic approaches and entrances to great metropolitan centers can be a fitting climax to a trip, heralded by glimpses of the skyline from far away, just as the spires of Chartres Cathedral are seen for miles across the plains. It

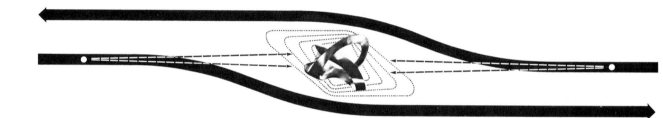

The line of sight in siting landmarks along a freeway; the road must aim the eye.

"Uncounted highways in all corners of the world have seen the family fleeing," a sculptural group in a rest area on the Vienna–Salzburg freeway, designed to be seen by the standing motorist. Sculpture of this size placed directly on the freeway, such as that of a saint on a bridge similar to the one in this view, has proven ineffectual, since it is out of scale for the rapidly passing motorist.

Perhaps giant sculpture (for which this example by Henry Moore might serve as a model) can be placed at strategic spots along the freeway to be seen by the moving motorist.

is an irreparable loss that driving for two hours on the new Interstate 95 from the New York city line to New London, hardly ever more than two miles away from the coast, one gets only a few short glimpses of the ocean, that, taken together, last less than four minutes.

For diversity and relief, the provision of stopping places off the non-stop freeways has long been considered essential. Many of these stops are purely physiological or

A distant panorama, seen from the freeway high on a ridge: Palisades Interstate Parkway approaching Bear Mountain Bridge.

mechanical in purpose—on a 70-mile stretch of the Ohio Turnpike it has been found that 34 per cent of the stops were for food, 28 per cent for toilet use, and 21 per cent for fuel or auto service. Aside from these services, there are rest turnouts for mere stopping and relaxation; physicians suggest that a change in position is desirable every two hours or so to restore proper blood circulation in the human organism. Some states have picnicking facilities at the rest turnouts, others provide direct access to state parks and beaches from the freeway system. It should be borne in mind that over 20 per cent of all automobile trips are social or recreational in purpose, and that a freeway is closely related to public open spaces which it connects and ties together.

Thus, from the social and esthetic viewpoints, much greater emphasis should be placed on roadside turnouts. Their spacing at two to three miles, as currently prac- ticed in Germany and Austria, may be too close for safety when traffic volumes are high, but an average of 30 miles seems definitely too long for most conditions. Be- sides, many of the existing turnouts have a dreary institutional look, crowded as they are into a narrow right-of-way. Crowds picnicking with their noses against a wire fence separating them from the landscape evokes images of a human zoo. To eliminate such degrading conditions, a minimum area of perhaps 15 acres should be provided

Where the line of sight permits only lateral views from a ridge, overlooks are appropriate, such as the Rockefeller lookout on the Palisades Interstate Parkway, with the Hudson River below.

for each turnout, not three as recommended, for example, by the State of Ohio. The turnout can then be developed into a small roadside park, isolated from the noise and the fumes of traffic. It should exploit an area of natural interest which can be further protected by scenic easements. The Federal-Aid Highway Act of 1938, as amended in 1940, provides that "the construction of highways by the States with the aid of Federal funds . . . may include the purchase of such adjacent strips of land of limited width and primary importance for the preservation of the natural beauty through which highways are constructed. . . ." Unfortunately, very little use has been made of this provision.

The problem of providing food and automotive services seems to be inadequately resolved by the present service areas on toll highways, because of their institutional character and monopolistic position. Particularly because of much shorter distances between interchanges, the new interstate freeway system will be able to depend in a more satisfactory way on existing commercial auto, restaurant, and motel facilities in neighboring communities. However, the clustering of commercial activity at interchanges poses a definite esthetic and planning danger, since municipal or county controls cannot be depended upon to regulate these properly. Some state control of the

An attempt at a positive approach to service areas on toll freeways. The restaurant
on a bridge becomes a landmark in the uneventful Oklahoma landscape.

freeway zone, as previously suggested, seems imperative. To a large extent, it can be accomplished, not by prohibition, but by the encouragement of healthy trends through organized commercial districts, and adequately designed frontage roads protected by a wide right-of-way, proper setback lines, and landscaped outer separators.

Though separated from adjacent development on a small scale, a freeway is, on a large scale, an integral part of the twentieth-century community—the interurban region. It cannot be planned and designed in isolation—as a line from A to B—but only as an intimate part of the growing arterial network, as part of a mesh with a future optimum density. Thinking in terms of areas rather than lines will prevent the high-

In the swamps of Florida, where the freeway is bounded by drainage canals, an attempt is made to introduce an artificial lake with trees and walkways as an amenity to enhance the otherwise dreary service area.

Scenic overlooks in Maryland and Oregon, with picnic areas. Access from the parking lot to Multnomah Falls in the lower view is via a pedestrian tunnel under the eastbound lane of Interstate 80 N.

way planner from neglecting to protect and control adjacent land use. It will prevent him from neglecting to build, rebuild, or at least provide for a far-reaching skeleton of feeder roads at the same time the freeway is constructed. At present, only connections from the freeway to the nearest road can be built with freeway funds—which is, of course, grossly inadequate. Thinking in terms of a future freeway mesh will prevent the planner from choosing the path of least real estate resistance and most traffic service today—he will locate it so that it will augment and be augmented by future freeways, to be built 20 to 40 years hence. Thinking in terms of ultimate spacing will prevent putting freeways too close together or too far apart.

There is also a word to be said for functional differentiation. Though parkways exclusively for passenger traffic are temporarily out of fashion, they require less excavation, and can fully utilize the visual appeal of relatively steep grades, to which passenger cars are immune. Many freeways for mixed traffic, built today, will be loaded to capacity two decades hence or sooner. They will require parallel facilities a few

A rare example of perfect integration of the freeway with recreational facilities: the Anthony Wayne area on the Palisades Interstate Parkway; facilities are provided for swimming, picnicking, and ball games.

A comprehensive network of freeways and parkways: the New York metropolitan region.

miles away. It seems quite irrational to duplicate a mixed traffic facility with another one nearby. But if today's freeways were located with a view toward this ultimate, much denser network, a consistent differentiation, tied in with land use, could be achieved between passenger parkways and commercial traffic expressways. This exists today to some degree only in the New York region.

To quote Paul B. Sears: "Our future patterns of land use will be based on that of our growing highway system as surely as the human body is molded about its skeleton. Since we are responsible for the physical framework of our future economy, it deserves the best thought and talent we can give it." A highway engineer cannot be a regional planner and an architect at once, but regional planners, economists, architects, sculptors, graphic designers, psychologists, biologists, and geologists can work together with the engineer and the landscape architect in visual coordination teams to integrate the freeway plan with an overall development plan of the urbanized landscape, and to make the freeway an enduring work of beauty.

Considering the relatively small added cost of esthetically refined design, the public driving on dull or ugly freeways is truly "not getting its money's worth." This is all the more frustrating, since the public in general believes its experts; if they say that $60 billion is needed to provide the ultimate in safety, it would hardly think of questioning their judgment if the experts said that $66 billion is needed to provide the ultimate in safety and beauty. Almost all the suggestions of this study have been, on occasion, successfully tried in the U.S. or abroad. Why shouldn't a firm effort be made to elevate all freeways to the visual standard of the best?

"For the road cannot be considered in isolation. It is not just a track for motorists; it is an all-embracing, all-penetrating network which together with the vehicles on it, the signs, the bridges, the roadside ancillaries, is an integral part of our life and landscape."—RAYMOND SPURRIER.

The drama of the approaching city: bridges and tunnels in New York and Chicago.

A new totality of the urban sculpture, experienced from the freeway: downtown Manhattan with the Statue of Liberty from Interstate 78.

PART FOUR

The Monuments of Technology: The Esthetics of Industry
and Commerce in the Landscape

1. Industrial Location

2. Industry as an Element of Urban Design
   Clarity of Massing
   Rhythmic Coordination
   Structural Expression
   The Use of Silhouette
   Articulation of Elements
   Integration with the Landscape

3. Commercial Facilities in the Urban Fringe

4. Possibilities of Planned Design

5. The Need for Visual Order

1. Industrial Location

Cradled by invention in the city (often in a backyard slum), the nation's manufacturing plants have come of age outside the old centers, but well within the metropolitan areas. They are now on their way back to the hinterland—to the fields and streams which saw the birth of the water-powered mill at the time of the Industrial Revolution. At the same time they have become significantly varied and extremely specialized, and their sites can never be casually chosen. Factories compete for land with agricultural, residential, and recreational uses; they bring more people to formerly rural areas; and they pay the tax bills in the fringe towns where they are located. These facts make them unwelcome in some communities and eagerly sought after in others. But most regions of the United States are actively seeking new plants, and it must always be remembered that the busy hum of machinery and the ring of tools on metal has made this country the leading industrial nation of the world. The siting of new technological facilities is a key factor in helping the economy to expand. It also involves unexplored areas of design in the accommodation of industry handsomely and well.

Although residential development is by far the largest user of urban land, and also accounts for the largest share of money invested in new construction (some 40 per cent); and although the rapidly growing freeway network, while accounting for a fraction of one per cent of the nation's street and road mileage, will soon be carrying close to one-third of the nation's vehicular traffic, industrial uses are a prominent and often disturbing feature in the urbanized landscape. Industrial land use includes the manufacture, processing, and storage of goods, extractive and disposal activities, as well as such utilities as water, gas, and electricity. On a regional scale, these functions may occupy some six to twelve per cent of the urbanized land and they account for 22 per cent* of the nation's investment in new construction.

The location of industrial activities is rather firmly determined by economic considerations. Industries in which the cost of transporting raw materials looms large, such as cement plants or paper mills, locate near their source of supply; processes in which the product gains rather than loses weight, and in which distribution to the consumer is a major cost factor (bakeries and bottling plants, for example) are market-oriented. For many industries, the point of minimum transport costs is by no means evident in advance, and has to be calculated from a careful consideration of alternate places of supply and alternate transport routes. A steel works, for example, will locate at a point where the total cost of shipping its ore, its coal, and its finished product will be at a minimum. The cost of transporting energy is in many cases an important factor: aluminum smelters, chemical plants using electrolytic processes, or atomic energy installations will locate near sources of cheap electric power; conversely, thermal power plants serving cities will locate as close to their consumer as possible, at a place where they have an ample supply of water for cooling purposes

* This figure includes utility lines under and over streets.

and, preferably, coal or oil deliveries by barge; losses of electric power in transmission are high.

Next to the differences in transport costs, differences in labor costs are an important locational factor. In some highly automated industries, such as oil refining, labor costs can be negligible, but other industries, such as textiles, are highly labor-oriented. Both the cost of labor and the quality of the labor force are important. The producers of precision instruments, for example, seek areas with a tradition of high skill; apparel manufacturers need pools of cheap female labor. Differences in tax, insurance, and interest rates, or in climate, topography, or social environment are, in essence, similar to labor costs, in that they are attributes of particular sites, and do not vary regularly with distance.

A third major locational factor concerns the economies of agglomeration: that is, economies (or diseconomies) that result from a large scale of operations, or those that accrue to a firm because it is located near other firms with which it either exchanges or shares certain goods, services, and facilities. For example, an isolated oil refinery may waste some of its byproducts which could, however, be utilized as raw materials by subsidiary chemical plants, if these were located next door. Small industries producing a non-standardized product, such as the fashion-oriented ladies' garment industry, are highly dependent on urbanized economies. Research-oriented industries prefer to locate near centers of learning, with which they can share reference facilities and highly trained personnel.

Recent years have seen the emergence of several interesting extra-economic locational considerations, such as the strategic defense policies of the federal government, or the factor of managerial taste. Proximity to airports for convenient use by executives, or access to a certain style of residential living for them and their wives seem to have affected more than one locational decision. One prestige-conscious firm went so far as to object to apartment development in the vicinity of its plant, because its corporate image might suffer from any environment but that of detached single-family homes.

The economic forces of location, strongly modified by the gradual nature of historic change, have shaped the industrial scene of present-day North America. Some ninety per cent of the primary metals industry (blast furnaces, rolling, drawing, and casting of steel and iron, as well as nonferrous metals) is concentrated in a fairly narrow belt that stretches from Connecticut to Allentown-Philadelphia-Baltimore, with a small gap at the Appalachians, through Pittsburgh, Youngstown, Cleveland, and Detroit to Chicago, encompassing Buffalo and Hamilton in Canada. The remaining ten per cent of the primary metals industry is about evenly distributed between Alabama and scattered locations in the West, such as Los Angeles or Utah. The smelting of nonferrous metals plays a relatively greater role in western locations, such as Montana, Arizona, or the Pacific Northwest, but even in this field the largest concentrations are in Baltimore and in the Mohawk and Connecticut Valleys.

The metal-consuming industries (fabricated metal products and machinery, including electrical) operate in symbiosis with the primary metals industry, and are located within the primary metals belt and around it: north into Massachusetts and the Mohawk valley, through Southern Ohio toward Louisville, Kentucky, and Evansville, Illinois, west toward Minneapolis and St. Louis. Outside the northeastern quadrant of the United States, the only metalworking centers to speak of are on the West Coast, with some oilfield machinery being produced in Texas. All of the automobile industry—except assembly plants near major markets—is located around Detroit. Aircraft assembly, on the other hand, is widely dispersed in Los Angeles-San Diego, Seattle, Wichita, Dallas-Fort Worth, and Baltimore-Hagerstown.

The chemical industry is much more evenly spread between the West Coast cities, the Gulf Coast, West Virginia, Tennessee, and the Manufacturing Belt, but the largest concentrations are still between New York and Baltimore. The latter stretch is also an important center for petroleum refining, the other three concentrations of oil refineries being near Chicago, in Los Angeles, and along the Gulf Coast. The glass industry is centered on the West side of the Appalachians between New York state and Ohio, while cement and brick plants are scattered across the country in rough proportion to the population distribution.

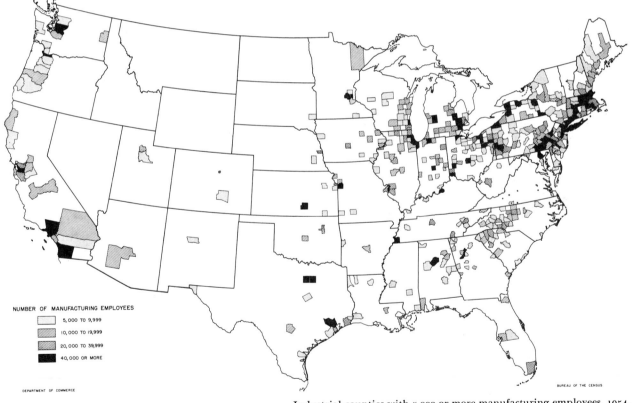

NUMBER OF MANUFACTURING EMPLOYEES

5,000 TO 9,999
10,000 TO 19,999
20,000 TO 39,999
40,000 OR MORE

DEPARTMENT OF COMMERCE   BUREAU OF THE CENSUS

Industrial counties with 5,000 or more manufacturing employees, 1954.

The textile towns form a string from Maine to the southern part of the Appalachian Piedmont. As for apparel, some 40 per cent of men's clothing and 70 per cent of women's apparel is produced in New York City, with secondary centers located around New York, and new centers emerging in Dallas and Los Angeles. The leather and shoe industry, likewise, is still heavily concentrated in the New England and the Middle Atlantic states, with secondary centers in the Midwest. Food processing, to the extent that it does not deal with perishable products such as bread or fresh milk, is located at the juncture of the major agricultural and industrial regions—the Corn Belt, California, Florida, the Gulf Coast states, and the Atlantic coastal plain. The lumber, furniture, and wood products industries closely follow the forested areas of the continent, with wood pulp production centered in the Pacific Northwest, the South, and in Canada—the largest producer of newsprint. To summarize, the bulk of the North American manufacturing activity continues to be heavily concentrated in the triangle between Boston, Baltimore, and Chicago, with very few cities outside this area having more than half of their labor force employed in manufacturing—even though the relative shift of population and employment to the South and West has been considerable.

On the scale of a single metropolitan area, locational factors have changed more radically in the past thirty years. Prior to the 1920s, most factories had to be accessible to sources of supply and to national and regional markets by railroad, and accessible to their labor force by walking or by public transport. Mechanical transmission of power and manual handling of materials within buildings favored compact multi-storey factories. These three factors led to a very high density of industrial land use, frequently in an unhealthy proximity to residential areas.

Today, for many goods, deliveries in a radius up to 500 miles are most economically accomplished by truck; high-value products can be shipped by air; and a railroad siding is often required merely to arrange more favorable financing. With a highly mobile labor force and roads free from congestion, anyone living within ten miles of the plant can reach it in less than half an hour. Conveyors and fork lift trucks within buildings require elbow room and an unbroken floor area on one level. With electric transmission of power to individual motors, a flexible plant layout can be provided. All this suggests a large site, to be found only in the urban fringe. There, in addition to greater productive efficiency, relatively low land values enable a firm to provide ample parking space, landscaped lawns, recreation areas for employees, and a land reserve for future expansion.

As a result, the density of industrial land use has dropped sharply. After the Second World War, densities of 75 employees per acre for labor-intensive industries and 25 employees per acre for extensive industries were typical in many urban-suburban areas. A widely accepted planning standard for new plants today is ten employees per acre, with some factories featuring an employment density as low as two workers per acre. Sometimes, the very low densities indicate a highly automated production process, but more often they reflect a propensity of management to acquire extra acreage for prestige and for possible future needs.

Very heavy manufacturing, such as an integrated steel works or an oil refinery, needs highly special site conditions—deepwater access, rail connections, proper base for foundations, and thousands of acres of flat land (the complex of refineries near

Typical large multi-storey plant from the earlier part of this century.

Smaller single-storey plant with a low lot coverage, characteristic of modern development in the urban fringe.

Linden, N. J., takes up as much land as Idlewild Airport, or as much as southern Manhattan below 50th Street); but such mammoth installations are few and far between. Of the more ubiquitous industries, only utilities depend on special topographic features: large power stations and sewage treatment plants need waterfront sites; water towers and telephone relay stations locate on hills. But the typical small- to medium-size manufacturing plant in the urban fringe is quite flexible in its choice of site: it does prefer good foundation conditions and moderately flat ground, but if sites are scarce firms do resort to rock excavation and other heavy site preparation. Other than that, it needs utilities: water (sometimes in large amounts or of a special chemical composition); electric power; sometimes gas and, unless it can build its own disposal system, a sewer connection. It also needs road access adequate for trucks and peak employee traffic volumes; actual freeway frontage is desirable mainly from the advertising standpoint.

Within the urban fringe, industries prefer to locate closer to the core of a metropolitan area, not at the farthest outskirts. The more mature areas have more highly developed community services, a more stable population composition, and higher density, which provides the plant with a larger labor pool within commuting distance. Besides, greater proximity to the core usually makes the plant more accessible to other urban functions, which it may need. Thus, metropolitan growth seems to proceed in two waves: in the first, settlement by residence takes place; in the second, industry moves in, providing the new communities with a local employment base. In low-density areas, large plants prefer not to locate too close to each other, so as not to compete for the labor market; and the general pattern for small plants (often representing infant industries) is to be located closer to the center, where they can make use of agglomeration economies, and for large, more stable and mature industries to be located further out. In our analysis of 169 Connecticut towns it was found that "new industrial plants with less than 50 employees" were positively correlated with measures of centrality, whereas just the opposite was true for "new industrial plants with over 1,000 employees." On a nationwide basis, half of all production facilities are still located within seven miles of a central business district, but this radius is steadily expanding. As we have seen, many formerly rigid physical siting limitations

Early nineteenth-century industrialists in Lowell and elsewhere took pride in creating a harmonious environment through interesting massing and detailing of their plants: *above,* a former textile mill in Chicopee Falls, Mass.; the landscaping is a later improvement.

have been relaxed by increased accessibility, less concentrated markets, and the growing importance of the human element in production. Some of the extra-economic locational considerations represent a deliberate attempt to attract the best available talent to a given firm.

2. Industry as an Element of Urban Design

While some "glamour" industries, notably pharmaceuticals and electronics, try to put a premium on visual design and on the architecture and site planning of their facilities, on the whole the esthetic record of twentieth-century American industry is rather uneven. All too often, visually prominent industrial installations are put together by engineers in what seems to them the most expeditious fashion, without any thought given to the appearance of the complex in the urbanized landscape. At the other extreme, straightforward industrial buildings are sometimes confused by incongruous and irrelevant "architectural" ornamentation, poor window detailing, or tasteless advertising displays. Site relationships to the surrounding development also

Today, even some of the most glamorous and advanced technological processes result in an utterly chaotic environment: *above,* plutonium recycle test reactor in the research and development city of Richland, Washington.

leave much to be desired: industrial scars in the landscape, particularly along railroads, do not contribute to the beauty of the country. Meanwhile, inherent in our advanced technology is a great potential of significant esthetic expression, which sometimes comes to the fore by accident, but should more often do so by design.

The visual complexities occasioned by the use of very refined techniques demand a far greater degree of design attention than did the industrial building of the last century. But new technological facilities often get a great deal less, since the modern producer often has little awareness of his responsibility for an important part of man's visual surroundings.

In attempting to set up some guide lines for the use of industrial shapes as design elements in the urbanized landscape, we shall continue to follow the concepts of internal and external harmony. Internal harmony in this context implies clarity of massing, rhythmic coordination, and structural expressiveness. External harmony implies compatibility in silhouette, articulation of elements, and integration with the landscape.

CLARITY OF MASSING

From the viewpoint of design, industrial structures can be classified in two groups: enclosures, housing men and machinery, and exposed machinery itself, standing in the open air. Representative of the latter type are petro-chemical plants or exposed electric generating stations. They are a classic type of design in which form really does follow function; hence, esthetic advice is redundant. In the design of enclosures, however, the engineer has considerable freedom, and a number of generalized formal suggestions can be made.

Foremost among them is the need for clarity and simplicity in massing. Partly from a desire for marginal savings in structure, partly perhaps from a twisted legacy of the functionalist school of architecture, even small factories with a simple production layout are often given the form of a complicated set of overlapping volumes. Meanwhile, a single volume, with one spacing of columns and a single structural system enclosing the production, storage, and administrative functions is usually the esthetically correct solution for small- and medium-size plants. If one incompatible element

Clarity of massing: the simple volume of the airframe assembly hall dominates; subsidiary masses are properly articulated; General Dynamics plant, Ft. Worth, Tex.

Confused massing, no clear dominance, no geometric order: General Dynamics plant, San Diego, Cal.; though the scale shown here is extreme, the principle holds true for smaller buildings as well.

such as the boiler house cannot be incorporated into the basic volume, it should be expressed as a separate, relatively freestanding mass, not "glued" onto or into the body of the plant. In the case of the factory pictured on p. 283—a typical situation— the office wing, "glued" to the front, should not have been expressed as a separate element because the expression is not strong enough. The office space should have either been made a freestanding pavilion with a corridor link or, more practically, the roof height and the building width should have been made the same throughout, with the office function perhaps indicated by a slightly different fenestration.

The principle of unity also holds true for façade treatment. The need for a "front" on small manufacturing establishments is felt by many businessmen, and this front is usually made of brick, the traditional building material of nineteenth-century industry, while the other sides are made of a less expensive material, like cinder block. Such a "fake front" is justified if the building is designed to be attached to others of the same type, or if a wall as high as the building encloses the side yards and the rear yard. This is unlikely to be the case. A freestanding building can be seen from many directions, and the sides are likely to be more prominent from the road than the front. Hence, there is no reason to discriminate against the "sides" and the "rear": all four walls should be made of the same material. If face brick on all sides is too expensive and a cinder block front appears to be emotionally unsatisfying, the front entrance can be accented by one or two brick panels, but the unity of the building should be preserved.

A technological solution that can give structural and formal unity to the factory shell is the use of prefabricated, modular panel elements in reinforced concrete,

The unity of massing in a dam provides magnificent linear contrast to the undulations of the surrounding topography, but the subsidiary volumes, such as that of the generator house, should be clearly articulated and should bear a firm geometric relationship to the basic mass, as below. The location of the generator house and the penstocks in the upper view appears visually tenuous and undefined; Shasta Dam on the Sacramento River in northern California, and Fort Gibson Dam on the Neosho River near Tulsa, Oklahoma.

Perhaps the complex massing of this abandoned factory which grew by sporadic additions has a certain nostalgic charm, but, unless handled with the utmost architectural skill, it should not be attempted in new construction.

Unity of a small mass destroyed by different materials, haphazard openings: a very typical condition.

Modular design, tilt-up panel construction in reinforced concrete: clarity of structure and mass; industrial and office building in Arizona.

metal, or asbestos. Employed almost exclusively on large installations, they are only gradually making their way into the construction of smaller plants, where the visual need for the kind of discipline they provide is acute. Unfortunately, some small entrepreneurs do not seem to like the anonymous simplicity of a ready-made building shell, and destroy its integrity by a "personalized" treatment of the front wall, usually provided by the display man.

RHYTHMIC COORDINATION

A very frequent condition in industrial design is the repetition of numerous identical or similar masses. Many of the visual principles relating to "order of pattern," discussed in the chapter on low-density housing, apply here. The danger of monotony, however, is much less acute in this case, since the number of identical elements in a group is usually limited by scale economies for a given facility. Hence there is no need to introduce deliberate breaks and variations into a straightforward geometric order. Moreover, variety and relief is usually provided by differences between groups of identical objects that result from the nature of the technological process. Linear elements, both vertical and horizontal (pipelines, stacks) are usually on hand to provide contrast, articulation, and accent. Thus, an integrated industrial complex will usually present an exciting visual image, on condition, first, that its plan possesses a governing geometric order (axial or grid), and second, that the various functions are laid out on this grid with a rigorous, conceptual logic. Even so, an architectural study is often needed, as in the case of sewerage treatment plants, where the pleasant contrast between cylindrical sludge digestion tanks and rectilinear aeration chambers in a landscaped setting could find a much more dramatic expression.

On the whole, however, the danger of chaos in industrial design is not in the large, integrated facility, but rather in the accumulation of small individual enterprises in one area, enterprises which have no functional reason to coordinate the design of their structures between each other, and whose financial means are limited. A row of assorted small factories of various shapes along a road, with untidy driveways, storage yards, and chain-link fences, can effectively ruin the appearance of a community. Perhaps the best answer to the disorganized sprawl of small industries intruding on residential and commercial areas is the "industrial park" or organized industrial district, usually promoted by a railroad, power company, real estate group, or chamber of commerce. If an individual industry chooses to occupy a district lot it is spared the task of engaging location experts, site engineers, and other specialists to investigate labor supply, taxes, and utilities. These planning services are provided by the district management, which may also offer financial and construction assistance. In such a location a manufacturer is assured that all needed physical facilities are available, and that his investment is protected through covenants governing land use and design quality.

Esthetic controls in an organized industrial district often require 100-foot setbacks and landscaping; they often regulate signs, parking, temporary buildings, and unmasked storage areas. Sizes range from 80 acres to 1,000 and more, and, though the

Rhythmic coordination: processing facilities and storage tanks of different sizes and shapes arranged in a rhythmic order within an overall rectilinear grid, clearly expressing the logic of the technological process: Cities Service refinery near Lake Charles, Louisiana.

Another strong, industrial rhythm: Grain elevators and railroad yards near Kansas City, Missouri; the sight is familiar, but seldom is the design so unencumbered with ancillary structures.

A clear, firm order of pattern, pleasantly set off by open space in the foreground, which is accented by horizontals: a pond (*above*) and a pipeline (*below*). It is important that the tanks not be defaced with advertising signs or discordant colors. The dark cylindrical crude oil tanks blend well with the landscape, while the reflective color of the spherical tanks, containing highly volatile products, emphasizes them as dominant rhythmic shapes; *above*, Oklahoma (Standard Oil), *below*, Texas (Socony-Mobil).

technique has come into prominence since 1940, a few districts date back before 1900. The technique has been beneficial in that it has limited disorganized industrial sprawl and has provided small industries with agglomeration economies which they could not achieve on their own, but the appearance of most of the districts still leaves much to be desired; they are "parks" in name only. Despite a moderate amount of esthetic control, most of the districts lack a clean order of pattern, and they lack rhythmic coordination of verticals and horizontals, often characteristic of a large facility; they lack adequate landscaping and a conceptual design plan. Visual unity in these developments can be fairly easily provided by insisting on the rule that rectilinear masses are not placed at odd angles to each other; that unified exterior treatment be provided; that structures of a similar size be arranged in groups; that plants with vertical elements be thoughtfully placed with regard to the ensemble; and that adequate landscaped spaces be provided in between.

Alternation of low buildings and parking lots provides some rhythmic relationship, but the rectilinear order is violated by an oblique angle; moreover, the green spaces are visually insignificant compared with the paved area, resulting in an appearance of congestion, particularly near buildings encroaching on freeway ramps; industrial park on Route 128, Mass.

STRUCTURAL EXPRESSION

For a work of engineering seen apart from its surroundings, an expressive structure is a most important source of beauty. Engineering structures have historically evolved from the more massive and static shapes, with low stresses per unit of cross-section, toward lighter and more dynamic shapes, with higher stresses and a more efficient utilization of material. Concomitant trends have been toward more efficient principles of support (arch, cantilever, or suspension, instead of the simple post and beam), and toward greater differentiation of function (frame for support and panels

Complex massing, rhythmically integrated with the site in a firm geometric order. Note successful use of landscaping to break up parking platforms, and pedestrian space around fountain which cools air-conditioning water. Natural articulation of the various horizontal levels is in harmony with the topography, and random planting of trees and shrubs tends to accent the even rhythm of cars and building façades, while the latter remain dominant because of elevation; model of a 90-acre research center in California, Thompson-Ramo-Wooldridge Corporation.

for enclosure, instead of the undifferentiated wall, serving both purposes). The engineering masterpieces of today are those where there is no enclosure, where form and structure are one, where the least possible amount of a chosen material is used to carry the highest possible stress.

The social preferences of our society, however, working through the market mechanism of the economy, have often counteracted this trend toward structural refinement. When materials are cheap, and labor—including design labor—expensive, the engineer is under constant pressure to substitute materials for labor, to use heavier, simpler, and more crude design solutions instead of those that are now made potentially feasible by the current state of mathematics and the engineering art. Moreover,

Orderly, rhythmical massing in an industrial park near Boston, Mass.

speed is expected from the design and construction organizations, since the investment of an industrial entrepreneur is tied up and brings no return until his facility is operating. The construction time for a typical factory is often only nine months, and the amount of creative thought that can be given to any single situation is limited. Finally, there is a widespread economic tendency—of questionable long-range wisdom —to favor maintenance expenditures at the expense of capital expenditures. In the case of industry, this tendency is reinforced by the fiscal policies of the government. For tax purposes, maintenance expense is included with manufacturing costs, to be subtracted from gross income to give taxable profits. Since the capital for new construction may come from profits, a low initial expenditure and consequent mediocre quality of design is favored, to keep taxes down. It is often possible for a producer continually to alter his cheaply built plant and count these outlays as maintenance. But if a new facility is to be used for defense production, the construction cost of the installation may be written off taxable profits in five years. This second policy encourages maximum initial expenditures consistent with good design. Yet, to achieve greater permanence and elegance in industrial design, a change in federal law would be obviously insufficient. What is needed is a change in attitudes, in which the prestige value of beautiful industrial facilities will be sufficiently important to the entrepreneur to encourage him to make economic sacrifices. Indications of such a trend are evident among some larger companies, but so far not among the smaller entrepreneurs.

The evolution of the American water tank (manufacturer, Chicago Bridge and Iron Company).

To come back to the subject of structurally expressive forms, several suggestions seem near at hand. For factories, recent engineering advances—stressed skin construction, reinforced concrete plates with a complex curvature, "space frames" and other three-dimensional trusses such as geodesic domes—allow us to visualize large, simple,

Exposed transformer, screened by planting, can be a very good neighbor in a residential community; accent and interest are added to the neighborhood. This is surely preferable to hiding the transformer in a colonial "house," as some telephone companies do with switching equipment. Design by Consolidated Edison Co. of New York.

lightweight, and permanent space enclosures which, almost totally divorced from the manufacturing process they are currently enclosing, would be immune to functional obsolescence. They would satisfy the requirement for "clarity of massing" and would be structurally much more expressive than the currently dominant post-and-beam or simple truss construction. On the other hand, whenever an enclosure can be omitted without undue increase in maintenance costs, this should be done. We have noted the dramatic effect of oil refineries and chemical plants, in which the processing apparatus stands in the open air. Repetitive structures—water tanks, telephone relay towers, and pylons carrying high-tension electric transmission lines—can be given much more expressive and stimulating shapes than many of those currently in use. To refine their form, design competitions should be arranged with top figures from engineering and the arts as critics, to reward the best designs and to discourage the use of designs which have been superseded. Television transmitters and telephone relay towers, which locate on the highest elevations, can be humanized by combining them with sightseeing towers and other recreational facilities. This practice has been very popular in Europe, but so far has not been thought of on this continent. As a combined technical and recreation facility, the tower can have a much more handsome and expressive structure, as the German concrete paraboloids with several tiers of cantilevered balconies convincingly show.

THE USE OF SILHOUETTE

Proceeding from the design of the industrial facility itself to its relationship with the environment, we should concern ourselves first with its outline, as seen against the sky. The scale of industrial installations being what it is, they are likely to be bigger than anything in their environment, and their skyline will characterize the landscape. In cases when physical location requirements are very rigid, not much deliberate esthetic use can be made of an industrial skyline—except for making the view more accessible, say, by orienting the alignment of a freeway in such a manner that motorists can enjoy the industrial panorama. In the case of smaller installations,

The electric generating station: enclosed (*above*) and exposed (*below*); locations are in the Midwest and in Texas.

One of the most beautiful structures in Scandinavia, this mushroom-like water tank on a granite rock dominates the residential area of Lauttasaari in Helsinki. The top is of prefabricated, prestressed concrete ribs; the stem is reinforced concrete poured in place.

however, sites can be chosen with a certain regard for deliberately changing—or preserving—the outlines of a landscape. The design plan of a community can point out spots where vertical accent is desirable and areas where such an accent would be in conflict with existing features, and this visual plan should affect the location and the zoning controls of industrial reserves in the community. With a view toward the deliberate use of industrial skylines for visual accent, we can roughly classify some typical industrial silhouettes:

FLAT, SINGLE STOREY (light manufacturing, warehousing): accentuates horizontality of flat land, may need trees for vertical accent; very unobtrusive if viewed from ground level; can be completely masked by trees, if desired. Viewed from an elevation, roof plane may be dull if too large.

FLAT, TWO-TO THREE-STOREY (research laboratory, specialized manufacture, such as instruments, combined factory-office building): visually, best sited on elevated ground, in moderately rolling topography; can be locally dominant element that does not disrupt the skyline of the background.

FLAT, WITH RAGGED OUTLINE (heavier manufacturing, usually involving thermal treatment of metals): larger facility, in need of railroad, with whose alignment the mass of the building should be coordinated in plan, so that the alignment of the mass does not look arbitrary; the outline is usually interesting both from the ground level and from an elevation; mass is of a size that cannot be concealed in the landscape; ample separation from adjacent development desirable.

THE SINGLE VERTICAL (water tank, chimney stack, relay tower, rocket-launching facility): a large array of facilities, each of them highly standardized in design, some always isolated, some frequently appearing in conjunction with horizontal elements. In each case, structural expressiveness and siting are very important, since this element always pierces the existing skyline. Chimneys, formerly indispensable attributes of factories, are much less frequent today: if well-proportioned, a single chimney can give a welcome accent to a highly horizontal development; when technically possible it should stand apart from an adjacent mass for maximum effect. Groups of chimneys of various heights (as in chemical plants) can create an interesting ensemble; a chimney and a tall element of a different shape, such as a water tank, are in conflict, however, and should be combined in one structure. In the absence of a stack, a water tank often can be the accent and the trademark of a low-slung factory; the siting of either element with regard to the horizontal mass should be carefully studied, to create a balanced composition; this is much easier in the case of the water tank, since its siting near a building is completely flexible. Freestanding water tanks in a flat landscape are effective as accent near bodies of water; they can serve as landmarks near freeways in rolling topography and accent the forested tops of hills in steeper terrain. Since the scale of water tanks and residential development is incompatible, the water tank on a hill amid residential development should have ample forested green space around it. On no account should it be placed amid houses, without any visual buffer. Relay towers, locating on fairly high hilltops, are usually automatically articulated from the surrounding landscape by a forested—or bare—setting, but their light steel structure is often visually too transparent to make their dominance convincing. Heavier towers of reinforced concrete, designed with structural elegance, are much more significant and interesting.

THE VERTICAL OF MISCELLANEOUS GEOMETRY (dish and radar antennas, and similar advanced facilities): these occur singly or in a group, and locate on elevated ground; whether the installations are military or civilian, they usually have an adequate reservation of open space around them. Their esoteric shapes make them dramatic focal points in the landscape. Little can be said, however, for the conventional radio transmitter. The thin, tall structures are quite weak visually, while the wire antennae and the guy cables present a confused appearance: the facilities become prominent at night with their aircraft warning lights, but should in general not be placed in a prominent spot in the urban landscape.

Telephone relay tower.

THE SINGLE, HIGH-BULK STRUCTURE (power plant, incinerator, boiler house): a highly ubiquitous use, in scale with the industrial landscape, but out of scale with any other use, unless articulated by a large amount of surrounding open space. Careful study of the massing composition and exterior treatment is important. Quite different in character, but perhaps the largest bulk structure in view, is the gasometer: it greatest visual danger is competition with the skyline of a central business district in a city.

FLAT, RHYTHMIC MASSING (oil and gasoline storage tanks; on a smaller scale, sludge digestion tanks in sewerage treatment plants): these do not have to be ugly if on flat ground (not cut into rock ledges as in the entrance to Stockholm harbor), if firmly arranged in a geometric order (without haphazard mixture of small and large tanks), and if given a quiet color, without advertising messages. If the waterfront is valuable for recreational, conservation, or visual open-space use, tank farms should be set back from the ship dock even at the expense of installing booster pumps to carry the petroleum products from ship to tank. Landscaping of the surrounding area is important, particularly in the case of sewerage treatment plants, where the facilities can be subtly blended into the sculptured land forms.

STRONG VERTICAL RHYTHMIC MASSING (steel mills, oil refineries, shipyards, mining): these are very large-scale, unique facilities, where deliberate esthetic manipulation is not possible, except for the provision of adequate buffer zones to prevent conflicts in scale with adjacent development, and the provision of adequate vantage points for the traveling public.

Three examples of characteristic industrial skylines: *top,* flat, one-story building with trees and flagpole as a vertical accent; *center,* strong vertical rhythmical massing; *below,* single, high-bulk building; a manufacturing plant near Montreal, an oil refinery near St. Louis, and a municipal incinerator in Wisconsin.

Successful siting of a water tank: *left,* as an accent and a trademark along the low-slung volume of an assembly plant (with harmony in color); *right,* as a dominant element on the waterfront (note reflection) where it gives focus to a residential community without disrupting its scale.

The horizontal "campus look" of this elegant medical supplies plant in New Jersey, vertically accented by trees, needs a dominant vertical accent; two are provided, in the competing chimney and water tower. A common European practice is to combine chimney and water tank in one structure, resulting in a stronger vertical dominant.

There is no need to study the profile architecturally in a facility with strong vertical massing, as above; it grows automatically out of the functional process.

The profile against the sky is an important consideration in the appearance of thin, rhythmically spaced verticals: *above*, derricks of the Standard Oil Company march across the flat Oklahoma landscape, evenly spaced on 1,400-foot centers (40 acres per well), a standard based on sound conservation practice; *below*, towers of a British 275,000-volt power transmission line. The Central Electricity Generating Board favors placement of transmission lines against a background of landscape, since seen against the sky they can be too obtrusive. This, obviously, is not always feasible, and the graceful design of the towers themselves is no less important.

ARTICULATION OF ELEMENTS

In discussing the industrial silhouette, we have had occasion to mention the importance of buffer zones to isolate elements which in scale or otherwise are incompatible with their surroundings. The plea for buffer zones was made earlier in connection with the street grid in residential development, and in connection with freeway design. The buffer zones are of the utmost visual importance in industrial design, where they can take many forms.

The simplest buffer is a fence. Opaque fences of substantial structural strength should be made mandatory in all industrial zoning provisions, where the screening of unsightly uses such as junk yards or material storage areas is involved. A subtler form of screening, to be recommended whenever enough space is available, and whenever a use is more permanent, are dense stands of evergreens, several rows deep, planted in a green reserve at least fifty to one hundred feet wide, depending on the size of the area to be enclosed. Any "token" buffer narrower than 50 to 70 feet will not read visually as a buffer, but rather as a meaningless and reluctant attempt to conform to a regulation. Since evergreens in buffers take time to grow up, the immediate screening effect can be enhanced by providing a moderately high bank of earth around the use to be screened; but care should be taken that the soil composition and moisture content in the bank be such as to support the projected planting.

To the extent that a use does not have to be hidden from view but merely set off and given proper perspective, adequate setback regulations, removing the building

Hints of the landscape of the future? Titan ICBM at Vandenberg Air Force Base (*above*), and AT&T antennae for overseas telephone communication in Florida (*below*).

line a substantial distance from the property line, are most important. The amount of the setback, again, must depend on the size of the facility, including both its area and its height. Fifty feet may be adequate for small factories of a few thousand square feet, and 100 feet may be a good standard for medium-size industrial development, but very large installations such as oil refineries need a permanently protected green zone more than a mile in width, not primarily for visual reasons, but for protection from odors and air pollution as well. Government authorities, both military and

Left, A well-meant attempt with inadequate maintenance: the embankment was built to screen the coal piles from the street, but the pine trees planted on top of it are all dead. *Right,* The ubiquitous chain-link fence: not too obtrusive if seen against the background of a dominating mass, but it becomes extremely obnoxious if prominent in itself. Solutions: wider mesh, if its value is mostly symbolic; if firmer protection is needed, an opaque color, helping to blend the fence with its background (the reflective quality of galvanized wire makes it so prominent); another possibility is stronger mesh and supports, with the fence used to carry vines.

civilian, and some private corporations recognize this need for adequate protection of facilities by open space; the U.S. Steel Corporation owns extensive amounts of land around its new Fairless Works on the Delaware River (though there is no guarantee that none of it will be sold in the future), and the National Aeronautics and Space Administration acquired more than 72,000 acres on Merritt Island in Florida for its new Missile Test Center adjacent to Cape Canaveral. Clearly, most of this area will serve the function of protective open space. However, by no means all large-scale,

noxious industries live up to the need to provide proper isolation of their installations from urban development, and since local or even state controls in this matter
would be clearly of very little help, the matter of establishing proper open-space
standards for chemical complexes, oil refineries, and steel mills should be a federal
responsibility.

To summarize, the construction of industrial facilities in the urbanized landscape
must go hand in hand with the provision of a differentiated matrix of open space, into

A junkyard, a fence, and a better fence.

which these facilities are to be set: park or forest-like greenbelts around major industrial zones, with none but agricultural conservation or recreation uses permitted;
within these zones, adequate green spaces between industries, to provide a humanized
setting; visually obnoxious uses screened by buffer planting. And, for the smaller
uses, if they are not incompatible with a residential or other more intensive urban
environment, a park-like "estate" setting assured by setback regulations, coverage
limitations, landscaping requirements, and localized buffer planting.

INTEGRATION WITH THE LANDSCAPE

A matrix or grid of open space and green buffers, while it serves to articulate the
industrial districts and individual industrial properties, simultaneously provides the
anchor that ties the technological environment to the natural environment. For this
tie to be successful, the continuity of the natural environment has to be preserved by
proper attention to continuity of land forms and to the composition of planting. In
an environment of higher density, such as a research center, the planting can be
formal, with fountains, flower beds, and closely cropped lawns; in a more extensive
setting, the informality of a more natural and rugged vegetation is logical. The most
important visual consideration, however, is the healing of industrial scars in the surface of the earth.

A proper balance must be preserved between the part of the property covered by
building, the part covered by parking, that devoted to storage, truck docks, and other
functional open areas, and that devoted to landscaping. In a study of 188 industrial

Industry, landscape, and a freeway: *top,* setback of several thousand feet—factory barely visible; *center,* setback of 500 to 1,000 feet —pleasant relationship; *below,* less than 100-foot setback—factory encroaches upon highway, cannot be well comprehended.

properties which covered, on the average, 45 per cent of the lot by buildings, the Los Angeles County Regional Planning Commission found an average of 3.8 per cent of the lot area devoted to landscaping. This low percentage is no doubt partly determined by the excessive watering requirements posed by an arid climate, but even under these conditions a considerable number of these industries was able to allocate more than eight per cent of the lot area to planting. In areas with more moisture and lower

Bethlehem Steel's integrated works at Sparrows Point, Md., with blast furnaces in the foreground, shipyard on the left: an example of a fortunate separation of a large-scale facility from adjacent development by a body of water: only intrusion of residences is at right.

densities, the dedication of substantially greater amounts of land to planted areas is being practiced—up to two-thirds of the lot and more in the case of some Eastern "prestige" industries. As a general rule, such high requirements would of course be very wasteful of land and maintenance effort, but minimum standards requiring between 10 and 25 per cent of the lot area in landscaping could be feasible and proper under most conditions.

Next to the amount of land devoted to landscaping, its distribution on the property is important. A large landscaped area in one lump is of little help if next to it the continuity of the landscape is violated by a depressingly large and monotonous expanse of parking. Parking areas, in industry no less than in commercial use, which will be treated later, must be broken up by trees and strips of grass to provide a more humanized and amenable environment.

Special attention should be paid to storage and disposal areas, and to areas in which the natural ground cover has been disturbed by fill or excavation. Tight enforcement of "no dumping" regulations, and the use of earth removal ordinances, requiring the loaming and reseeding of disturbed areas (as mentioned under "earth removal regulations" in connection with housing development design earlier), can be of help. Proper attention to sand and gravel pits is particularly important in this context. "Borrow" areas, as well as sand and gravel pits, should not be allowed to occur haphazardly throughout the community, and should be properly set back from uses that are prominent in the view, such as major thoroughfares. Beyond that, stringent

Integration with the landscape: the time-honored New England stone wall, natural planting left intact, and a man-made pond provide a proper buffer and a proper setting for this plant in eastern Connecticut; however, the surrounding environment is not legally protected against future development.

performance standards for the rehabilitation of the used part of the facility should be enforced. The National Sand and Gravel Association suggests that excavations made to a water-producing depth should have their banks graded to an acceptable slope, surfaced with topsoil and planted with trees, shrubs, grasses, or legumes. Excavations

Very extensive setback with a closely mowed lawn, typical of many modern industries in the East; placing of the formally cropped shrubs, however, is out of scale in this low-density environment.

Industry in the landscape: Ford assembly plant at Mahwah, N.J. about 30 miles from Times Square: freeway interchange, center; Ramapo mountains and Palisades Interstate Park in background; Motel on the Mountain, upper left. Major esthetic faults are the abrupt break between the lushness of the surrounding vegetation and the bareness of the Ford parking lots (which could have been broken up by vegetation to a greater extent), and the misalignment of the river—it was pushed around by adjacent uses, with no regard for its fate; another indication of the need for comprehensive visual planning in the macro-landscape.

Examples of careful garden landscaping near industrial facilities: Lockheed Aircraft research laboratory in Palo Alto, Cal. (*above*), and Edwards manufacturing plant in Norwalk, Conn. (*below*).

Exhausted strip mine rehabilitated through reforestation and the introduction of water becomes a valuable recreational asset examples by the National Coal Association.

that do not reach the water table should be either back-filled with non-noxious, non-combustible solids, or graded to a gently rolling surface in conformity with surrounding topography, covered with topsoil and planted, as above. Clearly, not many communities have taken the trouble to apply standards of this type, for the unused, eroding sand bank, often in uncomfortable proximity to adjacent uses, is an all-too-familiar violation of the landscape in the urban fringe. On a scale immensely greater than that of a gravel pit, some coal producers in the Midwest have achieved significant progress in the reforestation and rehabilitation of the man-made wasteland of open-pit coal mines. But here, too, much remains to be done by the public to bring most of the operations up to the level of the best.

3. Commercial Facilities in the Urban Fringe

Commercial activity in low-density urban areas makes a visual impact out of all proportion to the comparatively small area which it occupies. Typically, in a region as a whole, commercial use occupies about three per cent of the urbanized land and accounts for about six per cent of the investment in new construction. But commercial activities attract far more people per unit of area than any other land use; and because they want to be seen by and be accessible to the maximum number, they prefer to settle in conspicuous spots along major thoroughfares. Accordingly, we find here one of the most glaring problems of visual design.

Where in the urban fringe should retail stores and other commercial uses be placed? How can they be fitted into this evolving pattern of land use so that the new order looks better and works better than present commercial development?

Disorderly though commercial development may appear at first glance, it is actually a constellation held in shape by a dynamic balance of supply and demand. Excess capacity is removed by bankruptcy (in the case of a small independent trader) or withdrawal (in the case of a chain, which will find a more profitable outlet in some other district). Undercapacity, leading to the abuses of monopoly and uneconomic service, is now more likely to exist in a central city, where prime locations are limited, than in a fringe area where the car-borne shopper can easily break through political boundaries.

It should be realized that there will always be an underlying conflict of aim between the planner and the developer of commercial property (unless the planner is willing to conspire with the developer to give the latter a monopoly). For the planner, in trying to avoid waste, is always concerned to encourage an ordered and localized balance of supply and demand. The developer's opportunity for greatest profit, on the other hand, lies in discovering and exaggerating some point of imbalance where demand can be made to rise beyond the planned supply.

The anticipated trade area may be extended by lower prices or better value, more choice or more accessibility, pleasanter surroundings, or special promotions. The

An example of the ultimate harmony of art and nature: Reservoir dam of the New Haven Water Company, and the Hammonasset River.

trade area may also be extended in depth as well as width by discovering an opportunity where none was thought to exist—for example, by bringing in live theater, a ski store, a skating rink, or a restaurant with banquet rooms and catering service. Then the prevailing system of percentage rents will turn the developer's ingenuity to maximum profit.

Any viable pattern of commercial development which may be suggested for the urban fringe area must comprehend and acknowledge this underlying logic of a natural economic order. Retail trade, in the economists' jargon, is a market-oriented activity. The merchant would like to be placed wherever he can be reached most easily by the most customers. The customer wants the largest choice of goods and services at the lowest price and most convenient accessibility. Each party will, of course, eventually prefer some compromise within these extremes, because shopping is, after all, no more than an occasional activity.

Where is a store "most easily reached"? Accessibility is seldom accurately measured in terms of distance. A grocery store with small and awkward parking, even though it be only a half-mile down the street, is actually less accessible than a supermarket with ample parking three miles down the highway. The prosperity of a central business district (whether it be Chicago's Loop, or Main Street in a town of 3,000 people) depends upon its being the area most easily reached by the most people. Accessibility supports high land values, which tend to winnow out such bulky, low-density uses as warehousing and automobile showrooms. These move to cheaper and larger sites on the outskirts of the city. So do many of the city's residents; and the local service stores, which include supermarkets and automobile service stations, follow along to keep their company.

The most important type of shopping—measured in money, time, or space—is that for food. Only journeys to and from work are more frequent than those for shopping and personal business. The largest item in any shopping budget is food; it ranges from one-quarter to one-third of all household expenditures according to income level. This is more than goes for rent (or its equivalent—amortizing mortgage, maintenance, and depreciation) or for private automobile transportation, which are the next largest items on the expense list.

The consumer is therefore extremely conscious of the price of food at retail. This has led to a long and ingenious struggle for economy in food distribution. The large supermarkets, comprising less than ten per cent of the grocery stores, do more than 70 per cent of the total grocery business, on a profit margin of less than one per cent. The housewife is encouraged to economize by buying in quantity—cigarettes by the carton, peaches by the bushel, and dog food by the bag. Mechanization and self-service (i.e. making the customer do the work formerly done by hired help) have helped to offset the rise in wages, which have gone up faster than any other retail expense during the last decade.

Because a busy housewife has to go shopping for food frequently, convenience and accessibility become almost as important as price. So food stores have always been first among retailers to follow their customers to the suburbs, to the fringe, to the frontier new or old. This leads to economy in distribution, and also decreases highway traffic, as the movement from warehouse to store in large truck shipments decreases the length of individual shopping trips by car.

Most food items are comparatively bulky and low in value, and the average check in a supermarket is between five and six dollars. Walking sizable bundles home in an area zoned for one-acre single-family residence, or even taking them on a bus, is not usually practicable and certainly not convenient. Thus most shopping for food in an urban fringe area will be done by car.

Because of its high volume of sales per square foot—between $100 and $150, as compared with about $60 in a conventional department store—the supermarket

Cooling pond of a Standard Oil refinery in Texas.

usually requires a larger allowance of parking space in relation to floor area than other stores. When a family has only one car and the wage earner receives a weekly pay check, the bulk of the week's food shopping is done on Friday evening or Saturday morning. In many supermarkets as much as three-quarters of the whole week's business is done on those two days. This leads to a very high parking demand over a short period. With an expected increase in the number of two-car families, however, food shopping in higher-income neighborhoods may in future be more equally spaced through the week.

More easily than any other retailer, a grocer can afford to pioneer in following his customers out into the fringe, not so much because ample parking space is cheap there, but because each household spends such a large amount of its income on food. A supermarket doing a business of $2 million annually can be effectively supported by 2,000 families, if there is not much competition. With a lot area of one-half acre per family, this whole group of customers could be housed within a circle of less than one-mile radius.

Compare this with the facts of trade which face a large department store. It will have perhaps ten or more times the floor area of the supermarket, even in the case of

Crossroads shopping, old and new: *above,* crossroads settlement north of El Reno, Okla.; *below,* crossroads in Tucson, Ariz.

a suburban branch store, in order to provide adequate display and selling space for the many different and often bulky goods which it stocks. In the course of a year, however, each family will spend at the department store only about half as much as it spends at the supermarket. Moreover, this average family will go shopping for department-store goods perhaps once a month, as compared with two or three times a week for food. And at the department store they will charge it; at the supermarket they pay cash.

Obviously then, a department store, and the other stores included in the GAF category (general merchandise, apparel, and furniture), must draw on a much wider area than a supermarket for an equal volume of trade. So within a retail trade constellation there will be many more supermarkets than department stores, to maintain a natural economic balance. The wide accessibility which the GAF stores need was found until recently only at the center of an urban transportation system, that is, in the central business district. With wider dispersal of population, and the use of private cars in preference to public transportation, city department stores followed their customers to the suburbs and fringe areas beyond. Paramus, New Jersey, for example, when it was a little town with a population of around 15,000, suddenly found itself selected as the site for two regional shopping centers with $30 million of new store buildings, and parking space for more than 15,000 cars. This new shopping area has a potential market of one million people within ten minutes' driving time.

4. Possibilities of Planned Design

NEW COMMERCIAL CENTERS

In developing a pattern of commercial uses for the urban fringe we must not be led astray by the lurid and disorderly present of that area. Ultimately most of this region will become residential.

Highway traffic is not a good neighbor for housing, and stores in a low-density area (which we expect the urban fringe to remain, even when developed) can count on their supplies being delivered by truck and their customers by car. So any cluster of stores in this area will cause a great deal of traffic; therefore, it must be as far as possible insulated from residential areas and immediately accessible to large highways. A small community store group could probably be served by two feeder roads; a large regional center had best be placed at the crossing of two major freeways. A group of stores will almost inevitably do more business than would the same stores operating at a distance one from the other. Fortunately, this ecological clustering is good for business as well as for planning.

Commercial development is not only incompatible with the quiet, spacious, and safe green privacy which fringe dwellers are seeking for themselves and their children, but also raises almost insuperable problems of incompatibility in visual scale. A one-story supermarket 20,000 square feet in area might perhaps with difficulty be brought

Schematic representation of residential traffic flow to a planned commercial and community center.

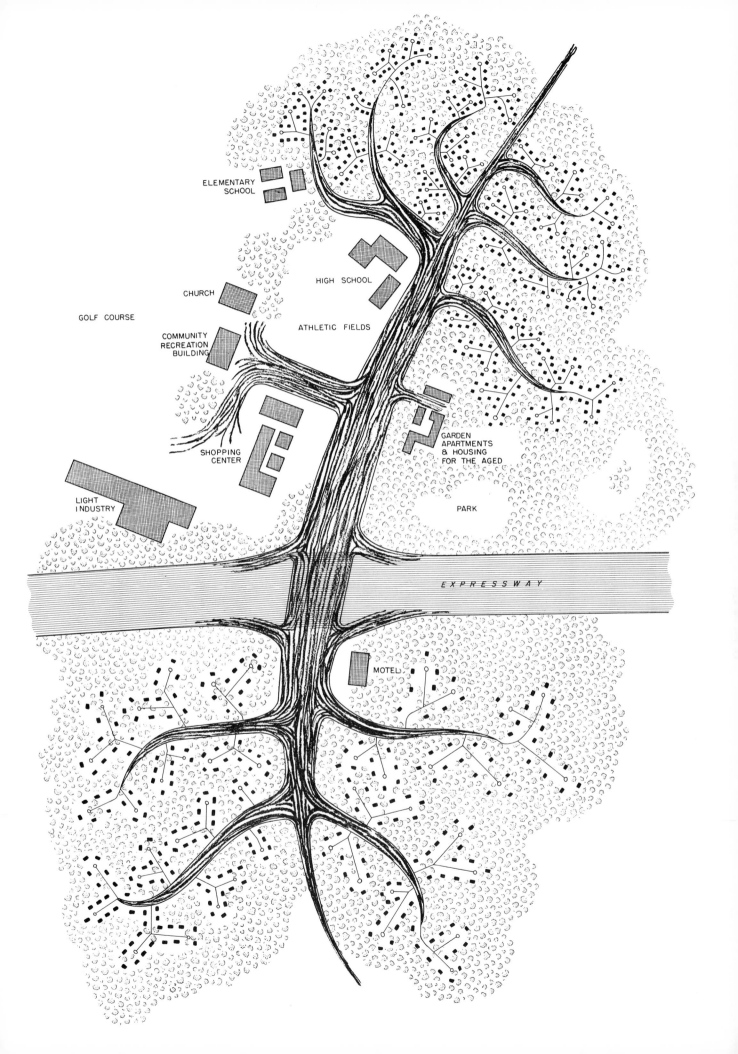

ELEMENTARY
SCHOOL

CHURCH

HIGH SCHOOL

GOLF COURSE

ATHLETIC FIELDS

COMMUNITY
RECREATION
BUILDING

SHOPPING
CENTER

GARDEN
APARTMENTS
& HOUSING
FOR THE AGED

LIGHT
INDUSTRY

PARK

EXPRESSWAY

MOTEL

into some pleasing relation with a settlement of single-family houses—but the parking area? It will have to be at least three times as large as the store building. Breaking it up into smaller, scattered lots with trees, bushes, and changes of level will usually hinder smooth and economical use.

Depending upon the highway to bring both customers and supplies, the store cluster should ideally be attached to a feeder road which collects traffic from the quiet residential cul-de-sacs as upland streams drain into a widening river. Because we are trying to allow unhampered movement, because we are concerned with time more than distance (so that "nearer" in miles may actually be farther in time), we must abandon the traditional self-contained neighborhood idea, and plan for much larger, fluid, overlapping communities.

Stores are not the only buildings which raise difficulties of traffic and scale. High schools with auditoriums and athletic fields serving the whole community, large recreation facilities such as bowling alleys and public swimming pools, churches, drive-in movies, hospitals, office buildings, and industrial plants, when placed in a low-density settlement, raise similar problems of traffic and scale. By grouping these structures we could also protect residential areas from traffic nuisance, and could design highway capacity sized for predictable loads. Land use should be zoned according to its traffic generation, so that the size of the commercial cluster can be fitted to the size of the highway network upon which it will depend. It may even be possible to arrange some overlapping use of parking space. A research laboratory, for example, with one shift and a five-day week, could help out the shopping center where peak parking loads come in the evenings and on Saturdays.

In the buffer area between this concentration of traffic and the single-family residential areas, there might be a golf course or a bird sanctuary, or a public park and a small village for the aged within walking distance of the stores. This would also be a suitable place for high-rise apartments. Bicycle paths and trails through a strip of public parkland should lead from residential areas to the recreational opportunities in this buffer strip.

There have been many suggestions that small grocery stores more frequently spaced would give better service and encourage small neighborhood groupings which would correspond to an elementary school "market area." Such ideas are based on a sentimental backward glance to the deserted city; they do not fit the actual habits of life in the urban fringe, nor do they correspond to the present economics of food distribution, as we have explained earlier. Walk-in trade is simply not practical with American driving habits and urban fringe density. Once in the car, any housewife will be willing to drive ten minutes rather than five, if she can thus find wider choice and better value. As 80 per cent or more of all retail buying is done by women, shopping convenience must also be planned into any new store group.

The minimum economic size for a chain supermarket dealing in food only has been gradually increasing and now stands at about 15,000 to 17,000 square feet. This would have to do a minimum business at $1½ million annually. If total food expenditure is $1,200 to $1,500 annually per household, a market area of at least 2,000 homes would be desirable, on the assumption that no single store will capture all household food spending.

A shopping center with two supermarkets, for a market area twice this size, would not cause unreasonably long driving distances and would give much better shopping service. For it would justify a full group of service stores, a variety store, children's clothes, even a junior department store. If other types of buildings were combined with the store group, as suggested above, there would be opportunity for a good restaurant, a sporting goods store, and more apparel stores, with a bank, a post office, and a public library. This would become a viable community center.

Alternatively such a site would be attractive to a discount department store, which is essentially a group of independent stores under one roof, their selling efforts, advertising, and pricing closely coordinated by an aggressive central management. With high turnover and low markup, such a store would draw on a much wider market area than the community shopping center and would thus cause a heavier traffic load. The discount store might also be expected to offer even better value than the standard supermarket by using its food department as a loss leader for promotion.

As for the other frequently cited justification of the corner grocery store, that it supplies the things you run out of, or forgot to get—the aspirin, the salt, the ice cubes, or the milk—this service could be made available 24 hours a day by a battery of vending machines at the local gas station.

THE OLD TOWN CENTER

So far we have considered commercial development in fringe areas as though it could be exactly placed by some all-powerful designer on a *tabula rasa*. Actually the residential areas to be served will often have grown up around an existing small town. What is essentially a crossroads store group will focus on the intersection of Main and the other shopping street. The first invader of this genteel symmetry will usually be a large supermarket. Needing a minimum area of 2 acres at a reasonable price and on one of the principal highways, it will be forced to settle at the far edge of the existing business center. For its car-borne customers it is more accessible there than it would be in the middle of town. But the supermarket encourages other new stores, and these string out along the highway in a strip 100 feet deep, zoned commercial. Meanwhile, the old town center, with inadequate parking space and shabby stores catering to the taste of vanished farmers, deteriorates still further. Yet land prices in the center remain high, thus discouraging any large-scale private development.

The municipal offices, and in some towns a courthouse, will remain as the nucleus of an office population; this is unlikely to expand much, but it does anchor some activity in the center. For the new fringe population, however, the greatest asset of the old center will be its character (even though the word be used in its theatrical sense). Here is an individual amalgam of huge old trees, nineteenth-century brick store blocks, a small park perhaps with a fretwork bandstand, a white-painted "Gothic" church, an iron fountain left over from some long-forgotten exhibition. Here is the flotsam of a small, undistinguished, but intensely individual history.

The scale of these old town centers is usually small. Remove the crust of shabby dejection, close some of the streets to cars and fit more small stores into the present street space, tear down the slum stores and refurbish any buildings with a strong visual character (not only the alleged Colonials, but those lively nineteenth-century revivals also—the Greek, the Egyptian, the Italian, or whatever), and finally—but first in importance—fit ample pockets of parking into the outer edges of this store group where they can connect immediately with the highways.

Every existing town center will, of course, have its own special (and seemingly insurmountable) problems of development. We can do no more here than suggest general principles based upon the idea that it is "character" and variety which can most profitably be exploited to help the old central business district compete with new shopping centers on its outskirts or in the next town.

The stores must also be encouraged to carry through this theme of individuality into their ownership and the merchandise which they carry. A large modern shopping center will favor national chain stores as tenants because their leases supply the credit base required for financing the development. This gives the small town center an opportunity for stressing the independent store or individual craftsman offering exceptional merchandise not available in chain stores. This new-old store group should have something of the quality of a City Market which provides an outlet for home-grown and homemade farm products.

How could all this be made to happen? Nothing short of intervention by local government will be sufficient to coordinate such a program of development. Land in existing small town centers is usually held in small parcels by individual owners, many of them short-sighted and jealous of their rights. To make possible the large-scale planning envisaged here, intervention by the town, with threats of forcible purchase by eminent domain, will almost certainly be required.

For the town center must boldly pass in a single leap from the traditional street grid to the new pattern required by the automobile age, where strolling pedestrians are separated from speeding cars by eliminating the shared street. Auto highway and pedestrian pleasance—journey and destination—are connected only through the parking lot.

If this change is to accomplish the objectives which we have outlined, the town will have to finance and control the development. This in turn means that the small town must have some new form of financing opened to it, as well as technical guidance in planning and management. Present urban renewal programs may not always fit the case.

FREEWAY SERVICE PARKS

Along the new freeways it is necessary to provide service areas for long-distance travelers. Each should be inconspicuously fitted into the larger rhythm of road and landscape, planned as an element in the traffic corridor of the highway. In some instances a service park might be used to shield local communities from the disturbance (both aural and visual) that such a highway is bound to provoke near residential areas.

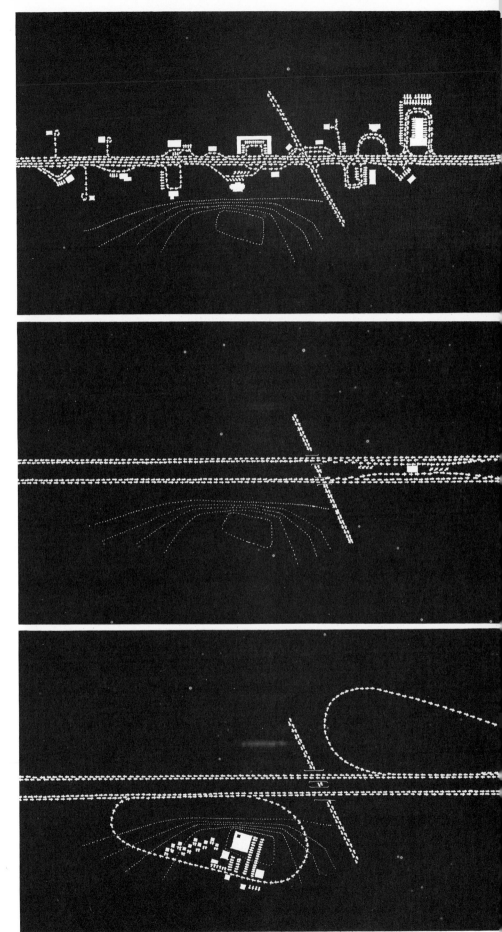

Past: typical commercial highway strip, showing the multitude of turns required to reach roadside services.

Present: limited access highway with austere concession-type service area in the median strip.

Possible: the same highway, with identical services on a loop, on either side, where motels, service stations, and restaurants as well as shops serving the traveler can be clustered.

These roadside service parks should provide gas stations, restaurants and motels. Craft and souvenir shops offering specialties of the area might also be included, particularly in vacation areas where visitors are always looking for "something to take to the folks back home." In places which attract hunters and fishermen a sporting-goods store would also be justified.

While these service parks should be designed primarily to serve the needs of long-distance motorists on the freeway, they can be placed for convenient use by neighboring communities as well. Such an enlarged and dependable year-round trade would make a more attractive opportunity and would justify a slightly larger cluster, which in turn would give more competitive service.

For the tired motorist's sleep and relaxation, the service park should be separated from the freeway traffic noise by trees and bushes, and by a difference in level. This should be one of the criteria used in picking such a site. On the other side, the service park should be cut off from neighboring settlement by a strip of parkland with picnic grounds, camp sites, and perhaps an overnight trailer park.

The lengthy acceleration and deceleration lanes required for connection with the freeway suggest an elongated strip plan along the frontage road. This would also give any neighboring settlement a maximum length of protection from the highway corridor. On the other hand, some special condition of topography or land ownership or existing development might suggest forming the service park as a deep pocket at right angles to the highway.

The location of these service parks must be attuned to the long-distance scale of the freeway; it must not be influenced (any more than the course of the road itself) by local pressures and jealousies of small taxing districts. Land purchase, construction, and management of the service parks should be coordinated with the highway program at the state level. The land, though not part of the right-of-way, should be retained in public ownership, with income distributed among all taxing districts which adjoin the freeway.

A SPECIAL PROBLEM: THE ROADSIDE COMMERCIAL STRIP

In theory, the combination of (1) regional shopping center, (2) community store group or old village center, (3) freeway service park, and (4) scattered auto service stations with vending machines, could fully satisfy the commercial needs of low-density fringe areas. In practice, however, the most noticeable commercial development in these areas is "Strip Commercial." Indeed, this is such a visually aggressive and ubiquitous feature that it is sometimes considered to be typical, even inevitable, in the urban fringe. It comprises everything from billboards to drive-in movies, from gas stations to motels, from diners to trucking terminals, from farm fruit stands (and even working farmland) to discount department stores, from junk yards to dine-and-dance. The highway offers good accessibility and good advertising display space along a practically unlimited frontage.

The composition of the roadside strip will depend on the character of the highway, with the road carrying a greater amount of through traffic having a higher propor-

Typical roadside commercial strip on Route 1 in Connecticut.

Three views of folk architecture on Route 99 in the Pacific Northwest.

tion of traveler-oriented facilities; but since the majority of traffic is always local, community-oriented stores will not hesitate to locate on a through road, if access is not restricted. As one would expect for comparable general merchandise and apparel stores in a more central location, 85 to 95 per cent of the shoppers in roadside stores in the urban fringe live within 30 minutes' driving time. In the absence of legal restrictions, the volume of traffic alone, regardless of its destination, will cause commercial development to spring up: it begins to develop in the presence of daily volumes of about 5,000 cars, and becomes very intensive with 10,000 to 20,000 volumes.

When highly developed, a roadside commercial strip can have the characteristics of a linear commercial center, combining regional, local, and travel-oriented uses, offering its customers, to some extent, the opportunity to shop while moving in the car (hence oversize signs and garish displays), and having the added advantage of flexibility for expansion. Any compact center, of the type we have favored above, has to be developed at one time, by one entrepreneur acquiring a large tract of land under his centralized control; he often has to accept initial losses until such time as the population growth of surrounding areas catches up with the store capacity he has provided. Possibilities of gradual growth are limited. A strip, by contrast, grows by gradual accretion, in tune with the gradual population growth and the pattern of individual land ownership. Land along highways is usually both undesirable and too expensive for residential use; there is no public agency interested in acquiring it for landscaped buffer zones; thus it becomes reserved automatically for commercial expansion, and the town fathers in search of "tax base" are frequently all too eager to abet this process by thoughtless ribbon zoning, designating for commercial use a strip only 100 feet deep along both sides of every major highway far in excess of possible demand.

The trouble with commercial ribbons is, of course, that vehicular movement and shopping are incompatible, both functionally and visually. The numerous turning movements generated by roadside uses (in the order of 50 to 300 a day for an average roadside business, much more for important stores) make the highway one continuous intersection: both speed and capacity are reduced, and accidents rise. The "psychological friction" created by lateral restrictions and distractions makes driving even more difficult. While traffic capacity drops, the volume of traffic rises because of trips generated by the new businesses, until complete congestion results. Contrary to popular opinion, there are remedies.

There is a growing trend to give more zoning power to counties, especially a veto power over zoning changes along county and state roads. Wherever appropriate enabling legislation is enacted, county planning boards can block further expansion of strip commercial zoning, and influence the towns to reduce the extent of existing strip zones. We should also make much wider use of the state highway departments' power to control access. For access control, a highway does not have to be four-lane, divided, with grade separations: any new conventional, two-lane county or state road classified as a local arterial should have access partially controlled through condemnation of the access rights of abutting property owners. This is more difficult along existing roads, where access rights may be very costly; but this is still a sound method of control, particularly in rural areas, where land values are low and zoning nonexistent. Landscaped buffer strips are also necessary. These may be secured by purchase (under an open-space acquisition program), or by requiring adjacent developers to dedicate the land.

In existing roadside commercial areas, frontage roads are necessary, separated from the main highway by landscaped strips 12 to 20 feet wide. In this way the number of access points can be much reduced and the highway edge defined visually.

From desert to desert in Tucson, Ariz.: The elaborately landscaped Hotel El Conquistador was promoted in 1930 by the city's leading businessmen; note also the verdant golf course across the highway. The new shopping center surrounded by blacktop and automobiles creates a different type of desert landscape.

Once roadside strips are effectively curtailed, where will new commercial establishments settle? It can be shown that a deep, large site is much better for shopping as well as for traffic than the traditional strip. If there is danger of unduly favoring a single landowner, future "designed commercial districts" might be put in a "floating zone" of stated area within a larger district. Any landowner within this district could then apply to have his property zoned commercial, if he pledges to build so many square feet of store area on that property within a limited period—say two years—and backs his ability and good faith with a performance bond. New permits for roadside commercial clusters would be refused until the existing ones were substantially filled.

5. The Need For Visual Order

A retail store, unlike a museum or a town hall, does not enjoy a monopoly position. It is usually clustered with other stores selling the same or similar goods; and a few minutes away by car will be a similar cluster, just as there may be another gas station selling the same brand of gas less than a mile down the road.

Retail stores therefore want to appear interesting, approachable, eager to serve. Reasonably enough each store wants to call attention to itself, some by obviously expensive and tasteful restraint, others by a cheeky, colorful gaiety, others by a "house style" which borrows prestige and good will from other links in the chain. These motives can all contribute to a pleasant brightening of our surroundings. We should be suspicious of those regulations which would impose a common drabness. What is needed is rather a framework of order within which the building designer can operate with greatest flexibility.

Where a group of stores is organized by an entrepreneur into a shopping center, the architect can impose a uniform character through the plan, the landscaping, and the structural framework of the store buildings. Widespread use of the mall plan is due to the persuasive efforts of shopping center architects. So is the landscaping, sculpture, fountains, and ordered space found in these shopping malls. Yet within this ordered framework freedom of design is encouraged. Signs, for example, will be restricted in number or in area but not in style.

With the coming of two-storey enclosed malls and discount department stores, the visual problems of aggressive merchandising may be at least temporarily contained. For the outside of such structures will normally be blank and windowless (reflecting the plan of perimeter storage areas and air-conditioned space within) decorated only by the wall texture and a sign which does not have to blare down competition. Fortunately also this large scale and increased height makes its possible for such a structure to dominate its parking area.

Through the zoning control offered by a "designed commercial district," even a number of small independent stores on separately-owned parcels of land may be converted from the old street-front pattern to an island store group with adequate parking area. Allocation of ground areas and control of bulk can thus be controlled by law; unity and grace of design will depend upon the persuasion of a skilled architect.

When parking areas are set side by side with buildings, there is an obvious discrepancy in scale between building and parking area. The building, which traditionally

The gas station of the past and the present.

has dominated its site (particularly when that site is featureless and flat), is now in fact dominated by a parking area which is at least three or four times greater in area than the building. The pale bright mosaic of reflective metal when the parking area is filled, or the flat black expanse when empty, is more visually aggressive than any well-mannered building; nor does it offer a restful background for human activity. Ideally, cars and buildings should be widely separated. For convenience, however, cars should be parked as close as possible to the building. Logically, therefore, parking areas should ring the building like a moat.

In general we must increase the apparent scale of the building and decrease that of the parking area. High parapet walls may be added to increase the building's

The gas station of the future? Example from San Mateo County, Cal.

height and hide all the mechanical clutter on the roof (which never appears on the architect's perspective). Several buildings may be combined into a group which is articulated by some feature such as a tower building or a dome. The apparent spread of the building may also be increased by using wings, colonnades, walks and lines of planting to unite separated buildings and to carry the building complex out among the parking areas.

Though a minimum setback from the road and some geometric order in the location of the structures is necessary, lining up all buildings on a building line is not, since the effect of isolated commercial buildings in a low-density area is not that of a street, and side façades may be more prominent than front façades. What is necessary, just as with small industries, is consideration of all four sides of the building, since the "rear" is very likely not to be hidden completely from public view; at present, rear walls of stores are notorious for their ugliness.

Trees, bushes, and fences are most effective in decreasing the apparent area of parking space. They are visually even more powerful when combined with changes of level, and modern earth-moving machinery can as easily step a site as smooth it. Evergreen trees not only shield from view; they also dissipate noise and smell. Their shadows will pattern the harsh texture of reflective bodywork and dapple the drab surface of an empty lot. The angular patterning of "hairpin" divider lines also decorates a drab blacktop surface.

Another approach, encouraged by high land costs, is to condense ground-level parking areas into a multi-storey garage. By concentrating cars in parking structures they can be forced to harmonize in style and scale with adjoining buildings.

The viewpoint of a passing motorist on the highway is more confined and predictable that that of a motorist who approaches the building as a visitor. Vistas can be staged with tree screens and levels and earth barriers. General rules such as fixed setback lines may not work effectively under all conditions of topography; and topography here must be extended in meaning to include existing trees and vegetation.

While the most effective way to minimize the impact of a sea of cars or a sea of blacktop without obscuring the advertising appeal of the main commercial structure is to depress parking or elevate the building (an expanse of colorful car tops generally looks much better than a row of fenders and grills), careful and adequate planting on commercial properties is also important to integrate them with the surrounding landscape. Frequently commercial development appears as a desert-like eyesore against a background of lush green vegetation. Requiring a certain proportion of the lot to be covered by grass, shrubs, and trees is imperative if such a development is to be a good neighbor. Even a gasoline station on a small lot can reasonably dedicate 20 per cent of the land to planting. Curbs to define the paved area might also be required.

Town and Country Shopping Center, Palo Alto, Cal.; the old trees have been retained and protected in the parking lots.

Parking lot for shoppers at Levittown, Pa.; where there are no trees existing, new ones can be planted.

Preservation of existing trees must be encouraged or their replacement by new planting enforced.

Finally, and always, there is the question of signs. What controls can enforce order without hampering initiative and changing taste? Probably the need is for a limitation of total area, so that signs may be in a single large unit or scattered smaller units (cf. the single large billboard and the old Burma-Shave series). Then there can be some control of location, and perhaps of the number of messages.

For example, a large sign with a short, simple message can be located in the grass strip between the highway and the commercial parking lot; or it can be located on the commercial structure; or the allowed area can be used up in several small signs, related to each other. In principle, we should insist upon ample freedom for experiment within a large-scale framework of regulated order.

Pedestrian mall, Old Orchard Shopping Center, near Chicago, Ill.; Loebel, Schlossman and Bennett, architects.

Levittown, Pa.: trees and planting in islands on the walkway; Lathrop Douglass, architect.

Left: Northland Shopping Center, Detroit, Mich., showing restrained lettering; Victor Gruen and Associates, architects. *Right:* Broadway Anheim, Cal., showing lavish planting and controlled signs; Welton Becket and Associates, architects. *Below:* Eastland Shopping Center, Detro Mich., with raised planting beds in walkway, and play sculpture visible in background; Victor Gruen and Associates, architects.

Northland Shopping Center, Detroit, Mich., showing pedestrian approach through parking areas.

Northland Shopping Center, Detroit, Mich., showing vehicular exit from one of parking areas.

Too many signs (*above*) versus one large sign and individual store identification (*below*), as at the Belvedere Shopping Center, Marin County, Cal. (John Lord King, architect; Thomas Church, landscape architect).

A profusion of advertising (*above*) versus no advertising (*below*), as at the South Bay Shopping Center, Redondo Beach, Cal. (Victor Gruen and Associates, architects).

The corporate headquarters—a novel and somewhat uncertain type of commercial activity in low-density areas—as an oasis of beauty and order in the urban fringe: Connecticut General Insurance Company's home office in Bloomfield, Conn., near Hartford, whose central business district is visible at the upper left; Skidmore, Owings and Merrill, architects.

The Family, sculptural group by Isamu Noguchi, on the parklike grounds of the headquarters.

PART FIVE

The Outlines of Open Space: Esthetics and Recreation

1. Present Trends in Recreation
   National Trends: The Use of National Parks and All-Day Facilities
   National Trends: Recreation in Motion
   Regional Differences
   Local and Individual Preference

2. General Factors Affecting Design
   Limitations Set by Nature
   The Human Factor
   The Problem of Multi-Purpose Use

3. The Framework of Open Space Design
   Esthetic Organization
   Materials of Open Space Design
   Organization and Scale
   Quantities
   The Imprint of the Designer

4. Opportunities for Design
   National or Regional
   State or County
   Local Measures
   The Cost

To John Bartram, the eighteenth-century father of American botany, open space was all outdoors. From his home in Pennsylvania he ranged the wilderness to Ontario and Florida, noting the variations in climate, soil, and wildlife, and exclaiming with pleasure at each new species found. But the French and British were already fomenting the Indian troubles, and Bartram's travels eventually became circumscribed by hostile tribes and warring frontiersmen. "Unspoilt Nature" and "The Natural Man" were already a dream before Rousseau made the illusion popular. Other mid-eighteenth-century men were crowding into cities, where communications between them were easier, and where the costs of congestion soon began to make themselves felt as open space disappeared. It took a hundred years for the cities to gain some semblance of green with the nineteenth-century park movement, but even so they have never caught up with the need.

Ironically enough, as we have already seen, there always was and still is plenty of open space in the United States as a whole, but not always in the places where it is most useful. Today, our problem in designing open space is to strike a balance between dispersal and congestion, to create deliberately a system or progression of open spaces which will bring optimum conditions for the life of the human community and at the same time preserve what is left of Bartram's plant and animal discoveries.

If we take his definition of open space as all outdoors, the suggestion that we are in a position to design it may seem preposterous. But it should be remembered that we are considering design as including conservation, the broad strokes of land allocation, and the siting of all the new facilities which must be disposed in space. Now that man has penetrated to every corner of the continent in modes of travel which would have astounded Bartram, we are indeed in a position to design the productive, protective, recreational and ornamental areas which make up the open land spread out before us. In fact, it would be irresponsible to omit design considerations in any future type of development—in watersheds, timberlands, oil fields, suburban home sites, or desert playgrounds.

This chapter is an attempt to show that open space is an inherent part of the design in any type of development. It is as much a part of the commercial or industrial landscape as of the residential, although these aspects have received relatively less attention from designers. We should be thinking of open space on the one hand as all the land which is not built upon, and on the other hand as sites which have a recreational potential of some kind. The first aspect has already been discussed in the parts of this book which deal with the highway, housing, and technology. In the following pages we shall advance some principles which can apply to open space in any context, but especially in the context of recreational use and enjoyment, which today is one of the most vital aspects of nature's "utility to man."

1. Present Trends in Recreation

The importance of open space today has been magnified by twin phenomena, working against each other: the urban expansion, consuming thousands of acres of

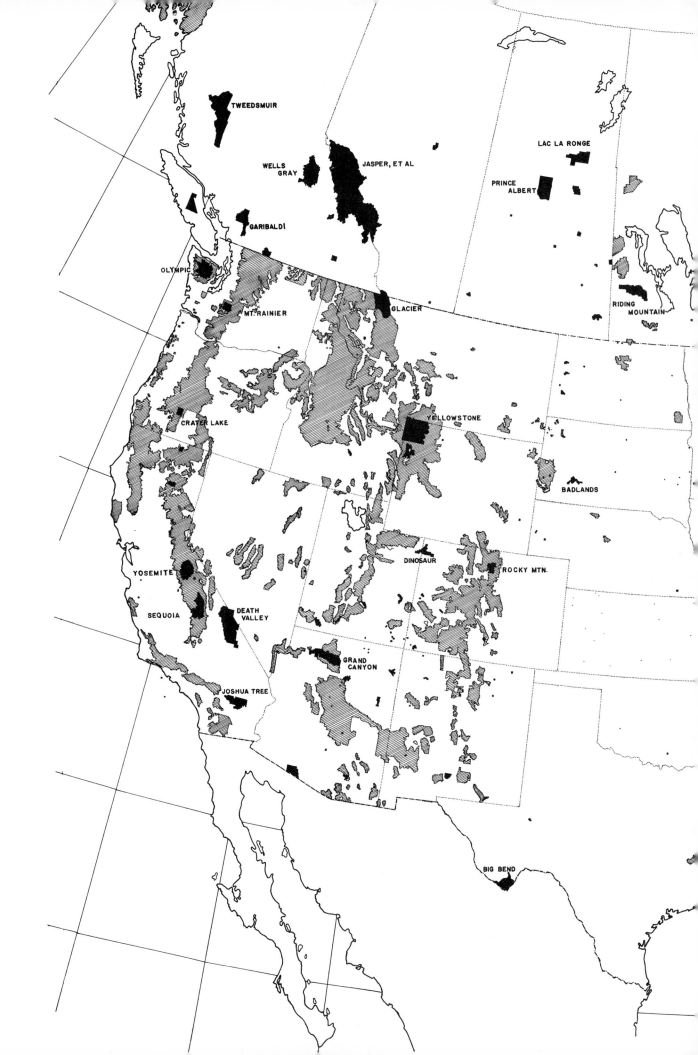

TWEEDSMUIR

WELLS
GRAY

JASPER, ET AL

LAC LA RONGE

PRINCE
ALBERT

GARIBALDI

OLYMPIC

MT. RAINIER

GLACIER

RIDING
MOUNTAIN

CRATER LAKE

YELLOWSTONE

BADLANDS

DINOSAUR

ROCKY MTN.

YOSEMITE

SEQUOIA

DEATH
VALLEY

GRAND
CANYON

JOSHUA TREE

BIG BEND

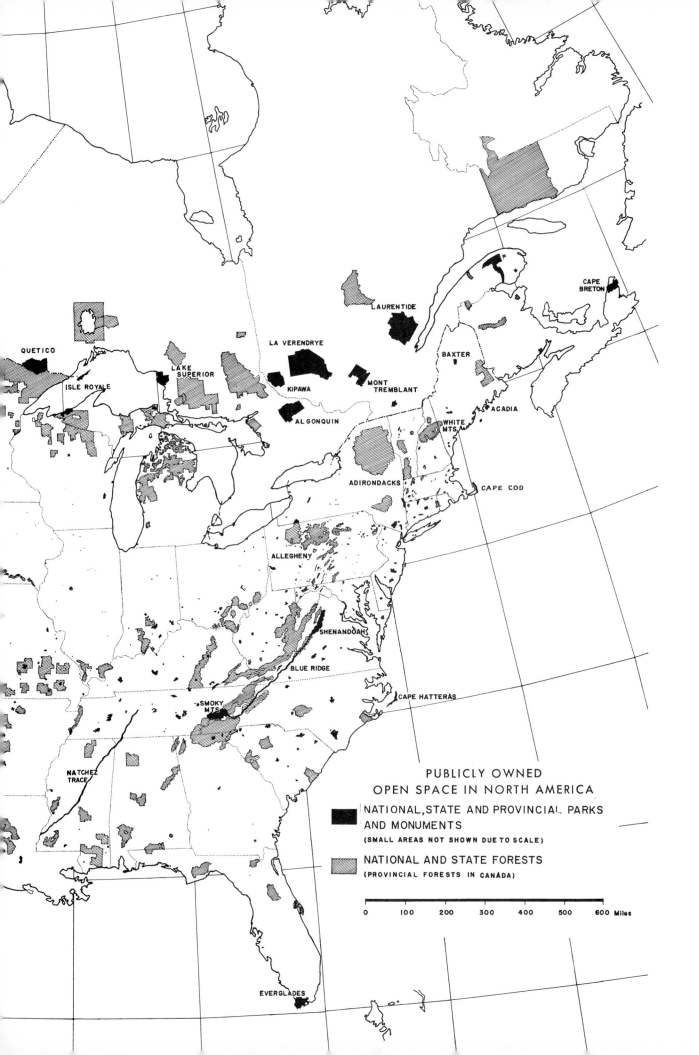

QUETICO

ISLE ROYALE

LAKE
SUPERIOR

KIPAWA

LA VERENDRYE

ALGONQUIN

MONT
TREMBLANT

LAURENTIDE

BAXTER

CAPE
BRETON

ACADIA

WHITE
MTS.

ADIRONDACKS

CAPE COD

ALLEGHENY

SHENANDOAH

BLUE RIDGE

CAPE HATTERAS

SMOKY
MTS.

NATCHEZ
TRACE

PUBLICLY OWNED
OPEN SPACE IN NORTH AMERICA

NATIONAL, STATE AND PROVINCIAL PARKS
AND MONUMENTS
(SMALL AREAS NOT SHOWN DUE TO SCALE)

NATIONAL AND STATE FORESTS
(PROVINCIAL FORESTS IN CANADA)

| 0 | 100 | 200 | 300 | 400 | 500 | 600 Miles |

EVERGLADES

former countryside; and an accelerating demand for more outdoor open space at every scale, from the house lot to the national park. When the same people want two results which are incompatible, discipline guided by knowledge is the best means of avoiding the mass frustration which is already upon us. The achievement of balance will be aided by formulating better-documented and more forceful standards of design. But before attempting to analyze the principles of design, it would be well to take stock of the pressures for and against the use and the preservation of open space —the opposing phenomena.

The first part of this volume has stated the general problem of urban fringe growth. People who have thought they were moving out to the country soon find themselves suffocated and hemmed in, although less than thirty per cent of the residential area is paved or covered with buildings, even in our inner suburbs. What is it that they long for, and do not have? Is it a wide, uncluttered view? Is it a playground conveniently near, or the old-fashioned vacant lot with its tangle of underbrush so fascinating to the young? Is it opportunities for specific outdoor pastimes?

To a considerable extent, we can find answers to these questions by tracing the activities of those who seek relief by one means or another. We cannot assume that all families share the desires of those who take action, and we will return to this problem later. Nevertheless, our society is very imitative, very well-informed of what the neighbors (near and far) are doing. Minority trends are often forerunners of mass demand. Some elements of the demand may be classified as national, with only minor variations. Others are subject to regional, cultural, or sometimes entirely capricious divergence.

NATIONAL TRENDS: THE USE OF NATIONAL PARKS AND ALL-DAY FACILITIES

A clue to the development of a taste for outdoor and natural surroundings is furnished by the frequent mention of leisure-time homes in newspapers and magazines. A recent magazine advertisement contained the words, "The second house, fast replacing the second car as a status symbol for the American family . . ."

Many families have acquired weekend and vacation homes, to be sure of bases from which they can enjoy and use outdoor areas in their myriad ways. Some of these homes are not on private land, but in national or state reservations, where this is permitted. *Westways*, a magazine published by the California Automobile Club, reports that "water skiers, campers, and fishermen who love the placid waters of Lake Isabella are making use of Greenhorn Mountain Park as a bedroom," and The California Outdoor Recreation Plan reports over 36,000 summer or vacation homes, of which about two fifths are on national forest lands. Does a family with these resources need an open space, a playfield or a park, within easy reach during the week?

The answer is yes. Apart from the park demands of the thousands of others in the cities and suburbs who cannot afford such luxury, there remain some basic needs which apply to all. Small children do not accommodate themselves to the concentrated weekend recreation orgy. Older children cannot find enough room for their games even on half-acre lots, and usually end up playing on suburban streets—just as children do on city streets. Everyone needs some visual relief from concrete, glass, and metal walls, within the orbit of usual daily activities. Sometimes, such opportunities are provided at the place of employment, either as "noon-hour parks" or as after-work playfields. Playground and other recreation activities are often part of the modern shopping center, as well as of the school; to some extent these have reduced the need for facilities close to the home. The small local parks and playgrounds are still needed, although they may be provided under other than governmental auspices.

Neighborhood playground in a residential district of Cleveland, Ohio; a restricted site creates the need for a protective fence.

Nationally, however, there are indications that *fewer people, in proportion to the total population, now depend on neighborhood or local recreation for their principal satisfaction.* Figures that have been gathered and published, for instance, by Richard H. Pough of Wildlife Preserves, Inc., and Marion Clawson of Resources for the Future, show that local parks have barely kept pace with the nearly four per cent yearly increase in visits "which would reflect the combined effects of growth in population and per capita income [1945–1956]," while visits to national parks and forests have increased eight to ten per cent, annually, with much greater increase in the "one-of-a-kind" sites and in the great multi-purpose open space reservoirs. The greatest increase in use is shown by those facilities which require one or two hours' drive from urban centers, and often those at a distance of 500 miles or more. People are becoming very knowledgeable about scenic and recreational features, through mass media as well as word-of-mouth reports from friends. They will travel quite a distance, if necessary, to enjoy a popular sport or unique scenery, though they would prefer to have such resources near enough for frequent enjoyment. Mission 66 and Operation Outdoors of the National Park Service and the Forest Service, respectively, and the all-inclusive study carried out under congressional direction by the Outdoor Recreation Resources Review Commission, headed by Laurance S. Rockefeller, testify to the federal government's awareness of the growing pressure.

In most parts of the country, the outdoor activities which lead in popularity, according to all available surveys, are picnicking and swimming or boating; the use of water for recreation has increased enormously in recent years. These activities require

natural features, not uniform site development or equipment; they are often indulged in by whole families, and need a minimum of supervision except for safety.
But a substantial percentage of respondents in some surveys have given "solitude,
rest, quiet, or watching others play" as their objective in the larger parks.

Left: Crowded ocean beach near Hyannis, Mass.; New York, 250 miles; Boston, 75 miles. *Right:* An inland bathing beach at Natres
State Park, Mass.

The type of picnicking that is so popular is a commentary on contemporary attitudes. The elaborate provisions made at up-to-date state or national parks, including
tables, benches, stone fireplaces with heavy iron grilles, shelters, and sanitary facilities,
indicate that the public takes its accustomed patterns from home and backyard to the
"natural" areas. The need for this paraphernalia is accompanied by a flexible attitude
toward accessibility, depending on whether a day's outing or a vacation is contemplated. National parks are for the most part used on vacations; only Shenandoah and
Yosemite are near enough to large urban concentrations so that any appreciable use is
made of them for day-outings. The average stays in each of five national parks surveyed were from one to three days, but the average number of days spent on the
whole trip varied from five to twenty-two. Over 35 per cent of the visitors to Grand
Canyon and over 18 per cent of those at Glacier came from more than 1,500 miles
away. The two-week vacation may nowadays be spent much farther from home than
formerly.

The increasingly frequent access to "natural" areas from urban or suburban homes
indicated by the surveys presents a new danger, not only of scenery being spoiled, but
of the experience of nature being whittled away into superficial glimpses of waterfalls
or mountain peaks on outings spent largely among urbanized surroundings—the
motels, eating places, amusement centers, and other accoutrements of our motorized
civilization, which follow the vacationer and in some cases set the demand.

NATIONAL TRENDS: RECREATION IN MOTION

A companion trend to the growing use of more distant parks is the emphasis on
travel itself as a form of recreation. The annual or occasional trip of several hundred

miles is one form. The contemporary result, as just described, is a stay of a much shorter duration indulged in by many more people than was the case in the early decades of the National Park System. Road travel on the national forest highway system has grown much more quickly than the recreational use of the forests themselves.

The backyard in the woods: overnight camping in Tolland State Forest, Mass.

Until 1936 such visits numbered less than recreational visits, but in 1952 they were more than twice as many, say Clawson and Held. Few can indulge in these long trips very often, many perhaps never; but the Sunday outing now takes place on Saturdays, holidays, and summer evenings also. There is probably no stronger evidence of our increased leisure time than the increase of recreational traffic on our highways.

One form of motorized recreation is the drive to an outlying park or resort. The drive to the more popular of these places may be a nightmare of slow progress, heat, and fumes. Many people have found an alternative in the "drive in the country" with a picnic at a roadside turnoff, or in an inviting barway or patch of woods, if these are

Left: Roadside picnic area on the Severn River, Anne Arundel County, Md., acquired as part of highway construction. *Right:* Typical roadside turnout with fireplaces and picnic benches on a Maryland highway.

Tourist routes can be designed to include and preserve fast-disappearing rural American scenery.

not posted against trespassing. The newer highways provide frequent stopping places, and turnoffs at scenic view points.

Some highway departments are marking Tourist Routes consisting of ordinary semi-local roads that will give the visitor a good view of local architecture, historic spots, or natural scenery. In the Boston region, where parkways joining the metropolitan or state reservations are not contemplated, there is an interesting substitute, the "Bay Circuit." This is a designated band, several miles wide, fifteen to twenty or more miles from downtown Boston. It is the declared intention of the State to acquire title or easements controlling land use in as much of this band as possible, to keep it open and green, with a suitable proportion of land accessible for public use. A system of existing semi-rural roads through the middle of this band is designated as a "tourist route"; it attempts to give the motorist a taste of rural village and farm life as well as scenery.

The slight delusion which the public permits itself on these tours is epitomized in a sign posted in a Bennington restaurant, "Ride Miles in the Primitive Country and Enjoy Vermont." The sign refers to riding horses for hire, but the tourist is far more likely to accept the invitation on his four rubber tires.

Some authorities, realizing that widespread use of country roads for touring can be very damaging to the life of the rural communities, have begun to consider the scenic drive as an actual park facility of county and state. Certain regional park systems join their large reservations with parkways, providing greenbelts around their outer suburbs. If the system is wide enough it will effectively mark the end of an urban cluster and provide a brief pause before entering an adjacent one. In the "continuous city" or inter-urban region this device of clustering development is particularly necessary to create some sort of orientation and sense of order. The Cleveland Metropolitan Parks District, while it has good access from present and proposed freeways, has a particularly notable system of parkways. The principal element is a continuous band joining the large reservations and forming what is there called "The Emerald Necklace." In 1959, there were seventy-four miles of parkway and park drives in this

Fresh water fishing.

jurisdiction, and more have been added since. On a much larger scale, West Virginia interests have submitted a bill to Congress calling for a new scenic highway to increase tourism in that state. To be called the Allegheny Parkway, it would run from Hagerstown, Maryland, through the Monongahela National Forest and on into Virginia, ending at the Cumberland Gap on the Kentucky-Tennessee border, a distance of 550 miles, mostly in West Virginia. The proposal is tied in with the opening up of spectacular mountain areas and a large increase in overnight camping facilities. Earlier examples of this approach are to be found in the Blue Ridge and the Natchez Trace parkways.

The National Park Service has proposed for some years a national parkway system, quite different in purpose from the interstate freeway system, but supplementing it. The Service has also proposed a public trail system for riding and hiking, through easements on private property and with public maintenance; but it should be remembered that the numbers of people using the existing trails, such as the Appalachian Trail from Kentucky to the Canadian border, the Long Trail through the Green Mountains in Vermont, and numerous trails in California mountains, are very few compared to the millions of motorists who drive through or stop to picnic in the parks.

Such proposals mean that all-day parks are not adequate in size and convenience for the urban public, and quite possibly are not adequate in variety. The "all-day-country" supplements them as an established resource; but, in the fringe and formerly rural areas especially, where the building of three new ranch houses along a country road may effectively cut off three hundred acres of view, this resource without proper design supervision, new highways, and effective controls may prove to be as ephemeral as the once-sought-after "rural retreat."

A new form of motorized recreation—the beach buggy; Sandy Neck, Sandwich, Mass.

REGIONAL DIFFERENCES

Our country is the richer for having been settled by people from many nations, collecting in regions whose culture became strongly colored by customs of the homeland. Where these traditions are fostered, recreation is given broader dimensions, not only for the participants, but for the spectators as well. Among these traditional customs are Caledonian Games, rodeos, Indian dances, folk dancing, and agricultural fairs. Other strongly regional "festivals" are inspired by principal crops or flowers, such as the Tulip Festival at Holland, Michigan, and the Tournament of Roses at Pasadena, California.

Regatta spectators, Marblehead, Mass.

Regional differences are obviously occasioned by geography as well as by ethnic or cultural inheritance. The children of almost every town on the seaboard are absorbed by some recreational use of water. Where there are sandy beaches, swimming is probably paramount. In the warmer waters, skin diving has become very popular. On the more rugged coast of the Northeast, boating is the absorbing passion. Rowboats, motorboats, sailboats, dot the waters; their occupants are fishing, racing, cruising, or just enjoying sun and water-cooled breezes. In setting up a schedule of needed areas, one cannot sensibly ignore the competition this resource offers to the conventional land playground.

Too often, there is a division between privileged and underprivileged in these activities. Towns are gradually realizing the need for acquiring community marinas. Their lateness in making such an effort has increased the tax-supported cost, yet such an expenditure might actually replace at least partially a similar sum spent on a land facility. Public and private marinas are springing up everywhere, east, west, and south. In one county, Suffolk on Long Island, forty-four new marinas are currently being planned. On the southern California coast, where natural harbors are infrequent, additional man-made marinas for almost 10,000 boats are operating at Long Beach, Balboa, and Newport. The new Marina del Rey will take 9,600 craft, and smaller private marinas are under development constantly.

Island Marinas, East and West: *left,* Avalon Bay at Santa Catalina Island; *right,* Edgartown Harbor at Martha's Vineyard.

Another geographic factor in regional habits is the presence of high hills or mountains. In summer such resources lead naturally to hiking, camping and horseback riding, as in the Rockies, or the Great Smokies, or the Green and White Mountain ranges of New England. In winter, these activities are replaced by skiing, a sport which has increased greatly. Skiing is no longer an unusual or exclusive sport in any region whose climate and terrain bring it within an hour's drive; school buses and instructors take pupils to the slopes, replacing an earlier reliance on family initiative.

If in some areas people are conditioned to prefer certain activities outdoors, it is probable that in others the residents are conditioned to a negative attitude toward any such activity. It is easy to imagine that in humid, hot areas there is little incentive toward prolonged exercise or exposure to sun. There is not really a sufficient body of data to substantiate a lower demand for playfields and game facilities in these areas of the U.S., but knowledge of the daily living pattern makes it clear that summer afternoons, the most common time for use of such facilities in cooler areas, are largely

spent in siestas, in seeking a cool, quiet place indoors or in the shade. Air conditioning of buildings must offer a strong counter-attraction to the outdoors in such a
climate. A compensating availability of swimming pools, beaches, and cooler camping
or day outing parks must be given greater emphasis in this case.

LOCAL OR INDIVIDUAL PREFERENCE

It is fairly easy to recognize the divergent interests of large blocks of people with
similar ethnic backgrounds, or of those who are strongly conditioned by the preval-
ence of certain natural features or climate. More difficult is the estimation of individual or small-group variation in demand.

Some evidence is provided by certain detailed use-surveys related either to simul-
taneously-gathered data on age, occupation, family status and other characteristics, or
to census data for the same areas. Until recently, there was not enough material on
the people who use public recreation facilities to make any such study. There is now
enough to make a beginning, and it should prove important for public policy, since,
in spite of the similarity of demand assumed by park and recreation advisors, there is
evidence of a real divergence among population groups in the kind, number, and
quantity of facilities wanted.

Unpublished surveys by the National Recreation School of family and individual
"extra-urban" recreation covered two small-city groups: one in New England and
New York, and one in Texas, Arkansas, and Oklahoma. While it was true that picnicking, swimming, and boating were almost always at the top of the list, both of
facilities used and those wanted, there were also indications of community individualism. Two northern cities (in each case the largest and most established city in its
group) showed a lesser inclination to go far afield. Golf was a leading recreation, more
so than in other places. Were the people of these cities well enough provided with
physically and financially accessible resources to eliminate much need for outlying
reservations? Or were they so set in a groove (perhaps the golf habit) that they simply
didn't think of expeditions to "natural areas"? A community known to have a high
percentage of engineers and of technical and skilled workers had the highest proportion of hikers, campers, and nature students. A southern city with no superficially obvious factors except geography and climate to differentiate it from its companions in
the study showed a marked indifference to and lack of participation in extra-urban
recreation. The question here becomes: do these people use local facilities more or
less than their counterparts in other cities? In general, where a high proportion of
people indulged often in any of the surveyed activities (which ranged from 16 to 20 in
number and covered all seasons) they were willing to travel farthest for good opportunities, sometimes as much as 80 miles each way for a day's outing. In addition, such
people apparently enjoy and want facilities for a larger number of different activities.

This information, incomplete as it is, supplements more recent local studies to
suggest that training and background have much to do with enjoyment of open
space, especially for adults. The unpublished survey of the National Recreation
School includes this statement:

Sankety Lighthouse and golf course, Nantucket Island.

More should be done by schools to help children develop interest in various forms of recreation and acquire skills that contribute to a more satisfying use of outlying recreation properties. Large numbers of people are denied the enjoyment of recreation activities primarily because they have never had an opportunity to observe or experience the satisfaction that results from participation in them. Local recreation authorities also have a responsibility and opportunity to expose people to forms of recreation that can be enjoyed outside the city.

In the absence of previous experience or education, people will bring their customary habits with them to any new experience. So we find the family turning the opportunity to immerse itself in the nearly-natural surrounding of a large park into a close approximation of its backyard barbecue. Similarly, people who are used to the facilities of metropolitan or state parks expect to find duplicates in wilderness reservations and even the one-of-a-kind national monuments. An uncritical attempt to satisfy the demands in ever-increasing quantity poses a very serious question of policy. If we assume that differences in taste and skill are not only existent, but worth fostering, we should base a regional open space plan, or even a community plan, on an appraisal of local habits and possible future modifications of those habits—not merely on a "standard" recreation pattern.

For those with built-in rural habits and tastes, we must presuppose privately owned home sites large enough to give some opportunity for dealing creatively with the land itself, as well as to furnish privacy from noise and view of close neighbors. We must also expect that they will want larger areas of open space, at a scale bearing some relation to what they have grown up in, so that the environment will provide the reassurance of familiarity. They will also prefer easy access to really wild or really rural areas. If access to such places is not easy, they will surmount obstacles to reach them anyway, and public pressure for good highways can be expected, with fresh complications following their construction.

Cranberry Harvest Train on Edaville Railroad near Cape Cod, Mass., a commercial tourist attraction.

On the other hand, families with a gregarious nature and a bias toward urban life as it is found in most European countries will have far more modest demands. Most of our cities do not even meet these modest demands, of course, but neither do many of our suburban fringe communities. Such families have the universal need for light and air and space enough for daily living; they would like small parks and promenades for sitting, strolling, and picnicking, and an occasional outdoor restaurant. Their only future need is for specific sports facilities for a few activities, including places to swim, and opportunities for an occasional outing or picnic. These are the people, incidentally, who are most apt to be found in group outings, organized camping, and social club activities. The National Recreation School surveys found them more prevalent in New York State than in New England or in the South. In Toronto, a postwar influx of Central European and Italian immigrants has resulted in an intensified use of in-city parks by people who value them more than the longer-established population, and who use them in ways that European parks are used—for strolling, sitting, and conversation.

Berkshire Music Festival at Tanglewood in Lenox, Mass., where the Boston Symphony Orchestra performs in summer; New York, 145 miles; Boston, 150 miles.

Cookout in Olympic National Park, Wash.

However, we can expect that present fashions and the publicity issued by the outlying resorts will result in an accelerating shift toward the "larger" outdoors. The final report of the Park, Recreation, and Open Space Project (of the Tri-State New York Metropolitan Region) says: "Public taste in recreation is running more and more toward pursuits which need a natural setting. Without wildlife and scenery what use will it be to go hiking, fishing, hunting, camping, bird-watching or picnicking?" Their conclusion is that we cannot make much more intensive use of the parks and forests now in public ownership, even though these are 79 per cent undeveloped (that is, in a natural state). Therefore, they say, we must acquire much more land to meet the increased demand and larger populations of the future.

2. General Factors Affecting Design

In spite of the fact that we need more measurable data on demand and use related to regions and major population groups, there is a fairly general understanding of the current pressures. This is not the case with respect to other factors that are equally important and far more permanent. These concern the limitations imposed by the processes of nature, by the built-in spiritual and physical requirements of mankind, and by conflicts arising from the use of land, especially multi-purpose use.

LIMITATIONS SET BY NATURE

There are some facts of nature which provide automatic limits to our freedom in planning. Some of these concern size. It is impossible to perpetuate a forest without a sufficient area to guarantee reproduction, allowing for variable climate, use, and accident. Some types of open woods or grazing land must be considered in relation to the number of animals which may feed on or trample them; this is a familiar limit to cattlemen of the Southwest. Game refuges must be large enough to furnish a complete habitat and maintain a balance of the complex indigenous life. If this seems of interest only to the naturalist, consider the effect on landscape of the many species that dig holes, build dams, chew wood, or eat leaves; or of the rank weeds that can overtake native growth on semi-urbanized land. Consider how much birds add to our enjoyment of nature. Birds need large areas of woods or underbrush, a variety of food and water, and a balance between predators and prey.

The attempt to use the "high deserts," such as the Mojave and the Arizona deserts, for living, for industry, and for recreation has been stimulated by the military and nuclear installations. Since it was discovered that with air conditioning the desert becomes quite habitable, it has been exploited. The land is, or was, cheap; the climate is, although hot in summer, almost always sunny and dry. The area has become a health resort for people with respiratory troubles. The scenery is spectacular.

But to what extent can urbanization proceed in the desert? Water is obtained, in most such areas, from ground wells. (The irrigation ditches furnish water for agricul-

The spectacular scenery of Maroon Lake, White River National Forest, Colo.; relatively untouched, this is becoming a popular recreation area, with parking and other facilities greatly enlarged.

ture.) But this water has been stored for centuries and the annual replenishment, from a rainfall of five to ten inches, cannot equal the demands which may be put on it if there is no check to development. At present the Federal government is holding back on further sales of surplus lands in the "high desert," pending completion of county plans and zoning ordinances.

It is becoming a more frequent experience to look down from a plane and see grids marked on the desert where unpaved roads have been laid out. Sometimes a single house or shack marks the lair of the speculator awaiting a growing demand for homes from a metropolis which may be fifty or a hundred miles distant. A closer look at communities like Hesperia and Apple Valley in San Bernardino County, California, which are well started though still not large in population, reveals house lots with neat green lawns, native shrubs including the unmistakable Joshua Tree, and sometimes willows or other deciduous trees that look uncomfortable in their desert context. These willows are a reminder that the flowering of the desert valleys is obtained

Mojave Desert country, California.

Wind sculpture in White Sands National Monument, N.M.

at a very high cost in water consumption and that the permanence of the supply is by no means certain.

In more temperate zones, if enjoyment of water is an objective of our planning, it may be necessary to protect and reserve a whole drainage basin, or at any rate the banks of a whole stream system. Preserving only a fraction leaves the door open to diversion, pollution, flood aggravation, and many other hazards, while a unified control can make possible fishing, swimming, boating, picnicking, or rambling; it can at times combine these with power production and navigation. All these are on the positive side, while the prevention of floods through good management of the water and adjacent land may prove an equal or greater benefit.

Joshua Tree National Monument, Cal.; Los Angeles, 140 miles.

No factor is more important to the planning of open space than the indigenous soils. Topography and geology are partly responsible for the distribution of soils, and are in themselves fairly obvious limiting features. But the ragged paths and bare-patched lawns often found on public land are evidence that the designer was unaware of the soil's capacity to withstand erosion or tamping, or that he had planned for a much lower level or use. Sandy soils are particularly sensitive to surface disturbance and erode very easily, yet their good drainage and ready submission to the bulldozer often lead them to be considered ideal for playgrounds and parks. The proper vegetation and the proper soil for each type of use should be diligently sought.

THE HUMAN FACTOR

Humanity makes some demands on its environment which are, in a sense, also ecological limits. Chief among these are the requirements for solitude, for privacy, for rest. When the natural area or the "naturally" landscaped park is so small in its dimensions that incongruous surroundings force themselves on our attention, the capacity of the green space to provide these requirements is much weakened.

But it is well established that the natural oasis is a requirement of even the densest urban area. Its provision on an adequate scale and in satisfying form is a part of human conservation. Thoreau wrote in his Journal for 1859, "Each town should have a primitive forest of five hundred or a thousand acres, where a stick should never be cut for fuel . . . let us keep the New World *New!*"

These green oases fulfil a human need. Human beings have some physiological needs which can be satisfied only by open space. They need, at times, relief from heat, from smoke or smog. The elevation, the orientation with respect to prevailing winds, and the density of trees will vary the size requirements for this purpose. Noise is more easily escaped when there is a fairly dense buffer of woods; but if openness for the sake of cooling breezes is even more desirable, a large area may be the only satisfactory solution. Then there are the needs of people for exercise of varying intensity. Each activity one could name has its own space requirements, as well as some controlling needs with respect to ground surface, buffer areas, and vegetation. There are quite well established recommendations for the amount of space of these kinds that should be planned for each thousand of urban population; yet these standards are often inappropriate for an outer fringe or a rural community. In addition, we have seen that not all groups have identical demands.

It has been thought that areas where lot sizes are over one acre might show a reduced need for playgrounds and playfields. This has not proved to be so. Information from Rockland and Westchester Counties in New York and Fairfield County in Connecticut indicates that in these low-density communities there is just as much desire for community facilities as in more compact suburbs. However large, the individual lots are seldom large enough or properly landscaped or surfaced for group play. If this is true, the problem of accessibility is magnified by the large lot sizes. Playfields are needed in the fringe areas because of a lack of contiguous, usable open space; while playgrounds provide the special facilities, such as swings, slides, paving, sprinklers, and pools for which individual families lack both space and funds.

THE PROBLEM OF MULTI-PURPOSE USE

There are many conflicts between primary uses of both public and private land. Forestry or water conservation may have points of conflict with recreation; wildlife conservation or management may impose restrictions on recreation and on forestry. A plan must be based on knowledge of future as well as present needs for the varying uses, and on an integrated group of decisions which will fill those needs. Some resulting decisions will be specific restrictions for a particular area, while others may allow considerable latitude so long as a prescribed total is allocated for each intended use.

There are even conflicts to be considered between supposedly similar uses of public land or commercial recreation facilities, going back to the differences in personality and background of groups and individuals. Some want to surround themselves with many of the conveniences of urban living, while others want to shed all reminders of their ordinary lives and immerse themselves in a near-wilderness. The leasing to a concessionaire by the State of California of the Squaw Valley facilities, built for the Winter Olympics, and the installation of new hotels, motels, restaurants, movies, and other entertainments, show that the California Division of Beaches and Parks expects to draw a good many of the gregarious, entertainment-seeking genus homo as well as the mountaineer and the skier. Advertisements of resorts stress the awe-inspiring scenery or the restful quiet, but many of them are actually calculated to attract patronage on the basis of "organized fun" or of sophisticated city-style shows.

Wildflowers and alpine fir in Paradise Valley, Mount Rainier National Park, Wash.

It would be wrong to assume, however, that multiple use is not often quite practical. Our national forests are managed principally for the maintenance of timber supply and water resources, and for the greatest current use and revenue consistent with these purposes. The Greenhorn Mountain Park, for instance, which was mentioned earlier as a "bedroom" for recreationists, is in Sequoia National Forest; the whole area is used for timber harvesting and livestock grazing, as well as for recreation and summer homes. Major ski resorts are located within some national or state forests, and the policy on tree cutting has been satisfactorily adjusted. Often such facilities become national or state property after a period in which a fair return on investment has been earned. Within these forests have been preserved many of our scenic treasures, and examples of our rare plant and animal life.

An outstanding example of secondary recreational uses is furnished by the great timber companies. The largest companies permit hunting and fishing in season on most of their land; in addition, many other pursuits are permitted in various locations. Sixty-five major companies have established a hundred and thirty-two public parks on their lands. These contributions to public recreation are part of an educational program in the care, management, and appreciation of forests, in order to reduce fires and other forms of waste, and to help maintain a sustained yield.

The conflict between use or preservation, inaccessibility and public enjoyment, comes to a head periodically in the internecine rivalry between the National Park Service and the Forest Service. The former fears that the economic considerations which, by law, must be given weight by the latter will lead to the destruction of some national scenic assets, including ancient forests, flora and fauna, and geological formations. The Forest Service, on the other hand, points out that the Park Service's policy of promoting the greatest possible public use of the parks poses a still greater danger to these resources. Each policy, that of use regulated in a manner to perpetuate the resource, and that of specimen preservation with appropriate facilities for observing, may be correct under certain conditions, but we believe that in view of the very large amount of undeveloped or nearly undeveloped land in the United States still existing, it would be conspicuous waste to put more than a small percentage of it behind glass, as a museum piece "untouched" or, as the opponents of the policy call it, "forever rotting." The number of such sites should be governed by their uniqueness and their area by the ecological requirements. There is little reason for the National Park Service to duplicate the same kind of facilities provided by the state park systems. Rather, it should stimulate a more rapid expansion of those systems, giving advice and coordinating all facilities at the various government levels.

3. The Framework of Open Space Design

ESTHETIC ORGANIZATION

Within the context of contemporary trends, demands, and tastes, and of certain limitations which are fairly immutable, we can look for standards and attempt a more rational organization of open versus built-up space. For this purpose, the setback of a house from its lot lines, the conservation of marshland, and the creation of a state or national park become part of the same concept—a design for open space.

Every time man builds a structure, he is designing the outlines of open space. He doesn't usually realize this. In fact, he quite likely feels that the idea of designing "open space," which he vaguely identifies with all outdoors, must be absurd. Yet here, as in other fields of man's activity, the refusal to formulate standards and live by them does not keep him from creating a pattern of sorts; it simply reduces the probability of a harmonious result to nearly zero.

One reason for man's failure to realize that he is thus executing a design is that our perceptual faculties are trained to appreciate the outlines of tactile objects, such as statues or buildings, more easily than the outlines of a space enclosing an object or surrounding the observer. Perception of this sort requires a somewhat more developed esthetic observation before it can be consciously registered and formulated. Nevertheless, unconscious perception can stimulate reactions just as pleasant or painful as though the cause were fully understood; and most people are at least partially aware that a landscape is attractive or distasteful. With a little practice in observing and describing the open shapes, their outlines and qualities, anyone can acquire a heightened perception and a degree of sophistication in this art.

At times we are only conscious of a single unit of open space, whose outlines we can recognize, and which we can bring into perspective with ourselves as the reference point. At other times, we may be able to see many such units at once, as from a plane or a high vantage point; or we may see them in succession, building up a composite picture as we move.

If the form of open space is susceptible to recognition and definition, can we formulate some elementary principles of design which can produce more satisfactory manifestations? To show that open space has shapes which are individual and comprehensible merely requires presenting a number of examples. To set up hypothetical rules is a vastly more exacting problem.

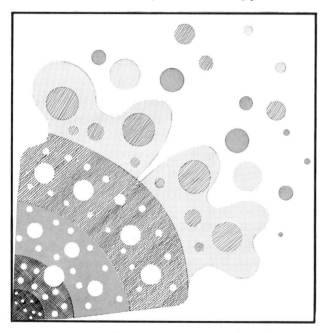

PROGRESSION IN SCALE AND TEXTURE FROM URBAN TO RURAL OR WILD LAND:

Schematically represented is a segment of a city and its surrounding countryside. The smallest circles represent small parks and playgrounds in mid-city. Hardly any playfields or larger parks will appear at the core. Gradually the size of the units increases, the distance between them becomes greater, and the texture of urban development becomes more open. The "fringe" includes the last ring in which the open spaces (white) form the pattern, and the first in which urban concentrations (villages, industrial parks, and the like) are the elements of design among farm lands or woods.

Because western civilization has traditionally seen man as either the center or the reference point of the known universe, the non-inhabited or unused areas have come to stand in contrast, sometimes in active opposition, to the man-made environment. The concept of "open space" is probably a necessary part of man's attempt to understand his environment by organizing his observations into categories. The easiest way to organize impressions is by dichotomies: that is, by opposites, which can be reduced to one positive quality and its absence, or negative value.

A second and more advanced framework for organizing observations is the continuum, a graduated scale from one extreme to the opposite, with no gap in the possible degree of intensity with which a given characteristic may occur. From classical times to the nineteenth century, the face of our world showed a rather clear-cut separation of urban and rural areas. The contributions of modern technology have changed this, so that more and more we are observing a gradual transition from "open," meaning natural or agricultural, to "urban," meaning closely developed for man's residence, his commerce, his industry, or his highways and airports.

By placing our observations in the context of the continuum, we can allow for a more complex kind of organization than the simple dichotomy. There is still a need, however, to make each category recognizable for the purpose of understanding the relationships of the whole. Just as in any chart or table, categories are more easily recognized if they are separated by substantial intervals. Translated into terms of the landscape, this means that if there is a blurred transition, it should be interrupted and redesigned, so that the open areas have shape, color, and other definite attributes. By contrast, if urban forms occur in an almost natural landscape, they may blend themselves inconspicuously into the background. Indeed, they should do so if the enclosing landscape is to count as an "open space" in contrast to some adjacent urban texture. Similarly, if a few carefully planned high-rise buildings are to be given light, air, and density contrast by surrounding blocks of very low structures, the latter must not be haphazardly interrupted by medium-height buildings, or by any which focus attention upon themselves as individual elements of architecture.

Beyond the conceptual requirements, we know that a view of space in nature must give satisfaction in some of the basic ways in which any beautiful object satisfies. Line, color, balance, and dynamic organization in one or more planes are some of the specific characteristics that affect us in pictures. Moving into analogies of plastic art, such as sculpture and architecture, we find that contemplation of mass, texture, and line are added means of satisfying our senses. All these are present in nature, though not necessarily in one segment.

But these esthetic qualities are much more satisfying when they have an internal relationship among themselves, and an external one with the viewer. The artist has always sought a technique of organization. In both graphic and plastic arts, perspective is the classic Western means of organizing, of creating the sense of space and position in space. Perspective is dear to the rational mind, for good reason: it assists the beholder to understand the relationship of parts in a complex whole. Through no accident, the term perspective is used to describe a perfected mental ability to comprehend related pieces of knowledge, sensation, or emotion, in much the same way. The opportunity to observe large or at least deep open spaces, with objects seen in receding planes, will be of great assistance in creating a mental perspective for natural phenomena.

In the Orient and in some primitive arts, perspective is replaced by sequence and rhythm. There are numerous writings on modern art exploring the kind of organization found in jazz, for instance, where repetition and a recognizable rhythmic framework permit free-form excursions almost at will, eventually coming in on the correct beat, as John Kouwenhoven has pointed out, drawing analogies between "skyscraper architecture" in the gridiron city and modern jazz. We must realize, then, that there are more ways to conceive of the organization of landscape than as a static picture.

Nature untouched is never disorganized. Provided one can reach a proper viewpoint, or series of viewpoints, there is always an observable order based on stream systems, on land types, on topography, climate, and so on. One does not have to expect organization in pictorial terms within a given small area. Nature's scale is often vast. It is when we impinge upon it that we must use intelligence to make the meeting ground harmonious with natural laws and with our own needs, simultaneously. In these "fringe areas" we must bring the original vast scale into terms related to ourselves, our buildings, our roads, and all the technical paraphernalia of the contemporary age.

MATERIALS OF OPEN SPACE DESIGN

Being more knowledgeable about the limits under which any design of open space must function, and about contemporary values, means a greater chance of success in the execution and permanence of design.

Farm lands in the Connecticut River Valley.

The building blocks of design, of course, are the various kinds of soil, rock, vegetation, water, and, at different extremes, even air or solid buildings—whatever seems open by contrast to what seems closed or dense. As we have seen, there must be contrast enough to form a dichotomy, or a continuum reduced to a few, well-differentiated components.

The units to be worked with will be of all sizes, shapes, colors, and textures: dazzling white sand or pebbles, the dense blue-green fir trees, the pale waters of a shallow river, the rippled surface of a lake, and the variations of grass and crops. These will normally be set off against houses, industrial plants, roadside business buildings, bridges, and important roads. On occasion, they may also be a foil for each other.

Water as an open space, created by a hydroelectric facility in Connecticut.

These materials occur in many forms or "land types"—gently rolling, flat, and rugged. Rock and mountain profiles depend greatly upon their geologic age and composition. The sharp black scallops and pinnacles of volcanic mountains in the Northwest, the perpendicular, flat-topped rocks and cliffs rising from the Central and Southwest deserts, and the undulating, misty blue or violet ranges of the Northeast are familiar to most of us in picture if not in firsthand experience.

Observing all this variety of land forms, it becomes apparent that an acre or a square mile of one type is not the equivalent of the same area of a different form. Before we conclude that wherever man puts down a cluster of dwellings, he must have his five acres of playground and playfield, his five acres of larger parks, and his ten acres of regional park per thousand, let us consider the difference in impact and in usefulness of various natural elements.

WATER

Why is a body of water almost always a prized feature in any landscape? This is so whether the water is the predominant component—surrounding an island—or the accent—a jewel in the midst of a forest or a jungle of concrete and asphalt.

Water gives pleasure by its ability to reflect and enhance surrounding colors and textures. It gives, symbolically and often literally, a refreshing sense of coolness and cleanness. A very interesting sidelight on our age-old appreciation of water, especially in fountains but also of trees, comes with the realization that the negative ions given off by aerated water or by the transpiration from leaves have been found to have a direct, immediate effect on the physical well-being of those nearby.

An even stronger reason for water's importance to landscape is its complete break in texture, color, and apparent density from any material which surrounds it. The continuum is thoroughly interrupted, and the sense of separation therefore increased. For this reason, a small area of water has an effect far greater than any other natural element in creating the illusion of distance. It is, for the same reason, a most effective boundary definition between parts of a design and is the best guarantee of a permanent open space one can have. A small piece of ground on its edge can, in the words of the late Charles W. Eliot, "open up great vistas of scenery, stores of fresh air." And it has power to stir the imagination with visions of far-distant shores.

Water can also provide the type of dynamic esthetic satisfaction that we get from traveling a scenic highway. The California Public Outdoor Recreation Plan contains a recommendation for scenic waterways similar to scenic roads, and specifically proposes that pollution and shore disfigurement be controlled on the Sacramento River and Sacramento-San Joaquin Delta to make these a recreational resource.

FOREST

Forests are among the largest homogeneous units of open space in the United States, thereby creating a paradox in design. Within their vast expanses the occasional clearings become the "open" units and give form to the design; it is immaterial in the forest macro-landscape whether the clearings are farmland, golf courses, or compact towns. This situation, however, rarely occurs on our urban fringes. As a rule, agriculture will have tamed the land and lumbering cleared all but the most inaccessible slopes long before the first suburbanizing wave reaches the primeval forest. In only a few cases has a combination of geography, climate, and delayed urban growth produced burgeoning cities directly surrounded by forest. There are some in the Northwest and in some mountainous sections of California and the Appalachian range. Here, an interesting interplay of urban and forest shapes can take place. At first, suburban clusters will be gracefully subordinated to the mass of trees, the rugged or rounded mountain profiles. The possibility of full development should be considered, however. A design of connecting and related woods or other green belts should aim to preserve for the period when they form a minority the essential grace or grandeur of the original, especially as to contours, horizons, and salient features.

The use of forests for recreational purposes may be quite independent of their function in the open space pattern. The tree canopy covers all but the tallest spires and beacons; thousands of hunters, hikers, picnickers, and nature students can be absorbed in a large forest with little change in its esthetic value. And where homes are largely clustered under or against the trees, it will be possible to concentrate on the civic center or the business and industrial complexes as the dominant open space design elements.

Golf courses are important as an open space in low-density areas: Palm Springs, Cal., seen from San Jacinto Mountain.

It would be a mistake to think of all forest areas as similar in visual effect, even in a limited geographic area. In and around some North-Central cities, for example, are found beech-maple forests on the high plateaus; hemlocks and other evergreens, with mountain maples, in the cool ravines; and flood plain forests in the river valleys. In the West, taller spruce and redwoods on high ground merge into the jack-pine, mesquite, and chaparral of the valleys and low-growing wind-stunted trees along the coast. The northern coast of Maine is the "country of the pointed firs," green-black spires against sea and sky. Each region has its distinctive forest cover. Nothing could be more dismal than a diffusion of these strong regional characteristics resulting from the introduction of alien species in any quantity.

DESERTS

The desert is no doubt the least useful of our natural area types, especially for recreation. It does have a grand scale and a richness of color, at times, which are a unique scenic attraction. It is second only to water in the sense of separation it produces. In general, discomfort is associated with the desert because of its temperature extremes. In some places, such as the Imperial Valley, where intensive planting and irrigation have transformed a desert, the resulting climate is said to be almost unendurable to nothern newcomers, who flee from it in summer if they can. However, where self-perpetuating vegetation can be developed (guided, perhaps, by the research in original vegetation now being done through study of pollens and carbon analysis of fossils), it is probable that the climate will gradually change and a stable forest or prairie result.

Although true deserts are not prevalent on this continent, we have a few of considerable size, as well as vast plains of semi-arid land that is half desert, half prairie. If it were not for the great changes wrought by irrigation, the desert would probably be irrelevant to a discussion of the "fringe." Urban growth, however, is infiltrating the desert, using air conditioning in homes as well as in offices and industries to compensate for the natural climatic extremes. While the contrast with conditions in other regions is often upsetting to the newcomer, many admit to a strong attractive force which holds them, once established.

There are many areas where the high desert is being transformed into industrially-based communities, and other places where development is primarily of a resort type. In all of these, development consists of quarter sections or groups of squares, sometimes in isolated clusters scattered over the wastes. Cultivation of trees and grass, made possible by irrigation, is often in jarring contrast to the sparse, low bushes and the tawny sands. However, there is no mistaking what is occupied and what is "open." And in this case the green areas are seldom the "open spaces."

Deserts, then, will be valuable forms of open space chiefly as "spectaculars," for their dramatic color and scale, for contrast to the table rocks that rise like islands from them, and for their occasional oases. Highways with viewpoints which give a continuous panorama and opportunities for close study of the significant mineral or vegetable species are the recreation resources to be developed. These are preserved now in national reservations such as Organ Pipe Cactus and White Sands National Monuments and Grand Canyon National Monument and Park. The high deserts with good climate will also be valued as vacation and health resorts. The Salton Sea, because of its large size, is a mecca for outboard motorboating, in spite of its location in a very low, hot desert.

Prairies and Grazing Lands

Although the waving prairie grass which delighted our early naturalists is hard to find nowadays, and even short-grass prairie has largely given way to the plow, sparsely covered grazing lands are more extensive than deserts on our continent. They are frequently interrupted with physiographic variations, and the effective units therefore are not so vast. The vegetation, sparse though it is, offers some variety in color and texture. The chaparral and sagebrush growth of the West and Southwest provides a characteristic regional landscape; although much of the land is known as "range," it takes acres to feed one head of cattle. Permanent settlements for human beings are handicapped by the same lack of water and soil fertility. Oil and other mineral resources have made it worth man's while to force urbanization in some of these lands. When this is done, the problem of providing recreational open space becomes almost entirely one of artificial landscape creation: the natural landscape is valuable only for its large scale and the sense of solitude, qualities not enhanced by developing recreational parks, except on a grand scale. Examples of the latter, which are sought for their uniqueness and educational value, are Grand Mesa and Wasatch National Parks.

Milksheds in the hinterland of large metropolitan areas provide a visual amenity as well as satisfying an economic need.

FARM LANDS

One of the pleasantest features in any landscape is a gently undulating series of fields, patterned with row crops, grass, ploughed furrows, or orchards in neat rows. They appeal to our visual sense by their richly varied texture, and their intricate interplay of lines and rectangles. They also carry symbolic messages that we have learned over the centuries to admire—messages of dedication to hard work, respect for the soil, production of abundance from the bare wilderness. With the silos and barns we associate the many farm animals now known to the young largely from picture books, but still loved. To many of us the sight of a wilderness may inspire awe and admiration, but it does not strike the warm response that a serene, well-cultivated farm landscape evokes. We tend to identify ourselves and our values with the scene, and are able to do so through the humanizing effect of agriculture.

Appreciation of such features is not uniform, of course, even when it is educated and experienced. It is surprising to find Sylvia Crowe, whose perceptive writing on the British landscape carries on the notable contribution made by Thomas Sharpe, advocating that a truck-garden be interspersed with a few trees scattered among the cabbage rows to avoid monotony. It may be because Americans are accustomed to a large-scale landscape that on this side of the water fields of row crops seem esthetically appealing in themselves. There is always a minor variation of size, texture, and color, with a skeleton of paths or tractor lanes, even on the vast plains of the Midwest. There are the horizons for frame, and the straight rows for orientation.

WETLANDS

Currently, wetlands are receiving more attention in general writing and legislation than they have for some time. The reasons are not hard to find, even though by some standards these are the most unusable, next to deserts, of our open spaces. A number of major floods in recent years, well publicized by newspapers, radio, and television, have helped at least some of the public to understand the need for any measures which will store water and help to reduce the maximum flow in both normal and extraordinary flood seasons.

The flood-prone or swampy borders of streams, or the narrow gorges which cut through the sandy plateaus of Virginia or the country north of Toronto, are not especially valuable, until suburbanization has made it profitable to fill home sites to a safe level. They are therefore the easiest of all natural open space units to buy outright or to control by purchase of "conservation easements" or by stream-encroachment legislation. Where a river basin consists of many tributary streams, a fine pattern of green belts can be preserved, if it is begun early enough, along the many fingers of the system. It offers good distribution and continuity, both valuable factors in design. The Toronto and Washington National Capital regional open space plans, among others, are based very largely on conservation of stream valleys, and they are also an important element in the Boston region.

The fact that hunting and fishing are perennially popular and that nature study, especially bird-watching, is a growing pastime gives support to the preservation of marshlands, reinforcing the other reasons which exist. It is sad but true that even this package of good reasons is not always sufficient to combat the influence of proposed industrial or highway development, or even of residential subdivision.

GOLF COURSES, PARKS, TECHNOLOGICAL INSTALLATIONS, AND OTHER MAN-MADE OPEN SPACE

The function of open spaces developed for so-called urban purposes is ambivalent in the national landscape. In the New York or Los Angeles metropolitan region such occurrences as golf courses, airports, developed parks, and even cemeteries perform

Airports provide open space but in turn need large buffer zones, and should not be encroached upon by incompatible uses: International Airport, Houston, Tex.

the same service as would natural forests or farm lands in the country. They provide almost the only open spaces noticeable in the macro-landscape. They are the chief providers of visual relief from the monotony of continuous buildings; often they have the allied usefulness of making the air a little cooler and cleaner for those lucky enough to live nearby. In some cases, they are entirely or partially available for physical use, in sport or passive recreation. In others, such as the enormous military reservations in Virginia, they are completely unavailable for use or circulation. Even highways and railroads provide a kind of open space in the closely-knit parts of the urban region.

In the open country, of course, and most noticeably in a desert, such technological developments are urban impositions on the natural terrain. Whereas in a vast city almost any such contrast is welcome, provided its side effects are not too annoying, it is a different matter in a predominantly rural landscape. In the fringe communities the residents are much more fastidious about the "open space" developments they will welcome. They should be, for they have been left with all kinds of blight from uses which could only technically be classified as "open space"—open-air storage depots, junkyards, gravel pits, and other commercial facilities, or from raucous carnivals, driving ranges, and race tracks.

In most such cases of blight, it is the details of arrangement which are most harmful, rather than the inherent nature of the use. Local regulations are slowly developing amenities of landscaping and spatial relationships. It is necessary for this kind of development to be clearly urban, that is, a product of man's culture; this requires that its edges be well marked and give a positive impression, at the same time indicating the type of use. While it is sometimes desirable that a large-scale open area be maintained through a juxtaposition of several such developments, this will not be pleasant to the eye if it is haphazard. Either the uses must be actually homogeneous, as in an industrial park, or great care must be taken to provide an exterior relationship, as in the case of the handsome Radnor Industrial Park, in Montgomery County, Pennsylvania, where three "light industrial" plants, two schools, a motel, and a golf course are neighbors in a unified total composition.

ORGANIZATION AND SCALE

When the cultural pattern of a nation is homogeneous, a pattern of optimum spatial organization appears spontaneously, like the farmstead or the fishing village. It is a conflict of ideals and choices which occasions the heterogeneous sprawl. What is it that makes organization preferable to chaos? The units are the same, but when organized they acquire a value that was lacking before. It is apprehended through the mind, and brings pleasure when it strikes the sympathetic reactions in our nerves, both primary and associative. These depend on the reference points (or basic values) which have become familiar and friendly.

It should be noted parenthetically that identical repetition of a single design unit cannot be called organization, though it may constitute a pattern. But when we have a large view, such a repetition within limited areas or at conscious intervals may give weight and texture to the whole composition.

Establishing Contrast

At the very least, man has made a distinction between his home, or refuge, and its setting, or his garden and its surrounding wilderness. In more complex cultures, many degrees and kinds of land use and land value can be detected. Either the simple dichotomy or the graduated "continuum" may be the basis for organization of the environment. In either, there should be one preponderant element, to constitute the background. In the landscape of basically two contrasting elements, whichever is in the minority should be the medium of design, should furnish the principal accents and have greatest impact on the eye. But the larger or "background" area should have a continuity and unity, even though full of minor diversions and patterns.

Orientation

Perspective and rhythm, discussed in an earlier section of this chapter, are two orientation schemes. Open spaces, like other design elements, are seen and felt rhythmically in relation to an axis of orientation; at the same time, they must be complete and realizable in themselves. By their relative size and character they will help us to identify the major features around which the regional landscape is organized.

On flat terrain, the grid seems the natural system of orientation. With no eminence from which to view a complex directional framework, straight lines and right angles are the simplest to project over a distance. There may be variations in form and direction within this framework, but if they have no functional reason, their nonconformity will not necessarily produce a pleasing variety. The farmsteads of the Midwest plains, set in their quarter sections or mile squares, are usually parallel and perpendicular to the die-straight roads that bound their lands. Their windbreaks of trees, often the only trees in the landscape, are straight or L-shaped and parallel to houses, barns, and barnyard fences. If they were not, these lonely works of man would seem arbitrarily adrift in the vast plain.

The diagonal modern roads, cutting across the well-established squares at oblique angles, are often unfortunate from an esthetic point of view. Their destination is unclear, their relationship to the scenery they traverse definitely hostile. Concessions should be made to following the field system, combined with a wider right of way, and to separation by landscape accents of the highway from its setting. Where there is a natural irregularity, such as a winding river or sculptural elements of hills and rocks, it offers an occasion for a logical departure from the grid—the opportunity to create a more discursive pattern, with more detail. It will still be important to maintain a sense of direction and location, with reference to the region and its foci, with a major road network, and with the type and size of open spaces and the variation in spacing of urban structures. Because of the effect physiography has had on urban locations, it is often possible to parallel natural features such as a river or a high ridge and still be heading for the nearest urban center. Thus can the highways, with their landscaped borders and their appended developments, afford to swing in graceful curves harmonious with the rivers and streams, or to hug the shoulders of mountain ranges. The landscape, viewed in perspective, will then have unity, and the traveler on the highway will be simultaneously conscious of the river, the goal of the river and his road, and his own progress.

Blocks of woods, landscaped grounds, golf courses, and other large open spaces whose boundaries are set by man should fit into the major physiographic features or the major urban features, whichever are predominant. As we have seen on the great plains, the road system, an urban imposition, is the only strong system of orientation.

In mountain valleys the green fields of the floor will reach, finger-like, into folds of the hills. If, in time, a town spreads over the valley, it also will reach out in fingers, while the forested slopes will be thrust downward between them. This should form the basis for any pattern of "green belts" or "green wedges" for that area.

In the case of Toronto, a decision for a modified linear plan, recognizing the lateral direction of urban growth along the lake, was considerably modified by the influence of the river valleys generally converging on the central city. Interruption of an indefinite urban spread is here furnished by a belt of agricultural land which is to surround "Metro" Toronto before any adjacent urban center fuses with it.

SCALE

In keeping with the basic need to integrate ourselves with our environment,

The open-space oasis in the heart of the big city: Boston Common and the Public Gardens.

whether we think of it as adjusting nature to our civilization or vice versa, is the need to establish and maintain a scale. At one end, the scale must relate closely to us. At the other, it may relate to the vast urban agglomeration, the great tower building, or the steel works or aircraft plant; or it may relate to the large open spaces interwoven with or beyond the fringe.

Creating such a scale so that everyone feels it, though unconsciously, demands expert design. Scale is not a matter of size only; it is composed of mass and distance (including time) as factors. Apart from the fact that all scales, for man's comprehension, must eventually relate to his dimensions, there may be within a given land area several scales operating simultaneously. There will be one scale for the individual property, another for the neighborhood or community, and others for the river-basin, economic or metropolitan region, physiographic region of the continent, and finally a continental scale. For instance, both the neighborhoods and the urban center are concentrations of living or working at high density. They need open areas and green spaces at frequent intervals for convenience.

Another factor of convenience is that too large an open space creates a barrier to neighborhood movement, on foot or in vehicles. But both Central Park, conceived over a hundred years ago as an outlying reservation, and the much smaller Boston Common and Public Gardens are well related to the urban scale. They afford relief, without negating the feeling of being in an intensely urban place. But an "in city" park on the scale of Olmsted's Central Park would not be practicable today. Officials in one of the largest cities canvassed in this study have been discussing the possibility of developing small "passive" areas in a number of its neighborhoods, convinced that people can learn to appreciate lawns and flower gardens as well as sculpture and the other elements of landscaping art. "We have become so much the victims of the fear of vandalism," one of the city planning commissioners writes, "that we have become vandals, in a sense, ourselves. For fear that grass and flowers may be destroyed, we are destroying them ahead of the vandals by providing only macadam-surfaced bleak bleak areas that we label playgrounds."

The Spree River, tastefully flanked by greenery, in an industrial section of Berlin; compare with industrial river landscapes in America.

The establishment of an urban character requires that the urban forms should predominate. Therefore, frequent small parks and landscaped grounds should serve to enliven the townscape. Today, they are a more important element in the urban pattern than the large central park, with its policing and maintenance problems. But as we approach the fringe, there will be some large areas still in a natural state. The open areas developed for recreation or other purposes should be related to these, with a suitable transition in scale and character.

How this can be done is best illustrated concretely. On a micro-landscape scale, there is a good example on the campus of Amherst College, in Amherst, Massachusetts. Here an urban green space, a small campus flanked by double rows of trees, is surrounded by nearly continuous buildings on three sides. On the fourth, paths converge on a memorial round terrace, a few steps lower than the green, with an unobtrusively flat round disc carrying the names of those who served in the armed forces

Transition from the micro-scale to the macro-scale: terrace at Amherst College, Amherst, Mass.

of the world wars. Unseen except by walking close to the balustrade, the football fields below separate the campus proper from the adjoining countryside. Large hemlocks frame the view on either hand. The transition is agreeably made, and a nice touch is the scent of evergreens, which evokes the right mood for appreciating the view of distant hills and valleys.

Scale at the higher levels will be created by broader strokes, largely by the placement of urban concentrations and the preservation of natural areas in shapes and quantities that make a positive contribution. Forests, for instance, may occur as great carpets, as smaller blocks, or as scattered trees. A continental scale can be felt immediately in a view of the great national or the larger state forest reservations. This scale is equally recognizable in the vast private holdings of the lumber companies, or on the great ocean beaches.

It is the job of the local and the regional planner and of those who execute plans to see that areas which are needed to create this scale are not fragmented by minor elements belonging to a much more local design. They must especially protect the edges of any large land use area from being shredded by more urban intrusions. The closer we are to such a boundary, the more essential is its firm outline to our understanding that it is a boundary. The maintenance of sharp edges and definite shape around homogeneous blocks is a different matter from assembling all urban development into one mass and shape. Sometimes we see an isolated residential development, tied no doubt to a city but physically separated by green country, and we recognize that it is fitted into and completely fills one quarter section. The other three quarters may be solid cropland or solid woods. The development usually has the curving, stylized roads now considered "good design." There is no attempt at a transition; one simply lives in the development and would not know whether it were near the edge or at the heart. Here, just as much as among ugly cross-roads "sprawl" or in an amorphous city suburb, one can only say with Gertrude Stein, "There isn't any there there."

Lewis Mumford, in a recent speech to landscape architects, aptly called the fringe, as presently known, "undifferentiated, low-grade tissue." But differentiation through open-space design is not impossible. Small green shapes should become progressively larger and less formal as they approach the edge of open country. Even if another sub-division is later built in an adjacent section, the reverse process should commence at the common boundary, preserving for both an outer breathing-space of natural ground and an inner focus which should be individual for each separate neighbor-hood or community.

Within the principal scale of any level we may want many minor variations. Inter-rupting a broad sweep with a sudden cluster of smaller, more intense forms has the effect of stepping up the rhythm and providing excitement; but the major composi-tion must be kept in mind. A minor element must not be so out of scale or so im-portant that it seems to be a major part of the design. A judicious transition in scale may be called for not only to establish a harmony with the area's regional position; it may be needed to relate different developments in a single community which, be-cause of anachronism or violent contrast in use or technology, are incongruous neigh-bors.

The most frequent cause of this problem, from the industrial revolution up to the present, has been the factory. Not only was the factory unwelcome next to typical urban forms because of its noise or dirt; it overwhelmed also by its height and land coverage. The old mill type, with dozens or hundreds of windows piled storey on storey, simply multiplied the façade of a dwelling. The new type introduces a more func-tional but still more incongruous monolith of concrete or glass. Either needs some-thing to bring it into focus with, say, an old New England town clustered around its Common. The only way to make this transition, without rebuilding much that may be worth preserving, is by maintaining a suitable distance between the two. If this dis-tance can be kept large, it may be left pretty much in its natural state. If smaller, it must get artificial help in making the transition.

For example, an old Massachusetts town of fair size was built up at nineteenth-cen-tury scale, with a few typical factories. It was an agricultural and trading center. Re-cently it was lucky, from a tax point of view, in acquiring the large administration building of a national insurance company. The simple, modern style, the enormous size compared to existing buildings, would have been most unhappy had not the new building been placed at the end of a good-sized lake, opposite the town center, and surrounded by a rolling lawn and marshy areas. Whether you look from the passing expressway and see the old town set off by the lake, or from the town toward the new building, the effect is agreeable and interesting.

Water is especially useful for this purpose, for reasons mentioned in the discussion of materials: it greatly increases the effectiveness of its actual area. A large plant of the American Optical Company at Southbridge, Massachusetts, set off from the highway by a pond, illustrates how effective water can be, with very little effort expended on other design methods.

When planting or building materials must be relied on, it is necessary first to sur-round the large-scale building (or group) with accents at its own scale; then, with small breaks created by lawn, changes in level, clustered trees, or whatever means are most suitable, to shift in stages to the scale of the surrounding environment.

QUANTITIES

Allied to scale, but affected by different factors, is the matter of quantities or total areas of open space. Here we come back to the standards of need and use discussed earlier.

By and large, our metropolitan areas fall far short of the minimum standards proposed by the National Recreation Association some years ago, and adhered to by most planners and park authorities up to now. Recently the Association has suggested an upward revision of the amount of land in larger parks, state or county controlled, from ten to twelve acres per thousand, and has stressed the need for preserving, in addition, all large areas which from a conservation, scenic, or historic point of view are irreplaceable, or which should be held in reserve where expanding urban populations might need them. In fact, the sudden alarm lest we crowd ourselves into vast suburban slums has produced the slogan "buy now, develop later," which has come close at times to meaning "buy now, plan later."

On the other hand, consider that our national overall density is 60 persons per square mile (over ten acres per person); that there are around 490 million acres of land in federal and state ownership, not including Hawaii, or Alaska, most of which is government owned; and that in even our most crowded cities, not more than 20 per cent of the total ground area is covered with buildings. Of course, from the point of view of productivity and ability of the land to absorb and store water, paving or dusty yards stripped of top soil are almost as bad as actual building coverage; nevertheless, in the fringe, where a growing percentage of our people live, houses and driveways together cover not more than ten to 20 per cent of the lots, leaving 80 to 90 per cent open. In the densely populated, industrial state of Connecticut two-thirds of the land area is now in forest; this is in addition to all open spaces found among farm or urban land uses.

The report of Edwards, Kelcey, and Beck for the Massachusetts Department of Natural Resources on Public Outdoor Recreation (1957) distinguishes between the residents of the larger cities and their suburbs, who have an average space 72 feet square, or about one-eighth of an acre each, and those in the remainder of the country, who have 23 acres per person. "It is not difficult," says the report, "to understand why dwellers in the city have an urge to get off their little 72-foot squares and go to places where they can stretch their limbs . . ."

The vastness of the federal land holdings is seldom kept in mind, even by westerners; but not much of the area is readily accessible to the urban dweller. About one-fifth of all the land area of the United States is federally owned; over half of Arizona, Idaho, Nevada, Oregon, and Utah—much of it semi-desert; nearly half of California; and five per cent or more of some twenty other states. The two largest blocks are managed by the Department of Agriculture Forest Service (167.5 million acres) and the Department of the Interior Bureau of Land Management (178.1 million acres). The National Park Service by contrast controls only 15 million acres. The Department of Defense controls 25.4 million acres, which are to a large extent inaccessible and sometimes not even visible to the public. (None of these figures includes Alaska or Hawaii.)

The states own only one-fifth as much, altogether, as does the United States as a whole. A considerable part of the state-owned lands once were federal grants, given as trust for the support of schools, but most states have disposed of all or a substantial part of these. In the central Midwest, little of the state-owned land was acquired for the development of any land program, distinct from the provision of facilities. In other states forestry, water conservation, agricultural improvement, or game management, as well as conservation in general, have been objectives. In most cases, each area is used for several of these purposes, and also for recreation.

In New York much of the land now held in the Adirondacks and Catskill State Forests had been sold by the state and reverted to it for non-payment of taxes. In many other states tracts were similarly acquired. In almost all, the policy for purchase of land for parks is to pay very low prices per acre when it cannot be obtained free. This, of course, decreases the already slim chances of an adequate distribution, under state auspices, in the metropolitan fringes. Some states, however, are assisting localities to purchase open space—New York has voted $75 million for this purpose in 1961. The National Housing Act of 1961 included an appropriation of $50 million in federal funds for this purpose.

Not only is the distribution of public land within states out of balance with population, but it is even more drastically unbalanced for the nation as a whole. This is partly because the preponderance of lands that can only be used at very low densities, or purely for recreation, lies in the western half of the country. Another reason is the timing of exploration and settlement, which started on the eastern seaboard.

How much of this area do we need to keep open, for use or for esthetic or other human needs? There is, of course, a need for "land banks," the judicious reservation of land where future extensions of residence, of business, or of industry will be most helpful in the total scheme of things. Incidentally, this presupposes regional and national planning for the best results. But this is not the particular concern of a study in design, except that it will mean a series of interim stages between formulation of the plan and its eventual completion.

In general, but keeping in mind the principles of scale and orientation discussed earlier, we would be right in asserting that the great majority of communities needs to provide playgrounds and ballfields at about the standards now recommended, which are based on distance and population. If the playground is to be reached by a trip of not over a quarter-mile, it must be centered on a neighborhood only a quarter as large as that served by a playfield, with its half-mile recommended limit of service. Since the minimum for both suggested by the National Recreation Association is two and one-half acres for each thousand of population, this means that playfields would tend to be about four times the size of neighborhood playgrounds; ten to twelve acres, in a half-acre minimum lot district, to serve somewhat over 4,000 people. A playground serving three hundred and forty families, or a half-mile square at a half-acre minimum lot size, would contain at least two and one-half to three acres. It would not be practical to develop many different facilities on such a small site, but if some parts of it are left in a natural state, children will create their own games; and a sprinkler, slide, and sandbox do not require much room or large investment, assuming that water is available. Playfields will be more thinly distributed as we move out in the fringe, and will be supplemented by the "all-day" type of park.

We have some experience in planning the small and the medium-size open-space system; but when we come to the macrocosm, the large region, few are experienced and there are not many guides. *The established standards are admittedly for urban and suburban places.* Until recently, the fringe or rural areas were not considered under enough pressure to require "standards." It is now vaguely suggested that they be "increased" for lower-density areas, but no one has established just how much. Furthermore, some authorities have established a sliding scale, with much lower standards for dense city neighborhoods. This is surely an abandonment of the human needs on which the ratios were founded. Let the areas be smaller, but more numerous, in the cities.

The National Recreation Association has advocated, in addition to ten acres of local public open space, an additional ten or twelve acres of park and conservation preserve per thousand people, as a minimum. This rather meager standard is hard to exact within convenient range of the greatest population concentrations, yet it does not begin to use up all the "open" land between some of our more widely separated metropolitan areas.

There are no standards at all on private or institutional open space, yet a cursory examination of any tabulated survey of open space, for an area of any size, will show that these provide a substantial and often preponderant amount of the total.

Some information on the degree to which regions follow published standards is available from several surveys completed within the last few years. Unfortunately, the surveys are not designed so as to be completely comparable, but many statistics are at least roughly so:

CLEVELAND

The Cleveland Metropolitan Park District is far ahead of most urban regions in having provided in its metropolitan parks, forming the famous "Emerald Necklace" around the city, 8.4 acres per thousand people in the Standard Metropolitan Area. For Cuyahoga County alone, the ratio is over 11 acres per thousand. There are no state or national parks in this area. Local parks and reservations provide a little over two acres per thousand. All institutional and private (i.e., club and commercial) open space doubles the amount, for a total of about 26 acres per thousand.

While central Cleveland lacks enough park or other open space, the outer city and suburbs are well supplied; the fringe communities border on the great metropolitan reservations, with a liberal sprinkling of institutional and private open space. There are possibilities for great improvement, especially along the Cuyahoga Valley, but in general the metropolitan area provides the kind of balanced design we have been talking about.

Systems of open space I, the classic greenbelt: Cleveland, Ohio. The "Emerald Necklace" consists of a park road string joining "beads" of regional reservations, in part wild and in part developed for recreation. River valleys are incorporated into the "greenbelt," and recent emphasis has been on reclamation of the Lake Erie shore as a scenic and recreational asset.

Systems of open space II, stream valleys and areas with parkway corridors: Washington, D.C. An extensive system of open space, incorporating stream valleys, parkways, and large institutional uses, mostly federal. Funds for added stream valley acquisition in the National Capital Region are available under Capper-Crampton Act.

Systems of open space III, stream valleys: Toronto. The existing system is fragmentary, consisting of two lower valley reservations and some lakefront parks; the "Metro" plan proposes expanded conservation of stream valleys for water supply, flood control, and scenic and recreational use.

Systems of open space IV, valleys, ridges, and park roads with proposed green zone: Greater Boston area. An old and well-established park system, administered largely by the Metropolitan Parks District. The shaded area outside the District and the circumferential Route 128 freeway is the so-called Bay Circuit, an area for which a variety of open-space conservation measures are proposed. A continuous tourist route is also planned, but the component roads and adjacent open space are to remain as far as possible under local control, often in private ownership. A major objective is to retain, for public enjoyment, the opportunity to see rural scenery and activities, as well as natural oases. Towns in the designated area are asked to participate through planning, acquisition of land or easements, and zoning.

Systems of open space V, areas connected by parkway corridors: New York. A comprehensive park and parkway system developed through the generosity of private individuals, such as the Harrimans and Rockefellers, on the one hand, and through the perseverance of energetic public servants, such as Robert Moses, on the other. Ocean beaches, mountain ridges, and the connecting parkway grid form the backbone of the system.

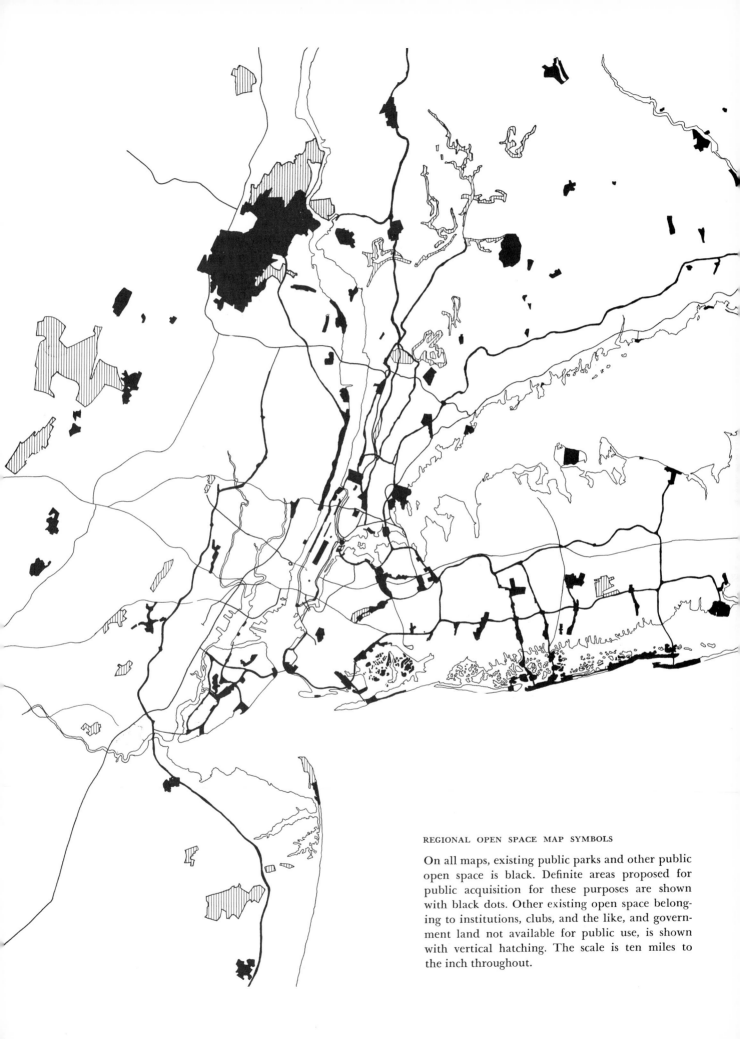

REGIONAL OPEN SPACE MAP SYMBOLS

On all maps, existing public parks and other public open space is black. Definite areas proposed for public acquisition for these purposes are shown with black dots. Other existing open space belonging to institutions, clubs, and the like, and government land not available for public use, is shown with vertical hatching. The scale is ten miles to the inch throughout.

Systems of open space VI, isolated areas: Los Angeles. The large area to the north is the Angeles National Forest; other than that there are only a few isolated parks. Some recreational use is made of flood control projects, but generally stream valleys do not play an important role, since the "arroyos" are dry gullies for most of the year. Wavy lines indicate large flood control basins used for land and water recreation; random dash pattern at the top indicates the Angeles National Forest boundary along the west slope of a high mountain range.

The total acreage owned by the CMPD is about 11,700 acres, or 14,500 including public golf courses and parkways. The report made for the District finds a need for 5,000 additional acres, by 1980, on the basis of present use and expected population. It provides significant indices of the age groups and the home location of those who use the parks, which could be applied to the Regional Planning Commission's population projections to determine size and location of new parks. Proposals for future acquisition show a compromise between the use-demand and the conservation point of view, which is usual in the fringe areas; the emphasis is on securing large areas susceptible of development for fairly heavy use, combined in some cases with the preservation of unusually interesting scenic features.

BOSTON

Boston's Bay Circuit concept of an outer ring of reservations joined by parkways is somewhat like the Emerald Necklace. But only fragments of the Bay Circuit are in public hands, while the inner park system is also incomplete. The continuous parkway scheme has been abandoned. The greatest success of the Boston metropolitan region has been in protection of its river and stream banks and its water supply lands, along with a good many of the outstanding scenic or historic sites.

NEW YORK

Turning to New York, we find that the Park, Recreation, and Open Space Project of the Tri-State New York Metropolitan Region reports that there are 151,725 acres of "all-day" parks in its area, of which almost 33,000 are municipal, the rest state or county-owned. Of the total, 130,187 are outside the core counties (New York, Bronx, Queens, Kings Counties in New York and Hudson County in New Jersey), hence at a radius of ten to fifteen miles from downtown Manhattan. The average acreage per thousand people is about 10 for the "all-day" parks, but about 12.6 for all parks, for the whole Region. It is the municipal quota which is below the NRA standard. In the densely developed part of the Region, however, meeting the standard is physically and financially almost impossible. As the Project report points out, to provide five acres of playground and playfield and five of larger parks per thousand people for Manhattan would require an area larger than the island itself.

In the fringe areas, mounting school costs make the citizens take a dim view of other capital projects. The best hope is to combine the acquisition of school sites with extra acreage for recreation.

Ten specific new regional parks are proposed by the Project, some of which have long been advocated by other groups and agencies. The recommended total additional acreage is 560,000 acres in state and county parks, and 176,000 in municipal parks. (State forests and fish and game lands are included with state parks.)

LOS ANGELES

In the Los Angeles Metropolitan area (Los Angeles and Orange Counties) 29 per cent of the land is publicly owned. The cities, counties and recreation districts hold 27,590 acres; the State Division of Beaches and Parks, 4,923 acres plus 437 in special facilities; the National Park Service, 582 acres in the Channel Islands National Monument (undeveloped); and the National Forest Service, 1,753 acres.

Among the unusual facilities of this region are 66 eighteen-hole golf courses, and marinas containing berths for almost 13,000 boats. To effect a standard of 6 acres of regional park per thousand people, the Region proposes acquisition of land to make a total of 54,000 acres. These would consist of 28,235 in regional parks, 11,865 in special areas, 8,000 in open space, 3,621 in recreation parks, and 2,280 in parkways. The latter are almost wholly lacking now; they would feature vista points and small picnic turnoffs.

These are all within the urbanized area of about 1,500 square miles. In spite of the enormous size of the Los Angeles-Long Beach metropolis and its explosive growth, its low density and high proportion of vacant land and nearly exhausted oil fields make it possible still to find some areas for large parks. The use of land, behind the earth dams built for protection from the rare peak floods, to create varied recreation facilities is especially noteworthy, as is the use of many irrigation reservoirs and some water supply reservations for public access.

THE IMPRINT OF THE DESIGNER

The principles of orientation, of scale, of actual and relative size, could be fulfilled and still create a monotonous, mechanical picture. The result might be functional. It would not necessarily be art, or even recreation in the fullest sense. We need not worry about the sections in which nature is untouched. It is the hand of man that may do mischief, alternating between irresponsible wilfulness and uncritical following of "models."

One sometimes reads statements from formalist architects, engineers, and planners affirming that they have taken "the whole physical environment of man" as their sphere of activity. Some of them may not know that landscape architects also are taking quite seriously the responsibility of their profession, now that vast sections of the country are overrun by the tide of urbanization. The land is being violated, they say with justice, and they have been trained to deal with it constructively. At last they feel that problems more challenging than the landscaping of a private garden or a park are beckoning them. The sad fact is that, except for an increasing number of industrial developments and our more lavish freeways, they are rarely given an opportunity to design at the regional scale. It is interesting to note here that in some European countries electric power companies are employing landscape architects to site the location of cross-country lines in order to integrate them with the natural scenery.

The ecologist—another neglected professional who, as a scientist of man's relation to his environment, should best know what results will follow specific actions—is also seldom consulted. He is forced to stand in the role of Cassandra, though sometimes he has a brief importance when called on to explain some catastrophe which already has befallen. The geographer writes and speaks on major trends, but is seldom in a position to direct positive action. The soil scientist is only just being discovered as a long-needed resource man, who knows for what use a given piece of land is best suited and who can predict some of our most embarrassing occurrences, such as the saturation of soil by septic tank overflow, or the lowering of the water table by too many wells too close together. He knows which soils should at all costs be saved for the production of food crops (including meat and milk), but he is seldom deferred to in this matter. *No plan for a region should be made without an ecological analysis of every open space larger than the ordinary city park.* Thus we would learn of interacting factors in the total environment, and could predict the effect of any proposed change—in the short and in the long run. We could also, with the help of the botanist, biologist, and geologist, know more accurately the value each piece of land holds for us, before we destroy that value forever.

All of these people can contribute to a pool of knowledge which the land planner ought to share, in order to design wisely. It is not just that design should be functional. The man who deeply understands the material he is working with will be better inspired in his plans than one who does not. For example, "earth sculpture," like rock blasting, is comparatively easy with modern machines. The results are sad, if the designer or engineer does not understand how the earth will seek to regain its former stability, or how the rock will split.

It would be calamitous if our entire continent, or even all of it that is not on steep mountain slopes or under water, should come under the influence of formalist design. Too often we hear of anti-sprawl panaceas, which suggest that all our dwellings should be bundled into high-rise towers or neat clusters or row-houses, surrounded by appropriate expanses of lawn, planting, and playgrounds. The old city centers, meantime, would be razed and replanted to grass and trees, resembling Nebuchad-nezzar's dream. The national highway system would consist of hygienically-sealed ex-pressways in greenbelts.

Such a pulling together and organizing of rural-suburban settlement would, of course, be less antisocial (in a fundamental sense) than urban sprawl. Yet the presence of a pattern is not the equivalent of a civilization.

If such schemes are not the ultimate in mediocrity and misplaced value, they seem to us to come close. They imply a total lack of respect for the diversity of human choice. They would take away the symbols and the orientation that have held our spider-web regional structures in place, yet would provide no effective substitutes.

Let us instead allow a very considerable amount of freedom, even at the risk of mistakes, in order to produce the sparks of originality, the contrast and alternation that we have noted as psychological necessities. We should use our natural and social scientist far more than we have done for education and guidance; and then let our designers shape, with technical advice from the various disciplines, the major out-lines of each functional area, whether it is in the small community or the great region. Rigid predetermination of details or even of all the major accents can lead only to disappointment with the results.

4. Opportunities for Design

The largest opportunity for design of open space that is likely to come to a suitably qualified person is a metropolitan park system or a river-basin multi-purpose develop-ment. The first is a skeletal part of a whole region, which will be *filled in* by others. The second is a large core, around which will develop both residence and enterprise. Recently, the city of Boulder, Nevada, with a large vacant area, was turned loose by the federal government to control its own destiny, after the lake, the power proj-ects, and the core community were complete. The only stipulation was that a plan for the whole area (over 30 square miles) should be prepared immediately with some restrictions on the sale of land, and requirements for a Capital Improvement Pro-gram. This, and a very few other communities that for one or another reason own most of their land, can exert as complete a control over development as they wish.

The important point is that, as at Boulder, there should be a plan. This is even more important for open space than for urban development, for open space will be the most noticeable element in the ultimate pattern of the region. It is also the medium which can least successfully be supplied on a second try—by redevelopment.

Next in importance is establishment by the governing body of the region, with informed support from its voters, of a priority list. This should work in two ways: a list of minimum necessary projects should be agreed upon, with alternates where these would really be equivalent, and a timetable should be established to secure first the areas which are most in danger of succumbing to competitive uses. Additional scheduling should preserve some force and coherence in the interim stages between wilderness or farmland and ultimate urban status.

There are a good many ways, besides the obvious one of purchase, whereby any region or community can effect the shaping of design, which goes on every time a piece of ground is sold for a different use, or an owner plants a tree or cuts one down. The following paragraphs show some of the more interesting possibilities, though they do not pretend to comprise anything like an exhaustive list. Though many of them may operate at several levels, they are grouped under the geographic or governmental unit which is most apt to furnish the opportunity to plan them.

NATIONAL OR REGIONAL SCOPE:

RIVER BASIN PROJECTS

These may be primarily for water supply to arid regions, flood protection, power, or navigation; often two or more are combined. Recreation has turned out to be such a large byproduct in these developments that extensive planning for highway access and camping or lodging facilities, boat launching units, exclusive fishing, swimming, and motorboating areas, and so on, are now required.

These projects are usually designed on purely engineering principles. More often than not, they turn out to be esthetically satisfying, at least on the scale of the macrolandscape. However, since the scenery is so drastically altered and often made much more interesting, local and regional planners should have a chance to help formulate the plans with a view to an ultimate plan esthetically and functionally successful *in detail.*

FOREST DEVELOPMENT

Healthy and orderly appearance of forests is a factor in our landscape on the continental scale. Long-term development is most apt to bring this about. Legislation to promote or assist the economy of tree farming and selective cutting is desirable at either federal or state levels, as is legislation which would encourage multiple use of forests.

Man-made recreational designs in nature: ski slopes at Stowe, Vermont.

AGRICULTURAL DEVELOPMENT

Because cultivated fields are a pleasing sight in themselves and often the only means of keeping an open view, any steps that will encourage continued and competent farming are strategic in the unified open space program. In some of our rapidly metropolitanizing regions, this is a difficult proposition indeed. Fundamentally, the bolstering of agriculture against competing needs for land is a matter of public and private finance. There is considerable literature on the subject. Carl Belser, the Planning Director of Santa Clara County, California, has expressed the importance of agricultural land and the urgency of the problem in *Green Gold: A Proposal for a Pilot Experiment in the Conservation of Agricultural Open Space.* William H. Whyte in *Securing Open Space for Urban America: Conservation Easements,* and Shirley A. Siegel in *The Law of Open Space,* have described a number of existing or proposed legal measures, as has Erling Solberg of the U.S. Department of Agriculture. Several of these have suggested variants of a proposal, made by Charles W. Eliot II, that farm land be taxed only as such while farmed, but that if sold, a severance tax be collected, somewhat as is done with forest lands when timber is harvested.

In part, the solution lies in a compromise: less total space for agriculture, but more intensive use. Truck gardens, berry farms (or ranches, as they are called in the West), and concentrated dairy farms are best able to withstand competition for land. This type of dairying is practically an industry, as carried on in the environs of Los Angeles and scattered locations elsewhere. Zoning regulations which recognize this type of operation are needed to make satisfactory transitions from such areas to other land uses, and to establish acceptable lot sizes and intensity of use.

It should be also borne in mind that on the national scale, the problem in North America is *too much* land under cultivation. In 1961 only 296 million acres out of the 458 million acres of cropland in the U.S. were actually harvested. The Department of Agriculture conservatively estimates that in 1980, all domestic and greatly expanded export needs for farm products could be produced on 51 million fewer acres of cropland and 19 million fewer acres of grassland than now available. At least this much, and probably more marginal agricultural land should revert to trees, to grass prairie, and to public parks and recreation grounds.

STATE OR COUNTY SCOPE AND LEGISLATION:

ACCESS TO WATER FOR PUBLIC RECREATION

The states which are well endowed are the ones which have laws protecting the citizens' right of access to their streams and lakes for recreation. Minnesota requires subdivision plans around lakes to show public access to the shore every half-mile, at least. Massachusetts has a long-standing Great Pond law, preserving all ponds over ten acres as public property. No landowner abutting these ponds can bar the public from access to them. It seems contradictory that the states in which water is a more precious commodity, and almost the only physiographic feature, have not taken even more effective steps to promote the recreational use of such ponds and rivers as they have. The muddy, brush-bordered streams of Illinois are now considered valuable assets to residential property, yet they are not protected for public benefit from private use and misuse. Furthermore, neither the state nor any counties own shore front on Lake Michigan.

MAKING THE MOST OF HIGHWAY PLANS

Some states permit "excess condemnation" in connection with acquisition of highway sites, if it can be shown to be in the public interest. It is certainly a public benefit to acquire, by purchase or eminent domain, land for small roadside parks. These may be larger than the traditional picnic sites, whenever a suitable opportunity for a small state park exists. They might even contain swimming or boating facilities. In other cases the apparent size of a small picnic area might be increased by the purchase of scenic easements, along with the highway right-of-way. New Hampshire, among other states, has done this in places where unchecked wilderness growth would otherwise have obliterated a fine mountain view.

Because of the financial policy governing purchase for state parks and the habit of building roads only to meet today's traffic desires, land is seldom acquired for large parks or forests adjacent to an expressway. Yet this is where they should be, accessible to the many, especially from urban centers, yet not located where crowds must drive through peaceful villages or rural roads in order to reach them. The moment a new major park is acquired, a right-of-way for a connecting highway should also be acquired; such a policy would soon make it apparent that locations reasonably near the regional highway network would be desirable. We are too ready to destroy the values inherent in an unspoiled country village and its surrounding landscape in order to make a different kind of recreational experience more easily accessible.

FOREST DISTRICTS OR ZONES

The states with vast timber resources which are important to their economic health have led the way with legislation that would be appropriate in any area. Minnesota, Wisconsin, and Michigan allow counties and townships to declare areas to be in exclusive forest districts, in order to round out or make more efficient existing timber holdings. This affords an opportunity to preserve outlines where they should be and prevent the waseful frittering away of forest resources through scattered, haphazard clearing.

EXCLUSIVE AGRICULTURAL ZONES

California is the state in which a head-on collision between lucrative agriculture and lucrative subdivision can best be seen. In that state, agricultural zoning districts, exclusive or combined with residence on large lots, have been created and upheld by courts, largely as a defense against involuntary annexation by cities looking for extra tax revenue. Some midwestern states have similar zoning, and there are a few isolated examples in the East. They should be more courageously used, wherever agricultural areas are still large enough to offer good operating and marketing conditions. As long as there are areas within the general region where residential subdivision can take place, there is little danger that the exclusion of all but farm houses from an agricultural district will be declared illegal.

EXCLUSIVE RECREATION OR OPEN SPACE DISTRICTS

Among exclusive zone districts, the most extreme example to date has been the exclusive Recreation District on some California beach land. This could only be upheld, in view of its rather discriminatory impact on the owners, because of public recognition that the remaining unbuilt stretches of shoreline must be saved for public use at all costs. In the West and on the eastern seaboard some communities have instituted open space or "O" districts, where various uses short of building are permitted. (Sometimes these also include "Official," i.e., municipal, buildings.) The legality and practicality of this measure depends on the economics of the area, the prevailing land pattern, and the fairness of the uses permitted.

Sometimes stream banks, flood plains, and marshes are included in the "O" districts. Sometimes they are zoned separately in "Flood Protection" districts, since this is obviously a kind of safety measure. Stream banks may be zoned against building, or, in some states, water resource authorities are permitted to establish "encroachment lines."

All these measures are extremely useful in creating a meaningful pattern, especially if they are applied on a regional rather than a purely local scale. This may involve action as a county, a metropolitan district, or a cooperative region, or merely through informal consultation between local communities. Toronto "Metro" and Northern Virginia are examples of regional design making maximum use of the regional stream system, as is the Boston Metropolitan Park District.

LOCAL MEASURES:

CONSERVATION EASEMENTS

Reference has been made in this chapter to a technique which is considered by some to be more lasting than zoning, and which does not cost so much as full purchase. This is the purchase of development rights or "conservation easements." The state or a smaller division may pay a fair price to secure the open character of land, or its availability for hunting or fishing. The owner continues to use it, within whatever restrictions are agreed on. Usually this is intended as a permanent arrangement, and "runs with the land," in legal terminology, but sometimes it is a prelude to acquisition, perhaps as a bequest, at the owner's death or when he no longer cares to use the property. Whereas some tax assessors will not reduce assessments on property whose development is restricted by zoning (claiming it can be changed at any time without much difficulty), they cannot ignore the binding force of easements or other covenants. Golf clubs, private institutions, and some woodlands and farmlands can best be conserved in this manner. Covenants between private individuals to maintain open space are only enforceable by parties thereto, except in Wisconsin, which has a law permitting the state to enforce restrictions on private land.

MAKING USE OF LARGE LOTS

One other technique of keeping land out of rapid subdivision by zoning is the "acreage" or large-lot district. Courts have variously upheld from one- to five-acre minimum lots in residence districts, depending on the prevailing type of land holding. For the purpose of keeping land rural or open in appearance, unless it is heavily wooded, nothing less than five acres is effective. To preserve farms for diversion to other use, a still larger minimum is needed. Therefore, it is safer to rely on other means in our transitional fringe areas.

However, the objective of discouraging large-scale subdivision can be secured by a minimum of one to two acres, depending on local conditions. The outward pressure of population and the amount of land available elsewhere will affect the support of such a policy. Sometimes it is used as a declared interim policy, to prevent the waste of land and public services, by keeping development within a reasonably compact area adjacent to existing development. This procedure was used at Clarkstown, New York, several years ago. A more drastic proposal along the lines of a British housing estate is suggested by Marion Clawson, in the *Journal of the American Institute of Planners* (May, 1960), and by Charles Abrams and others. This involves actual purchase and resale of the land; it would require legislation and constitutional amendments in most states.

Such approaches can be useful in creating large, predominantly green areas in contrast to a village type of growth. Not only is this more economical for the community, it reduces premature despoiling of natural areas or farms and results in a more interesting and beautiful landscape.

MAKING THE WHOLE COMMUNITY A GREEN SPACE

One way in which the public sanction of one- or two-acre lots as a minimum could be made more equitable would also make the resulting pattern of more effect. Usually, it is the owners of a rural or "estate" section of a town who want the higher minimum requirement. When proposing such a district, local zoning authorities could make conditions resulting in the rear half, more or less, of lots remaining unbuilt upon, though otherwise unrestricted. Thus, a deep "superblock" would be created, saving road maintenance and providing a sizable area, all in one piece, of gardens, lawns, and woods.

Green space as a key to community design.

In this way we might again get the kind of benefit to a larger area which was once afforded by the suburban estates around Boston, of which the late Charles W. Eliot wrote: "Boston, at the end of the list (of people per park acre, in 1880) boasts uncommonly attractive suburbs which have served some of the purposes of a park . . . ." Boston still has such suburbs; Brookline was one of the earliest, and now Weston and Lincoln are assuming a similar role at the current lower densities. Parts of Greenwich and Fairfield, Connecticut; Purchase, New York; Gates Mills outside Cleveland, Ohio; Palos Verdes Estates and Pasadena in the Los Angeles area; Santa Barbara as a separate community; and Hillsborough or Woodside in the San Francisco metropolitan region, might be cited, among others. In these, the residents have determined to preserve a pastoral or handsomely landscaped residential haven from urban clutter, no matter what the cost in taxes. These are at the very least a welcome interruption of suburban monotony. In proportion to their accessibility to the urban region, they are a visual resource, and often act as pace-setters for more run-of-the-mill developments.

The front and rear yard requirements also should be set with a view to creating the maximum amount of continuous green space on the rear. Front setbacks have been overdone in many instances. Their purposes are to keep homes at a reasonable distance from the traffic, fumes, and other street nuisances, and to provide enough light and air for rooms on the street side; they may also be set with some consideration of the possibility that the street may need widening in the future. But the creation of a handsome street, including a border of grass and trees and shrubs, should be kept in proportion to the most important living space, and the greater contribution to total open space, which the rear yards provide. And if the appearance of the street is important to the whole community, is it fair to effect it through demands on adjacent property owners, rather than through adequate width and planting of the public way?

THE PRIVATE ESTATE AS OPEN SPACE AND AS A DEVELOPMENT TRACT

The extreme in open-space value provided by the individual lot is the case of the large estate, from fifty up to thousands of acres in extent. These are generally considered to be relics of a bygone age; however, the recently increased appreciation of the value of open space may spur the use of various devices to encourage large private holdings with suitable assurance of their withdrawal from the development market.

An important point about such estates is that they give a rare opportunity for large-scale, unified planning when, if ever, they are opened for development. Many subdivision and zoning regulations require submission of the entire plan of any large tract to the planning body for approval, whether it is for residential or other use.

Perhaps the ultimate in such opportunities is the Irvine Ranch, between San Diego and Los Angeles. Thousands of acres of choice orchard and grazing land have been retained in one family for three or four generations, but are now on the verge of development, presumably under a single plan for the whole area.

Another large tract which was recently opened up is Sterling Forest, N.Y. This adjoins parts of Harriman and Bear Mountain State Parks, and is close to Tuxedo Park, so that an additional large area of greenery, merging into wilderness, is preserved on the fringe of metropolitan New York (about an hour from mid-city). Sterling Forest is projected as a balanced community; it combines some areas for private homes with large tracts for research plants, where Union Carbide Corporation and New York University already have installations; all the development is based on long leases rather than sale. Income and advertising value are being derived ingeniously from the gardens. These, a separate business corporation, have been developed as a tourist attraction, with seasonal displays. The setting is a small marshy plain between rocky spurs of the mountains; it has been drained to form a series of small lakes.

Sterling Forest Gardens form a far outpost of extremely urban sophistication. It is well done in its genre. Whether this kind of thing is a violation of the regional landscape depends somewhat on the surrounding area. If a good-sized cluster of homes and smaller research plants develop, and these are more logically tied to the highway

View of Sterling Forest Gardens, Tuxedo, N.Y., an extensive private development

system than now, one could make a good case for an extension of the urban core in this manner out into the fringe. The transition, as we have said in the section on principles of design, should be gradual and orderly.

It is not only the private individual estate which provides a large, ready-made planning unit. Sometimes a university or similar eleemosynary body owns a larger property than is required for its immediate purpose. Stanford University, at Palo Alto, is a case in point. Here, the University owned acres which it could not, under deed of gift, sell, but did not need for the campus. The solution was an admirably conceived research and industrial park, with a much smaller area devoted to residences, all on a long-lease basis.

Another view of Sterling Forest Gardens, Tuxedo, N.Y.; this comprehensive real estate development includes industrial research facilities, private housing, and floral displays open to the public for a fee.

A university which had the custody of open space thrust upon it was Antioch College in Ohio. That college manages a large tract which includes a small wilderness, with a stream valley, falls, and rapids, and typical ravine growth. Other features are a tree-farm demonstration area, where the Yellow Springs citizens may select and cut their Christmas trees each year; and an area under cultivation, demonstrating good farm practice. The entire tract, known as Glen Helen, forms a teaching resource, and is used by groups from all over the country.

One of the best known and handsomest of the single-tract developments is the headquarters of the Connecticut General Life Insurance Company, in Bloomfield, Connecticut (a suburb of Hartford). Here, 160 acres of former farmland have been turned into a spacious park; the much-photographed building occupies a very small part of the whole tract, even with its parking spaces, pools, gardens, and sculpture. Here is a fine, permanent open space in a fringe rapidly filling up with residence, business and industry.

THE RESIDENTIAL ASSOCIATION

There are numerous instances of residential areas protected by private covenants which are more restrictive than the local zoning. As distinct from whole communities that set high standards, these are often exclusive, in a literal sense; gatekeepers or locks bar all except those with legitimate reasons from access. Tuxedo Park, New York, is one of the older and better known of these, but there are many. When an entire community is controlled in appearance by covenants, as in Shaker Heights in suburban Cleveland, the result is seldom distinguishable from the "high class" community which has chosen this path through elective decisions.

THE LOCAL USE OF REGULATORY POWERS

The various measures of authorization which were mentioned at the State level are often carried out on the local scene. In much of the country, this may be under county auspices, when not in the jurisdiction of an incorporated city. In the Northeast, the towns are the principal unit for local government, including zoning, subdivision regulations, and other powers for the public good or protection.

The good sense shown in preparing plans, the imagination in design of large and small land areas, and the fairness with which conflicting interests are treated are called for first and last at this level. It is the only scale at which many of us will ever think of design. Our experience at home will condition us to cooperation or indifference in a broader sphere.

THE COST:

It is the opinion of many speakers and writers on open space that the public must adjust itself to the purchase of much larger land totals than formerly, in order to exercise adequate control over future development. This requires revised legislation in many states, liberalizing the conditions under which a governmental agency can "go into the real estate business," including the exercise, when warranted, of eminent domain powers.

A long-term view of the financial burden and benefits is also needed. A seemingly excessive outlay in terms of the next five years may provide a huge saving over a period of twenty-five or fifty.

The Cleveland Metropolitan Park system has cost an average of $430 per acre because it was started before land values for subdivision soared. Since future purchases will be in relatively less congested areas, it is estimated that 300 acres should be acquired, on an average, in each of the next twenty years, at a cost not very much more than the past average per acre. The Cleveland Metropolitan Park District is unusual in having its own tax levy for capital outlays. Periodically this has to be renewed; in a recent year the voters again approved a tax of one-tenth mill for continued purchase and development of the system.

The New York Metropolitan Region, on the other hand, has before it the proposal of the Park, Recreation, and Open Space Project for acquisition of 574,000 acres for recreation (not counting "conservation areas," which are usually obtainable at much lower costs because of their limited usefulness). The estimated cost is $1.9 billion, indicating an average cost per acre ten times as much as for the Cleveland Metropolitan system. It must be remembered, of course, that this includes parks which are considered essential in the core of the region, where land values have reached very inflated proportions. Nearly 40 per cent of the New York region's all-day recreation areas were acquired by gift, transfer from other agencies, or tax delinquency; but it must be pointed out that almost all of these are outside the core counties.

In general, cities and counties have no continuing budget for acquisition of open space. Sometimes a large outlay is financed over many years by a bond issue; this practice is being used by the northern Virginia communities and their new Regional Park Authority. New York State has passed by referendum a provision for a $75,000,000 bond issue to assist localities in acquiring parks and open space, and New Jersey has a similar "green acres" bond issue. Wisconsin is embarking on a very broad program of open space planning and acquisition.

States sometimes authorize large spending programs of limited duration. One of the most comprehensive state open-space programs is that proposed for Massachusetts in the report made for the Department of Natural Resources in 1957, which incorporated many projects suggested earlier and added some new ones. One million dollars a year in bond issues for four years has so far been authorized for purchase. No money has been appropriated for purchase of land or easements in the Bay Circuit, but land in the area could be acquired under the general state program, so long as it is outside the Boston Metropolitan District. Massachusetts has also appropriated $50,000 to assist communities to buy conservation lands; towns must contribute one-half of the cost, with a maximum of $15,000 to one town in the biennium.

The Federal Government in the Housing Act of 1961 authorized assistance to localities in acquiring open space, with a $50 million appropriation to carry out the provision. A local comprehensive plan is a condition for receiving a grant. President Kennedy has advocated a land bank, for future development and recreation. It is worth noting that the grants under the Housing Act can be used for acquiring open space for any public purpose, not necessarily for active recreation or developed park.

With the higher levels of government and taxation alerted to the need, communities will have a relatively easier time in financing their open space programs. It would be unfortunate, however, if the present tendency to give aid should reduce local initiative to meeting the minimum requirements for obtaining such assistance. The "common land" of today is needed for a vastly more intricate and complex society than the old New England common of our ancestors, and we should be willing to devote a far greater proportion of our energies and wealth to its achievement and protection.

Space that is "open" today is subject to such a variety of pressures that our communities and our regions should lose no time in setting up positive open space programs. But in so doing, they should not rest content with securing quantity. The devices of acquisition, restriction, negotiation for easements, and the rest can be many times more effective if they are preceded by intelligent design, treated as an art rather than as a science. The frequency of use may depend heavily on *quantity,* but the nature and intensity of the "recreational experience" are based firmly on the *qualities* of the environment.

The designed open space: Sebago Beach, Harriman State Park, N.Y.

PART SIX

Something for the Future: The Preservation of Visible History

1. Changing Attitudes

2. Losses and Gains

3. Inventory and Design Survey

4. Method
    Restrictive Covenants
    Bulk Zoning
    Tax Abatements
    Historic District Zoning

5. Preservation and Renewal

6. Private Enterprise Preservation and Urban Design

A WELL-KNOWN HISTORIAN of medieval society, Eileen Power, once remarked that history is not only written down, but is also built up. A visit to Mount Vernon in Virginia reveals a great deal about President Washington's daily life; and a tour of the restored Saugus Iron Works in Massachusetts provides a very good idea of the struggles of the early metals industry in the United States.

Unlike the dynamic inventor of mass production, Henry Ford, who observed that "History is bunk," most Americans take pleasure in their past and receive a considerable amount of instruction from visiting historic sites. (It is to be noted that Ford actually enjoyed this aspect of history, too, and made a hobby of buying up old houses which had belonged to famous people and moving them to his "Greenfield Village" in Dearborn, Michigan.) Although the proportion of those who use their leisure time to visit these sites is smaller than that for out-door recreation of the more active type, the numbers are steadily growing, and with them the numbers of buildings open to the public and the organizations dedicated to preservation in its various forms. In the last decade, Mount Vernon has had well over a million visitors a year.

In spite of its attractiveness, however, this feature of American life suffers from an incompatibility similar to that which limits our enjoyment of open space. For the reminders of the past are being torn down faster than they can be preserved. Just as in the case of natural sites, they, also, are in the way of the new development occasioned by population expansion. The attack comes from all sides. In a newspaper one recent morning the citizens could read of an historic literary shrine being threatened by a new motel, their oldest market by an expressway, and the character of their best residential district by apartment towers. The literary shrine was saved by a non-profit corporation organized by a group of private citizens, who bought it; the others were beyond the resources of any private group to save, although previous public regulation could have prevented the intrusions. The problem has now grown beyond that of individual buildings, and even beyond historic districts, to include esthetics and the preservation of whole cities, streets, and views. It therefore deserves consideration in any account of the man-made American scene.

1. Changing Attitudes

The preservation of our older fabric in both town and countryside has so far been done largely for the sake of history with a capital "H." Old Salem, North Carolina (a Moravian settlement), Williamsburg, Virginia (the first capital of that Dominion), Nantucket, Massachusetts (home of the whaling industry) and the historic districts of Charleston and New Orleans are outstanding examples, preserved or restored under private and public auspices in differing ways. We can be grateful to John D. Rockefeller, Jr., for Williamsburg, and to the architect Albert Simons of Charleston who spearheaded the move to create an historic district there, but their lead has only been slowly and painfully followed since the 1930s. Since every city, town, and village in

Catskill Mountain House, a favorite 19th-century resort, in its present state.

the United States possesses some items of historic interest, these early examples might have shown the way in countless communities all over the country, but it so happens that more worthwhile buildings have been pulled down in the years that followed the re-establishment of Williamsburg than in any one previous generation. History, it seems, is not enough, unless the building happens to be a president's birthplace or the home of a popular hero.

An old Cape Cod house remodeled under commercial pressure as part of a motel.

Recently, however, there has occurred the marriage of art and economics—a union which considers esthetic as well as historical contingencies. It is now eighty years since Charles Follen McKim first informed Americans that they had an interesting architectural heritage; knowledge of fine building has spread very slowly, but in the last thirty years has come to be considered an investment of value. At the same time Americans have begun to accept building controls, "look-alike" and non-"look-alike" ordinances and esthetic regulations, which, small steps as they are, have in some communities made people much more aware of the values of a rule of taste. Throughout the country, cities and Chambers of Commerce are realizing not only that our cities could be more attractive but that in fact bad esthetics means bad business. Consequently many towns seek to enhance the physical texture of their downtown areas; the gamut of changes runs from the planting of trees to the creation of large malls. Although the effort to make the central business district a more pleasing place is only one example of this growing interest in urban esthetics, it is a popular and well-publicized example. An interest in improving the overall appearance of cities is shown in the material gathered in Fagin and Weinberg's *Planning and Community Appearance,* in which there are excerpts from seventy-five municipal regulations concerning community appearance.

Moreover, these attempts to make our cities visually more pleasing are not only private and promotional but they have become matters for public action. Formerly any esthetic question was of private concern. As Judge Swayze put it in *Passaic* v. *Paterson Bill Posting Co.* in 1905, "esthetic considerations are a matter of luxury and indulgence rather than of necessity. . . ." If trees were planted along a street, it was often done through private philanthropy rather than public action. Esthetics was an individual concern. Each man's house was his castle and, as the judge stated, "no case has been cited, nor are we aware of any case which holds that a man may be deprived of his property because his tastes are not those of his neighbor." Since then, however, the interpretation of public welfare and interest has changed, and esthetic considerations have managed to get a legal foothold. The beauty of surroundings which once constituted a "valuable property right" is today "no longer doubted . . . an appropriate consideration within the statutory criterion of the general welfare. . . ." But the fact that esthetic factors have been found by medical science to be vital to our psychophysical health and have been declared by the courts to be a proper component of general welfare does not mean that the esthetic dimension has been exhausted. The necessity for considering the esthetic side of our lives becomes clear when we realize how little we have concerned ourselves with beauty and order in our physical surroundings, despite the findings of the public health profession and the justifications of the jurists.

As our country is sprawling into indiscriminate colonies of split-level houses, our cities are bulging with slums and luxury apartments. Both are esthetically unsatisfactory. Yet they need not be. Through planning it should be possible to make our physical surroundings attractive, so that community beauty is the rule rather than the exception. Although it is a hopeful sign that one hundred or so communities have, on their own initiative, investigated and taken action to ensure community beauty, yet on the other hand it is disturbing to consider the number of towns and metropolitan areas that are ignoring the whole issue of urban esthetics. Although there is now an awareness of the necessity for esthetically pleasing surroundings, there is still a long road ahead in attempting to achieve attractive cityscapes and urban regions. This is a challenge to the planning profession, which as yet has not been fully explored, and which will be discussed in the following pages.

2. Losses and Gains

Why is so much that is historic and esthetically pleasing destroyed, and what are the present means of preventing this?

Perhaps the New York metropolitan area exhibits the most flagrant disrespect of its landmarks and past. Here, where financial stakes are high, the architectural or historic value of a building holds little weight. Buildings like the Hunt Studio, Mark Twain's House, the Rhinelander Gardens, and the old Commerce building on Bowling Green have all been torn down recently. But New York City is too easy to single out. The suburbs and the fringe, as well as the city itself, have suffered in the same way. The only visible reminders of the Dutch Colonial era in northern New Jersey and southern New York are the Dutch Colonial house with its sandstone first floor, frame second floor, and gambrel roof with projecting eaves. Yet house after

Above: Rhinelander Gardens on West 11th Street, New York City, now destroyed. *Right:* Replacement for the Rhinelander Gardens—a new elementary school.

Terhune House, Hackensack, N.J., now demolished, and its replacement, a parking lot.

house has been destroyed until, today, there is only an occasional house held by an
historical society or by the state. The Terhune house, for example, was razed for a
parking lot; this house, the oldest in Hackensack with the first known gambrel roof,
adjoined a small park bordering the once scenic Hackensack River. The house had
been conceived as a pleasant addition to the park, and when it came up for sale interested groups and individuals tried to buy it for preservation. They, however, could
not compete with the price offered by a national chain store which was anxious to
acquire it to provide an addition to the main parking lot adjoining its store which is
across a four-lane highway. Despite the traffic hazards involved and the loss to the
park system as well as to the cultural history of the area, the company now has the lot.
This example is typical of what is unfortunately happening all too often in small
towns as well as large cities.

Fraunces' Tavern, New York City.

The turnover of buildings within cities is usually a spontaneous process motivated
by the prospect of increased profits. If more money can be made out of a piece of land
by tearing down what is there and putting up a new building, or even erecting
nothing (commercial parking lots can be extremely profitable enterprises), the pressures to do so are very strong. Further, the inventory of worthwhile buildings is
particularly numerous near the centers of cities, in the old residential districts, where
these old buildings fall in the path of new commercial development and new feeder

highways. It has been found in many cases that the refurbishing of older buildings can be more profitable than pulling them down and rebuilding, as in the restored residential area of Savannah known as the Trustees' Garden Village, but more often the possibilities of renovation are overlooked or ignored. All too often where buildings *are* preserved and put to new uses, they are rendered visually unattractive by signs, weatherboarding, and general disfigurement of the original structures.

Structures with strong historical significance have the greatest chance of survival. Such buildings have a patriotic overtone and can, according to former Secretary of the Interior Harold Ickes, "instill a love of the country and maintain morale." These buildings are what Ickes called "shrines." Included in this category are places like Mount Vernon and Hyde Park, both of which have been so popular that their floors have been about to give way. Serious problems begin to arise with buildings and sites which have more esthetic and cultural than patriotic value. Here the decision of preservation has not until recently appeared necessary. Should the Rhinelander Gardens have been saved? If this building had had the patriotic connections of Fraunces' Tavern, for instance, there would have been less questioning of its worth for preservation. But as it is now there is little way of measuring these less tangible values of a building: it remains a matter of the standards and taste of the community considering the problem. Although some areas have done outstanding work in preservation due to local interest, there is a need to create an overall system of inventory, value determination, and possible methods of preservation. This should not only be done, but it should be done quickly, for the longer the delay the more damage the wrecking ball and bulldozer can do.

Time may be running out on the preservation movement but its popularity is fortunately rising. In 1931 only two cities had historic preservation districts; in 1959, less than thirty years later, almost twenty towns had these districts, with fifty other towns or cities considering the adoption of such districts. This surge of interest has resulted from many factors, but perhaps the most basic is the increasing awareness of cultural heritage in our surroundings. As the interest in preservation has increased so has the base of this interest been broadening. In the past, only the most zealous architectural historian and Colonial Dame was involved with preservation. Now this group has expanded to include real estate leaders, bankers, planners, ministers, municipal officials, and lay citizens. Yet even though the interest has increased in almost every way, many of the efforts at preservation are sporadic and poorly coordinated.

In tracing the history of the preservation movement, it will be found that every level of government has tackled the problem in one form or another. The federal government has been involved with preservation ever since 1906 when the Antiquities Act was passed. The President through this bill could designate monuments historically worthy of preservation on federal property or property to be acquired by the federal government for preservation. However, it was the Historic Sites Bill of 1935 that stated most forcefully the federal policy toward historic preservation: "It is a national policy to preserve for public use historic sites, buildings, and objects of national significance for the inspiration and benefit of the people of the United States." This policy was to be administered by the Secretary of the Interior through the National Park Service, which was empowered to collect historical data, survey historical buildings and sites, make investigations, accept gifts and bequests, contract with individuals or local governments to protect important property, restore property of national significance, erect commemorative tablets, manage archaeological property, and organize a corps to further all these purposes. The National Park Service operated single-handedly on the federal level until 1949 when an auxiliary organization, the National Trust for Historic Preservation in the United States, was chartered to handle the preservation problem. The National Trust, though financed privately, has on its board of trustees the Secretary of the Interior, the Attorney General, and the Director of the National Gallery. The Trust has been an excellent aid to local communities interested in the historic preservation of buildings, which so far has been its major concern.

The National Park Service, on the other hand, has the national park system as its primary concern, with the preservation of historic landmarks as a sideline. Yet the Park Services' efforts in preservation should not be belittled, as will be seen in the section on Inventory.

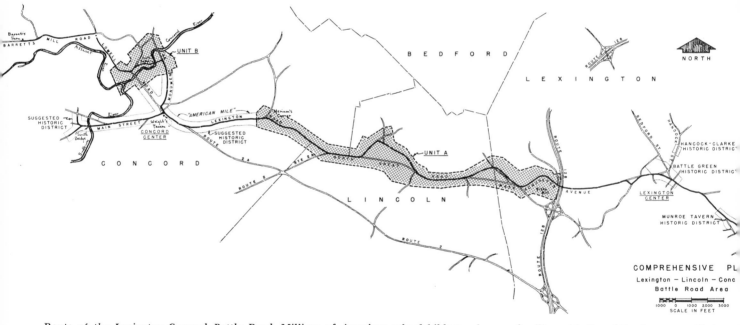

Route of the Lexington–Concord Battle Road. Millions of American schoolchildren who are familiar with Longfellow's poem will be able to see with their own eyes the sites of numerous incidents which took place on the eve of and during the day that opened the War of the American Revolution, when this new national historical park is well advanced or completed by the 200th anniversary of the event in 1975. By 1962, three million dollars of an authorized five million for land acquisition had been appropriated by Congress. This linear park, which runs through suburban and fringe territory, will contain a total of 750 or more acres of private property on some of which existing modern structures will be removed. In immediate charge of this unique project for the National Park Service is Mr. Edwin W. Small, who prepared the initial study for the Boston National Historic Sites Commission urging creation of the park.

The other forms of preservation are many and varied, ranging from strict public control to laissez-faire private development. What preservation action is taken largely depends on what type of building or complex of buildings one is dealing with, where they are, who owns them, what they are used for, what their history is, and what they are intended for. What should be done in New Harmony, Indiana, and what should be done in Wooster Square, New Haven, are two quite different problems. Yet whether one is dealing with a tight complex like a Virginia courthouse compound or a sprawling area like Georgetown, one has to choose tools from the same kit. Therefore, despite the differing aims and intentions of preservationists as well as differences between areas to be preserved, several broad types of preservation can be discerned.

These, broadly speaking, can be broken down into public, private, and a combination of public and private efforts. Public preservation can be for museum purposes, for example, Independence Hall in Philadelphia under the federal government; Spring Mill Rock, Indiana, under the state government; the Audubon House in Montgomery County, Pennsylvania, under county government; and Old Town in San Diego, California, under municipal government. Buildings and areas can also be retained by the federal, state, and local governments for non-museum purposes, like the White House in Washington, City Hall in New York, the Virginia courthouse compounds, and San Juan Antiquo in San Juan, Puerto Rico.

Private preservation, on the other hand, can also be for museum purposes. Historical associations, private corporations, and eleemosynary institutions can tackle on-the-site restorations such as Williamsburg, Virginia, or complexes of old buildings brought together as in Old Sturbridge, Massachusetts, and the Shelburne Museum in Vermont. Private institutions can also retain buildings for non-museum purposes as the University of Virginia has done in Charlottesville, the Moravian church in Bethlehem, Pennsylvania, and the Mormon church in the West. Another approach to private preservation can be found in the formation of associations of neighboring owners of property of historical and architectural value for the purpose of preserving the buildings for their mutual interest. This has been done in places like Elfreth's Alley in Philadelphia and Louisburg Square in Boston.

A combination of public and private interests is most desirable in preservation, which is so closely involved with both. Any private action in preservation involves the matter of property rights, which in turn involves law and public policy. Therefore, it is only a matter of the degree of public involvement which separates public and private approaches in the field of preservation, and this degree of public involvement can probably best be measured by the amount of financial support for the project which is given by the government. The protection and preservation of Independence Hall in Philadelphia was made possible through public funds, whereas the preservation of Williamsburg, Virginia, was achieved by private funds. However, the combination of both public and private interests can be seen in the historic districts set up for the preservation of areas through zoning, districting, or other municipal regulatory measures including tax abatements; and public interests have become even more involved with preservation now that public money is available through federal and state urban renewal legislation for slum clearance and rehabilitation. As a result, both public and private interests are very much enmeshed, to the benefit of both. Projects like Society Hill in Philadelphia; College Hill in Providence; Portland, Maine; Newport, Rhode Island; Nashville, Tennessee; and Wooster Square, New Haven, are the products of this happy combination of interests.

3. Inventory and Design Survey

Although the approaches to preservation are many, they all share the common initial problem of establishing an inventory and rating system of the outstanding buildings in the area involved. Before any preservation program can be begun, this basic problem must be met. In fact, the process of preserving and discarding presupposes a knowledge of all structures and features of the area. Values cannot be assigned to some structures unless an overall knowledge of all structures is first obtained and then a relative value system worked out. Consequently, preservation needs not only a thorough inventory but an intelligent rating system to make its operation a meaningful one; otherwise, the retention of historically, architecturally, and esthetically outstanding buildings and features becomes an arbitrary matter.

While this sounds almost too elementary, there are very few examples of comprehensive inventories of existing buildings and features within cities in this country. Areas like Charleston and Beacon Hill, which are dotted with outstanding buildings, have undertaken such inventories prior to establishing a historic district. These inventories can often lack comprehensiveness, since they usually deal with a small geographic area and not a total town. As a result of these sporadic and limited inventories, many scattered pockets of interesting buildings which are not numerous enough to warrant an historic district are ignored and made easy prey for the demolition crews.

Attempts have been made, however, to work up inventories on every level from the local historic district to the whole nation. The Historic American Buildings Survey was initiated in 1933 as a national plan for obtaining and preserving records of existing structures of historic and architectural significance. This was conceived as a means of relieving unemployment among architects, "so that generally structures were selected for recording in areas where unemployed architects were available; in areas where architects were not available, it was not possible to include many equally important structures in the survey," according to the National Park Service. The survey operated through the coordination of the National Park Service, the American Institute of Architects, and the Library of Congress. The National Park Service acted as planning and coordinating agency, organizing field work, providing standard drawing material, approving the finished records, and transmitting them to the Library of Congress, which acted as repository for records and public agency for the use and distribution of copies of the records. The American Institute of Architects provided "lay supervising representatives or preservation officers of the Survey in the area." This survey was actively carried out from 1933 to 1941 and has recently been resuscitated in the Mission 66 program of the National Park Service, begun in 1957. It includes approximately 26,000 measured drawings and 30,000 photographs, covering about 7,600 houses, churches, public buildings, mills, bridges, and other types of structures important to the cultural and economic history of the United States.

Areas like College Hill in Providence profited from this survey, for in that city 400 photographs were taken of 150 outstanding buildings. Other projects in the revived survey are the Schuylkill River Valley; Mill Creek One Hundred in Delaware; Greenville, Tennessee; Chester County, Pennsylvania; and a survey of lock buildings on the Chesapeake and Ohio Canal at Harper's Ferry in West Virginia and Maryland. It can be seen that this is a regional approach which does not neglect the preservation problems of the countryside.

The other inventory tried on a national scale is the Historic American Buildings Inventory. This was started by the same organizations as the Survey—the National Park Service, the American Institute of Architects, and the Library of Congress, as well as the newly created (1949) National Trust for Historic Preservation. This inventory was begun when the Historic American Buildings Survey was defunct and before the Mission 66 program was launched. "It is a much simpler project [than the Survey] and comprises only a one-page form which is filled out with the pertinent data . . . ," according to a representative of the American Institute of Architects. He goes on to say, "This project has been very largely under the direction of the Committee on the Preservation of Historic Buildings of the AIA, although all the sponsors have taken an active part in it, the Library of Congress serving as a depository for the originals of the completed forms. Much of the work that has been accomplished has been done by the local AIA representatives in the various AIA chapters. In one case, in Virginia, the National Trust was able to secure a foundation grant to meet special needs. Some 3,000 forms have been completed in Virginia on this particular project. . . . There has been fairly good coverage in Rhode Island, New York City (where, of course, it was essentially a Municipal Arts Society project, and they used the HABI forms for reporting to us), Michigan, Illinois, and Connecticut. . . . As of January 18, 1960, we have 4,518 forms. Deducting the 3,000-odd forms from Virginia, you can see that not too much has been accomplished in the rest of the country. This is undoubtedly due to the fact that it is a volunteer project." This information shows that the results of this cooperative project are unfortunately spotty, and it is to be hoped that it will be greatly expanded.

Aside from these national inventories, there have been many local and some state inventories. The most notable state attempt to record all structures of historic and architectural interest has been, as stated above, in Virginia. Here, with the aid of a grant of $16,000 from the Old Dominion Foundation, Virginia is trying to speed up the Historic American Buildings Survey as well as to select the most outstanding buildings for protection. Few other states have demonstrated such interest in preservation.

Local inventories have been far more numerous than state inventories and have until recently been primarily spurred by private interests. For instance, the AIA has published some interesting descriptions of significant buildings in cities where their national convention is annually held. But more often it is such groups as the Municipal Art Society of New York City, the San Antonio Conservation Society, or the Preservation Society of Newport County which have worked up an inventory of outstanding architectural and historic buildings. Such privately sponsored surveys have been invaluable, for they have frequently not only been well done but have been the only surveys of their kind in the city involved.

Recently there has been a display of official municipal interest in taking inventories of existing structures. For instance, Chicago's City Council created a Commission on Chicago Architectural Landmarks to "*a,* prepare criteria for determining and evaluating structures, and architectural landmarks; *b,* prepare a system of identifying and marking such landmarks; *c,* listing and identifying landmarks; *d,* prepare a policy and framework for preservation; and *e,* take steps to stimulate public education and interest." Philadelphia, Baltimore, Boston, St. Louis, Sacramento, and lately New York, among others, are following suit.

Providence is perhaps a good example of this new public interest in preservation and in particular in surveys of historic buildings. Here the City Plan Commission, with the support of the Providence Preservation Society and with government money, was able to conduct a survey of "extant buildings" in the College Hill area, recording date, style, architectural worth, condition, and amount of alteration. These factors were then indicated on maps showing the overall areas of concentration of buildings of each period, the architectural worth of all buildings in the area, and the buildings of historical importance. This could not have been possible if it had not been for the active *private interest and money* which aroused public action in Providence, which in turn activated the National Park Service to experiment in the College Hill area with their revived HABS program. College Hill's inventory stands out as a thorough and thoughtful method of surveying and evaluating the structures within an area. This is a necessary first step for any comprehensive work in preservation and planning which is too often sidestepped. The surveying efforts undertaken in Providence, Philadelphia, Newport, and Baltimore are important strides in planning history in this country.

Unfortunately, in most cases historic buildings *only* have been considered, although gradually the worth of architecturally outstanding buildings has warranted their inclusion in these inventories. It is our opinion that such inventories must be broadened to include esthetic considerations other than historic and architectural factors, such as vistas, groupings, and open spaces, a matter to which we have given some attention.

Various methods have been worked out for visual design surveys in which historic and architectural inventory takes its proper place in the scheme. In the method used by us, the city or region to be analyzed is broken down into Design Districts and Design Axes, which sometimes interpenetrate. This recognizes the fact that worth while structures, landmarks, and interesting building groups are not necessarily found together in convenient, well-defined neighborhoods, but may occur in discontinuous strips or belts within the urban pattern, along avenues and waterways, or following an extension of the original nucleus. A Design Axis can in most cases be treated as an attenuated linear district; for example, although Beacon Hill and the Back Bay in Boston might be considered as separate Design Districts, the axis of Beacon Street, which interpenetrates them both, deserves special consideration throughout its length as a museum of changing architectural taste through a whole century of Boston building, from its early granite houses through Bulfinch brick to the brownstone Eastlake style. Both districts and axes will contain landmarks which provide accent (church towers, squares, distinctive buildings) as well as contrast in materials, color values,

Houses on Beacon Hill, Boston.

repetitive elements, and scale relationships. All these are recorded in the Design Survey, which should employ a variety of techniques, including the building of scale models to demonstrate the worth of the area. These models have value beyond that of recording worthwhile areas for preservation—in some European cities a developer is required to produce a model of his proposed scheme at the same scale, so that it can be fitted into place on the master model. It is there examined by the appropriate design review board for suitability to its surroundings.

It has been said that if American architects and builders were required to do the same thing many incompatible relationships between old and new buildings would be discovered in time to produce changes in the design. This method could only work, however, if the city or suburbs established effective height and bulk regulations as well as design regulations governing the use of materials, fenestration, and street furnishings. A beginning has been made in some American cities under redevelopment and renewal powers which can be used to control development from this point of view.

4. Method

Once the inventory and accompanying rating system has been worked out, it is then possible to embark on a comprehensive preservation program. This inventory would establish the priorities of the different structures as well as their historic or esthetic values, making the timing aspect of preservation more systematic. The first consideration is the prevention of the destruction of the valuable buildings and features which have been recorded in the inventory. Some cities like Philadelphia and New Orleans have attempted to prevent this demolition of historic buildings. Philadelphia, for example, passed an ordinance in 1955 attempting to regulate the demolition of historically significant structures through careful permit checks on all structures listed by the Advisory Commission on Historic Buildings. After the life of the valuable buildings has been assured of protection, means should then be explored to preserve these buildings in the most worthwhile and feasible manner. This is when the most important aspect of planning begins and becomes an action program.

The methods of preservation can be negative and limited or positive and general depending upon the situation. The early work in preservation, as in zoning, was primarily preventive. Gradually, however, preservation has assumed not only a more comprehensive but a more positive role, as we shall see.

RESTRICTIVE COVENANTS

Perhaps the most negative preservation method is the use of restrictive covenants, the first method tried. Legally speaking, a restrictive covenant is a contract and a reciprocal negative easement. While zoning spells out legal duties by ordinance, a covenant describes legal duties by contract. The obligation of a restrictive covenant must be with the land. In general, a restrictive covenant is seen as a legal device attached to land, detailing certain practices to be carried out. This can be done for individual pieces of property or can be done for larger composite parcels of property.

Louisburg Square, Boston.

Elfreth's Alley, Philadelphia.

Restrictive covenants have been used effectively in certain prestige neighborhoods where there has been a concern to preserve the area. Elfreth's Alley in Philadelphia is an example of this as well as Louisburg Square in Boston. In Louisburg Square, for instance, a restrictive covenant runs with all the properties facing the Square and is used as a lien on the title of all these properties. This is a common practice in England, but here it is rather unusual. The use of restrictive covenants is only possible in places like Louisburg Square and Elfreth's Alley, where owner interest in maintenance of a certain character is high.

Although restrictive covenants have been harshly criticized and hence considered something to avoid, there are some good things to be said about them. In the first place, they are often expedient and quick. Quite often, time is an important concern in preservation planning; in fact, by the time a zoning ordinance is passed, buildings may all be razed. Buildings can be torn down in days, while it takes months to enact zoning regulations. With restrictive covenants, however, there need not be the long delays as so often occur from the time of the proposal to the time of completion, such as the approval procedures that are mandatory in renewal programs and other forms of public action. Another good feature of restrictive covenants is that they can be very particular and, therefore, avoid the pitfalls of the vagueness found in many ordinances. Yet all restrictive covenants presuppose interest in the part of the property owner who arranges the covenant. This initial interest must be there and it is not always easy to find. Even the most ideal restrictive covenant proposed in the most ideal circumstances cannot be comprehensive in nature, for its use is for particular properties for particular reasons. Consequently, the employment of restrictive covenants can be interpreted as a hit-or-miss approach to preservation since they depend on the individual property owner's initiative, and not necessarily on any public program.

BULK ZONING

Zoning, on the other hand, is a means of controlling use and bulk in a comprehensive public program. The control of use and bulk may not appear to be the most direct means of tackling the problems of preservation, but it is a workable measure which deserves attention. Zoning usually involves a use and density designation for an area. "Use" zoning may protect a residential neighborhood from industrial or commercial invasions, but it does not necessarily mean that the house owners in the neighborhood are not going to tear down their 1760 salt boxes to erect 1960 apartment houses unless the zoning density is the same as the density of existing development. Although bulk zoning does not prevent the destruction of buildings within a zone, it does make new construction economically unprofitable. This density or bulk regulation is a new approach, not only to zoning but also to preservation. In fact, the first time it has been considered in terms of preservation is in Greenwich Village, and then only as a stopgap measure.

In Greenwich Village the local Community Planning Board pressured the New York Planning Commission to amend the zoning maps in such a way that the residen-

Streets in Greenwich Village, New York City.

Patchin Place, Greenwich Village, New York City.

tial side streets in the Village would have a lower bulk limitation than was previously possible. The purpose of this amendment was an attempt to preserve the existing atmosphere in the Village. By limiting the allowable bulk on a given piece of land, builders would be discouraged from demolishing groups of old houses for towering and bulky new apartment houses. New buildings are going up all over the Village, and as a result the whole scale of the Village is being changed as well as the rent level and general atmosphere. Situations like that on MacDougal Alley result, where the small, old buildings are overwhelmed by the towering screen of the new buildings.

MacDougal Alley, New York City, now terminated by the cliff of a new apartment house.

The bulk limitation for Greenwich Village has been incorporated in a weakened form into the 1961 Zoning Resolution for New York City. This amendment can be seen as a means of attempting to ensure that the "residential side streets of Greenwich Village *may* be spared for a little while longer," according to Robert C. Weinberg, chief protagonist of the new regulations.

TAX ABATEMENTS

The use of tax abatements is frequently mentioned as a potential method of not only holding on to buildings, but also of insuring their continued existence. "The question of taxation is one of life or death for many historic properties," says Stephen V. Jacobs, one of the most active figures in the American preservation movement.

"Local decisions governing taxes are unfortunately based on the current method of making an economic balance sheet. The tax assessment pattern now in use does not reflect the true economic value to the community of historic and artistic buildings and sites. . . . One of our major needs is for some realistic system—and by realistic I mean financially rewarding—for distinguishing 'amenity values.' At present there seems to be no middle ground between the publicly owned monument which must be expensively administered by public or private agencies, and the fully taxed property. If a more honest appraisal of income-producing elements in the real estate line could be achieved, there might be a rebate to properties which are attractions of our older cities." However, it must be stressed that any form of tax abatement should presuppose an overall inventory of buildings, since assignment of tax relief would depend on the value of the building. Tax abatement would be helpful primarily for historic and architecturally valuable buildings, since their value is more obvious than a building or feature of mere esthetic value. Since this method has some legal problems in the way of economic discrimination, unusually strong proof of public welfare would be necessary.

Few cities have tried to use tax relief for preservation. For structures of historic and architectural value, the Vieux Carré Commission may make recommendations for tax exemption to the city of New Orleans. If granted, the exemption may remain in effect over a period of years. A provision of the exemption states that owners of these buildings may not change or destroy them without the approval of the Commission.

HISTORIC DISTRICT ZONING

The most popular and probably the most successful method of preservation has proven to be the historic preservation zone or district. These districts have been tried in all parts of the country in all types of circumstances. In most cases these districts have been set up independently of an overall zoning plan or map—usually after a zoning plan has been set in operation. Rarely have these ordinances been written into the original zoning plan, for historic districts are a relatively new innovation in zoning, often requiring special state enabling legislation. However, Lititz, Pennsylvania, is a town which has recently incorporated an historic zone in its first zoning plan. This is an unusual happening. Lititz, though a small town with a population of approximately 6,000, has an interesting number of Moravian buildings. This Lancaster town has been watched and guarded by many an architectural historian, and now, through the foresight of Dr. Carl Drepperd and the drive of its town manager, the Moravian Settlement has become a historic district within the town's total zoning plan.

In all cases historic districts have required specific zoning ordinances for their establishment, whether a part of the original zoning plan or not. These ordinances follow a similar pattern throughout the country. First of all, they define the boundaries, which in almost all cases, form a rectangular or rounded district. In other words, these districts are compact geographic sections of the city, not linear or discontinuous districts within the city. We have already pointed out that historic areas follow the growth patterns of a city which may not necessarily correspond to any solid shape.

The validity of the purposes of these districts as well as the justification of their use as a reasonable exercise of police power was put forward by the City Attorney for Richmond, Virginia, in October 1949 preceding Richmond's enactment of an historic district:

> Changes of times and progress cannot and does not mean that everything of the past must be obliterated in its path. The bringing in of the new does not mean that all of the old, regardless of merit, must be destroyed. For all change is based on history in part, and history has always served as a guide by which we judge the value of the present and determine the future. It encompasses that which still exists on earth in the form of a building or area as well as that which is written. If history in the form of a building or area is allowed to stand, it will serve at some time to illustrate the importance or unimportance, the goodness or bad- ness, the truth or the folly, of the change itself. If this be true then value has been illustrated, and if value has been illustrated we are certainly custodians of the past, for it belongs not to us alone but to time. To permit destruction of this value is to violate a trust. And to allow these concrete examples of history to be destroyed is also certainly to relegate history in large measure to the printed page, and abrogate forever the opportunity of all those who seek truth to see and feel a greatness as it existed.

Historic districts are seen here as producing material advantages for the community as well as encouraging an appreciation of the culture and heritage of the area. The Richmond report goes on to say: "We must not overlook the fact that the visiting of historic places is of a very great commercial value. Our tourist trade has been esti- mated at over $5,000,000. These people did not visit Richmond because it possesses nothing by which it can be distinguished from other cities but because it possesses his- torical landmarks which are treasured by many." The same sentiment was expressed in Massachusetts in the Justices' Opinion to the Senate in 1955 concerning the his- toric preservation district in Nantucket. Here it was stated that the general welfare of the inhabitants of the towns was promoted through preservation and development of the appropriate setting, but also "through the benefits resulting to the economy of Nantucket in developing and maintaining its vacation-travel industry through the promotion of these historic associations." Therefore, the popularity of these districts does not stem wholly from a cultural-sentimental interest, but also from this hard- headed commercial interest. As Jacob Morrison has put it, "The new blend of the dollar sign with the marks of antiquity has contributed much to the maintenance of historic landmarks, buildings, and sites."

The administration of these districts centers on the review of plans for construc- tion, alteration, repair, moving, or demolition of structures within the district by a review board.

The mechanics of this operation are clearly defined in the zoning ordinances for each district. The usual process allows the "Board of Review to pass upon the ap- propriateness of exterior architectural features of buildings and structures hereafter erected, reconstructed, altered, or restored in the Historic District wherever such ex-

terior features are subject to public view from a public street or way [Annapolis]."
"Evidence of such required approval shall be a Certificate of Appropriateness issued
by said Board [Winston-Salem]." In other words, each application for a building permit or for building activity within an historic district must be approved by a review
board of the district.

Variations in this process occur in every district, since the timing and administration arrangement differs from district to district. Some ordinances include "signs and
other exterior features" among exterior features, while most ordinances refer merely
to general exterior features "subject to public view from a public street, way, or place
[Winston-Salem and Alexandria]." Exactly what is meant by exterior features has
been the subject for many a court case.

As the duties and powers of the Historic District review board vary from district
to district so does the setup of the review board itself. The review boards are entitled
Board of Architectural Review, Historic District Commissions, Architectural Commissions, Board of Historical Review, and so on. Five to seven members is the usual
size of the board, although some have more; the Vieux Carré Commission has a nine-
member board. In some cases, these board members are merely residents of the city
appointed by the mayor or city council, as is the case in Annapolis and Providence.
More often the board members are specified representatives of different professional
and lay organizations. For instance, the Beacon Hill Architectural Commission is
composed of five commissioners appointed by the Mayor of Boston as follows: one
from two candidates nominated by the Beacon Hill Civic Association, one from two
candidates nominated by the Boston Real Estate Board, one from two candidates
nominated by the Boston Society of Architects, one from two candidates of the Society
for the Preservation of New England Antiquities, and one candidate selected at large
by the Mayor. The terms of the commissioners are of varying lengths and permit a
constant rotation of commissioners on the board. A residence requirement is often included, requiring board members to reside within the district, or within city or
county limits. Winston-Salem, however, requires "one but not more than two members of the Board [to] reside in the Old Salem area." This clause could prevent personal interest from interfering with decisions within the district.

The review of the plans and the issuance of certificates of appropriateness or approval for building plans is central to every ordinance for historic zoning. As in most
zoning regulations, the standards for determining appropriateness are often stated in
negative terms, listing what should not be allowed. Elements which would be considered incongruous in the district cannot be allowed, yet rarely are these elements
spelled out. The ordinances all emphasize that the new construction should "relate
to the old" and that the "quaint and distinctive character" of the area should be
maintained.

In reviewing the plans, most ordinances state that the commission or review board
"shall consider among other things the general design, arrangement, texture, material, and color of the building or other structure in question and the relation of
such factors to similar features of buildings in the immediate surroundings [Winston-

Salem]." In fact, these very words appear in most ordinances. Some districts have lengthier statements: "In passing upon the appropriateness, the commission shall consider, in addition to any other pertinent factors, the historical and architectural value and significance, architectural style, general design, arrangement, texture, material, and color of the exterior architecture, features involved and the relationship thereof to the exterior architectural features or other structures in the immediate neighborhood [Beacon Hill]." This relationship of the new building to the old is the crux of the preservation problem. The recent Lititz historic district simply states that the "Board of Historical Review shall authorize the issuance of a building permit only if it finds that the architectural style, general design, arrangement, location, and materials meet the following standards: *a*, they must be harmonious with the exterior architectural features of other structures in the immediate surroundings; *b*, they must be complimentary to the traditional architectural characteristics of the Historical District."

The prevention of "developments obviously incongruous to the historic aspects of the surroundings," is the main purpose of these review boards. Therefore, the review boards by ordinance have two interrelated goals: *1*, to prevent incongruous developments in districts since they might mar the existing character of the historic districts, and, *2*, to encourage the continuation of this character by allowing only buildings and additions which would blend into the character of these districts.

Until recently there has been little mention of the style of architecture to be used in these districts. The only architectural standard mentioned in most ordinances is the appropriateness of the new building to the existing surroundings. Incongruous developments have been understood as architecture which differed from the predominant style. This, of course, assumes that there is a predominant style of architecture in the district, rather than a mixture of styles, which is sometimes the case.

The Western ordinances are different from most of the earlier Eastern ordinances in that the Western ordinances setting up historic districts carefully spell out the style of architecture required in the historic district. They are both specific and rigid in their requirements. Santa Fe is a good example of this. In the statement of purpose for the Santa Fe historic zoning ordinance, it clearly states that one of its aims is to maintain a "continued construction of buildings in the historic styles." The ordinance then goes on to describe the Santa Fe styles of architecture, these being the "Old Santa Fe Style" and the "Recent Santa Fe Style," which are discussed in imperative terms. "The extent of this style (Recent Santa Fe Style) is to achieve harmony with historic buildings by retention of similarity of materials, color, proportion, and general detail. The dominating effect is to be that of adobe construction." The discussion of this Recent Santa Fe Style carefully stresses necessary details like "no door or window in a publicly visible façade shall be located nearer than three feet from the corner of the façade. . . . No cantilevers shall be permitted except over projecting vigas, beams, or wood details, or as part of the roof treatment. . . . Flat roofs shall not have more than thirty inches overhang." As in most districts a review committee, in this case the Historical Style Committee, will pass on permits for alteration, demoli-

Examples of old Santa Fe buildings: Mexican house of the 1860s (*top*); Old Shopping Plaza (*center*); Early Mexican Territorial architecture (*below right*); a Shrine (*below left*).

tion, and new construction within the district. This Historical Style Committee "shall judge any proposed alteration or new construction for harmony with adjacent buildings, preservation of historical and characteristic qualities, and conformity to the Old Santa Fe Style." This is the most specific historic zoning ordinance in terms of defining the style of architecture to be followed in new construction.

Most districts, however, leave the question of what is appropriate and harmonious to the discretion of the review committee, resulting in the continuance of the predominant style of architecture—since that has been what the review boards have considered appropriate. In other words, the look-alike requirement which is now associated with historic districts is basically a matter of local interpretation of appropriateness and not a matter of following any standards written in an ordinance, as in the Santa Fe ordinance. The boards of review are composed of specialists in this field, in the eyes of the law, and consequently are qualified to make this decision.

The result of these ordinances has been the continuation of one style of architecture despite the possible existence of several styles of architecture within the district.

The first divergence from this pattern has been in Providence. In its recent College Hill study, Providence has taken the step of trying to encourage a diversity of architectural styles within a historic district. This study states, "the Commission shall encourage that the making of alterations and repairs to structures on these lists (of architecturally and historically valuable buildings) be made in the spirit of their architectural style, but that additions to structures may be made in styles other than the one in which the structure was built." This idea was included in the state enabling bill, which stated, "It is not the intent of this act to limit new construction, alteration, or repairs to any one period of architectural style." As in most districts, College Hill "does not have a concentration of any one style. . . . This fact emphasizes the validity of the statement that it makes no sense to prevent the design and construction of any one style of architecture. Good design should be encouraged so that this era's philosophy of architectural design can take its place among those of our forebears."

This is the first case of an historic district encouraging different styles of architecture and providing a variety and diversity so that both the old and new can be appreciated. This natural diversity is possible in most historic districts as far as the ordinances are concerned. Therefore, what is needed is a new interpretation of "appropriate" style of architecture and a rethinking of the relation of the old and the new.

The general consensus is that these districts are well liked by the people who have been connected with them. The Beacon Hill Civic Association, prior to the 1955 passage of the act establishing the Beacon Hill district, sent a questionnaire to four groups—the Chamber of Commerce, the Real Estate Board, the local chapter of American Institute of Architects, and the city official responsible for the enforcement of the law, in the following cities which had operating historic districts: Charleston,

Buildings in the "New Santa Fe Style" and variations: House (*upper left*); Motel (*upper right*); Commercial building (*lower left*); Office building (*lower right*).

South Carolina; New Orleans, Louisiana; Alexandria, Virginia; Williamsburg, Virginia; Winston-Salem, North Carolina; Georgetown, District of Columbia; Natchez, Mississippi; and Annapolis, Maryland. In compiling the answers to the questionnaire the replies from Williamsburg and Natchez were discounted. Everyone who answered the questionnaire had been residents of the city when the local law for preservation was passed and had also been in favor of it. When asked to "please state in not over two words how, in general, you consider the law has worked out," the replies were all positive, varying from "fair" to "excellent." Charleston, New Orleans, and Georgetown had the highest percentage of enthusiastic answers. All answered that the laws had been beneficial to the area involved and to the city as a whole; the architecture of the areas had been preserved, and civic pride had been increased. The only discordant note was one from Alexandria's Chamber of Commerce, which, while approving the idea of preservation, believes that control of exterior architecture has 'hindered progress.' In some cases, city officials' enthusiasm was dampened by "problems of enforcement."

Above, left & right: Beacon Hill, Boston.

Right: Preserved and restored buildings in Charleston, S.C.

Although there were a few disgruntled comments from local merchants, most of the replies were highly favorable. This is the best test of the operation. Such districts were primarily locally motivated for local reasons, and if the local inhabitants feel the districts to be successful, then the districts have achieved the purpose for which they were established. What better testimonial could they get?

5. Preservation and Renewal

Historic preservation zoning is one of the many legal techniques like restrictive covenants, bulk zoning, and tax relief which can aid preservation. Recently, however, the scope of preservation planning has been expanded by the new federal programs in urban renewal. The urban renewal interest has not only produced new opportunities for preservation, but has encouraged a planning approach to community problems. Mere zoning does not meet all the social and economic problems which tag along with the physical problems of a community. An area with a concentration of architecturally and historically valuable buildings is not usually insulated from the normal problems of communities; consequently, the treatment of it should include all the regular planning techniques. This is not always the case. Far too often, these areas with historic and architecturally outstanding buildings are treated in an isolated manner without considering the rest of the city of which they are a part. It is imperative that a comprehensive approach be taken to the physical, economic, and social problems of historic areas if they are to fit into the framework of contemporary cities. The historic areas need not be made into museums, but rather can be incorporated into the everyday pattern of living. The Virginia courthouse complexes are a good example of fitting historic buildings into the contemporary pattern of activity within a city. Accompanying this text are photographs of the courthouse complex in Charlottesville, county seat for Albemarle County. The courthouse is the large building with the pillars and sits in the center of a square on the top of the hill. Facing it on all sides are small brick buildings which are architecturally controlled and house the bulk of the lawyers for the whole county.

Problems such as traffic circulation and parking, for example, must be dealt with in an historic area along with the problems of esthetic controls. This overall approach to planning, recently stressed by the requirements of the urban renewal programs, carries over into preservation planning, especially as certain of these federal programs are directly applicable to planning of historic areas.

Courthouse (*above*) and surrounding buildings on the square at Charlottesville, Va.

Some of the government programs which can be used in preservation planning are housing for the aged, cooperatives, public housing, and urban renewal clearance, rehabilitation, and conservation programs. A comprehensive approach to any community area involving historic and architecturally valuable structures might well include several of these government programs. Not only are many social and physical problems met by this variety of programs, but communities will often find the use of them financially advantageous as well. For instance, Newport is considering, among other things, the incorporation of housing for the aged in its plan for the preservation of its older section. New Haven, on the other hand, while not creating a special zoning district for historic preservation, has used the tools of rehabilitation to renew one of its older areas, Wooster Square. Although code enforcement is the ostensible aim of the program in Wooster Square, a more thorough rehabilitation has occurred. "Actually much more than correction of code violation is taking place. Once a home owner sets out to make his property meet the Code, he puts in many improvements beyond those required." The correction of code violations is closely supervised by the planning expert as well as the buildings expert. Helpful suggestions for economy and for structural and buildings mechanics as well as esthetics are offered. The basic policy of the Wooster Square Rehabilitation Program is one of persuasion rather than force. But in order for this persuasion to be effective, it is necessary first to build up a strong neighborhood feeling. Pride and civic responsibility have to be encouraged to the point where home owners are anxious to improve their neighborhood. A community relations officer spent two years in the neighborhood achieving this objective before the program started.

This persuasive method has no control over esthetics. All that can be hoped for is that the home owners will heed the advice and the sketches of the planning specialist. This planning specialist "studies the house in relation to the others on the block and, with his knowledge of the desires of the owner in question, makes further suggestions for improvements which will make the property harmonize with others in the block, as well as give the property the attractive and dressed-up appearance that is essential for thorough and lasting rehabilitation. To achieve this, he prepares perspective

drawings of each block. In addition, where it is appropriate, he prepares freehand perspectives in color of individual properties which he gives to the owners. These simple, clear illustrations have been most effective in communicating ideas and inspiring the owners." For the most part these suggestions have been taken. The accompanying photographs show some of the buildings in the Wooster Square area before and after rehabilitation.

Sketch of Wooster Square, New Haven, Conn., before renewal.

This and opposite page: Examples of rehabilitation in the Wooster Square area of New Haven, Conn., before and after.

6. Private Enterprise Preservation and Urban Design

Apart from the official programs, there are some cities with historic areas which have spontaneously renewed themselves. In such cases, there is no need for stepped-up programs of code enforcement, esthetic controls as in the historic zones, tax abatements, restrictive covenants, and the other devices used by cities and towns to preserve their older features. This is an ideal situation. Cambridge, Massachusetts, is an example of such a community, where the old is automatically preserved and the new is also encouraged. Brattle Street is a famous street lined with well-kept old houses. The accompanying photographs illustrate some examples of spontaneous preservation in Cambridge.

Sometimes this spontaneous preservation can be very much aided by a large institution like a university in a community. Middletown, Connecticut, has been fortunate in having Wesleyan University move in and preserve an older section. Here the buildings have not only been preserved but have been integrated into the university. Some of the buildings have had additions put on them in the rear, and parking has been well camouflaged in the rear also.

This spontaneous renewal of architecturally and historically valuable buildings is a highly unusual happening in this country and cannot be counted on. Usually this continuity has to be enforced; therefore, most places require definite action to preserve the worthwhile older features. The type of action taken depends upon the individual situation; in some cases, zones are the answer, in others rehabilitation programs or restrictive covenants, or the other tools available for preservation. But in all cases a comprehensive planning approach with a high degree of flexibility is mandatory.

Old houses, showing additions, on Brattle Street in Cambridge, Mass.

Historic houses at Middletown, Conn., sensitively restored by Wesleyan University for use as an Honors College and an Art Center.

The purpose of preservation is to preserve "those parts of the old fabric of our towns which have some value apart from their use as living space, and which can play a part, even if it is a purely esthetic part, in the life of the community as it actually is," remarks James Lees-Milne of the British National Trust. Yet before this can be begun, a policy has to be made as to what is worth keeping.

The importance of the surroundings to preservable structures is recognized by France in its Law of 1943 which provides for the protection of preserved buildings. The recognition of surroundings spelled out in this law indicates the value that France places on the total atmosphere and surroundings, rather than just on the preserved building itself. This law states: "any building or land within a range of 500 meters of either class of building (scheduled or listed, the two French categories of preserving) may itself be scheduled (preserved), and any building or land within sight may be listed (preservation desirable but not mandatory). The Minister and local authorities have power to purchase compulsorily any building or land which forms an essential part of the setting of a protected building. No new building operations or alterations to any existing buildings within sight of a scheduled or listed building may be undertaken without the approval of the Ministry or of the local authority. No advertising is allowed on any scheduled or listed building or on any building or land within 100 yards of such a building or on any building which, although on neither of the schedules, is of architectural or esthetic significance as part of the urban or rural scheme." This is a philosophy which considers the townscape and not just individual buildings.

Left and below: Old Merchant's House in New York City, shown in its unfortunate present-day surroundings.

Whether dealing with a whole distinctive area or with only a distinct feature like
an unusual doorway, it must be realized that these features are all part of a larger unit
whose total welfare is foremost. It is the total city fabric which is all important.
Therefore, each esthetic feature must be blended into the existing city fabric so that
it can be fully appreciated. The advantage of working with an inventory is that the
total picture is clear and it is therefore possible to work out a long-range preservation
program which is all-inclusive. Today, either a whole historic district is treated or, on
the other extreme, the individual historic building, yet rarely are they taken in their
proper perspective or in the context of the total city. This can be done by coordinating the design survey and program with the comprehensive plan of the city. By so doing it is possible to integrate historic structures and buildings of architectural merit
into the contemporary city, and avoid the isolated museum approach which can be
found in incongruous surroundings, like the Old Merchant's House in New York.
These old buildings can have varied functions in a city. In New York, there is the already-mentioned example of Fraunces' Tavern at the base of Broad Street on the
fringes of the downtown business area. This building is probably the earliest residential building remaining in Manhattan. It now has a restaurant on the ground
floor which is open at lunch and is extremely popular with Wall Street business men.
Rather than just being a museum, this building thus serves a necessary function in the
downtown area in New York.

In New Haven, the old Bishop house is being used for business purposes; in fact,
the U.S. Army recruiting office is located there.

Bishop House on Elm Street in New Haven, Conn., restored for commercial use with the advice of
Yale art historian John Hoag.

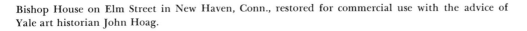

At all times, it must be remembered that preservation programs are essentially public programs for a public city. In many cases, private groups can be extremely helpful in arousing interest, getting programs going, and providing labor and money. Yet all such action should be coordinated with public programs—housing for the aged, rehabilitation programs, etc.—as well as with the comprehensive plan. Professional groups like the American Institute of Architects and local historical societies can provide invaluable assistance. Just as urban renewal rehabilitation work has found it imperative to have local cooperation, so in preservation it is necessary to arouse public interest and cooperation. Usually such interest has been spurred on by private groups. In general, public programs can well use private assistance, and likewise the work of private groups can often be more effective if integrated with the total community plans.

An encouraging sign which may prove a decisive spur to preservation is the recent proliferation of privately-operated, non-profit trusts. These trusts may accept tax-deductible gifts, and they may acquire, own, manage, and sell properties and set up restrictions as to their future use. A typical clause in the articles of incorporation of such a trust may read: "to acquire by purchase, gift, bequest, devise, or otherwise any properties having historical, educational, or general cultural significance and to restore such properties to, and maintain them thereafter in, their historic condition and uses, whether residential, commercial, religious, civic, monumental, educational, or otherwise." They may also erect new buildings—a useful tool in rehabilitation, since often many of the buildings are unsound and cannot be preserved or re-erected, except at prohibitive cost. Among the recently-formed spontaneous groups of this nature are Historic Boston, Incorporated, the New Haven Historic Preservation Trust, and the Canadian Heritage of Quebec. The last-named is empowered to operate anywhere in Canada, and, as well as preserving old buildings, has acquired historic and scenic land on the Gaspé Peninsula and elsewhere.

Such groups are usually extremely well-informed in the rehabilitation of older buildings, since they have been called into being primarily through an interest in preservation. In the only example we shall cite here, expert planning and architectural advice was obtained by a private individual for an entire residential block, consisting of old houses, some of which met all criteria for preservation while others were architecturally valueless. In the gap left by the demolition of some of the houses in the latter category, a new three-story apartment house was decided on, domestic in scale and in keeping with the surrounding architecture. The only additional structures needed were garages, which were planned in groups away from the streets and entered from driveways located on the site of demolished buildings. This combination of new buildings with rehabilitated older ones is to be put on the market for individual purchase, and a residential association formed to protect the character of the block and to take care of the upkeep of the pooled open space in the center, which is being relandscaped as a common garden.

If such private endeavors are protected by historic district zoning, bulk zoning, and the other devices mentioned heretofore, they stand a better chance of maintaining their character and values. In this connection it may be said that the values of properties on Beacon Hill have risen steadily since the inception of the Historic District in 1955.

In spite of the fact that educated private enterprise is at last pointing the way, and that cities and states are beginning to accept preservation as part of planning and enforcement procedures, the crucial problem of relating the new with the old remains particularly vexing. We have seen throughout this book that new development can be wayward and intractable in matters of scale and detail, and have suggested measures needed for a more conforming spirit, including the necessity for visual standards and design control over bulk, materials and fenestration. Many of the design criteria already mentioned apply here, also, especially those relating to order of pattern, articulation of groups, and architectural consistency.

Revitalized block on the Hill in Providence, R.I., discussed in the text; an example of private enterprise in restoration and renewal; Davis, Cochran, and Miller, architects, in association with Tunnard and Harris, planning consultants.

This task falls within the province of urban and regional design. It is not the responsibility of the urban designer to undertake the preservation of old buildings—this is a job for specialists: architectural historians, antiquarians, municipal art societies, the local officials responsible, and private preservation groups—but he must take cognizance of them in his plans and weave his new designs around them. They

The new Royal Orleans Hotel in the Vieux Carré, New Orleans, La.; Curtis and Davis, architects, with Richard Koch and Samuel Wilson, Jr., associated architects.

must be clearly identified in the city pattern. If a group of historic buildings is not separated by a street from new development, it will probably be necessary to introduce green space or an enlarged walkway like the Paul Revere Mall in Boston's North End, to give a sense of definition, especially if the new buildings are of a different scale and design. The historic buildings can then form sub-groups within a larger pattern. Too great a contrast between the old and the new formed by sudden changes of scale or material is at all costs to be avoided. In cases of individual buildings or monuments it may be important to create a focal axis leading to them, in order to rescue them from isolation or incongruous neighbors, or to link them with some other interesting element of the cityscape. In some instances a focal element can be a whole historic district, as in the Vieux Carré, rather than a small group of individual buildings. In such a case, care must be taken not to destroy the scale of the larger entity by unsympathetic intrusions, such as a tall hotel. The exterior of the Royal Orleans Hotel in the Vieux Carré is admirably handled from the point of view of scale, materials, and detail.

As distinct from a purely commercial beehive, a living and vital city or town will always retain some elements of the past and significant examples of urban design. If we let these examples fall in the path of expansion we are not only demolishing an important part of our visual inheritance—we are putting a lower value on man himself and blighting his aspirations for the future.

Covered wooden-bridge, paralleling a span of the New York Thruway over the Wallkill River in the Catskills. Protection and preservation of interesting old wooden and iron bridges is an important though neglected way of enhancing the rural landscape.

An inspiring entrance to New York City for travelers by rail: Grand Central Terminal (Warren and Wetmore, Reed and Stem, architects). The sixty-storey Pan American Building has been built over the tracks at the rear of the main concourse. The Terminal was saved from demolition by public pressure, but its interior is not yet safe from further commercial and advertising desecration.

CONCLUSION

The Emergence of Form: Esthetics and Planning

Shaping the Urban Region
    Basic Tasks
    The Prevention of Violations
    The Preservation of Continuity
    The Relationship of Elements
    The Attraction of Talent

THE ELEMENTS of the urbanized landscape discussed in this book—low-density residential areas, freeways, industry and commerce, open space, and preservation of the older urban fabric—have been chosen either because they are phenomena new on the American scene or demand new techniques in the exercise of control and development. Each contributes, or can contribute, to the emerging physical environment of the nation, which, as we have seen, is radically changing in our own century into a larger, looser confederation of settlement patterns, or, as we have chosen to call them, urban regions.

Many people seem to be frightened by the prospect of continuous low-density urban belts stretching from Maine to Virginia, from Toronto and Pittsburgh to Milwaukee, and from Amsterdam to Frankfurt and Mannheim. Dutch planners suggest establishing barriers to prevent their cities from growing together, and many American planners would like to do so, if they could. However, there seems to be no reason why, properly organized and interlaced with greenbelts, freeways, natural reservations and sites of historic interest, and accented vertically by occasional high-rise elements, these low-density urban regions of tomorrow should not be more livable and effective in satisfying the totality of human values than the transitional urban forms of today.

To achieve this form, of course, the urban regions must be shaped consciously with an end in view, rather than evolving, as they do now, from the haphazard results of thousands of uncoordinated private, corporate, municipal, and higher governmental decisions. Not only is comprehensive planning needed on this new scale so that the decisions can follow a more cooperative pattern, but regional planning must be given a visual, esthetic dimension; otherwise no one will be aware of its presence, no matter how successful the decisions may be within an administrative or economic framework. Although we can envisage successful planning on a state and interstate level, with the counties or their equivalents actively participating in and coordinating development on the township and municipal level, a negative result esthetically would not win it any friends or result in the "utility to man" which we have emphasized as the underlying philosophy of all successful physical design. To this end, designs must be economically and socially based, and, in a democracy, the pleasures and satisfactions of many men must always be considered. This is why we have taken pains to show that a highway which is used by so many people should be beautiful as well as convenient; and that the rural-urban fringe, the fastest growing part of the urban region, can be better designed.

In actuality, then, design and community decisions should always be considered together, because of the close relationship between man's thought and creative spirit and his needs for a better living and working environment. With this necessity in mind, in the following summary we shall outline the basic tools for shaping the urban region.

Shaping the Urban Region

BASIC TASKS

It is first necessary to calculate a generalized, optimum location pattern for centers of employment and social activity, together with an optimum density distribution of the residences which focus on them, taking into account geography, the level of technology, and regional social values. This is a job for many experts, but especially for the planner and the regional scientist. The administrative, financial, and legal tools which can effect this result should be designed to conform, and not run counter to, this pattern. In most cases they will have to be re-examined to make possible new zoning techniques, new taxation policies, and appropriate public safety and health standards, among other social and economic devices.

It will also be necessary to design and execute in a carefully staged time sequence a coordinated regional transportation system, geared to the newly-established density and location pattern. This involves a clear and systematic grid of freeways to take care of the dispersed movement, and a high-speed radial system of rail lines linking the centers, sub-centers, and transfer hubs (subway, rail to air, and auto to rail), taking care of highly concentrated traffic volumes.

A third essential is to acquire and design, or otherwise firmly control, a system of open space to outline and define urban development. This system should range from the continental scale (the Appalachian chain from the Canadian border to Tennessee as a continuous national preserve would successfully define the Atlantic Urban Region, for instance), down through the state, county, municipal, and neighborhood scales to form a comprehensive matrix of green space for all urban development. Rather than following a static greenbelt concept, which would encircle and confine metropolitan areas forever, this system would be so oriented as to allow urban areas to grow and expand in an orderly fashion.

A fourth task is to direct and coordinate the location of utility extensions in the urban region, paying special attention to such high-cost facilities as trunk sewers and other utility trunklines and power distribution installations.

The undertaking of these four tasks—fiscal and legal land use control and development, the transport system, the open space matrix, and the utility grid—will ensure that the general image of the urban region will be established. Private and corporate enterprise will undertake the filling-in of the mosaic, with devices such as development timing and design review boards seeing to it that the pieces are fitting, esthetically and otherwise. Only such a system of freedom within a general order can be satisfactory and appropriate in a democratic society.

With the general framework set by planning (the locational design of the urban region), the esthetic design principles set forth in this book can come fully into play. In practice, they should be employed in the following critical areas:

THE PREVENTION OF VIOLATIONS

As we have seen under industry and residence, much that is unpleasant in a visual sense can be controlled either by prohibition or administrative enforcement of simple county or municipal regulations. The "littering" of the landscape with uncontrolled methods of waste disposal, for instance, can be avoided by the prohibition of open dumps and a requirement for incinerators, sanitary fill, and other controlled and confined methods of disposal. Unnecessary violations of the landscape and its surface cover can be prevented by earth removal regulations stipulating that fill cannot be excavated in certain areas, and, where it is allowed, that re-topsoiling, reseeding, or replanting must be employed to rehabilitate exhausted strip mines, gravel pits, and clay fields. Finally, screening by fences or other means can be required for otherwise objectionable uses like junkyards, automobile wrecking graveyards, and outdoor storage facilities, which are a necessary adjunct to the local economy. Mere eyesores, like billboards on arterial thoroughfares, should be prohibited outright, and overhead wiring in residential areas should be replaced by more modern methods of power supply.

THE PRESERVATION OF CONTINUITY

Design is a positive factor in achieving the overall continuity of the urbanized landscape and the proper integration of the man-made features within it. Although in the denser urban areas continuity may be obtained by buildings, streets, walkways, and paved areas, among other devices, in low-density development the man-made structures should be set like jewels in a background of nature, achieving the look of a well-planned "campus" or village green. The idea of the continuum discussed under open space can be achieved in various ways, the first of which is the setting of minimum standards for major earth-form changes, such as community-wide grading regulations to achieve smoothly-flowing, gentle, well-rounded slopes, which we have seen as being important in subdivisions, highways, industry, and commerce, and in avoiding abrupt changes and violations caused by thoughtless introduction of new facilities. Next is the articulation and separation of the man-made elements themselves so that they do not conflict with each other—by wider rights-of-way on freeways, buffer zones on arterial streets, adequate setbacks for industry and commerce (but not too wide on residential streets). Then there should be planting standards to cut out once and for all the unrelieved deserts of the parking lots and to integrate again the man-made and natural forms. Finally, there is the preservation of as many diverse natural areas as possible by open-space acquisition or zoning—wetlands, mountain ridges, farm lands—and historic preservation for spiritual richness, which again demands buffers and proper articulation to avoid conflict with newer developments, which may be quite different in scale.

THE RELATIONSHIP OF ELEMENTS

Stress must be laid on considering man-made elements not as isolated entities but rather as components of a larger visual pattern; this demands much greater attention to site location and relationships in plan and silhouette. We have emphasized the importance of order of pattern in groups of detached houses, the coordination with the environment in highway design, and the importance of rhythmic coordination of masses in industrial design. We have advocated the careful location of vertical elements and of focal points in the master design plan. This process cannot be legislated as readily as in the above two areas, but it can be greatly improved through the use of regional and community design plans, design review boards, manuals, and recommendations to entrepreneurs. It involves the total "texture" of a region, from the silhouette of the shopping center to the relationship between a factory and a body of water.

THE ATTRACTION OF TALENT

Finally, there is a need for better design of the man-made elements themselves. As we have noted, vast areas of the urbanized landscape receive no attention from design-oriented experts. By showing some of the coordinating principles we hope that further interest may be generated. This is a matter in which regulation is least applicable and where specific rules do not apply; to go more deeply into the architectural principles of the one-family house, for instance, would demand a textbook on architectural design. What is required here is the attraction of top talent to the field of mass building, which architects have hitherto avoided in favor of unique, high-cost structures; and of visually-trained designers into engineering and the design of other objects in the landscape, from which they have been excluded.

The development of a nationwide concern for a better visual environment must be stimulated by education and by economic measures. No one should imagine that any comprehensive remedy will be forthcoming without cultural and fiscal pump-priming. If economic abundance increases, and with it leisure-time occupations, there is hope that both desire and resources are likely more and more to be devoted to esthetic satisfactions, but, without proper direction and a determined effort to raise the level of popular taste, the gains may fall far short of any modest ideal.

Twenty years ago we would have said that the time was not yet ripe for an effort to educate large numbers of people in esthetic matters; public indifference to public beauty was then widespread, although most people looked forward to a brave new postwar world. Since then, a disillusionment with public programs of redevelopment and a growing realization of the ephemeral nature of the better things of life in uncontrolled surroundings have made more groups and individuals aware that something should be done about our communities to make them more attractive. Even the New York taxi-driver, the owner of the small corner store, and the lowest-paid school teacher has saved enough to make a trip to Europe and come back with the image of beautiful communities and a more gracious way of life than his own. Attendance at art museums has soared, and there is now a respectable number of people interested in historic preservation. Usually this interest has not been related to contemporary living, although the postwar appearance of action groups like Keep America Beautiful, Los Angeles Beautiful, Inc., and back-yard improvement societies is an indication of a new interest in amenity. However, and without disparaging these efforts, it can be fairly said that the approach has been on the level of cosmetics, and that the cleaning up of dirt and litter will not bring anything but palliative results. What is needed now is a leadership effort which will channel the new interest in a more beautiful environment by showing how more fundamental esthetic problems can be solved by the various fiscal, administrative, and design tools suggested in these pages.

This leadership must be given on the national level, not only by government but by private groups, committees for economic development, national municipal associations, and other organizations which deal with resources and fiscal policy as well as appearance. As will be seen on the accompanying chart showing private and public investment in construction, the share of the gross national product being devoted to

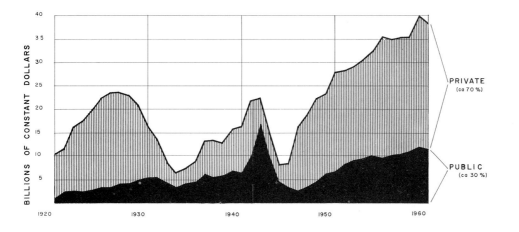

DOLLAR VALUE OF NEW CONSTRUCTION IN 1947-1949 PRICES

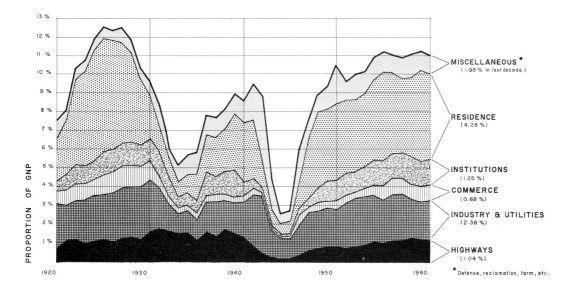

INVESTMENT IN NEW CONSTRUCTION AS PART OF THE GROSS NATIONAL PRODUCT

the physical shell of the environment is less now than in the '20s, even though the rate of population growth was slower then. It is perhaps significant that a greater share is now going to institutions (churches, schools, hospitals, and the like) and less to commercial development, but it is unfortunate that a smaller percentage is going to housing and highways, and of course much more should be going to conservation and open space.

Desirable changes would involve less spending on durable and non-durable articles of consumption, and more public spending on investment in environmental facilities. These would include more carefully designed highways with much wider rights of way, new and efficient rail transit systems in areas of high population density, more durable and better-looking houses, much more money for landscaping, park maintenance and street trees, better and more widespread sanitary facilities, and massive open space acquisition, which in an urbanized society is at least as important as the billions now spent on supporting marginal farmers. This capital investment would require more labor to sustain it, but the new spending and the new jobs would be depression-proof and stable, unlike the present over-emphasis on consumer goods, which contributes to over-expansion of capacity and periodic recessions. The new emphasis can thus be justified both on cultural and economic grounds.

With education, most Americans would no longer tolerate big, flashy automobiles crowded on ugly highways seen against a background of fields littered with their just-discarded predecessors; they would prefer modest and durable vehicles on expansive freeways with views of well-landscaped surroundings. They would no longer tolerate cheap wood-and-plasterboard boxes, destined to fall apart in thirty years and create urban renewal problems of colossal magnitude. And they would not regard with equanimity the prospect of everyone on a half-acre lot with public open space squeezed down to almost zero, preferring the advantages of a variety of compact as well as low-density settlement patterns, with plenty of open space reserved for public use.

All this implies a change in our social values, as well as a corresponding re-allocation of resources. It has become fashionable in recent years to talk of goals for Americans, in recognition of this country's obligations to its citizens and to the rest of the world. A not inconsiderable task among these goals, and one that will require a dedicated national effort with an extensive mobilization of talent and energy, is the creation of surroundings in which our civilization can flourish and the ideals of human dignity be upheld. Our free economy prides itself in its efficiency, rarely stopping to think of "efficiency for what?" For processing and discarding and reprocessing more and more materials, merely to keep the economic system running? Or for creating machines and artifacts to delight the spirit? As the freedom from want and fear is increasingly taken for granted, our society will stand or fall on the question: Freedom for what?

Freedom for making the richest country the ugliest in the world?

Or freedom, among other freedoms, for shaping an environment worthy of man?

Photographic Credits

This volume contains 176 drawings and 398 photographs; sources for the latter are given below by page and location:

t—top
b—bottom
c—center
l—left
r—right

Page	Credit	Page	Credit
5	National Park Service	116b	Finch and Barnes, Architects
7	Fairchild Aerial Surveys	117t	John Reed
9	Jack Amman	117c	Authors
11	Authors	118l	Philip C. Lin
14	Philadelphia City Plan Commission	118r	Philip C. Lin
16t	John Reed	119t	Del Ankers Photographers
16b	Roger G. Ferriter	119b	John Reed
20	Aero Service Corporation	120	John Reed
22c	Roger G. Ferriter	123	Philip C. Lin
22r	Richard Dahn	124	John Reed
25	Regional Plan Association	125t, b	Walter D. Harris
30	Standard Oil Company of New Jersey	126t	Philip C. Lin
32	Picturesque America	126b	Stadtbauamt Wien
33	Picturesque America	127	Los Angeles City Planning Department
34	Deerfield Academy	129t	Joseph Loughman
35	Aero Exploration	129b	George Chappell
44	Joseph F. Loughman	130t	Charles R. Schulze
45t	Crimilda Pontes	130b	Authors
45b	Toni Cooper McElrath	131t	Charles R. Schulze
46t	Richard Dahn	131b	John Reed
46b	Roger G. Ferriter	132t	Charles R. Schulze
47	Fairchild Aerial Surveys	132b	John Reed
48t	Crimilda Pontes	133	John Reed
48c	Louis P. Klein	135l	Charles R. Schulze
48b	Crimilda Pontes	135r	Authors
49	Richard Matson	136t	Mackle Company
50t	William R. Farrell	136b	Fred Wehrman
50b	Richard Dahn	137t	Eichler Homes, Marvin Rand
51	Richard Dahn	137b	Eichler Homes, Ernest Braun
52	William R. Farrell	138	John Reed
75	Jack Amman	139	John Reed
77	Fairchild Aerial Surveys	140	John Reed
87t	Jack Amman	141t	Charles R. Schulze
87b	Air-Photo Co.	141b	John Reed
96	Los Angeles City Planning Department	142	John Reed
97t	Mackle Co.	144	Philip C. Lin
97c	George Heilpern	147	Aero Service Corporation
97b	Todd's Camera Shop, Fairfield, Conn.	148	Mackle Company
100t	Fairchild Aerial Surveys	149t	Mackle Company
100b	Fairchild Aerial Surveys	149c, b	John Reed
101t	Skidmore, Owings and Merrill	150t, b	John Reed
101b	Air-Photo Company	151b	Hugh Pomeroy
103t	Charles R. Schulze	152	Fairchild Aerial Surveys
103b	Charles R. Schulze	153	Fairchild Aerial Surveys
106t	Authors	154t	Neue Heimat
107	Standard Oil Company of New Jersey	154b	Tunnard and Harris
108t	Portola Studio	155	Helsinki City Planning Commission
108b	Philip C. Lin	156	Aero Service Corporation
112	Photo-Art Commercial Studios	161t	Landesbildstelle Berlin
114	Architectural Review	161b	John Reed
116t	Del Ankers Photographers	163t	New Jersey State Highway Department
116c	Authors	163b	Long Island State Park Commission

Page	*Credit*
166	Charles R. Schulze
176	California Department of Public Works
177	Museo de Arte Moderna, São Paulo
178l, r	Aero Exploration
184l	New York Thruway Authority
184r	Long Island State Park Commission
188	New York Thruway Authority
189t	Aero Exploration
189b	Ohio Department of Highways
196t	New York Thruway Authority
196b	Long Island State Park Commission
199t	Charles R. Schulze
199b	State Highway Commission of Kansas
200t, b	Hans Lorenz
202	Ohio Department of Highways
203t	Wisconsin Highway Commission
204t	Palisades Interstate Park Commission
204b	John Reed
207t	New York State Thruway Authority
207b	Authors
208t	New York State Thruway Authority
208b	Long Island State Park Commission
209t	State Highway Commission of Kansas
209b	John Reed
210l, r	John Reed
211t, b	John Reed
212t	New Jersey Turnpike Authority
212b	California Department of Public Works
213t	Cook County Highway Department
213b	California Department of Public Works
214t	New York City Department of Parks
214b	California Department of Public Works
215	New York City Department of Parks
216t	Cook County Highway Department
216b	Charles R. Schulze
221t	California Department of Public Works
221c	New Jersey State Highway Department
221b	Charles R. Schulze
223	California Department of Public Works
228t	John Reed
229b	Pückler—Muskau, Andeutungen über Landschaftsgärtnerei
230t	Florida State Road Department
230b	Maryland State Roads Commission
232t, b	Malcolm Strachan
233l, r	Charles R. Schulze
234t	Charles R. Schulze
234l	Authors
234r	California Department of Public Works
236	California Department of Public Works
237	New York State Department of Public Works
238t	New York State Thruway Authority
238b	Oregon State Highway Department
239t	Florida State Road Department
239b	Long Island State Park Commission
241t	Standard Oil Company of New Jersey
241b	Authors
242t, b	New Jersey State Highway Department
246b	California Department of Public Works
247t	California Department of Public Works
247c	Massachusetts Turnpike Authority
247b	New Jersey State Highway Department
248	Standard Oil Company of New Jersey
249t	Malcolm Strachan

Page	*Credit*
249 (4 views)	Charles R. Schulze
251t, b	Charles R. Schulze
252t, b	Charles R. Schulze
254	Fairchild Aerial Surveys
255	New York City Department of Parks
256t	Fairchild Aerial Surveys
256b	Long Island State Park Commission
260t	Charles R. Schulze
260b	Charles Brickbauer
261	Authors
262t	Authors
262b	State Highway Commission of Kansas
264t, b	John Reed
265l, r	Charles R. Schulze
266l	New Jersey Turnpike Authority
266r	New York Thruway Authority
268	Palisades Interstate Park Commission
269	Palisades Interstate Park Commission
270t, b	Oklahoma Turnpike Authority
271	Florida State Road Department
272t	Maryland State Roads Department
272b	Oregon State Highway Department
273	Palisades Interstate Park Commission
275t	John Reed
275b	Cook County Highway Department
276	John Reed
283t, b	Ralph Warburton
284	Johnson & Johnson, Incorporated
285	General Electric Company
286	General Dynamics Corporation
287	General Dynamics Corporation
288	Portland Cement Association
289t, c	Ralph Warburton
289b	Portland Cement Association
291t	Cities Service Corporation
291b	Standard Oil Company of New Jersey
292t	Standard Oil Company of New Jersey
292b	Socony-Mobil Oil Company
293	Cabot, Cabot & Forbes Company
294t	Thompson—Ramo—Wooldridge
294b	Authors
295	Chicago Bridge & Iron Company
296	Consolidated Edison Company of New York
297t	Dravo Corporation
297c	Caterpillar Tractor Company
297b	Authors
299	American Telephone & Telegraph Company
300t	Johnson & Johnson Company
300c	Socony-Mobil Oil Company
300b	Combustion Engineering
301tl	International Harvester
301tr	Chicago Bridge & Iron Company
301c	Johnson & Johnson Company
301b	Shell Oil Company
302t	Standard Oil Company of New Jersey
302b	Central Electricity Generating Board, London
303t	American Machine & Foundry Company
303b	American Telephone & Telegraph Company
304tl, tr	Ralph Warburton
304bl	Charles R. Schulze

Page	Credit	Page	Credit
304br	American Chain & Cable Company	360	National Park Service
307	Bethlehem Steel Company	364	Massachusetts Department of Commerce
308	Authors	365	Dieter Hammerschlag
309t	Johnson & Johnson Company	367	Palm Springs Chamber of Commerce,
309b	New York Thruway Authority		Boltz Photo
310t, c	Dorothy Moore	369	Eric M. Sanford
310bl, br	National Coal Association	371	Fairchild Aerial Surveys
312	John Reed	374	Massachusetts Department of Commerce
314	Standard Oil Company of New Jersey	375	Authors
315t	Standard Oil Company of New Jersey	376	Dorothy Moore
315b	Fred Wehrman	389	Bob Bourdon
323t	Lewis Roscoe	393	Dorothy Moore
323b	Authors	395	Sterling Forest
325	Fred Wehrman		(City Investing Company)
327	Richard A. Sabin	396	Sterling Forest
328	Authors		(City Investing Company)
329	Geoffrey Baker	399	Palisades Interstate Park Commission
330	Geoffrey Baker	404	John Reed
331t, b	Geoffrey Baker	405l, r	Authors
332	Geoffrey Baker	407t	New York Times
333	Geoffrey Baker	407c	Ann Satterthwaite
334t	William Farrell	407bl	Rubel Photo
334b	Geoffrey Baker	407br	Ann Satterthwaite
335t	Ben T. Field	408l, r	Ann Satterthwaite
335b	Geoffrey Baker	415	Ann Satterthwaite
336t	Connecticut General Life Insurance	416l, r	Ann Satterthwaite
	Company	418	Ann Satterthwaite
336b	Ezra Stoller	419	Ann Satterthwaite
343	Dorothy Moore	424	Ann Satterthwaite
344l	Massachusetts Department of Commerce	425	Ann Satterthwaite
344r	Kelsey Studio	426	Ann Satterthwaite
345t	Massachusetts Department of Commerce	427	Ann Satterthwaite
345bl, br	Maryland State Roads Commission	428	Ann Satterthwaite
346	Massachusetts Department of Commerce	429t	Ann Satterthwaite
347	Massachusetts Department of Commerce	429b	David Gosling
348	Massachusetts Department of Commerce	430	New Haven Redevelopment Agency
349	Massachusetts Department of Commerce	431	New Haven Redevelopment Agency
350l	All Year Club of Southern California	432	Ann Satterthwaite
350r	Massachusetts Department of Commerce	433	Ann Satterthwaite
352	Massachusetts Department of Commerce	434	Ann Satterthwaite
353	Massachusetts Department of Commerce	435	Ann Satterthwaite
354t	Massachusetts Department of Commerce	437	Davis, Cochran & Miller
354b	National Park Service	438	Koch & Wilson, Architects
356	U.S. Forest Service	439	New York State
357t	Fairchild Aerial Surveys		Department of Public Works
357b	National Park Service	440	Authors
358	National Park Service		

Bibliography

Selected references consulted in the preparation of this study are listed below. The items, including books on esthetics and design as well as technical background material, are grouped according to the parts for which they are the most pertinent, although in some cases the work may have relevance throughout.

PART 1: THE URBANIZED LANDSCAPE

Berman, Eleanor Davidson, *Thomas Jefferson Among the Arts; an Essay in Early American Esthetics,* New York, Philosophical Library, 1947.

Bogue, Donald J., *Metropolitan Growth and the Conversion of Land to Nonagricultural Uses,* Oxford, Ohio, Scripps Foundation for Research in Population Problems, 1956.

———, *The Structure of the Metropolitan Community: a Study of Dominance and Subdominance,* Ann Arbor, University of Michigan Press, 1950.

Chapin, F. Stuart, *Urban Land Use Planning,* New York, Harper & Brothers, 1957.

Clawson, Marion, *et al., Land for the Future,* Baltimore, Johns Hopkins University Press, 1960.

Dickinson, Robert E., *City Region and Regionalism,* London, Oxford University Press, 1947.

Duncan, Otis Dudley, "Population Distribution and Community Structure," *Cold Springs Harbor Symposia on Quantitative Biology,* Vol. XXII, 1957.

Duncan, Otis Dudley, *et al., Metropolis and Region,* Baltimore, Johns Hopkins University Press, 1960.

Garrison, William L., *et al., Studies of Highway Development and Geographic Change,* Seattle, University of Washington Press, 1959.

Gibberd, Frederick, *Town Design,* 2nd ed., London, The Architectural Press, 1959.

Gras, N. S. B., *An Introduction to Economic History,* New York, Harper & Brothers, 1922.

Gulick, Luther Halsey, *The Metropolitan Problem and American Ideas,* New York, Alfred A. Knopf, 1962.

Gottmann, Jean, *Megalopolis: the Urbanized Northeastern Seaboard of the United States,* New York, The Twentieth Century Fund, 1961.

Higbee, Edward C., *The Squeeze: Cities Without Space,* New York, Morrow, 1960.

Hoover, Edgar M., and Raymond Vernon, *Anatomy of a Metropolis,* Cambridge, Harvard University Press, 1959.

Horwood, Edgar, and Ronald Boyce, *Studies of the Central Business District and Urban Freeway Development,* Seattle, University of Washington Press, 1959.

Isard, Walter, *Location and Space Economy,* New York, John Wiley, 1956.

———, *Methods of Regional Analysis: an Introduction to Regional Science,* New York, John Wiley, 1960.

Jacks, G. V., "The Influence of Man on Soil Fertility," *Annual Report of the Board of Regents of the Smithsonian Institution,* Washington, Government Printing office, 1957.

Janus, P. E., and C. F. Jones, *eds., American Geography: Inventory and Prospect,* Syracuse, N.Y., Syracuse University Press, 1954.

Lynch, Kevin, *The Image of the City,* Cambridge, Mass., The Technology Press & Harvard University Press, 1960.

Martin, Walter T., *The Rural-Urban Fringe; a Study of Adjustment to Residence Location,* Eugene, Ore., University of Oregon Press, 1953.

McKenzie, R. D., *The Metropolitan Community,* New York, McGraw-Hill, 1933.

McIver, Robert, *Community, a sociological study,* London, Macmillan, 1917.

Nairn, Ian, *Outrage,* London, The Architectural Press, 1955.

———, *Counter-Attack Against Subtopia,* London, The Architectural Press, 1957.

Netzer, Dick, "The Property Tax and Alternatives in Urban Development," (paper presented at the annual meeting of the Regional Science Association), New York, December 1961.

Perloff, Harvey, *et al., Regions, Resources and Economic Growth,* Baltimore, Johns Hopkins University Press, 1960.

Rodwin, Lloyd, *ed., The Future Metropolis,* New York, Braziller, 1960.

Santayana, George, *The Life of Reason,* vol. IV: *Reason in Art,* New York, Charles Scribner's Sons, 1905.

Thomas, William L., *ed., Man's Role in Changing the Face of the Earth,* Chicago, University of Chicago Press, 1956.

Tunnard, Christopher, "America's Super-Cities," *Harper's Magazine,* Vol. 217:1299, August 1958.

Tunnard, Christopher, *ed., The Atlantic Urban Region,* New Haven, Yale University Graduate Program in City Planning, 1956.

Tunnard, Christopher, and Henry Hope Reed, *American Skyline,* Boston, Houghton Mifflin, 1955.

Whyte, William H., *et al., The Exploding Metropolis,* New York, Doubleday, 1958.

Wiener, Norbert, *The Human Use of Human Beings; Cybernetics and Society,* 2nd ed., Boston, Houghton Mifflin, 1954.

Wood, Robert C., *Suburbia; its People and their Politics,* Boston, Houghton Mifflin, 1958.

PART 2: THE DWELLING GROUP

American Society of Civil Engineers, *Land Subdivision,* New York, 1949.

American Society of Planning Officials, *Model Zoning Ordinance,* 2nd ed., Chicago, 1960.

American Society of Planning Officials, Planning Advisory Service, *Reports:*

No. 6, "Architectural Control," September 1949.

No. 37, "Minimum Requirements for Lot and Building Size," April 1952.

No. 38, "Installation of Physical Improvements as Required in Subdivision Regulations," May 1952.

No. 46, "Public Open Space in Subdivisions," January 1953.

No. 86, "Land Development Ordinances," May 1956.

No. 96, "New Developments in Architectural Control," March 1957.

No. 102, "Subdivision Design—Some New Developments," September 1957.

No. 124, "Subdivision Manuals," July 1959.

No. 135, "Cluster Subdivisions," June 1960.

No. 145, "Regulation of Mobile Home Subdivisions," April 1961.

"The Architect and the Homebuilder," *American Institute of Architects Journal,* Vol. XXXVI, No. 3, September 1961.

Beyer, Glenn H., *Housing: a Factual Analysis,* New York, Macmillan, 1958.

Church, Thomas D., *Gardens are for People,* New York, Reinhold, 1955.

Clark, Colin, "Urban Population Densities," *Journal of the Royal Statistical Society,* Series A, No. 114, London, 1951.

Coughlin, Robert, and Walter Isard, *Municipal Costs and Revenues Resulting from Community Growth,* Wellesley, Chandler-Davis Publishing Co., 1957.

Eckbo, Garrett, *The Art of Home Landscaping,* New York, F. W. Dodge Co., 1956.

Fagin, Henry, and Robert Weinberg, *eds., Planning and Community Appearance,* New York, Regional Plan Association, 1958.

Gallion, Arthur B., *The Urban Pattern; City Planning and Design,* New York, Van Nostrand, 1950.

Göderitz, Johannes, Hubert Hoffman, and Roland Rainer, *Die gegliederte und aufgelockerte Stadt,* Tübingen, Verlag Ernst Wasmuth, 1957.

Kelly, Burnham, *Design and the Production of Houses,* New York, McGraw-Hill, 1959.

Kostka, Joseph V., *Neighborhood Planning,* Winnipeg, 1957.

———, *Planning Residential Subdivisions,* Winnipeg, 1954.

"Land Planning in a Democracy," *Law and Contemporary Problems,* Vol. 20, No. 2, Raleigh, N.C., Spring 1955.

Lautner, Harold, *Subdivision Regulations,* Chicago, Public Administration Service, 1941.

Lees, Carlton B., *Budget Landscaping,* New York, Henry Holt, 1960.

Lustron Corporation, *The Lustron Planning Guide,* Columbus, Ohio, (n.d.).

Massachusetts Department of Commerce, Division of Planning; *Preparation of Earth Removal Regulations,* Boston, 1957.

———, *Suggested Rules and Regulations Governing the Subdivision of Land,* Boston, 1959.

Merriam, Robert E., *The Subdivision of Land,* Chicago, A.S.P.O., 1942.

Meyerson, Martin, Barbara Terrett, and William Wheaton, *Housing, People and Cities,* New York, McGraw-Hill, 1962.

Mobile Home Parks and Comprehensive Community Planning, University of Florida, Public Administration Clearing Service, Studies in Public Administration No. 19, 1960.

National Association of Home Builders, *Home Builders' Manual of Land Development,* Washington (n.d.).

National Association of Home Builders Builder Survey, reprint from the March, April, June, and July 1960 issues of the *NAHB Journal of Homebuilding,* Washington, 1960.

"New Ideas in Land Planning," *National Association of Home Builders Journal of Homebuilding,* Vol. XVI, No. 5, May 1962.

New York State Department of Commerce, *Control of Land Subdivision,* Albany, 1954.

Peets, Elbert, "Studies in Planning Texture," *Architectural Record,* Vol. 106, No. 3, September 1949.

Rose, James, *Creative Gardens,* New York, Reinhold, 1956.

Simonds, John Ormsbee, *Landscape Architecture; the Shaping of Man's Natural Environment,* New York, F. W. Dodge Co., 1961.

Spread City; Projections of Development Trends and the Issues They Pose, the Tri-State New York Metropolitan Region, 1960–1985, New York, Regional Plan Association, 1962.

Stein, Clarence S., *Toward New Towns for America,* New York, Reinhold, 1957.

Twin Cities Metropolitan Planning Commission, *Metropolitan Land Study,* Planning Report No. 4, Saint Paul, Minnesota, April 1960.

U.S. Housing and Home Finance Agency, Division of Housing Research, *Construction Aids:*

"House and Site United," Washington, June 1952.

"Septic Tank Soil Absorption Systems for Dwellings," Washington, February 1954.

U.S. Housing and Home Finance Agency, *Suggested Land Subdivision Regulations,* 2nd ed., Washington, 1960.

Urban Land Institute, *Technical Bulletins:*

No. 32, "The Effect of Large Lot Size on Residential Development," July 1958.

No. 40, "New Approaches to Residential Land Development," January 1961.

No. 42, "Density Zoning—Organic Zoning for Planned Residential Developments," July 1961.

Urban Land Institute, *The Community Builder's Handbook,* 2nd ed., Washington, 1961.

PART 3: THE PAVED RIBBON

American Association of State Highway Officials, *A Policy on Geometric Design of Rural Highways,* Washington, 1954.

———, *A Policy on Arterial Highways in Urban Areas,* Washington, 1957.

———, *A Policy on Landscape Development for the National System of Interstate and Defense Highways.* Washington, 1961.

Crowe, Sylvia, *The Landscape of Roads,* London, The Architectural Press, 1960.

Deakin, Oliver A., *New Jersey's Garden State Parkway* (reprinted from *The Town Planning Review,* vol. xxvii, No. 1, Liverpool University Press, April 1956).

Forschungsgesellschaft für das Strassenwesen, *Richtlinien für Strassenbepflanzung,* Köln, 1960.

———, *Richtlinien für die Anlage von Rastplätzen an Strassen und Autobahnen,* Köln, 1960.

Hafen, Paul, *Das Schrifttum über die deutschen Autobahnen,* Bonn, Ferd. Dümmlers Verlag, 1956.

Hanes, J. Carter, Connors, Charles H., *eds., Landscape Design and its Relation to the Modern Highway,* New Brunswick, N.J., Rutgers University College of Engineering, 1953.

Kasper, Hugo, Walter Schürba, and Hans Lorenz, *Die Klothoide als Trassierungselement,* 3d ed., Bonn, Ferd. Dümmlers Verlag, 1961.

Lorenz, Hans, *Aesthetische und optische Linienführung der Strasse,* XI Internationaler Strassenkongress, Rio de Janeiro, Sektion 1, 1959.

———, *Moderne Trassierung* (reprint from *Der Querschnitt,* Spezialheft 3, Strassenbau- Planung und Ausführung, n.d.).

Lorenz, Hans, and F. A. Finger, *eds., Trassierungsgrundlagen der Reichsautobahnen,* Berlin, Volk und Reich Verlag, 1943.

Matson, Theodore, Wilbur Smith, and Frederick W. Hurd, *Traffic Engineering,* New York, McGraw-Hill, 1955.

Outdoor Advertising Along Highways—a Legal Analysis, Highway Research Board Special Report No. 41, Washington, 1958.

Ranke, Victor, *Perspektive im Ingennieurbau insbesondere Strassenbau,* Wiesbaden, Bauverlag, 1956.

Snow, W. Brewster, ed., *The Highway and the Landscape,* New Brunswick, N.J., Rutgers University Press, 1959.

Steinman, David B., and Sara Ruth Watson, *Bridges and their Builders,* New York, Dover Publications, 1957.

Wells, Nelson Miller, "Landscaping," Section 28 in *Highway Engineering Handbook,* Kenneth B. Woods, ed., New York, McGraw-Hill, 1960.

PART 4: INDUSTRY AND COMMERCE

Ahearn, Vincent P., *The Zoning Problem and Its Significance to the Sand and Gravel Producer,* Washington, National Sand and Gravel Association, 1958.

Alexandersson, Gunnar, *The Industrial Structure of American Cities,* Lincoln, University of Nebraska Press, 1956.

American Society of Planning Officials, Planning Advisory Service, *Reports:*
    No. 51, "Motels and Motel Regulation," June 1953.
    No. 103, "Outdoor Advertising," October 1957.
    No. 120, "Planned Industrial District Zoning," March 1959.
    No. 140, "Gasoline Station Location and Design," November 1960.

Baker, Geoffrey, and Bruno Funaro, *Shopping Centers, Design and Operation,* New York, Reinhold Publishing Co., 1951.

———, *Parking,* New York, Reinhold Publishing Co., 1958.

Bennett, Wells, ed., *The Design of Industrial Plants,* Ann Arbor, Univ. of Michigan, College of Architecture and Design, 1952.

Bone, A. J., and M. Wohl, *Economic Impact Study of Massachusetts Route 128,* U.S. Bureau of Public Roads, Massachusetts Department of Public Works, Massachusetts Institute of Technology, Preliminary Report, January 1958.

Branch, Melville C., "Planning Environment for Research and Development," *The Princeton Engineer,* Vol. XVIII, Nos. 1 & 2, 1957.

Crowe, Sylvia, *The Landscape of Power,* London, The Architectural Press, 1958.

Gruen, Victor and Larry Smith, *Shopping Towns U.S.A.,* New York, Reinhold, 1960.

Jonassen, C. T., *The Shopping Center versus Downtown,* Columbus, Ohio State University, Bureau of Business Research, 1955.

Kelley, Eugene J., *Shopping Centers; Locating Controlled Regional Centers,* Saugatuck, Conn., The Eno Foundation for Highway Traffic Control, 1956.

Munce, James F., *Industrial Architecture,* New York, F. W. Dodge Corp., 1960.

National Industrial Zoning Committee, *Principles of Industrial Zoning,* Columbus, Ohio, 1951.

Pasma, Theodore K., *Organized Industrial Districts,* U.S. Department of Commerce, Area Development Division, Washington, 1954.

Smith, Herbert L., Jr., *Buildings for Research,* New York, F. W. Dodge Corp., 1958.

Urban Land Institute, *Technical Bulletins:*
    No. 19, "Planned Industrial Districts," October 1952.
    No. 23, "Space for Industry," July 1954.
    No. 30, "Shopping Centers Restudied," 2 pts., February & May, 1957.
    No. 41, "Industrial Districts Restudied," April 1961.

Whitney, F. L., "Newer Trends in Industrial Buildings," *Buildings for Industry,* New York, F. W. Dodge Corporation, 1957.

Wiedemann, Glenn K., "Borrow Pits Can be Assets," *Landscape Architecture,* Vol. 52, No. 2, January 1962.

PART 5: OPEN SPACE

California Department of Natural Resources, Division of Beaches and Parks, *Program for California's Beaches and Parks,* 1961.

Clawson, Marion, *Methods of Measuring the Demand for and Value of Outdoor Recreation,* Washington, Resources for the Future, Reprint No. 10, 1959.

———, "Public Land Administration for the Next Generation," *Northeastern Logger,* October 1960.

Cleveland Regional Planning Commission, *Open Space in Cuyahoga County, an Introduction,* 1961.

———, *New Gems for the Emerald Necklace,* Report for the Cleveland Metropolitan Park Department, 1961.

Crowe, Sylvia, *Tomorrow's Landscape,* London, Architectural Press, 1956.

Eliot, Charles William, *Charles Eliot, Landscape Architect,* Boston, Houghton Mifflin, 1902.

Ise, John, *Our National Park Policy; a Critical History,* Baltimore, Johns Hopkins Press, 1961.

Kepes, Gyorgy, *The New Landscape in Art and Science,* Chicago, Theobald, 1956.

Kouwenhoven, John A., *The Beer Can by the Highway, Essays on What's American about America,* Garden City, N.Y., Doubleday, 1961.

Massachusetts Department of Natural Resources, Edwards, Kelcey and Beck, Consultants, *An Inventory and Plan for Development of the Natural Resources of Massachusetts,* Part II, "Public Outdoor Recreation," Boston, 1957.

Metropolitan Regional Council and Regional Plan Association, *Park Recreation, and and Open Space Project of the Tri-State New York Metropolitan Region:*
Shirley Adelson Siegel, "The Law of Open Space."
Marion Clawson, "The Dynamics of Park Demand."
William A. Niering, "Nature in the Metropolis."
Project Staff and Committee, "The Race for Open Space," New York, Regional Plan Association, 1960.

Metropolitan Toronto Planning Area, Metropolitan Toronto Planning Board, 1959.

National Advisory Council on Regional Recreation Planning, *A User-Resource Recreation Planning Method,* Hidden Valley, Loomis, California, 1959.

The Nature Conservancy, *Preserving Natural Conditions in a World of Technological Dominance, a Symposium.* Annual Report, 1957.

National Recreation Association, *Planning Recreational Facilities,* New York, 1957.

National Recreation Association, *Standards for Neighborhood Recreation Areas and Facilities,* New York, 1943.

Outdoor Recreation Resources Review Commission, *Outdoor Recreation for America; a Report to the President and to Congress,* Washington, January 1962.

"Recreation in the Age of Automation," *Annals of the American Academy of Political Science,* September 1957.

Regional Planning Commission and Parks and Recreation Department of Los Angeles, *Regional Recreation Areas Plan* (n.d.).

Regional Planning and Economic Development Commission of Northern Virginia, *Parks, Recreation and Open Space,* 1960.

Sanderson, Ivan T., *The Continennt We Live On,* New York, Random House, 1961.

Santa Clara County Planning Department, *Green Gold: a Proposal for a Pilot Experiment in the Conservation of Agricultural Open Space,* 1959.

Sears, Paul B., "Exploitation and Conservation of Land," *Journal of Soil and Water Conservation,* Vol. 12, No. 2, March 1957.

———, "The Appraisal of Natural Resources," *The Science Teacher,* Vol. XXI, No. 4., September 1954.

———, "Changing Man's Habitat: Physical and Biological Phenomena," *Yearbook of Anthropology,* Wenner-Gren Foundation, 1955.

Sharpe, Thomas, *Town and Countryside: Some Aspects of Urban and Rural Development,* London, Oxford University Press, 1937.

Thomas, William A., Jr., *ed., Annals of the Association of American Geographers,* Vol. 49, No. 3, Part 2, Supplement, September 1959.

U.S. Department of Agriculture, National Forest Service, *The Program for the National Forests,* Washington, 1959.

U.S. Department of Agriculture, *The Proposed Food and Agriculture Act of 1962, a Summary.* Washington, February 1962.

U.S. Department of the Interior, National Park Service, *Remaining Shoreline Opportunities in Minnesota, Wisconsin, Illinois, Indiana, Ohio, Michigan, Pennsylvania and New York,* and *Our Fourth Shore,* reports prepared by the Great Lakes Shoreline Recreation Area Survey, Washington, 1959.

———, National Park Service, *A Report on the Seashore Recreation Survey of the Atlantic and Gulf Coasts,* Washington, 1955.

Urban Land Institute, *Technical Bulletins:*

No. 36, William H. Whyte, "Securing Open Space for Urban America: Conservation Easements," December 1959.

Watts, May Theilgaard, *Reading the Landscape: an Adventure into Ecology,* New York, Macmillan, 1957.

PART 6: HISTORIC PRESERVATION

Bard, Albert S., "Aesthetics and the Police Power," *The American Journal of Economics and Sociology,* Vol. 15, No. 3, 1956.

Codman, John, *Preservation of Historic Districts by Architectural Control,* Chicago, American Society of Planning Officials, 1956.

Colean, Miles, and William W. Nash, *Residential Rehabilitation: Private Profits and Purposes,* New York, McGraw-Hill, 1959.

Feiss, Carl, "Historic Town Keeping," *Journal of the Society of Architectural Historians,* Vol. XV, No. 4, 1956.

Jacobs, S. K., *Historic Preservation in City Planning and Urban Renewal,* Washington, National Trust for Historic Preservation, 1959.

Jones, Barclay Gibbs, *The Historic Monument in City Planning,* Society of Architectural Historians, Pacific Section, Spring Meeting, Eugene, Oregon, 1958.

Lees-Milne, James, *ed., The National Trust; a Record of 50 years' Achievement,* London, B. T. Batsford, 1946.

Lillibridge, Robert M., "Historic American Communities: their Role and Potential," *Journal of the American Institute of Planners*, Summer, Fall, 1953.

Margolis, Alfred L., "'Esthetic Zoning—the Trend of the Law," *Western Law Review*, 7:171, March 1956.

Massachusetts, Commonwealth of, *The Establishment of Historic Districts Within the Commonwealth*, House Document No. 2935, The Legislative Research Council, 1957.

Morrison, Jacob H., *Historic Preservation Law*, New Orleans, Pelican Publishing Co., 1957.

Mumford, Lewis, *City Development: Studies in Disintegration and Renewal*, New York, Harcourt, Brace, 1945.

Municipal Art Society of New York, *Index of Architecturally Historic Structures in New York City*, 1957.

New Haven, City of, *Wooster Square Redevelopment and Renewal Plan*, 1958.

Providence City Plan Commission with the Providence Preservation Society and the Housing and Home Finance Agency, *College Hill: a Demonstration Study of Historical Area Renewal*, 1959.

Rodda, Clinton, "The Accomplishment of Aesthetic Purposes under the Police Power," *Southern California Law Review*, Vol. 27, 1954.

U.S. Department of the Interior, National Park Service, *Historic American Buildings Survey*, Washington, 1941.

Wertenbaker, Thomas J., *The Founding of American Civilization: the Middle Colonies*, New York, Charles Scribner's Sons, 1938.

Woodbury, Coleman, *Urban Redevelopment: Problems and Practises*, Chicago, University of Chicago Press, 1953.

Woodbury, Coleman, ed., *The Future of Cities and Urban Redevelopment*, Chicago, University of Chicago Press, 1953.

In addition to the articles in periodicals listed above, the following professional journals and magazines were consulted during the preparation of the work and will prove of continuing interest to the reader:

ARCHITECTURE

American Institute of Architects: *Journal* (monthly)

Architectural Forum (monthly)

Architectural Record (monthly)

Progressive Architecture (monthly)

House and Home (monthly)

Architectural Design (London—monthly)

Architectural Review (London—monthly)

The Architects' Journal (London—weekly)

Royal Institute of British Architects: *Journal* (London—quarterly)

Bauen und Wohnen (Zurich—monthly)

Architektur und Wohnform (Stuttgart—8 issues annually)

L'architecture d'aujourd'hui (Paris—6 issues annually)

Neue Heimat: Monatshefte für neuzeitlichen Wohnungsbau (Hamburg—6 issues annually)

PLANNING

> American Institute of Planners: *Journal* (quarterly)
> *British Housing and Planning Review* (London—6 issues annually)
> *Town and Country Planning* (London—monthly)
> Town Planning Institute: *Journal* (London—monthly)
> *Town Planning Review* (Liverpool—quarterly)
> *Urbanisme: révue française* (Paris—irregular issues)
> *Urbanistica* (Turin—irregular issues)

ENGINEERING

> *The American City* (monthly)
> *Civil Engineering* (monthly)
> *Engineering News Record* (weekly)
> *Public Works* (monthly)

TRAFFIC ENGINEERING

> American Association of State Highway Officials: *The American Highway* (quarterly)
> Highway Research Board: *Proceedings* (annual)
> Highway Research Board: *Roadside Development* (annual)
> U.S. Bureau of Public Roads: *Public Roads* (6 issues annually)
> Institute of Traffic Engineers: *Traffic Engineering* (monthly)
> *Traffic Quarterly*
> *International Road Safety and Traffic Review* (London—quarterly)
> *Road International* (London—quarterly)
> *Strasse und Autobahn* (West Germany—monthly)

LANDSCAPE ARCHITECTURE

> *Landscape: Magazine of Human Geography* (3 issues annually)
> American Society of Landscape Architects: *Landscape Architecture* (quarterly)
> Institute of Landscape Architects: *Journal* (London—quarterly)

HISTORIC PRESERVATION

> National Trust for Historic Preservation: *Historic Preservation* (quarterly)
> *Journal of the Society of Architectural Historians* (quarterly)

Index

Abrams, Charles, 392
Acadia National Park, Thunder Cave, engraving, 32
Acceleration lanes, 165, 234, 240, 322
Access, 36, 76–77, 80, 146, 151, 313; Highway. *See* Limited Access Highways
Adirondack State Forest, N.Y., 28, 379
Advertising, 257–61, 265, 283, 434. *See also* Billboards; Outdoor advertising
Agglomeration, economies of, 280, 283–84, 293
Agrarianism, 24
Agriculture, 8, 24–27, 36, 38, 63, 379, 389–91
Agricultural areas, map, 37
Air conditioning, 55, 351, 368
Aircraft industry, 281, 374
Air Force Academy, plan for, 101
Air polution, 304
Airports, 18, 63, 76, 280, 370, 371
Air transportation, 160, 282
Alameda County, Cal., photo., 213
Alaska, 10, 28, 257, 377, 378
Alexandria, Va., 3, 422, 426
Allegheny County, Pa., 93, 94
Allegheny Mountains, 167
Allegheny Parkway, 347–48
Aluminum smelters, 279
America, comparison with Europe, 11–12
American Association of State Highway Officials (AASHO), 181; regulations and standards, 181, 191, 198, 201, 224–26, 254
The American City, 111
American Institute of Architects, 412, 413, 436
American Institute of Steel Construction, competition, 244
American Optical Co., Southbridge, Mass., 377
American Society of Landscape Architects, 170
Amherst College, 375–76, photo., 376
Amusement centers, 14
Anchorage, Alaska, 10
Angeles National Forest, 384, map, 384
Annapolis, Md., 421–22, 426
Anshen and Allen, design by, 110
Antioch College, 396
Antiquaries Act of 1907, 409
Apartments and Apartment Houses, 22, 61, 62–63, 84, 106, 146–48, 318, 406, drawing, 71, photos., 149, 151, plan, 155. *See also* Garden apartments; Highrise buildings; Multi-family structures
Apathy, public, 4, 446
Appalachian Mountains, 11, 30, 444
Appalachian Trail, 348
Apple Valley, Cal., 356
Architects, 15, 17, 23, 56, 63, 67, 135, 155, 274, 326, 386, 412, 446
Architectural Forum, quoted, 55
Architectural historians, 437
Architectural Review, 67, quoted, 23
Architecture, 8, 67, 115–21, 148, 405, 423–24. *See also* Building; Design; Housing, types; Industrial design
Argentina, 165, 168

Arizona, 11, 26, 32, 134, 355, 378
Arkansas, 24
Arroyo Seco, Cal., 12
Arroyo Seco Freeway, 165
Art collections, 21
Arteries, 78, 104, 152, 153, 155
Arterial streets, 88, 89, 148, 151–52. *See also* Collector streets; Feeder roads
Articulation. *See* Freeways, articulation; Highways, articulation; Housing, articulation; Industry, articulation
Aschaffenburg-Nürnberg *Autobahn,* 168, 182, 193, 205, diagram, 188, photo., 189
Astoria, N.Y., photo., 16
Atlanta, Ga., map, 88
Atlantic Urban Region, 30, 40. *See also* individual states
Attached houses, 61, 67, 72. *See also* Garden apartments
Atomic energy installations, 279
Aubock, Carl, 126
Auden, W. H., 43
Austria, 168, 268
Autobahnen, 164, 165; Aschaffenburg-Nürnberg, 168, 182, 193, 205, diagram, 188, photo., 189; Breslau-Vienna, 181; Frankfurt-Darmstadt, 164. *See also* Freeways; Parkways
Automobiles, 36, 57, 59, 65–66, 67, 80, 135, 159–60, 164, 174, 313–14
Automobile industry, 281
Autoroutes, Brussels-Ostende, 165; *de l'Ouest,* 165. *See also Autobahnen;* Freeways
Autostrada, 164; Florence-Viareggio, 164; Genova-Serravale, 164. *See also Autobahnen;* Freeways
Avenida General Paz, 165
Avus (Automobil-Verkerhrs-und-Übungsstrasse), 163–64, photo., 161

Balboa, Cal., 350
Ballfields. *See* Playfields; Playgrounds
Baltimore, Md., 59, 414
Baltimore-Washington Parkway, 167, 193, 205, diagram, 188, drawing, 203
Banking, 38, 41, 65, diagram of, in Connecticut, 41
Barnett, Joseph, 167
Bartram, John, 339
Bassett, Edward M., 162
Beaches, 268, 376, 382, 391, photos., 344, 348
Beach buggy, photo., 348
Beacon Hill. *See* Boston, Beacon Hill
Beacon Hill Architectural Commission, 422
Beacon Hill Civic Association, 422, 425
Bear Mountain Bridge, 268
Bear Mountain State Park, N.Y., 394
Beauty spots, 31–35. *See also* Focal points; Landscape
Beirut, Lebanon, 12
Belgium, 59, 165, 168
Belser, Carl, 389
Belt Parkway, 165

Bennington, Vt., 347

Berlin, Germany, photos., 161, 375

Berman v. *Parker*, quoted, 56

Bethlehem, Pa., 411

Bethlehem Steel Works, Sparrows Point, Md., photo., 307

Bicycle paths, 318

Billboards, 3, 44, 76, 135, 162, 165, 175, 257, 259, 265, 322, 330, 445, drawing, 259, photos., 50, 51, 52, 260, 261. *See also* Advertising; Outdoor advertising

Bill, Max, sculpture by, photo., 177

Bixby Creek Bridge, Cal., photo., 236

Black dirt area, N.Y., photo., 9

Blast furnaces, 234

Blight, 17, 21, 83–84, 162, 371

Bloomfield, Conn., Connecticut General Life Insurance Co., 396, photo., 336

Blue Ridge Parkway, 159, 348

Boarding houses, 21

Boating, 349–50

Bogue, Donald, 64, quoted, 38

Bonita Springs, Fla., photo., 129

Borglum, Gutzon, 6

Borrow pits, 123, 227. *See also* Gravel pits

Boston, Mass., 43; Back Bay, 3, 414–15; Bay Circuit, 346, 382, 384–85, 398, map, 382; Beacon Hill, 412, 414–15, 423, 425, 437, photos., 415, 426; Common and Public Gardens, 375, photo., 374; Commonwealth Avenue, 160; Historic preservation, 412, 414–15, 423, 425, 437, 439; Louisburg Square, 411, 417, photo., 416; Park system, 346, 370, 382, 384–85, map of, 382; Paul Revere Mall, 439; Regional open space system, 346, 370, 382, 384–85, 398, map, 382; Suburbs, 393

Boston Metropolitan Park District, 382, 391, 398

Boston National Historic Sites Commission, 410

Boston Real Estate Board, 422

Boston Society of Architects, 422

Boston Symphony Orchestra, 354

Bottling plants, 279

Boulder, Col., 387

Boyden, Frank L., 35

Brazil, 168

Breslau-Vienna *Autobahn*, 181

Bridges, 165, 194, 220, 235, 237, 238, 239, 240, 243, 265, 266, 268, photos., 223, 234, 236, 237, 238, 239, 242, 266, 439, plans, 235; Abutments, 228, 231, 235, 246, 247, drawings, 246, photos., 246, 247; Detailing, 243, 248; Lighting, 242; Railings, 224, 231, 244, 249, 254, drawings, 244, 245, photos., 249. *See also* Overpasses

British National Trust, 434

British Town and Country Planning Act, 13

Broadway Anaheim, Cal., photo., 332

Bronx River Parkway, 160–62, photo., 255

Bronx River Parkway Commissioners, 162

Bronx River Valley, N.Y., 161–62

Bronxville, N.Y., 21

Bronx Zoo, 161

Brookline, Mass., 393

Brooklyn, N.Y., 165, photo., 215

Broome County, N.Y., 93

Brussels-Ostende *Autoroute*, 165

Buenos Aires, Argentina, freeway, 165

Buffer zones, 88, 145, 148, 152, 153–55, 210, 300, 302–05, 308, 318, 320, 371, 445

Builders, 78, 84, 132, 134

Building, 9, chart, 62; Boom, 57; Codes, 55; Controls, 405; Esthetics, 56, 405–06; Industry, graph, 79; Materials, 55, 117, 118, 120, 165, 175, 241, 242, 261, 287–90, 377. *See also* Construction

Bulk Zoning, 417–19, 427, 436. *See also* Zoning

Bureau of Labor Statistics, 78

Bureau of Public Roads, 167, 170, 184, 188, 258, 261

California, 12, 24, 26, 37, 64, 94, 134, 137, 348, 350, 378; Highways, 165, 245, 250–52; Regulations and controls, 123, 167, 257, 391. *See also* Los Angeles

California Automobile Club, 342

California Public Outdoor Recreation Plan, 342, 366

California State Division of Beaches and Parks, 360, 385

Cambridge, Mass., 431; Brattle Street, 431, photos., 432

Camping facilities, 248, 322, 348, photo., 354

Camus, Albert, 227

Canaan, Conn., 43

Canada, 11, 28, 168

Canadian Heritage of Quebec, 436

Canton, Mass., 93

Cape Cod, Mass., 11; Cape Cod house, 115, photos., 405

Capper-Crampton Act, 381

Catskills, highway in, photo., 184

Catskill Mountain House, photo., 404

Catskill State Forest, N.Y., 379

Cement plants, 279

Cemeteries, 370; photo., 48

Census, land use, 85

Census of 1950, 59, quoted, 17

Census of 1960, 59

Central business district, 13–17, 22, 38, 40, 65, 299, 313, 316, 320, 405

Central Electricity Generating Board, 302

Chain stores, 320

Chandigarh, India, 105

Channel Islands National Monument, 385

Charlottesville, Va., 411, photos., 427, 428–29

Charleston, S.C., 31, 412, 425–26, photos., 426–27

Chartres Cathedral, 266

Chemical industry, 281

Chemical plants, 279, 280, 286, 296, 305

Chesapeake and Ohio Canal, 413

Cheshire, Conn., development, 142, photo., 142, plan, 143

Chester County, Pa., 413

Chicago, Ill., 37, chart of daily transportation related to density, 65, photo., 275; Lakeshore Drive, 162; Loop, 313; Old Orchard Shopping Center, photo., 331; Riverside, 90, plan, 91

Chicago Bridge and Iron Company, 295

Chicopee Falls, Mass., textile mill, photo., 284

Chimney stacks, 298
Christaller, Walther, 38, 40, diagram by, 39
Church, Thomas, 334
Churches, 65, 145, 146, 318, 448, photo., 148
Circular arcs, 179–80, 182, 183, 186, 187, diagrams, 179, 180, 187. See also Freeways, alignment; Highways, alignment
Circulation facilities, 77–78
Citrus fruit industry, 64
Cities, 4, 24, 38, 41, 72, 84, 160, 266; Density of, 57–58, 59, map showing patterns of, 73; Parks, 17, 18, 339, 342–43, 370, 375, 380–86, 387, diagram, 362, maps, 381, 382, 383, 384. See also Parks; Planners and planning, 4, 15, 219; Preservation, 6, 434–35. See also Historic preservation; Transportation within, 58–59. See also Transportation
Cities Service refinery, near Lake Charles, La., photo., 291
Civic design, 155
Civic groups, 19
Civic responsibility, 428
Clark, Colin, 58
Clarke and Rapuano, 167, 399
Clarkstown, N.Y., 392
Clawson, Dr. Marion, 29, 59, 343, 345, 392
Cleveland, Ohio, regional open space system, 347, 380–84, 397, map of, 381; Suburbs, 393
Cleveland Metropolitan Park District, 347, 380–84, 397
Climate, 55, 280
Clothoid. See Transition curve
Cloverleafs, 160, 162–63, photos., 163, 204, 213. See also Freeway, interchanges; Interchanges
Clusters, 109–14, 145, 347, drawing, 69, plans, 111, 113, 114, photo., 112; Commercial, 151, 325–26; Regulations, 96. See also Streets, alignment; Zoning
Colean, Miles, 63
Collector streets, 88, 89, 151, plan, 113. See also Arterial streets
Cologne-Bonn highway, 164
Colorado, 11, 28, 31, 257
Columbia River Valley, Wash., 31
Columbia, Cal., 32
Commercial centers, 15, 22, 316–19, 444. See also Shopping centers
Commercial developments, 23, 153, 311–19
Commercial facilities, 5, 20–22, 311–18, 359, 360, plan, 321. See also Freeways, commercial facilities; Roadside commercial strip; Shopping centers
Commercial zoning, 326. See also Zoning
Commission on Chicago Architectural Landmarks, 414
Communication lines. See Utility lines
Communities, 13, 38
Community, centers, 145; design plans, 298, 446; esthetics, 56, 405–06; facilities, 44, 79, 145–46, 359, photos., 148–49. See also Churches; Schools; Libraries; Shopping Centers
Community Planning Services Inc., Pittsburgh, Pa., design by, 122

Commuting, 21, 43, 57
Company towns, 36. See also Factory towns
Concrete, 164, 248, 289. See also Building materials; Pavements
Connecticut, 40, 43, 78; Advertising controls, 257, 261; Banking centers, diagram, 41; Factories, 284, photo., 308; Highways, 165, 167, 184, 224, 227, graph, 185, photo., 166; Historic preservation, 413; Lot size, 94; Open space, 378; Population density, 72–74, map, 73; Retail centers, diagram, 40; Regional centers, diagram, 40; Rights-of-way, 254–55; Roadside commercial strip, photo., 323; Subdivision, photo., 123; Telephone calls, diagram, 42
Connecticut General Life Insurance Co., Bloomfield, Conn., 396, photo., 336
Connecticut River Valley, photo, 364
Connecticut Turnpike, 205, 227, 267, diagram, 188, drawing, 267
Conservation, 7, 8, 18, 127–28, 161, 370, 392, 398, 428, 448. See also Open space; Preservation
Conservationists, 63, 64
Consolidated Edison Company of New York, 296
Construction, 55, 61, 64, 66, 78, 279, 447–48, graphs, 447. See also Building
Contour maps, 227
Conurbation. See Urban regions
Coombe Hill, Kingston, England, photo., 114
Corbusier, Le, 71, 72
Corner lots, diagrams, 102
Cotton growing, 25–26
Country roads, 78, 80, 88, 151. See also Tourist routes
Country clubs, 21, 145
Covered bridge, photo., 439
Crest curves, 190, 191, 193, diagram, 194. See also Curves; Vertical curves
Cribbing, 124. See also Retaining walls
Cron, F. W., quoted, 197
Cropland, 64. See also Agriculture; Farms
Crowe, Sylvia, 370, quoted, 242
Cul-de-sacs, 90, 104, 109, 143. See also Streets, alignment
Cultural facilities, 21, 22
Cumberland Gap, Tenn., 347
Curbs, 127, 165, 261, 329
Curtis and Davis, 438
Curvature, 162, 164, 165, 167, 176, diagram, 187. See also Freeways, alignment; Highways, alignment
Curves, 178, 180, 181–95, diagrams, 179, 180, 183, 194, 195, 197, drawing, 182, graph, 185, photos., 178, 184, 208. See also Highways, alignment
Curvilinear street plans, 89, 90, 104–05, 122, diagrams, 104, 105, photo., 100, plans, 111, 122. See also Streets, alignment
Customs, 59
Cuts and fills, 222, 224–26; table of standards for, 224. See also Embankments; Freeway, embankments; Highway, embankments; Slopes

Dairy Valley, Cal., 26
Dairy industry, 389

Damascus, Syria, 12
Dams, 265, 288, photos., 288
Davis, Cochran, and Miller, 437
Davistown, Fla., plan, 154
Deakin, Oliver, 167
Dearborn, Mich., Greenfield Village, 403
Deceleration barriers, 227
Deceleration lanes, 234, 240, 320
Deerfield Academy, 35, photo., 34
Deerfield, Mass., 32, 35, photo., 34
Defense: Department, 378–79; Highways, 167, 168,
   201. See also Interstate highways; Policies, 280;
   Reservations, 63
Delabarre Glacier, Wash., photo., 5
Delaware, 261
Delaware County, Pa., 93, 94
Den Haag, Netherlands, 165
Denmark, 168
Density. See Gravity pattern; Housing, density;
   Population, density
Department of Agriculture, Forest Service, 378
Department of Defense, 378–79
Department of the Interior, Bureau of Land Man-
   agement, 378
Department stores, 38, 313, 314–16, 326
Depression, The, 86, 90
Deserts, 6, 10, 355–58, 367–68
Design: Axes, 414–15; Craftsmen, 55; Districts,
   414–15; Experts, 446; in Nature, 8; Plans and
   planning, 15, 16, 17, 23, 44, 63, 80; Principles, 444;
   Regulations, 415; Review Boards, 444, 446
Designed commercial districts, 325–26. See also
   Roadside commercial clusters
Designed residential districts, 96. See also Zoning
Desire lines, 43, 65, 217–20. See also Traffic
Detached houses. See Single-family houses
Detroit, Mich., 15, 16; Eastland Shopping Center,
   photo., 332; Northland Shopping Center, photos.,
   332, 333
Detroit-Pontiac highway, 162
Deutsch, Karl, quoted, 44
Developers, 56, 79, 81, 86, 89, 90, 128, 139, 145, 155
Development: Controls, 83–85, 145; Discontinuous.
   See Leapfrogging, Sprawl; Districts, 85. See also
   Zoning; Location of, 80–85; Scale, 76–82; Scattered,
   83–84. See also Leapfrogging, Sprawl; Scheduling,
   85; Timing, 444. See also Subdivision; Zoning
Dickinson, Robert E., 40, diagram by, 39
Die Strasse, 170
Diners, 11, 322
Directional ramps, 167
Discount stores, 319, 322, 326
Divided highways, 160, 162, 186, maps of, 168, 169.
   See also Freeways; Limited Access Highways
Dordogne, France, 31
Dormitory suburbs, 39
Douglas, Justice William O., quoted, 56
Douglass, Lathrop, 331
Downtown Merchants' Associations, 17
Drainage, 127, 210; Ditch, photo., 141. See also
   Freeway, drainage; Highway, drainage

Dreppert, D. Carl, 420
Drivers and driving, 159, 171–77, 181, 184, 206, 264,
   265
Drive-in movies, 23, 318, 322
Driveways, 68, 88, 151
Drought of 1930's, 6
Drugstores, 146
Dual highways. See Divided highways; Freeways;
   Highways
Duluth, Minn., 59
Dumps, 23, 445, photos., 45, 46. See also Junkyards
Du Pont Highway, 162
Durham County, N.C., 93

Earth removal, 121–22; Regulations, 122–23, 261,
   308–11, 445
Easements: Agricultural, 26; Conservation, 370, 392;
   Scenic, 263, 269, 390
Eastchester, N.Y., 119
Ecologists, 386
Economic forces, 3, 4
Economists, 38
Edaville Railroad, photo., 353
Edgartown, Mass., photo., 350
Educational facilities. See Schools
Edwards, Kelcey, and Beck, 188; Report by, quoted,
   378
Eichler Homes, 137
Electric generating stations, 286, photos., 297
Electrical World, 138
Electronics industries, 284
Eliot, Charles W., 389, quoted, 366, 393
El Reno, Okla., photo., 315
Embankments, 220–26, 240, diagrams, 225, drawings,
   222, 226, photos., 221, 222, 223, 234, 304. See also
   Slopes
Emerald Necklace. See Cleveland, regional open
   space system
Enclosure, 134–35, 286, 294, 296, photos., 135, 136
Engineers and engineering, 8, 9, 56, 98, 170, 190, 386
England. See Great Britain
Environment, 3, 4, 51, 55, 206, 280
Erosion, 6, 25, 123, 140, 221, 222, 227, 358, photos.,
   221
Estates, 394–96
Esthetic legislation, 35, 118–19
Euler's Spiral. See Transition curves
Europe, 11–12, 29, 59, 138; Cities, 18, 59, 86, map
   showing density of, 60; Freeways and Highways,
   162–65, 168, 170, 182, 190, 193, 205, 206, map of,
   168. See also Autobahnen; Autoroutes; Autostrada
Everglades, 10, 28
Evergreens, 231, 302, 328–29. See also Trees
Excavations, 76, 308–11. See also Borrow pits; Earth
   removal; Gravel pits
Exclusive zone districts, 390–91. See also Zoning

Factories, 3, 65, 234, 263, 282, 283, 295, 298, 377, 446,
   photos., 283, 289, 300, 301. See also Industrial
   design
Factory towns, 36. See also Company towns
Factory workers, 19, 37

Fagin, Henry, 405
Fair Lawn Industrial Park, Radburn, N.J., photo.,
    20
Fairfield, Conn., 393, map of, 82, photo., 97
Fairfield County, Conn., 359
Farmers, 24
Farms and farming, 6, 7, 24–27, 39, 76, 80–81, 143,
    369–70, 373, 389–90, 448, photos., 7, 25, 364
Federal-Aid Highway Act of 1938, quoted, 269
Federal-Aid Highway Act of 1958, quoted, 258
Federal Housing Administration, 89, 90, 91, 92, 94,
    106, 125; Housing insurance, 90; Land Planning
    Section of, 90
Federal land holdings, 378
Federal Reserve Bank of Boston, study by, 66–67
Federal 701 programs, 23
Feeder roads, 15, 148, 316, 318. See also Arterial
    streets
Feld, Myron X., plans by, 111
Fences, 68, 134, 302, 304, 328, 445, photos., 304–05,
    343
Field system, 373
Finch and Barnes, 116
Fire protection, 66
Fire regulations, 134
Fire stations, 145. See also Municipal structures
Flattened slopes, 222–26, 231, 233. See also Slopes
Flooding and flood control, 140, 141, 381, 384, 388,
    391. See also Open space, preservation
Florence-Viareggio Autostrada, 164
Florida, 10, 26, photos., 136, 271
Florida Turnpike, 205
Flushing, N.Y., photo., 100; World's Fair site, 165
Flynt, Helen G., 35
Flynt, Henry N., 35
Focal points, 140–48, 155, 446. See also Landmarks
"Folk art" and architecture, photos., 120, 323
Fontana, Cal., photo., 7
Food: Distribution, 313–16, 318; Processing industry,
    282; Supply, 64
Ford Assembly Plant, Mahwah, N.J., photo., 309
Ford, Henry, quoted, 403
Forest Hills Gardens, N.Y., 90
Forests, 8, 355, 366–67, 376, 379, 388, 390–91; Con-
    servation of, 359–61; Zoning, 390–91. See also
    National Forests
Forest Service, 361
Fort Gibson Dam, Okla., photo., 288
Fort Worth, Tex., photo., 286
Foundation planting, 130–32, 134, photo., 132.
Fountains, 17
Fragmented land ownership, 80, 82–83. See also
    Leap-frogging; Scattered development; Sprawl
France: Dordogne, 31; Highways, 162–63, 165, 168;
    Law of 1943 for protection of preserved buildings,
    quoted, 434
Freeways, 3, 15, 77–78, 88, 106, 116–17, 146, 148–53,
    159–275, 279, 386, 443, 448. See also Highways
    Acceleration lanes, 165, 234, 240, 322
    Access. See Limited access highways
    Advertising on, 257–58, 261, 265, 283; Controls of,

Freeways (cont.)
    257–61. See also Outdoor advertising
    Alignment, 177–206, 212–17, 220–33, 265–66, 296,
        444, diagrams, 179, 180, 186, 187, 188, graph,
        185, photos., 178, 184, 200, 212, 213, 216
    Articulation of elements, 165, 175, 176, 240–63,
        263–65, photos., 254, 255
    Buffers, 210, 320
    Commercial facilities, 263, 269–71, photos., 270
    Deceleration barrier, 227
    Deceleration lanes, 234, 240, 320
    Depressed, 234
    Drainage, 222, 224, 231, 234–35, 241
    Elevated, 233–34, 235
    Embankments, 220, 224, 240, diagrams, 225, draw-
        ings, 222, 226, photos., 221, 223, 234, 304
    Esthetics, 98, 159, 168–69, 177, 179, 206–75
    European, 162–65, 168, 170, 182, 190, 193, 205, 206,
        drawing, 267, map, 168
    External harmony of, 164–65, 176–77, 206–75
    Gradients, 164, 165–67, 190–94, 197
    Guide rails, 224, 231, 244, 249, 254, drawings,
        244, 245, photo., 249
    Interchanges, 15, 59, 146, 160, 224, 255, 258, 261–63,
        269, drawing, 259, photos., 204, 261, 309, plan,
        253
    Internal harmony, 177–206
    Interstate, 76, 167, 168, 169, 201, 258–61
    Landmarks, 160, 263–65, 266, 270, 298, diagrams,
        266, drawing, 267, photos., 265, 266, 270
    Landscaping, 159, 164–65, 170, 217, 220, 227–33,
        259, 265, photos., 166, 202, 227, 228–29, 230
    Location, 217–19, diagram, 219
    Maps of, 169, 274, 383
    Median dividers, 160, 164, 165, 167, 176, 201–05,
        230, 231–33, 240, 241, 255, drawings, 203, photos.,
        202, 203, 204
    Overpasses, 160, 234, 240, 242–48, drawings, 243,
        244, photos., 214, 234, 246, 247, 249
    Reflectors, 242
    Residential development and, 148–53, 250–52
    Rights-of-way, 148, 152, 217, 250–57, 271, 373,
        390, 445, 448, photos., 251, 252, 255, 256
    Roadside rest areas, 267–69, 322, photos., 271, 273
    Safety records, table of, 205
    Scenic turnouts, 263, 267–69, 272, 346, 390, photos.,
        269, 272
    Service areas and parks, 259, 261, 263, 269, 320–22,
        photos., 270, 271, 273, plan, 321
    Setbacks, 250, 259, 261, 271, 283, drawings, 306
    Shoulders, 164, 226, 230, 231, 240, 241, 254
    South American, 165, 168
    Speed limits, 165, 167
    Superelevated, 180, 181, 183, 198
    Vertical alignment, 190–94
    Visual field of, 172, 175, 206, 220, 260–63
Frontage roads, 325
Frost, Robert, 6
Furniture industry, 282

Game refuges, 355, 379

Garages, 11, 15, 59, 110, 113, 114, 329

Garden apartments, 61, 67, 72, 106, photos., 150, plan, 151

Garden State Parkway, 167, 186, 201, 205, 224

Gardens, 132, photos., 132, 133, 310

Gas stations, 11, 21, 162, 263, 313, 319, 322, 326, 328, 329, photos., 327, 328. *See also* Freeways, service areas

Gasometers, 234, 265, 299

Gaspé Peninsula, Canada, 436

Gates Mills, Ohio, 393

General Dynamics plant, San Diego, Cal., photo., 287

General Electric model residence, photos., 125

Generator plants, 36, 286, photos., 297

Genova-Serravale *Autostrada*, 164

Geographers, 38, 386

George Washington Parkway, drawing, 203

Georgia, 30

Georgetown, D.C., 411, 426

Germany, 35, 224, 268, 296, photos., 35, 375; Highways, 163–65, 167, 170, 181, 182, 184–85, 190, photos., 35, 161, 262. *See also* West Germany

Ghost towns, 11

Glacier National Park, 344

Glass industry, 281

Glen Helen, Ohio, 396

Goederitz, Rainer & Hoffman, 60

Golden Gate Bridge, photo., 223

Golf courses, 21, 76, 112, 145, 318, 351, 370, 373, 385, 392, photos., 97, 367

Gosling, David, drawing by, 429

Government land, 381, 382, 383, 384, maps, 381, 382, 383, 384

Grades, 164, 165–67, 190–94, 197

Grade crossings, 163

Grade separations, 160, 162, 164, 233

Grading, 123, 445. *See also* Embankments, Slopes

Grain elevators, photo., 291

Grand Canyon National Monument and Park, 344, 368

Grand Central Parkway, 165

Grand Mesa National Park, 369

Gras, N. S. B., 38

Gravel pits, 23, 29, 44, 76, 308, 311, 371, 445, photos., 47, 48

Gravity pattern of residential density, 41–43, 72, 76–77, map, 73, photo., 77, plan, 74

Great Britain, 13, 31, 59, 168

Great Lakes, 78

Great Plains, 373

Great Smokies, 31, 350

Greenbelt, Md., 184

Greenbelts, 31, 67, 373, 381, 443, 444, maps, 381–384. *See also* Parks; Open space, regional systems

Greenhorn Mountain Park, Cal., 342, 360

Green Mountains, Vt., 348, 350

Greenville, Tenn., 413

Greenwater Lake, Mass., photo., 207

Greenwich, Conn., 393, photos., 149

Grey areas, 44, photos., 16. *See also* Middle Ground

Gridiron street plans. *See* Street plans, rectilinear

Grocery stores, 313, 318, 319

Group housing development. *See* Housing, group development

Guide rails, 224, 231, 244, 249, 254, drawings, 244, 245, photo., 249

Guilford, Conn., 93

Gwynne, Patrick: design by, 114, photo., 114, plan, 114

Hackensack, N.J., Terhune House, 408, photo., 407

Hafraba (Association for the Motor Road Hanseatic Cities Frankfurt-Basel), 164

Hamilton, J. R., 172

Hammonasset River, Conn., photo., 312

Hancock, Mass., Shaker Village, 32

Harbors, 12

Harpers Ferry, W. Va., 413

Harriman family, 382

Harriman State Park., N.Y., 394, photo., 399

Harris, Walter, 125

Hartford, Conn., 41, 43, 141, photo., 77

Haussmann, Baron Georges Eugène, 3

Hawaii, 257, 261, 378, 379

Headlight glare, 201, 227, 231, 234, 250

Hedges, 134, 231–33. *See also* Buffers; Fences; Highway, landscaping

Held, Burnell, 345

Helix, 195–96, diagrams, 195, 197, photos., 196. *See also* Curves

Heller, Fritz, 170, 197

Helsinki, Finland, photo., 297

Helsinki City Planning Commission, 155, plan by, 155

Hénard, Eugene, 162

Henry Hudson Parkway, 165

Henry, Patrick, 6

Henson Creek Valley, Md., 141

Heritage Foundation, 35

Hesperia, Cal., 356

Hexagonal market areas, diagrams, 39

Hidden dip. *See* Highways, vertical alignment

High density areas, 66–67, 84, 104, 138, 144

High-rise buildings, 61, 72, 146, 148, 318, 363. *See also* Apartments

Highways, 5, 15, 19, 23, 27, 31, 35, 44, 59, 63, 64, 76, 159, 160, 169–70, 443. *See also* Freeways; Parkways Access. *See* Limited access highways
Administration, 169–70
Advertising on, 257–61, 265, 283, photos., 50, 335; Controls of, 257–61. *See also* Outdoor advertising
Alignment, 15, 166, 189–90, 265–66, 373, photos., 166, 184, 189, 212, 213, 214, 216; Continuity of, 180, 181, 185–87; Horizontal, 162, 164–65, 167, 176–90, 194, 227, 265, diagrams, 179, 180, 183, 186, 187, 188, 189, 194, 195, 197, drawings, 182, graph, 185, photos., 163, 178, 184, 208; Three dimensional, 194–201, diagram, 198, photos.,

Highways, alignment (*cont.*)
199, 200; Vertical, 190–94, 195, 197–99, 202
Articulation of elements, 165, 175, 176–77, 240–63, 263–65, photos., 254, 255. *See also* Highways, structure
Buffers, 325. *See also* Buffer zones
Costs, 167, 240
Cross section, continuity of, 220–27, diagrams, 222, photos., 221
Defense, 167, 168
Drainage, 190, 191, 227, 230
Embankments, 220–26, 240, diagrams, 225, drawings, 222, 226, photos., 221, 222, 223, 234, 304
Engineers, 17, 169, 227, 240, 274
Esthetics, 122, 159, 165, 168–70, 177, 179, 240
European, 162–65, 167, 168, 170, 182, 190, 206, drawing, 267, map, 168, photo., 35
Gradients, 164, 165–67, 190–94
Harmony with Nature, 176, 206–10, photos., 207–11
Interstate, 76, 167, 168, 169, 201, 258–61
Landscaping, 159, 164–65, 170, 217, 220, 227–33, photos., 202, 233
Location of, 190, 206–10
Overpasses, 160, 234, 240, 242–48, drawings, 243, 244, photos., 214, 234, 246, 247, 249. *See also* Bridges
Planning and design, 88, 159, 162–64, 169–71, 180, 181, 186, 201, 271–73
Radial, 15, 72, 76, photo., 75, plan, 74
Radial acceleration, 180, 181
Reflectors, 242
Roadside rest areas, 32, 267–69, 322
Rights-of-way, 148, 152, 217, 250–57, 271, 373, 445, 448
Safety records, table of, 205
Scenic. *See* Parkways; Tourist routes
Shoulders, 164, 226, 230, 231, 240, 241, 254
South American, 165, 168
Structure, 165, 169, 175, 240, 241, 242, 261
Superelevated, 180, 181, 183, 198
Tolls, 164, 167, 269
Highway Act of 1956, 168
Highway Research Board, 170
Hillsborough, Cal., 393
Historic American Buildings Survey, 412–13, 414
Historic Boston, Inc., 436
Historic preservation, 5, 32, 35, 143, 346, 403–39, 445, 446; Zoning, 416–19, 420–26, 427–29, 431, 436
Historic Sites Bill of 1935, quoted, 409
Historical societies, 436
Hoag, John, 435
Holland, Mich., 348
Hollywood, Cal., 12
Home ownership, 23, 60–61, 62, chart, 62
Home rental, 61, 63
Horsbrugh, Patrick, 230, quoted, 160
Hospitals, 318
House and Home, article in, 81–82, survey, 83
Housing, 55–155, 250–52
Codes, 18, 55

Housing (*cont.*)
Construction, 86. *See also* Building materials; Construction
Costs, 21, 66
Density, 57–63, 65, 69–71, 72–80, 85, 94, 109–10, 444, drawings, 68–71, map, 73
Developments, 37, 56, 72, 76–85, 145, 444. *See also* Subdivisions
High density. *See* Apartments; Multi-family houses
Low density, 55–72, 95, 98–155, 359, 443, 445
Growth, 57–72
Grouping, 37, 72, 86–97, 98–155; alignment, 86–97, 99, 103–05, diagram, 103, photo., 103; architectural consistence, 67, 115–21, 148, drawing, 115; articulation, 107–14, 124–35, 146; cluster, 96, 109, 117, 145, 347, plans, 111, 113, photos., 112, 114; esthetics, 55–57, 67, 145–46, 148; integration with environment, 119, 121–55; order of pattern, 63, 98–109, 121, 148, 155, 446, 448, diagrams, 99, 101, 102, 103, photos., 100, 106, 108, plans, 101, 106; unity of variety, 98, 119–20
Landscaping, 68, 127, 128–34, 144
Location, 80–85
Medium density, 66–67
Setbacks, 66, 96, 99, 109, 115, 119, 134, 259, 394, drawing, 110
Types, 120–21, chart, 62
Apartment, 22, 61, 62–63, 84, 106, 146–48, 318, 406, drawing, 71, photos., 149, 151, plan, 155
Attached. *See* Garden apartments; Row houses
Cape Cod type, 115, photo., 405
Detached, 92, 446. *See also* Single-family houses
Garden apartments, 61, 67, 72, 106, 150, plan, 151
High rise, 61, 72, 146, 148, 318, 363
Multi-family, 60, 61, 65
Owner built, photo., 22
Ranch type, 115, 348
Row, 61, 67, 72, 117, drawing, 70, photo., 108
Single-family, 12, 21, 55, 61, 63, 65, 72, 78, 93, 104, 106, 107–09, 116, 148, 446, chart, 62, drawing, 68, photo., 151
Single storey, 115
Split-level type, 115, 120, 406
Two-family, 92, chart, 62
Two-storey, 115, 120, drawing, 70
Housing Act of 1961, 398
Houston, Tex., 59; International Airport, 371
Hudson River, N.Y., photos., 238, 269
Hudson River Valley, 31
"Human Limitations in Automobile Driving," 172
Hungary, 168
Hurd, Frederick W., 201
Hutchinson River Parkway, 205
Hyannis, Mass., beach, photo., 344
Hyde Park, N.Y., 409
Hydroelectric facility, photo., 365
Hydroelectric power, 28

Ickes, Harold, 6, quoted, 409
Idaho, 24, 378
Illinois, 390, 413
Imperial Valley, Cal., 368
Incinerators, 132, 299, photo., 300
Indiana, 64
Indiana Turnpike, 205
Indianapolis Metropolitan Planning Commission, 84
Individual dwellings. *See* Housing, single-family;
    Single-family houses
Industrial areas, 72, 234, map of, 281
Industrial design, 284–311
    Articulation of elements, 288, 293–94, 302–05,
        model, 294
    Buffer zones, 300, 302–05, photo., 308
    Clarity of massing, 286–93, 296, photos., 284, 286,
        287, 288, 289, 296, 301
    Esthetics, 284–85, 290
    Landscaping, 290, 293, 305–08, photos., 284, 296,
        310, 375
    Location, 21, 279–84, 296–98
    Order of pattern, 289, photos., 292
    Parking lots, 282, 305, 308, 309, model, 294, photos.,
        293, 309
    Relationship with environment, 296, 305–11,
        photos., 307, 308, 309, 310, 312, 314
    Rhythmic coordination, 290–93, 446, photos., 291,
        293
    Setbacks, 283, 290, 302–05, 445, drawings, 306,
        photo., 309
    Silhouettes, 296–302, photos., 300, 301, 302
    Structural expression, 287–90, 293–96, photos., 286,
        289, 296
    Zoning, 216, 298. *See also* Industrial buffer zones
Industrialization, 24, 58
Industrial parks, 290–93, 372, 396, photos., 293, 294
Industrial revolution, 55
Industrial scars, 285, 305
Industrial technology, 56
Industry, 5, 36, 64, 65, 72, 153, 234, 279–330, 386, 443.
    See also Factories
Inner Connector Loop, 15. *See also* Highways
Institutional buildings, 18, 448. *See also* Hospitals;
    Schools
Instrument manufacturing buildings, 298
Insurance companies, 43, 396, photo., 336
Insurance rates, 280
Interchanges, 15, 59, 146, 148, 224, 255, 258, 261–63,
    269, drawing, 259, photos., 176, 252, 261, 309, plan,
    253
Interest rates, 280
Intersections, 89, 90, 162–63; Separated. *See* Grade
    separations; T, 89, 90, 105
Interstate highways, 76, 167, 168, 169, 201, 258–61
Interurbia. *See* Rural Urban Fringe
Iowa, 6, 24
Irrigation, 26, 368. *See also* Soil conservation
Irvine Ranch, Cal., 394
Isard and Coughlin, 66
Isard, Walter, 39, 40, diagram by, 39

Isfahan, Iran, 8
Italy, 164, 168

Jacobs, Stephen V., quoted, 419–20
James, Henry, quoted, 19–21
James River, Va., 31
Japan, 6, 29, 168
Jefferson, Thomas, 4, quoted, 8, 51
Jones Beach, N.Y., 165
Jones, Victor, 12
Joshua trees, 356
Joshua Tree National Monument, photo., 358
Junkyards, 23, 44, 302, 322, 371, 445, photo., 304. *See
    also* Dumps

Kaiser Steel plant, Fontana, Cal., photo., 7
Kansas City, Mo., photo., 291
Kansas Turnpike, 205
Kassel, Germany, plan for community near, 154
Keep America Beautiful, 446
Kelly, Dean Burnham, quoted, 67
Kennedy, John F., 85, 398
Kentucky, 261
King, John Lord, 334
Koch, Richard, 438
Koester, Hugo, 199
Kostka, V. J., design by, 110
Kouwenhoven, John, 364
Kulosaari Island, Finland, plan for development on,
    155

Labor costs, 280
Lakes, 140, 142. *See also* Water
Lake Erie, 381
Lake Forest, Ill., 21
Lake Isabella, Cal., 342
Lake Michigan, 390
Lake Mondsee, Austria, 190
Lakewood, Cal., photo., 96
Lancaster, Pa., 59
Land Bank, 85, 379, 398
Land development standards. *See* Development
    controls; Zoning
Land form, 121, 122, 364, 365. *See also* Landscape;
    Nature and natural features
Landmarks, 8, 104, 140, 160, 263–65, 266, 270, 298,
    409, 410, diagrams, 266, photos., 265, 266, 270. *See
    also* Focal points
Land ownership, fragmented, 80, 82–83. *See also*
    Leap-frogging; Scattered development; Sprawl
Land platting, 59, 86, 92. *See also* Speculation
Landscape, 4, 5–12, 24–27, 72, 121, 140, 363. *See also*
    Open space; Nature and natural features; Rural
    areas
Landscape architects, 56, 67, 128, 129, 155, 162, 274,
    386
Landscaping, 8–16, 68, 127, 128–34, 144, 375–76, 448,
    photos., 131, 144. *See also* Planting; Commercial,
    328–29, model, 294, photos., 331, 332; Freeway and
    highway, 159, 162, 164–65, 166, 170, 217, 220,
    227–33, 259, 265, photos., 166, 202, 227, 228–29,

Landscaping (*cont.*)
230. *See also* Freeway, landscaping; Highway, landscaping; Industrial, 290, 293, 305–08, photos., 284, 296, 310, 375
Land speculation, 55, 59, 82–83, 85, 86
Land use, 13, 29, 35, 218, 219–20, 386–87, 444
Land values, 23, 61, 80, 81–83, 84, 96, 135, 146, 250, 282, 313
Lansing, Mich., 93
Lansing Tri-county Regional Planning Commission, 81
Lawns, 59, 134. *See also* Yards
Lawrence Park, Pa., photo., 147
Leadville, Colo., photo., 11
Leap-frogging, 29, 66, 80–82, diagrams, 81. *See also* Fragmented land ownership; Scattered development; Sprawl
Lebanon, 12
Lebanon County, Pa., 93
Lees-Milne, James, quoted, 434
Leisure time activities, 19, 23, 446
Lenox, Mass., Tanglewood, photo., 354
Levittown, N.J., 138
Levittown, Pa., photos., 117, 119, 120, 153, 330, 331
Levittowns, 77, 79
Lexington-Concord Battle Road, Mass., 410, map, 410
Liard River, Canada, photo., 30
Libraries, 145. *See also* Municipal structures
Library of Congress, 412, 413
Limited access highways, 159, 160–62, 163, 164, 165, 167, 168, 324–25, maps of, 168, 169, plan, 321, photo., 163. *See also* Divided highways; Freeways
Limited access streets, 90, 151, 152
Lincoln, Mass., 393
Linden, N.J., 282–83
Lititz, Pa., 420, 423
Living hedge, 227
Ljubljana-Belgrade *Autoput*, 168
Lockheed Aircraft research laboratory, Palo Alto, Cal., photo., 310
Loebel, Schlossman and Bennett, 331
London, England, 19
London County Council, 19
London-Birmingham Motorway, overpass design, drawing, 244
Long Beach, Cal., 350, photo., 96
Longfellow, Henry Wadsworth, poem by, 410
Long Island, 24, 162, 167, photos., 152, 184
Loops, 90
Lorenz, Hans, 181, 182, 185, 187, 188, 198
Low density areas. *See* Housing, density; Rural-urban-fringe; Suburbia
Low-rise apartments. *See* Garden apartments
Los Angeles, Cal., 165, 227, 370–71, 393; Park system, 384, 385–86, map, 384
Los Angeles Beautiful, Inc., 446
Los Angeles County, Cal., 93, photo., 96
Los Angeles County Regional Planning Commission, survey by, 305–07

Lösch, August, 40
Lot coverage, 107
Lot size, 92–96, 109, 127, 144, graph, 95, table, 93
Loudon, J. C., *The Villa Gardener*, quoted, 133
Lowell, Mass., 284
Lumber industry, 28, 376
Lynch, Kevin, 177

Madison, James, 51
Maine, 28, 167, 258, 261, 367
Maine Turnpike, 205, 258, overpass design, drawing, 244
Mahwah, N.J., photo., 309
Malls, 17, 143, 326, 405, photo., 331
Manahawkin Bay Bridge, N.J., photos., 242
Manufacturing, 15, 36, 38, 40, 279, 283, 298; Cities, 39; Employment density, map, 281
Marblehead, Mass., photo., 349
Marin County, Cal., drawing, 117, photos., 117, 334
Marinas, 10, 112, 145, 349–50, 385, photos., 149, 350
Markets, 26, 36
Market areas, 13, 40, diagrams, 39. *See also* Regional centers; Retail centers
Market mechanism, 56, 77
Maroon Lake, Colo., photo., 356
Marshes. *See* Wetlands
Maryland, 261; Highways, graph, 185, photo., 272
Maryland-National Capital Park and Planning Commission, 141
Massachusetts, 32, 78, 127, 257, 390; Open space program, 30, 346, 370, 382, 384–85, 398, map, 382. *See also* Boston
Massachusetts Department of Natural Resources, 378
Massachusetts Institute of Technology, 66, 201
Massachusetts, Justices' Opinion to the Senate, 1955, quoted, 421
Massachusetts Turnpike, drawing, 243, photo., 207, table, 205
Massing, 286–93, 296, model, 294, photos., 284, 286, 287, 288, 289, 296, 301. *See also* Industrial design
Mass production, 55
McBride Associates, 20
McIver, Robert, 13
McKim, Charles Follen, 405
Meadowbrook Parkway, 165, 254, photos., 163, 254
Median dividers, 160, 164, 165, 167, 176, 201–05, 230, 231–33, 240, 241, 255, drawings, 203, photos., 202, 203, 204
Medical supplies plant, N.J., photo., 301
Merkel, Herman, 162
Merritt Island, Fla., 304
Merritt Parkway, 165, 227, 257, photos., 166, 233, table, 205
Metal consuming industries, 280–81
Metropolitan areas, 93, 94, 283, 444
Metropolitan centers, 40, diagram, 41
Metropolitan community, 36
Metropolitan park systems, 387. *See also* Open space, regional systems; Parks
Mexico, 168

Michigan, 391, 413
Middletown, Conn., 431, photos., 433
Middle Ground, 17–19
Middle West, 10–11, 40
Milan, Italy, 164
Milk industry, 26
Milkshed, photo., 369
Mill Creek One Hundred, Del., 413
Milwaukee, Wisconsin, 37
Mineral resources, 28
Mines, 300
Minimum visible object, 171–72
Minneapolis-St. Paul Metropolitan Area, 93, 145, graph, 95
Minnesota, 26, 390, 391
Mississippi River Valley, 32
Mobile homes. *See* Trailers
Mobility, results of, 31
Mojave Desert, 10, 355, photo., 357
Mohawk River, photo., 208; Bridge, photo., 237
Monongahela National Forest, 347
Montgomery County, Pa., Audubon House, 411; Radnor Industrial Park, 372
Montreal, Canada, factory near, photo., 300
Moore, Henry, sculpture by, photo., 267
Moravian buildings, 420
Morrison, Jacob, quoted, 421
Moscow Outer Ring, 168
Moses, Robert, 165, 382
Motels, 10, 263, 322, 344
Mott, Seward, 90, design by, 91
Mountains, 364
Mount Christie, Wash., photo., 5
Mount Desert Island, Me., Thunder Cave, engraving, 32
Mount Rainier National Park, Paradise Valley, photo., 360
Mount Vernon, Va., 403
Mount Vernon Parkway, 162
Mount Washington, N.H., engraving, 32
Multi-family houses, 60, 61, 65. *See also* Apartments
Multnomah Falls, Ore., photo., 272
Mumford, Lewis, 43, 72, quoted, 376
Municipal art societies, 437
Municipal costs, 66–67, 96
Municipal planning agencies, 128
Municipal services, 83. *See also* Utilities
Municipal structures, 145
Museums, 21
Muskau Park on Neisse River, Germany, print, 229

Nantucket, Mass., 31, 32, 403, 421, photo., 352
Nashville, Tenn., 411
Nassau County, N.Y., 162, photo., 100
Natchez, Miss., 426
Natchez Trace Parkway, 348
National Aeronautics and Space Administration, 304
National Association of Home Builders, 67, survey by, 78
National Capital Region, regional open space system, 370, 381, map, 381

National Coal Association, 310
National Forests, 28, 29–30, 31, 343, 345, 347, 360, 384, map, 384, photo., 356. *See also* Forests; National Parks
National Forest Service, 343, 361, 385
National Housing Agency, development of, photo., 112
National Housing Act of 1961, 379
National Industrial Zoning Committee, 216
National Interregional Highway Committee, 1944 report, quoted, 222
National Monuments, 344, 352, 368, 385, photos., 357, 358. *See also* National Parks
National Parks, 5, 6, 28, 29–31, 342–44, 345, 368, 369, engravings, 32, 33, photos., 5, 354, 360. *See also* National Forests; National Monuments; Parks
National Park Service, 348, 361, 378, 385, 410, 413, 414, quoted, 412; Mission 66 program, 343, 412, 413
National Recreation Association, 378, 379, 379–80, 385
National Recreation School, survey, 351–53, quoted, 352
National Sand and Gravel Association, 308
National Socialist Party (Germany), 164
National Standards, 258–61
National System of Interstate and Defense Highways, 167, 201
National Trust for Historic Preservation, 410, 413
Native industries, 32
Natres State Park, Mass., photo., 344
Nature and natural features, 5–9, 28, 37, 127–28, 145, 364, 365, 443. *See also* Landscape
Nebraska, 261
Neighborhoods, 318, 343, 375
Netherlands, 6, 59, 165, 168
Nevada, 378
Nevada Proving Grounds of Atomic Energy Commission, 28
Newark-Trenton highway, 162
New Deal, 90
New England, 10, 11–12, 43, 59, 78
New Hampshire, 261, 390
New Harmony, Ind., 411
New Haven, Conn., 41, photo., 126; Bishop House, 435, photo., 435; Wooster Square, 19, 411, 428–29, drawing, 429, photos., 430–31
New Haven City Plan Commission, survey by, 134
New Haven Historic Preservation Trust, 436
New Haven Water Company, reservoir dam, photo., 312
New Jersey, 10, 24, 201, 235, 398, photos., 20, 301
New Jersey Turnpike, 205, 263, bridge railing design, drawing, 245
New London, Conn., 43
New Orleans, La., 416, 426; Vieux Carré, 31, 439, photo., 438; Vieux Carré Commission, 420, 422
Newport, Cal., 350
Newport, R.I., 411, 414, 428; Preservation Society, 413; White Horse Tavern, photo., 48
New Rochelle, N.Y., 118–19

New towns, 38
New York, State of, 41, 43, 96, 145, 353, 379; Highways, 162, 164, 165, 167, 201, 224, 227, 254, 258, 261, 382, drawing, 245, graph, 185, maps, 274, 383. *See also* New York Thruway; Park systems, 30, 382, 385, 397–98, map, 383
New York City, 10, 26, 40, 57, 59, 63, 148, photos., 156, 275, 276, 407
    Bowling Green Commerce Building, 406
    Central Park, 160, 375
    City Hall, 411
    Fraunces' Tavern, 409, 435, photos., 408
    Grand Central Terminal, 440, photo., 440
    Greenwich Village, 417–19, photo., 418
    Historic Preservation, 406, 409, 414, 417–19
    Hunt Studio, 406
    MacDougal Alley, 419, photo., 419
    Mark Twain's House, 406
    Municipal Arts Society, 413
    Old Merchant's House, 435, photos., 434
    Pan American Building, 440
    Patchin Place, photo., 418
    Rhinelander Gardens, 406, 409, photo., 407
New York City Planning Commission, 417
New York Metropolitan Region, 93, 370–71, 406–07; Freeways and Parkways, 162, 164, 165, 382, maps, 274, 383; Lot sizes, 93, 95, graph, 95; Regional open space program, 382, 385, 397–98, map, 383; Regional Plan Association, 95
New York Thruway, 167, 193, diagram, 188, photos., 188, 208, 439, table, 205
New York University, 394
Nock, Albert Jay, quoted, 51
Nodal regions, 38, 72
Noguchi, Isamu, sculpture by, photo., 336
"No look-alike" ordinances, 118–19. *See also* Zoning
Non-farm dwellings, chart, 62
North Dakota, 261
Northern State Parkway, N.Y., photo., 208
Northern Virginia, Regional Park Authority, 398
Norwalk, Conn., photo., 310
Nuclear installations, 355
Nyack-Tarrytown Bridge (Tappan Zee Bridge), 238, photo., 238

Oak Park, Mich., 155
Off-street parking facilities, 17, 18. *See also* Garages
Office buildings, 318, photo., 289
Ohio, 64, 224, 261, 380, photo., 189. *See also* Cleveland
Ohio River Valley, 32
Ohio Turnpike, photo., 202, table, 205
Ohio Turnpike Commission, 258
Oil cracking plants, 10
Oil derricks, photo., 302
Oil pipelines, 217
Oil refineries, 280, 281, 282–83, 296, 300, 304, 305, photos., 291, 300, 314
Oil tanks, 234, 300, photo., 292
Oklahoma, 6, photos., 270, 302
Oklahoma Turnpike, 205

Old age housing, 19, 428
Old Deerfield Village, Mass., 35, photo., 34
Old Dominion Foundation, 413
Old residential areas. *See* Historic preservation; Middle ground
Old Salem, N.C., 403
Old Sturbridge, Mass., 411
Old town centers, 319–20. *See also* Village greens
Olmsted, Frederick L., 90, 105, 160, plan for Riverside, 91
Olympic National Park, 5, photos., 5, 354
One-family houses. *See* Single-family houses
One-way streets, 89
Open lots, 12, 60
Open-pit coal mines, 311
Open space, 19, 23, 31, 63, 64, 84, 96, 109, 143, 144, 148, 233, 339–98, 443, 444, 448, diagram, 39. *See also* Parks
    Aquisition, 145, 325, 386–87, 397–98, 445, 448
    Bonuses. *See* Zoning
    Buffer zones, 153, 304–05. *See also* Buffer zones; Zoning
    Design, 361–87, 387–98
    Fragmentation, 96
    Planning, 148, 379–87, 387–97; Local, 392–97; National, 389–90; State, 390–91
    Pooling, 109, 112, photo., 112, plan, 113
    Preservation, 145, 342, 346, 359, 378
    Programs, 29–30, 141, 398
    Recreational, 339–42, 366–67. *See also* National Parks; Parks
    Regional systems, 30, 346, 347, 353, 370, 379–85, 388–90, 397, 398, 444, maps, 381, 382, 383, 384
    Standards, 379–80
Optical guidance, 198, 227, 231
Orange County, N.Y., photo., 9
Oregon, 24, 257, 261, 378
Organ Pipe Cactus National Monument, 368
Outdoor advertising, 257–61, 265, 283, photos., 50, 260, 332, 334, 335. *See also* Billboards; Roadside commercial strip
Outdoor movies. *See* Drive-in movies
Outdoor Recreation Resources Review Commission, 343
Overhead wiring, 66, 135–38, 296, 445, photos., 138, 140. *See also* Utility lines
Overlooks, scenic, photos., 269, 272. *See also* Freeways, scenic turnouts
Overpasses, 160, 234, 240, 242–48, drawings, 243, 244, photos., 214, 234, 246, 247, 249. *See also* Bridges
Owner-built houses, 78, photo., 22

Palisades Interstate Park, photo., 309
Palisades Interstate Parkway, 167, photos., 204, 268, 269, 273
Palm Springs, Cal., 12, photo., 367
Palo Alto, Cal., photos., 310, 329
Palos Verdes Estates, Cal., 393
Paper mills, 279
Paramus, N.J., 316

Parapets, 244, 327–28. *See also* Guide rails

Paris, France, 18, 59, 165

Parking lots, 11, 15, 153, 282, 305, 308, 314, 318, 326–27, 328–29, 408, 445, photos., 293, 294, 309, 329, 330, 333, 407

Parks, 18, 19, 21, 28, 72, 145, 161–62, 269, 318, 361, 378, 379, 390, 448, *See also* Open Space
   City, 17, 18, 339, 342–43, 370, 375, 380–86, 387, diagram, 362, maps, 381, 382, 383, 384
   National, 5, 6, 28, 29–31, 342–44, 345, 368, 369, engravings, 32, 33, photos., 5, 354, 360
   State, 30, 268, 342, 344, 361, 394, photos., 309, 344, 399

Parkways, 159, 160–62, 164, 165, 167, 169, 186, 193, 201, 205, 224, 227, 254, 257, 273, 274, 347–48, 384–85, diagram, 188, drawing, 203, map, 274, photos., 163, 166, 204, 208, 209, 228–29, 232, 233, 254, 255, 256, 264, 268, 269, 273

Pasadena, Cal., 12, 348, 393

Passaic County, N.J., 76, photo., 75, plan, 74

Passaic v. *Paterson Bill Posting Co.*, quoted, 405–06

Pavements, 66, 165, 169, 175, 240–41, 261, photo., 241. *See also* Highways, structure

Peets, Elbert, 90

Pennsylvania, 6, 24, 30, 261

Pennsylvania Turnpike, 165–67, 205

Pentagon, road network, 167

Peripheral vision, 172–74

Perspective, 200, 363, 372

Pharmaceutical industries, 284

Philadelphia, Pa., 15, 16, 59, photo., 14
   Advisory Commission on Historic Buildings, 416
   Elfreth's Alley, 411, 417, photo., 416
   Historic preservation, 411, 414, 416
   Independence Hall, 411
   Penn Center office building, photo., 14
   Society Hill, 19, 411
   Suburbs, photo., 16

Picnic areas, photos., 35, 272, 345. *See also* Roadside rest areas

Picnicking, 343, 344, 351, 358

Pima County, Ariz., 93

Pipelines, 23, 217, 290

Pitkin and Mott, 91

Planned residential districts, 109–10. *See also* Zoning

Planners, 17, 44, 63, 93, 135, 155, 378, 386, 444

Planning agencies, 89, 93, 110, 148

Planning and Community Appearance, 405

"Planning Neighborhoods for Small Houses," 91

"Planning Profitable Neighborhoods," diagram from, 92

Planting, 123–24, 128–30, 134, 329, 330, 377, 445; Highway, 159, 164–65, 170, 217, 220, 227–33, photos., 227, 230. *See also* Landscaping

Playfields. *See* Playgrounds

Playgrounds, 79, 144–45, 342–43, 350, 359, 375, 376, 379–80, diagram, 362, photo., 343

Police protection, 38, 66

Police stations. *See* Municipal structures

Policy on Geometric Design, quoted, 181

Political groups, suburban, 21

Pollution, 3

Ponds, 140. *See also* Water

Population density, 23, 40, 57–63. *See also* Housing, density

Population growth, 4, 7, 28, 31, 57, 78, map, 58

Population potential, belts of, 36

Port Charlotte, Fla., photos., 97, 148–49

Portland, Me., 411

Portugal, 168

Pough, Richard H., 343

Power, Eileen, 403

Power lines. *See* Overhead wiring; Utility lines

Power plants, 279, 283, 299

Power supply, 37, 38, 139, 444. *See also* Utilities

Prairies, 368–69

Precision instrument industry, 280

Prefabrication, 78, 79, 80

Premature subdivision, 80, 86

Preservation: Historic, 5, 19, 32, 35, 143, 346, 390, 403–39, 443, 445, 446; Natural resources, 28, 31–32, 127–28, 140, 141, 143, 144, 145, 330, 355–58, 378

Preservation trusts, 436–37

Prestige areas, 80

Prestige industries, 280, 284–85, 307

Primary metals industry, 280

Prince George's County, Md., "Tantallon" development, plan, 146

Privacy, 99, 134, 135, 358

Probability pattern. *See* Gravity pattern

Production, 3, 7, 36, 38, 40

Profiles. *See* Highways, alignment; Streets, vertical alignment

Providence, R.I., 43; College Hill, 411, 413, 414, 425, drawing, 437; Historic preservation, 411–14, 422, 425

Providence City Plan Commission, survey of historic buildings, 414

Providence Preservation Society, 414

Public health, 66, 95, 444

Public housing, 21, 22, 63, 428, photos., 149

Public land, 378–79; Laws, 145. *See also* Parks; Public open space

Public open space, 143, 145, 155, 268, diagram, 362, map, 340–41, photos., 147, plan, 146. *See also* Open space; Parks

Public recreational facilities, 31, 344, 351–55, 359. *See also* Parks; Public open space

Public Roads Administration, Information Chief, quoted, 167

Public Service Company of New Jersey, 138

Public transportation, 18, 65–66, 282

Puerto Rico, 257

Purchase, N.Y., 393

Queens County, N.Y., 162, 165

Radar antennas, 299

Radburn, N.J., 67, 90, 104, 105, photo., 20

Radburn plan, 72, 92

Radial highways, 15, 72, 76, photo., 75, plan, 74

Radial acceleration, 180, 181
Radio telescopes, 265
Radio transmitters, 299
Railroads, 12, 36, 57, 59, 146, 159, 160, 180, 215–16, 282, 298, 444, 448, photos., 16, 216; Yards, 72, photo., 291
Railings. *See* Guide rails
Rainer, Roland, 126
Ramapo Mountains, photo., 309
Ranch houses, 115, 348
Ranke, Victor von, 200
Recreation, 31–32, 43, 339–55
Recreational facilities, 5, 31–32, 318, 344, 351–55, 359, 391, 397–98. *See also* Parks; Playgrounds; Roadside rest areas
Redevelopment programs, 15–18, 446
Redondo Beach, Cal., photo., 335
Redwood Freeway, photo., 223
Reforestation, 6. *See also* Forests
Regional centers, 36, 38–40, diagrams, 39, 40. *See also* Central business districts
Regional differences, 10–11, 32, 348–51
Regional open space systems. *See* Open space, regional systems
Regional Plan Association, N.Y., 95
Regional planners, 274
Rehabilitation planners, 428–29
Relay stations, 10, 146
Research centers, 305, 318, 394, model, 294
Research industries, 280
Research laboratories, 298
Residential associations, 396–97
Residential density. *See* Housing, density
Residential developers, 67
Residential development, 67, 70–72, 77–78, 80, 92, 140, 279, diagrams, 81, 92. *See also* Housing
Residential subdivisions. *See* Subdivisions
Resorts, 345, 360
Resources for the Future, 343
Restaurants, 11, 14, 263, 322, photo., 270. *See also* Freeways, commercial facilities, service areas
Restrictive covenants, 416–17, 427, 431. *See also* Preservation; Zoning
Retail centers, diagram, 40. *See also* Commercial centers; Regional centers; Shopping centers
Retail stores, 326
Retaining walls, 124–26, 240, 250, photos., 124, 126. *See also* Embankments; Slopes
Rhine River valley, Germany, 32
Rhode Island, 167, 413. *See also* Providence
Richland, Wash., photo., 285
Richmond, Va., engraving of, 33; City Attorney, quoted, 421
Rights-of-way, 29, 86, 90; Highway, 148, 152, 217, 250–57, 271, 373, 390, 445, 448, photos., 251, 252, 255, 256
Rivers and river valleys, 140, 155, 373, 388, photos., 49, 238, 269. *See also* Nature and natural features; Water
Riverside, Cal., 12

Road maintenance, 66
Roads, 76–77, 78, 80, 151. *See also* Highways; Tourist routes
Roadside, 206; Commercial clusters, 325–26; Commercial strip, 76, 162, 322–26, photos., 334, 335; Rest areas, 32, 259, 261, 263, 267–69, 272, 322, 390, photos., 35, 269, 271, 272, 273, 345
Rockefeller, family, 382
Rockefeller, John D., Jr., 403
Rockefeller, Laurance S., 343
Rocket launching facility, 298
Rockland County, N.Y., 359
Rock formations, 143, 210, photos., 210, 211
Rocky Mountains, 10, 350
Rohe, Mies van der, quoted, 56
Rollercoaster profile. *See* Highways, vertical alignment
Rome, Italy, approach to, photo., 260
Roof lines, 115–20, drawings, 115, 117, photos., 116, 117, 118
Roosevelt, Franklin D., quoted, 263
Roscoe, Lewis, plan by, 113
Rousseau, Jean Jacques, 339
Route Europe 5, photos., 178
Route selection, 190. *See* Highways, location of
Row houses, 61, 67, 72, 117, drawing, 70, photo., 108. *See also* Garden apartments
Royce, Josiah, 13, 51, quoted, 51
Rural areas, 24–27. *See also* Wilderness
Rural-urban fringe, 17, 21, 19, 22–24, 26, 43, 72–97, 148, 376, 443
    Buildings in, 146
    Commercial facilities, 23, 311–19
    Development, structure and location of, 23, 72–85, diagrams, 81, photos., 22, 25, 75, plan, 74
    Housing in. *See* Housing, low density
    Industry in, 283
    Lot size, 92–96
    Open space in, 23, 96, 145, 380
    Street systems, 86–90, 148, 151
    Subdivision design, 90–96
    Zoning, 95, 96
Rush, Earl, 102
Ryder, A. J., quoted, 43

Sacramento, Cal., 414
Sacramento River, 366
Sag curves, 190, 191, 193, 194, diagrams, 194, 197. *See also* Curves; Highways, vertical alignment
Sahara Desert, 6
Salton Sea, Cal., 368
Salzburg-Vienna freeway, 190, drawing, 267
San Antonio, Tex., Conservation Society, 413
San Bernardino County, Cal., 11, 356
San Bernardino Mountains, 12
San Diego, Cal., 411, photo., 287
Sand pits. *See* Borrow pits; Gravel pits
Sandwich, Mass., photo., 348
San Francisco, Cal., 10, 393; Golden Gate Bridge, photo., 223

Sanitary facilities, 448

San Jacinto Mountains, 367

San Jose, Cal., 82

San Juan, Puerto Rico, San Juan Antiquo, 411

San Mateo, Cal., photos., 87, 328

Santa Barbara, Cal., 393

Santa Barbara County, Cal., 93, 94

Santa Catalina Island, Cal., marina, photo., 350

Santa Fe, N.M., Architectural style, 423–24, photos., 424, 425; Historic preservation, 423–24

Santa Monica Mountains, photo., 127

Santayana, George, quoted, 4

Saugus, Mass., Iron Works, 403

Savannah, Ga., 31; Trustees' Garden Village, 409

Sawtooth effect, 99, diagram, 103, photo., 103. See also Housing, alignment

Scandinavia, 84–85

Scarsdale, N.Y., 118–19

Scattered development, 83–84. See also Fragmented land ownership; Leap-frogging; Sprawl

Scenic Areas, 145, 155, 347, 360, 366; Easements and overlooks, 263, 267–269, 272, 346, 390, photos., 269, 272. See also Landscape; Nature and natural features; Parks

Schmitt, Ingo, design by, 154

Schools, 18, 44, 65, 76, 79, 80, 95, 145, 146, 318, 448, photo., 407

Schuylkill River Valley, Pa., 413

Scott, Geraldine, 231

Screens, 134, 135. See also Fences; Privacy

Screw curve, 195, diagram, 195. See also Curves; Highways, three dimensional alignment

Sculpture, 177, 265, 267

S-curve, photo., 208

Sears, Paul B., quoted, 274

Seattle, Wash., 138, photos., 116, 135

Section line roads, 86

Sequoia National Forest, 360

Septic tanks, 66, 94, 140. See also Sewage disposal

Service areas and parks, 259, 261, 263, 269, 320–22, photos., 270, 271, 273, plan, 321

Service stations. See Gas stations

Setbacks: Commercial, 328, 329, 445; Highway, 250, 259, 261, 271, 283, drawings, 306; Industrial, 283, 290, 302–05, 445, drawings, 306, photo., 309; Residential, 66, 96, 109, 115, 119, 134, 394, drawings, 110

Settlement patterns, 3–13, 24, 28, 29, 36–44, 55, 74, 76

Sewage disposal, 23, 66, 79, 80, 84, 94, 95, 96, 140, 283, 444

Sewage treatment plants, 283, 290, 300

Shaker Heights, Ohio, 397

Sharecropping system, 26

Sharpe, Thomas, 370

Shasta Dam, Cal., photo., 288

Shenandoah National Park, 344

Shelburne, Vt., 411

Shipyards, 300

Shoe industry, 282

Shopping, 313–14

Shopping centers, 10, 13, 17, 21, 79, 146, 316–19, 320, 326–30, 446, photos., 329, 331, 332, 333, 334, 335

Advertising, 326, 330, photos., 332

Design, 326–28, 343

Landscaping, 326, 328–29, 330, photos., 331, 332

Parking areas, 314, 326–29, 408, photos., 329, 330, 333

Setbacks, 328, 329, 445

Shore frontage, 80, 381, 390

Shoulders, 164, 226, 230, 231, 240, 241, 254

Shrubs, 68, 132, 134. See also Hedges; Landscaping; Planting; Trees

Siegel, Shirley A., 389

Sight distance, 191, 199, 231. See also Vision

Silhouette. See Skylines

Simonds, John, 125

Simons, Albert, 403

Single-family housing, 12, 21, 55, 61, 63, 65, 72, 78, 93, 99, 104, 106, 107–09, 116, 148, 446, chart, 62, drawing, 68, photo., 151

Site planners, 56, 67, 128

Site planning, 80, 95, 96, 121, 134. See also Development, location of; Zoning

Skating rinks, 145

Skidmore, Owings, and Merrill, 101, 336

Skiing, 350, 360

Skylines, 296–302, photos., 300, 301, 302. See also Roof lines

Skyscrapers, 3, 72

Slums, 3, 15, 17, 18, 55, 121, 144, 159, 406

Slopes, 123, 124–25, 222–26, 231, 233, 240, diagrams, 225, drawings, 226. See also Embankments; Grading

Small, Edwin W., 410

Smelting industry, 280

Smoke stacks, 290

Society for the Preservation of New England Antiquities, 422

Sociologists, 63

Socony-Mobil Oil tanks, photo., 292

Soil conservation, 6, 23, 358

Soil scientists, 386

Solberg, Erling, 389

Somerset County, N.J., photo., 25

South America, 165, 168

Southbridge, Mass., American Optical Co., 377

Southern New England Telephone Company, 43

Souvenir shops, 322

Space definition, 99, 105–09, 128–30, 175

Space perception, 174. See also Vision

Sparrows Point, Md., photo., 307

Specialty shops, 65

Speculation, 55, 59, 80, 82–83, 85, 86

Speed limits, 165, 167

Spirals. See Transition curves

Split level houses, 115, 120, 406

Sprawl, 22, 80–81, 84, 387, maps showing patterns of, 82, 83. See also Fragmented land ownership; Leap-frogging; Scattered development

Spree River, Germany, photo., 375

Spring, Bernard F., quoted, 134
Springfield, Mass., 43, photo., 129
Spring Mill Rock, Ind., 411
Spurrier, Raymond, quoted, 275
Squares, 17, 19, 89, 145. *See also* Village greens
Squaw Valley, Cal., 360
Standard Metropolitan Areas, 36, 57, 64
Standard Oil Company, 302; Refinery, photo., 314;
    Tanks, photo., 292
Stanford University, 396
State forests, 28, 345, 376, 379, 390–91, photo., 345.
    See also Forests
State land, 342, 379
State parks, 30, 268, 342, 344, 361, 394, photos., 309,
    344, 399. *See also* Parks
Statue of Liberty, photo., 276
St. Augustine, Fla., City Gate, engraving, 33
Steam heat, 66
Steel mills, 279, 282, 300, 305, 374
Stein, Clarence, 90
Stein, Gertrude, quoted, 376
Steinman, David B., 239
Sterling Forest, N.Y., 394; Gardens, 394, 396, photos.,
    395, 396
St. Louis, Mo., 414
Stockholm, Sweden, 300
Stone walls, 143, photo., 308
Storage areas, 302, 445
Storage tanks, photos., 291, 292
Store cluster. *See* Shopping centers
Stores, 316, 319, 328. *See also* Commercial facilities
Stowe, Vt., photo., 389
St. Paul-Minneapolis Metropolitan Area, 93, 145
Streams, 140, 141, 145, 210, 381, 384, 391, photo., 141.
    See also Nature and natural features; Water
Streets, 66, 86–97, 104, 122, 148, map, 88, photo., 87.
    See also Rights-of-way
    Alignment, 99–104, 212–14
        Clusters, photos., 112, 114, plans, 111, 114
        Cul-de-sacs, 90, 104, 109, 143
        Curvature, 89, 90, 104–05, 122, diagrams, 104,
            105, photo., 100, plans, 111, 122. *See also*
            Curvilinear street plans
        Grades, 94
        Loop, 101, 152, plan, 113
        Rectilinear, 86, 89, 98, 104, 105, 112, 114, 122,
            148, 179, 214, map, 88, photo., 100, plan, 111
    Arterial, 88, 89, 148, 151–52. *See also* Collector
        streets; Feeder roads
    Buffers, 445
    Collector, 88, 89, 151, plan, 113
    Construction, 80, 89
    Design, 89, 90, 92, 151
    Esthetics, 152, 153
    Land service, 151, 152
    Patterns, 212–14, diagrams, 99, 101, 102, 103, maps,
        89, photos., 100, 101
    Residential, 89, photo., 393
    Standards, 89
    T-intersections, 89, 90, 105

Streets (*cont.*)
    Width, 152
Strip commercial. *See* Roadside commercial strip
Strip mines, 11, 445, rehabilitated, photos., 310
Stufa (Society for the Study of Motor Road Construc-
    tion), 164
Subdividing, 29
Subdivisions, 4, 21, 44, 56, 67, 76, 77, 81, 82, 86, 90,
    94, 98, 376, 377, map, 82, photos., 20, 22, 119, 131,
    142, 147, 152, plans, 91, 143
    Design, 91, 134–35, 143–48
    Premature, 80, 86
    Regulations, 55, 84, 85, 86, 89, 127–28, 152, 392–93,
        397. *See also* Zoning
    Residential, 76, 77, 79, photos., 75, 77, plan, 74
Suburbanites, 19
Suburbanization, 41
Suburban living, 65–66
Suburbia, 3, 15, 17, 19–22, 57, 60, 146, 393–94. *See also*
    Rural-urban-fringe
    Commercial facilities, 20, 21, 22, 311–19
    Density, photos., 96, 97
    Development, 57, 64
    Dormitory, 39
    Open space in, 19, 21. *See also* Parks; Playgrounds
Subway tunnels, 17
Suffolk County, N.Y., marinas, 350
Superblocks, 90, 393
Superelevation, 180, 181, 183, 198
Supergrids, 88, 148
Superhighways. *See* Freeways
Supermarkets, 313–16, 316–19
Surface mining, 7
Suspension bridges, 235. *See also* Bridges
Swamps. *See* Wetlands
Swayze, Judge Francis J., quoted, 405–06
Sweden, 168
Swimming pools, 112, 145, 318, photo., 149

Tabor, Baby Doe, cabin of, photo., 11
Taconic Parkway, 162, 167, 227, photos., 209, 228–29,
    232, 264, table, 205
Tangents, 166, 178–83, 184–85, 187, diagrams, 179,
    180, graph, 185, photos., 166, 178. *See also* High-
    way, alignment
Tanglewood. *See* Lenox, Mass.
Tankut, Gonul, plan by, 113
Tappan Zee, N.Y., 238, photo., 238
Taste, 4, 56, 67, 121
Tax abatements, 419–20, 427, 431
Taxation, 19, 61, 85, 280, 444
Technology, 3, 4, 25–26, 36, 37, 55, 58, 66, 139, 363
Telephone antennas, photo., 303
Telephone calls, 41, 43, diagram, 42
Telephone relay towers, 283, 296, photo., 299
Telephone wires, 66, 139. *See also* Overhead wiring;
    Utility lines
Television transmitters, 296
Tennessee, 30, 257
Tennessee Valley Authority, 8, 38

Terracing, photos., 125, 126, 127. *See also* Retaining walls

Texas, 6, 10, 11, 64

Textile industries, 280, 281–82

Thompson-Ramo-Wooldridge Corporation, research center, model, 294

Thoreau, Henry David, 28, quoted, 359

Throgs Neck Bridge, plan, 235

Thurstone, Louis L., 172

Tilney, Bradford, 142

Timber companies, 361. *See also* Lumber companies

T-intersections, 89, 90, 105

Tolland State Forest, Mass., photo., 345

Toll highways, 164, 167, 269

Toronto, Ontario, 353, 373, 391; Regional open space system, 370, 381, map, 381

Tourism, 32, 347–48, 421

Tourist attractions, 32, engravings, 32, 33, photos., 11, 353

Tourist routes, 346, 382, photo., 346. *See also* Country roads

Tourists, 28, 343, 344, 345, 346, 347

Towers, 265, 296, 298–99, 302, 328, 374, photos., 139, 299, 302. *See also* Water towers

Towns, 27, 41

Trade, 312–13

Traditions, 59

Traffic, 15, 18, 77, 89, 90, 105, 148, 155, 241, 316, 318, 324, 345, 444; Arteries, 19; Circles, 261–63; Congestion, 17, 22, 160, 162; Desire lines, 43, 65, 217–20; Engineers and engineering, 15, 219; Flow plan, 316; Noise, 231, 234; Planners and planning, 218–20; Signs, 262, photos., 262

Trailers, 56, 79, chart, 62, photo., 44

Trailer parks, 10, 11, 322, photos., 48, 129, plan, 102

Transformers, 296, photo., 296

Transition curves, 122, 167, 180–87, 188, 191, 199, diagrams, 180, 187, drawings, 182, graph, 185. *See also* Curves

Transportation, 26, 58, 65, 76–78, 282, chart, 65; Costs, 37, 58–59, 78, 83, 279–80; Public, 18, 26, 44, 58–59, 65–66, 282, 316, 444

Travel, 343–45, 351

Trees, 68, 108, 109, 130, 131, 159, 227, 230, 231, 265, 330, 373, photos., 130. *See also* Landscaping; Nature and natural resources; Planting

Trellises, 134. *See also* Fences; Screens

Triboro Bridge, 165

Tri-State New York Metropolitan Region, report by, quoted, 355. *See also* New York Metropolitan Region

Trolley lines, 57, 162

Trucks and trucking, 190, 282, 322

Tuckahoe, N.Y., 21

Tucson, Ariz., 93, map, 88, photos., 315, 325

Tunnard and Harris, 154, 437

Tunnels, 207

Tuxedo Park, N.Y., 394, 397. *See also* Sterling Forest, N.Y.

Twin Cities Metropolitan Planning Commission, 95

Two-family houses, 92, chart, 62

Two-storey houses, 115, 120, drawing, 70

Union Carbide Corp., 394

Union of Soviet Socialist Republics, 61, 65, 168

Unions, 37

United States Economic Mission to Austria, 126

United States Soil Conservation Service, 64

United States Steel Corporation, 304

Urban: Centers, 375; Esthetics, 160, 405–06; Expansion, 57, 59–60, 64, 342, 368; Planning, 8; Regions, 7, 17, 26, 36–44, 57, 59, 160, 443, diagram, 39, maps, 37, 58; Renewal programs, 320, 411, 427, 428, 436; Revolution, 4

Urbanism, 24

Urbanization, 29

Urban Land Institute, 66

Use zoning, 417. *See also* Zoning

Utah, 378

Utilities, 65, 66, 83, 84, 138, 139, 261, 283, 444

Utility poles, 76, 135–38, photos., 138, 139, 140

Utility lines, 23, 63, 66, 135–39, 217, 279. *See also* Overhead wiring

Vacant lots, 28, 29, 80, 85

Vacation homes, 342

Valona, Cal., photo., 176

Vancouver, Wash., photo., 112

Vandenberg Air Force Base, Cal., photo., 303

Venezuela, 168

Vermont, 3, 30, 31, 32, 261

Verrazano Narrows Bridge, plan, 235

Vertical curves, 190, 191–94, 197, 266, diagrams, 191, 192, 193, 194, 197. *See also* Curves

Vertical elements, 118, 301, 446, photos., 301

Vertical separation of roadways, 202. *See also* Grade separations

Victor Gruen and Associates, 332, 335

Via Appia, Italy, 159

Viaducts, 206, 240. *See also* Bridges; Overpasses

Vienna, Austria, 18; Veitingergasse, photo., 126

Vienna-Salzburg freeway, 190, drawing, 267

Village greens, 11, 143, 145. *See also* Old town centers

Villages, 11, 31, 32, 390

Virginia, 165, 167, 257, 261, 370, 371, 391, 411, 413, 427

Vision, 171–77, 191, 199, 231, 265, diagrams, 173, 175

Vistas, 17, 104, 117, 145, 146, 176, 265, 266, 329

Visual control zones, 260, 261. *See also* Freeways

Visual design plans, 15, 98, 414–15, 446

Voorhees, Alan M., 80

Wallkill River, N.Y., photo., 439

Walls, 134, 135, 143. *See also* Fences; Retaining walls

Warehouses, 12, 15, 298, 311

Warren and Wetmore, Reed and Stem, 440

Wasatch National Park, 369

Washington, D.C., 261; White House, 411

Washington National Capital Region. *See* National Capital Region

Waste, 3, 4, 45; Disposal. *See* Dumps

Wasteland, 28–29, 31. *See also* Land use

Water, 140, 366, 377, 386, 446; Access to, 390; Conservation, 63, 355–59, 360, 379, 385; Courses, 206–07; Falls, 140; Fronts, 300, photo., 215; Pollution, 161; Supply, 23, 66, 80, 94, 96, 386; Towers, 146, 265, 283, 296, 298, photos., 295, 297, 301. *See also* Towers

Wayne Township, N.J., map, 83

Weiler, Rachel, drawings by, 68–71

Weinberg, Robert C., 405, 419

Wells, H. G., 38, quoted, 27

Wells, Nelson Miller, 167

Welton Becket and Associates, 332

Wesleyan University, 431, photos., 433

Westchester County, N.Y., 94, 162, 250, 255, 359, photo., 161

Westchester County Park Commission, 162

West Coast, 11, 59, 78, 96, 165, 167

West Germany, 59, 61, 168, 241. *See also* Germany

West Hartford, Conn., 93, photo., 97

Weston, Mass., 393

West Side Highway, N.Y., 165

West Virginia, 30, 167, 261, 347–48

Westways, quoted, 342

Wetlands, 370

White collar workers, 21

White Mountains, N.H., 350

White Plains, N.Y., 118–19

White River National Forest, Maroon Lake, photo., 356

White, Stanford, 4

Whitestone Bridge, 165

Whitestone Parkway, 165

White Sands National Monument, 368, photo., 357

Whittlesey, Derwent, quoted, 38

Whyte, William H., 389, quoted, 18

Wilderness areas, 28, 29–31, map of, 29, photo., 30. *See also* National Forests; National Parks; Open space

Wildlife conservation, 24, 28, 355, 359

Wildlife Preserves, Inc., 343

Willamette River, Ore., bridge over, photo., 238

Williams, Donald A., quoted, 64

Williamsburg, Va., 32, 403, 405, 411, 426

Wilson, Samuel, Jr., 438

Windbreaks, 373

Windsor, Conn., 93

Winslow, Paul, 167

Winston-Salem, N.C., 422, 426

Wisconsin, 24, 26, 257, 261, 391, 392, 398

Wood, Richardson, 22

Woodbridge, N.J., 162, photos., 47, 163

Woodside, Cal., 393

Worcester, Mass., 43

Wright, Frank Lloyd, 4

Wright, Henry, 90

Wuppertal, West Germany, overpass near, drawing, 243

Wynn, Houston, 65

Yards, 19, 59, 92, 96, 106–07, 132, 134–35, 394, photos., 107, 108, 137, 140, plans, 106

Yellow Springs, Ohio, 396

Yellowstone National Park, Giant Geyser, engraving, 33

Yosemite National Park, 344

Yugoslavia, 168

Zoning, 18, 21, 55, 56, 76, 80, 84, 85, 92–96, 106–07, 109, 118–19, 135, 153, 257, 318, 356, 392–93, 397, 416, 420–27, 444, 445
Agricultural, 26, 389, 391
Bulk, 417–19, 427, 436
Commercial, 326
Forest, 390–91
Historic District, 420–29, 431, 436
Industrial, 216, 298
Open space, 391
Recreational, 391
Restrictive Covenants, 416–17, 427, 431
Ribbon, 324
Roadside, 324–25. *See also* Outdoor advertising, controls
Staged, 84